THE AGING WORKER

THE AGING WORKER

Research and Recommendations

Mildred Doering
Susan R. Rhodes
Michael Schuster

Withdraw
England Library
USP

SAGE PUBLICATIONS
Beverly Hills / London / New Delhi

Copyright © 1983 by Sage Publications, Inc.

All rights reserved. No part of this book may be reproduced or utilized in any form or by any means, electronic or mechanical, including photocopying, recording, or by any information storage and retrieval system, without permission in writing from the publisher.

For information address:

SAGE Publications, Inc.
275 South Beverly Drive
Beverly Hills, California 90212

SAGE Publications India Pvt. Ltd.
C-236 Defence Colony
New Delhi 110 024, India

SAGE Publications Ltd
28 Banner Street
London EC1Y 8QE, England

Printed in the United States of America

Library of Congress Cataloging in Publication Data

Main entry under title:

Doering, Mildred.
  The aging worker.

  Bibliography: p.
  1. Age and employment—United States. I. Rhodes,
Susan R. II. Schuster, Michael R. III. Title.
HD6280.D63   1983   658.3'042   82-23176
ISBN 0-8039-1949-2

FIRST PRINTING

HD
6280
D652a

TO OUR PARENTS

CONTENTS

Preface   9

  1. Introduction   11

I.   CHARACTERISTICS OF THE OLDER WORKER   29

  2. Psychological Characteristics of the Older Worker   31
  3. Work Behaviors of the Older Worker   61

II.   STAFFING, CAREER PLANNING AND
      DEVELOPMENT   83

  4. Staffing   85
  5. Career Planning and Development   105

III.   COMPENSATION, PENSIONS, AND
      RETIREMENT   121
  6. Compensation   123
  7. Pensions and Retirement   141
  8. Summary and Implications   187

Appendix: Summary Tables of Studies of Age in
          Relation to Work Variables   201

References   353

Index   377

About the Authors   391

PREFACE

The objective of the book is to provide background information for the academic researcher interested in pursuing research on aging and work, and for the human resource planner engaged in planning for an aging work force. To accomplish this purpose, the book examines in-depth the current research evidence on the aging worker based on a comprehensive literature review.

The book represents a joint endeavor. The listing of the authors' names is not meant to represent the order of contribution; rather, we have arbitrarily listed our names alphabetically to reflect the shared nature of the effort.

The research for this book was supported by funds provided by the General Electric Foundation. We wish to acknowledge in particular the coordinating role of Mr. William Orme, Secretary.

Professors Walter Beattie, Jr. and Neal Bellos of the Syracuse University All-University Gerontology Center were instrumental in stimulating our initial interest in research on aging. Also providing support and encouragement for the research was Dean L. Richard Oliker of the Syracuse University School of Management.

Of great value were the comments of George Milkovich of Cornell University and Richard Steers of the University of Oregon on portions of a preliminary draft of the manuscript. Their interest and contributions are appreciated.

We are grateful to our graduate students—Richard Stazesky, Dorothy Marge, Linda Michalopoulos, Blake Strack, and Stewart Feitel—for the hours they spent in the library tracking down and reading articles and books. Kathryn Tucker and Christopher Miller also made important contributions in locating material and in some preliminary writing. Nancy Yaunches and Larry Knickerbocker put our bibliography in order—a massive undertaking. In addition, Warren Pfister proofread the manuscript. Finally, we would like to express our appreciation to Mary Jo Chase, who at various times typed portions of the manuscript.

CHAPTER 1

INTRODUCTION

American work organizations are faced with a potential crisis of major significance. The labor force is becoming older, the demands of government to protect and enhance older elements of the labor force are more stringent, and the expectations of older workers are changing. The interaction among demographics, governmental regulations, and employee expectations presents a challenge for human resource management. If appropriate managerial responses are not developed, organizational effectiveness may be adversely affected. It is important that strategy and planning begin immediately. As a result of our work, there is now sufficient information to begin the process of organizational adaptation to the changing work force. At the same time, we have identified both significant gaps and critical conflicts in the research literature on older workers.

This book seeks to provide the background information necessary for researchers to study the impact of aging on workplace behavior and for organizations to begin the process of adaptation to the changing work force. Toward this end, we have produced the largest compilation of literature to date on aging and work. We have examined the research literature in order to identify age-related differences in employees with regard to critical issues facing organizations as the composition of the work force begins its historic shift. The book presents a detailed discussion of the current scientific evidence on older workers. This extensive gathering of information has enabled us to provide recommendations for organizational action. Where we have identified gaps in the research literature, specific future research needs are identified. In view of this two-pronged approach, the book should be of interest to academicians in organizational behavior, psychology, law, sociology, economics, gerontology, and personnel and industrial relations. In addition, governmental and organizational policymakers, as well as practicing managers, may benefit from the summary of research findings and recommendations presented here. Before turning to the specific topic areas, we briefly explore the bases of the problem, discuss some factors to be considered in the examination of the age-related differences, and outline the structure of the book.

The Bases of the Problem

DEMOGRAPHICS

Over the next four decades, the age composition of the work force will change dramatically as those born immediately after World War II advance in years. The postwar baby boom began during 1947. In that year, the number of births increased from 2.75 million in the previous year to 3.8 million (Johnston, 1976). The expanded population growth continued until 1961 when the number of births reached a peak of 4.35 million. During this period, from 1947 to 1962, there were 60 million births in the United States, compared to 40 million in the previous 15-year period (1932–1946) and 54 million in the subsequent period (1962–1976).

During the 1970s, the average worker was just entering the work force. In contrast, the work force of the 1980s will be characterized by 25–34-year-olds; the 1990s will be dominated by early-middle-agers (35–44 years) and the first two decades of the twenty-first century by older workers, late-middle-agers, and retirees (45 years and over). The discussion below highlights the expected changes in population and in the composition of the labor force.

Table 1.1 summarizes the expected shift to an older population. This table, as well as the other three presented in this section, are based on middle growth assumptions by the U.S. Bureau of the Census and Department of Labor, Bureau of Labor Statistics. The table presents the percentage changes for seven age categories over each decade for the period 1960–2020. Two distinct generational cohorts are shaded to highlight their progression over time. The cohort highlighted in the dotted area is the group with the largest rate of increase. The cohort immediately following it is even larger, but its rate of increase is somewhat smaller. These groups comprise the aging work force. As shown in the table, there will be a 42 percent increase in the population age group 35–44 during the decade 1980–1990. This cohort will continue to move through the population until retirement.

TABLE 1.1 Decennial Percentage Changes in U.S. Population, 1960-2020

Age	1960-1970	1970-1980	1980-1990	1990-2000	2000-2010	2010-2020
Under 18	+8%	-9%	+7%	+5%	-1%	-6%
18-24	+53	+18	-15	+ 5	+11	- 7
25-34	+10	+43	+13	-16	+11	+ 5
35-44	- 4	+11	+42	+13	-16	+11
45-54	+13	- 3	+11	+42	+13	-16
55-64	+19	+13	- 3	+12	+42	+13
65 and over	+20	+22	+18	+ 6	+ 9	+29

Source: U.S. Bureau of the Census, *Current Population Reports*, Series P-25, No. 601, "Projections of the Population of the United States: 1975 to 2050." Washington DC: Government Printing Office, 1975. Adapted from Table E (Series II) and Table 11 (Series II).

TABLE 1.2   U.S. Population (in millions), 1960-2020

Age	1960	1970	1980	1990	2000	2010	2020
Under 18	64.5	69.7	63.3	67.6	71.2	70.2	74.2
18-24	16.1	24.7	29.4	25.2	26.3	29.2	27.1
25-34	22.9	25.3	36.2	41.1	34.5	38.4	40.6
35-44	24.2	23.1	26.7	36.5	41.3	34.8	38.6
45-54	20.6	23.3	22.6	25.2	35.7	40.4	34.1
55-64	15.6	18.7	'21.0	20.5	22.9	32.5	36.7
65 and over	16.7	20.1	24.5	28.9	30.6	33.2	42.8
Total	180.7	204.9	222.8	245.1	262.5	278.7	294.0

Source: U.S. Bureau of the Census, *Current Population Reports*, Series P-25, No. 601 "Projections of the Population of the United States: 1975 to 2050." Washington, D.C.; Government Printing Office, 1975. Adapted from Table E (Series II) and Table 11 (Series II).

The second cohort (indicated by diagonal lines) represents the decline in the number of younger persons that has already begun to effect the elementary and secondary education systems. The smaller size of this cohort will soon affect enrollment in colleges and universities, and later on will result in fewer entry-level workers.

Table 1.2 presents the actual and projected population for the period 1960–2020. In 1960, there were 16.1 million persons aged 18–24. This same age group nearly doubled to 29.4 million in 1980. That same year, there were 43.6 million persons aged 45–64. In contrast, it is expected that there will be 72.9 million people in this group in the year 2010. Considering the 1980 situation once again, there were 24.5 million persons 65 and over. By the year 2020, this group is expected to grow in size to 42.8 million.

Tables 1.3 and 1.4 demonstrate the changes that will begin to take place in the number of people and the age composition of the labor force. In contrast with Bureau of Census projections, the Department of Labor only makes labor force projections to the year 2000, and the projections for 1995–2000 are unofficial. In 1980 there were 21.2 million persons in the labor force aged 35–44, and 17.0 million aged 45–54. In the year 2000, there will be 36.5 million workers aged 35–44 and 27.9 million workers aged 45–54. This represents a 73 percent increase over 1980 in the 35–44-year-old labor force and a 64 percent increase in the 45–54-year-old labor force. There will be a 13 percent (3.3 million) decline in the number of workers aged 16–24 in 1995 as compared to 1980.

Table 1.4 shows that in the year 2000, the overall composition of the labor force will be significantly older. In 1980, 21.2 percent of the

TABLE 1.3 Civilian Labor Force by Age

Age	1975	1980	1985	1990	1995	2000
16-26	22.0	25.1	24.4	22.6	21.8	24.3
25-34	22.3	30.4	32.9	35.0	33.0	30.3
35-44	16.8	21.2	25.9	31.3	34.9	36.5
45-54	17.1	17.0	16.9	19.3	23.8	27.9
55-64	11.2	12.0	11.8	11.1	11.0	12.5
65 and over	2.9	3.0	3.0	3.1	2.9	2.8
Total[1]	92.6	108.7	115.0	122.4	127.5	134.2

1. Column numbers may not equal the total due to rounding error.

Source: U.S. Department of Labor, Bureau of Labor Statistics.

labor force was aged 35–44, and 17.0 percent were 45. In 2000, 36.5 percent of the labor force will be 35–44, and 27.9 percent will be 45–54.

GOVERNMENT REGULATION—THE AGE DISCRIMINATION IN EMPLOYMENT ACT (1967)

President Lyndon Johnson, in his January 23, 1967, Older American message to Congress recommending passage of the Age Discrimination In Employment Act (ADEA) of 1967, stated:

> Hundreds of thousands not yet old, not yet voluntarily retired, find themselves jobless because of arbitrary age discrimination. Despite our present low rate of unemployment, there has been a presistent average of 850,000 people age 45 and over. They comprise 27 percent of all the unemployed, and 40 percent of the long-term unemployed. In 1965, the Secretary of Labor reported to the Congress and the President that approximately half of all private job openings were banned to applicants over 55; a quarter were closed to applicants over 45.
>
> In economic terms, this is a serious—and senseless—loss to a nation on the move. But, the greater loss is the cruel sacrifice in happiness and well-being which joblessness imposes on these citizens and their families [Public Papers of the Presidents, 1968].

The ADEA followed a period in which federal efforts to deter employment discrimination against aging workers centered only on the use of the government's purchasing power to require federal contractors to comply with regulations prohibiting age discrimination.[1] Congress enacted the Age Discrimination in Employment Act[2] in order "to prohibit discrimination in employment on account of age in such matters as hiring, job retention, compensation, and other terms

TABLE 1.4   Percentage Civilian Labor Force X Age

Age	1975	1980	1985	1990	1995	2000
16-24	24.1	23.1	21.2	18.5	17.1	18.1
25-34	24.1	28.0	28.6	28.6	25.9	22.6
35-44	18.1	19.5	22.5	25.6	27.4	27.2
45-54	18.5	15.6	14.7	15.8	18.7	20.8
45-64	12.1	11.0	10.3	9.1	8.6	9.3
65 and older	3.1	2.8	2.6	2.5	2.3	2.1

Note: The columns may not sum to 100 due to rounding error.

Source: U.S. Department of Labor, Bureau of Labor Statistics.

and conditions of employment."[3] The legislation was targeted to promote the employment of older persons based on their ability rather than their age, to prohibit arbitrary age discrimination in employment, and to assist employers and workers in finding ways of meeting the problems arising from the impact of age on employment.[4]

ADEA Coverage. The Act originally prohibited discrimination by employers, employment agencies, and labor unions[5] against workers in the 40–65-year age bracket. The raising of the mandatory retirement to age 70[6] increased the size of the ADEA-protected group.

The provisions against employer discrimination make it unlawful for an employer:

(1) to fail or refuse to hire or to discharge any individual or otherwise discriminate against any individual with respect to his compensation, terms, conditions, or privileges of employment, because of such individual's age;

(2) to limit, segregate, or classify his employees in any way which would deprive or tend to deprive any individual of employment opportunities or otherwise adversely affect his status as an employee, because of such individual's age or;

(3) to reduce the wage rate of any employee in order to comply with this chapter.[7]

Employment agencies are prohibited from refusing to refer individuals or from classifying them on the basis of their age.[8] Discrimination by labor unions is prohibited when those organizations use age to (1) exclude or expel individuals from membership; (2) classify individuals or refuse to refer individuals because of age; or (3) cause or attempt to cause an employer to discriminate on the basis of age.[9]

ADEA Exceptions. There are four major exceptions to the prohibitions of the ADEA. What might otherwise be illegal personnel practices are legitimate under the Act where (1) age is a bona fide occupational qualification reasonably necessary to the normal operation of the particular business; (2) the differentiation is based on reasonable factors other than age; (3) the employer is observing the term of a bona fide seniority system or a bona fide employee benefit plan which is not a subterfuge to evade the purposes of the Act; and (4) the employer is discharging an employee for good cause.[10]

The ADEA permits an employer to differentiate on the basis of age if "age is a bona fide occupational qualification (BFOQ) reasonably necessary to the normal operation of the particular business."[11] Court decisions and EEOC guidelines have indicated that the BFOQ exception is to be of limited scope and application.[12] The BFOQ defense has generally only been available for employment practices involving bus drivers, firefighters, police officers, and airline pilots, arising in the context of a hiring or mandatory retirement policy.

The BFOQ defense is given the greatest deference by courts where safety factors are involved in the particular job, such as those listed above. In general, such instances require the employer to show only that a rational basis exists to believe that the discriminatory practice serves to reduce the risk of harm to the public.[13] When safety is not involved, the employer has to establish a sound factual basis for any broad discriminatory policy, thereby significantly limiting the defense's utility for a non-safety-related policy.[14]

The "reasonable factors other than age" defense requires employers to establish that an employee was unable to perform a test or satisfy a valid job requirement, and that inability, not age, was the determining factor in the employment decision.[15] The "reasonable factor" differentiation is broad-based and has been decided on the basis of particular factual situations. Reasonable factors have ranged from the lack of basic job skills or initiative to companywide economic maladies.[16]

The ADEA permits an employer to observe a bona fide seniority system or employee benefit or retirement plan which is not a subterfuge to evade the purposes of the Act, providing the plan does not compel the involuntary retirement of employees prior to age 70.[17] While the validity of an employment action under such a plan depends on the facts of an individual case, there are several common factors that will establish a plan as bona fide.

Courts will look to see if the retirement plan has been in existence for some time, as opposed to being conceived just prior to an employee's "retirement." The court will also consider whether the plan pays substantial benefits or merely provides nominal amounts. Additionally, the courts will determine if the employer has actually followed the terms of the plan, or whether the employer has "loosely" interpreted the plan's language.[18] Finally, the employee's choice to retire must always appear to be voluntary.[19]

The "good cause" defense is a more specific restatement of the "reasonable factor" defense. The two defenses are often indistinguishable in their treatment by defendants and courts.[20]

ADEA Procedures. For an individual to bring a private action under the ADEA, a charge alleging unlawful discrimination must first be filed with the Equal Employment Opportunity Commission (EEOC).[21] The charge must be in writing or reduced to writing, and filed with the EEOC within 180 days of the alleged unlawful act of discrimination. Some states have enacted legislation prohibiting age discrimination and have created administrative agencies to adjudicate these rights. Moreover, at least one state (California) has eliminated the mandatory retirement age for all public and private sector workers. In these instances, an aggrieved employee must first pursue relief through these state administrative agencies. The employee can file charges with the EEOC within 30 days of termination of the state proceedings, or within 300 days of the alleged unlawful conduct, whichever is earlier.[22]

The EEOC is then allowed 60 days to investigate the charge and eliminate any illegal practices by informal methods. At the end of this period, the individual is permitted to bring a private suit in federal court.[23] Available remedies for an aggrieved plaintiff include back wages and benefits, as well as an equal amount of liquidated damages.[24] Liquidated damages, however, are only available upon showing a "willful violation" of the ADEA.[25] A "willful violation" is defined as a "knowing and voluntary violation of the Act."[26] The Act also provides for attorneys' fees to a prevailing plaintiff.[27] All of these forms of relief have been incorporated into the ADEA from the Fair Labor Standards Act.[28]

ESTABLISHING AGE DISCRIMINATION: THE BURDEN OF PROOF

The establishment of a prima facie case of age discrimination is not a matter of statutory law. Hence, many of the federal courts that have dealt with the issue have not always agreed on the appropriate formula to govern the plaintiff's attempt to establish his or her case.[29] However, it has become clear that the Fifth Circuit has greatly influenced the formulation of the prima facie case.[30] That court originally listed four elements to be proved as requisite for establishing a prima facie case: (1) the employee's membership in the protected group; (2) his or her discharge; (3) his or her replacement with a person outside the protected group; and (4) his or her ability to do the job.[31] These elements parallel the elements of the prima facie Title VII case discussed in McDonnell-Douglas Corp. v. Green.[32] Recently, the Fifth Circuit held that it is not necessary for a plaintiff who was laid off during a reduction in force to show actual replacement by a younger employee.[33] In fact, it now appears that even the replacement of the plaintiff by an older worker may not foreclose the establishment of a prima facie case.[34]

These four elements do not establish "an immutable definition of a prima facie case. The concept simply refers to evidence sufficient for a finding in the plaintiff's favor unless rebutted."[35] In Marshall v. Goodyear Tire and Rubber Co., the Fifth Circuit noted, as recognized in McDonnell-Douglas, that the prima facie proof required will vary with the applicable facts in each case.[36] Thus, the courts will not simply borrow from the McDonnell-Douglas guidelines and apply them automatically, but will seek to tailor the burden of proof in age discrimination cases so that relief will be granted only in those cases where actual discrimination is found.[37]

To maintain a prima facie case, the plaintiff must provide evidence sufficient to support an inference of discrimination.[38] Evidence which tends to identify age as the "likely reason" for the employment decision qualifies as sufficient.[39] The types of evidence found sufficient to establish a prima facie case of a violation of the ADEA can vary. The evidence may consist solely of specific incidents of discriminatory conduct,[40] or there may be a combination of discriminatory conduct and statistical evidence.[41] Examples of evidence sufficient to establish a prima facie case include proof that a plaintiff was within the protected age bracket and that the defendant has: placed an advertisement in a newspaper seeking a replacement for the defendant, and the advertisement explicitly seeks young applicants;[42] filled an opening, for which the plaintiff was qualified, with a younger person with similar qualifications;[43] engaged in a pattern of age discrimination by never hiring individuals within the protected age brackets;[44] or amended a pension plan to require employees to retire at age 62 rather than at age 65.[45]

Once the plaintiff has established a prima facie case, the defendant has the burden of going forward with evidence that reasonable factors, other than age, were the basis for the alleged discriminatory employment practices.[46] As previously discussed, an employer-defendant can accomplish this in various ways. The plaintiff retains the burden of proving the case of discrimination by a preponderance of the evidence.[47] That is, the plaintiff bears the burden of persuasion throughout the trial.[48] The defendant need only "articulate some legitimate nondiscriminatory reason" for the adverse employment decision.[49] An exception is the BFOQ defense, which is an affirmative defense, where the employer bears the burden of persuasion. As to all other defenses, the plaintiff bears the ultimate burden of proving that the employer acted with a discriminatory motive and that age was a determining factor in the employment decision.[50]

EMPLOYEE EXPECTATIONS

When Congress raised the mandatory retirement age, it was in response to the effective political pressures of older Americans. Protection from discriminatory treatment and the lifting of the retirement age, along with increases in pension coverage, pension benefits, and provisions for early retirement, have provided workers with more options than they have had in the past. Older workers appear to be exercising their rights with increasing frequency. For example, the EEOC (*Aging and Work,* 1981) reported that age discrimination complaints had increased significantly since June 1, 1979 when the EEOC assumed responsibility for administering and enforcing the ADEA. The EEOC reported that 8779 individuals filed complaints during Fiscal Year 1980, compared to 5734 in Fiscal Year 1979. This represented about a 60 percent increase in only one year. Employees also have come to expect career growth, development, and planning opportunities from their employer. The option of phased retirement is another employee expectation that will continue to increase.

It is most difficult to project the number of employees desiring to remain at work. At the present time, blue collar workers are seeking retirement at progressively earlier ages. At the same time, white collar and clerical workers appear more anxious to continue employment. These trends, should they continue, would further exacerbate the projected shortage of blue collar and oversupply of white collar workers.

Current projections fail to account for potential changes in the environment of the workplace. Most workers, particularly blue collar, have sought retirement in order to end careers in less desirable work. Should workplace conditions continue to improve, inflationary pressures continue unabated, or employee retirement benefits become insufficient, the participation/retirement mix could change across all occupations.

For the 25–54 age group, projected to have the largest increase, the potential for career growth may be severely limited. As career growth is an employee expectation, one might, in the absence of sound policy alternatives, expect some degree of frustration. Career frustration is not just a problem for the employee, but also impacts on the organization as the individual's work performance, emotional health, and physical health may be adversely affected. Frequently, the frustration is resolved by the individual lowering his or her goals or decreasing his or her self-expectations. The loss in human resource potential for the organization is clear. Organizational innovations to meet changed employee expectations include more flexible retirement programs, life-cycle planning, and career change programs.

Sources of Age-Related Differences

Age-related differences in work attitudes and behaviors may be caused by several factors—age, cohort, and period. An understanding of each of these concepts is essential because it forms the foundation for the study of aging workers. Therefore, each of these concepts is discussed.

AGE EFFECTS

Age effects are developmental in nature; that is, they are ontogenetic or systematically related to time (Goulet and Baltes, 1970). Causes of age effects influencing work attitudes and behaviors include psychosocial aging, such as social role changes, and biological aging.

Psychosocial aging refers to systematic changes in personality, needs, expectations, and behavior, as well as changes in status and roles and changes in relation to others. Super (1980) identifies nine life roles which people play at various life stages: child, student, "leisurite," citizen, workers, spouse, homemaker, parent, and pensioner. These roles carry with them certain expectations for behavior and have an influence on an individual's needs. For example, health insurance benefits may be particularly valued by those involved in the parent and spouse roles.

Biological aging refers to anatomical and physiological changes that occur with age. For example, the capability to reproduce offspring is a phenomenon associated with biological aging. Changes in sensorimotor performance, muscle strength, brittleness of the skeletal structure, visual acuity, reaction time, and balance are other examples of biological aging which may influence work attitudes and behavior.

COHORT EFFECTS

In a general sense, a cohort consists of persons born at the same time and who age together (Riley, 1973; Riley et al., 1972). A more precise definition is offered by Rosow (1978: 67):

> As a sociologically meaningful entity, a social cohort: (1) consists of people who share a given life experience; (2) this experience is socially or historically structured; and (3) it occurs in a common generational framework; (4) its effects distinguish one generation from another; and (5) these effects are relatively stable over the life course.

Cohort itself is not actually a variable, but serves as an index for the underlying factors which affect the attitudes and behavior of a given cohort. Past experience, such as the Great Depression, the women's movement, and the physical fitness movement, the size and structure of the cohort, and the educational level of the cohort may be factors contributing to age-related differences in work attitudes and behaviors. For example, we might expect cohorts of women who matured prior to the women's movement to have substantially different experiences than those going through the women's movement. As a result, work attitudes and behaviors of these groups may be quite different.

PERIOD EFFECTS

A period effect is a time-of-measurement difference representing environmental effects. A period effect is temporal in nature as distinguished from the stable cohort environmental effect. Among the period influences that may affect work attitudes and behaviors with age are changes in the work and nonwork environment, age-related expectations of others, and practice effects due to prior measurement. Examples of changes in the work and nonwork environment include changes in the nature of supervision, the reward structure, and labor market conditions.

SEPARATING AGE, PERIOD, AND COHORT EFFECTS

A multitude of causal factors may be responsible for any age difference in work attitudes and behavior. Needless to say, knowing why age differences exist is important for practical reasons. To the extent that differences in attitudes and behaviors are age effects, we would expect that the attitudes and behaviors of young adults would become similar to older adults as they age. On the other hand, if differences in attitudes and behavior are reflective of cohort effects, the best predictors of future attitudes and behaviors of a cohort are current attitudes and behaviors.

Using statistical techniques to separate age, period, and cohort effects requires three types of data: cross-sectional, longitudinal, and time-lag (Palmore, 1978). Cross-sectional data are comprised of age and cohort effects. Longitudinal data may reflect both age and period effects. Time-lag differences (that is, a comparison of people who are the same age in different time periods) contain cohort and period effects. Even when these data are available, the identification of each of the three effects is possible only under specific conditions or given certain assumptions (see Palmore, 1978, for a discussion). One assumption that has been relied on is that age, period, and cohort effects are additive. However, an interactive model may be more realistic. That is, not only are the effects of membership in a given cohort likely to differ through time, but the effects of growing older may vary greatly among birth cohorts (Glenn, 1976). Therefore, any analysis of age, period or cohort should draw heavily on existing theory and, where possible, rely on measures of causative factors associated with each type of effect (Glenn, 1976; Maddox and Wiley, 1976; Palmore, 1978).

The Structure of This Book

We structured this book along topical considerations. Part I addresses the "Characteristics of the Older Worker." Chapter 2 discusses the psychological characteristics. Empirical research on the values, needs and preferences, job attitudes, and behavioral intentions of older workers is examined. Chapter 3 focuses on the workplace behaviors of older workers. The research literature on the performance, turnover, absenteeism, and accident experience of older workers is provided. These two chapters present important background information for Parts II and III.

Part II, "Staffing, Career Planning and Development," consists of two chapters. Organizational staffing activities are explored in Chapter 4. Activities include recruitment, selection, testing, interviewing, and performance appraisal, as well as placement and job design. Chapter 5 focuses on career planning, training, and development. Topics such as career stages, middle career, mid-career changers, learning, and post-training performance are examined. Preretirement programs are also discussed.

Part III is devoted to a discussion of "Compensation, Pensions, and Retirement." In Chapter 6 we examine the literature on age and pay, employee pay preferences, pay satisfaction, and incentives. In Chapter 7 we discuss pensions and retirement by presenting the literature on pension trends, retirement income, the decision to retire, and the impact of social security on the labor force participation rates of older workers. Also contained in this chapter is an examination of retirement policies in other industrialized countries. We conclude in Chapter 8 with an integrative summary of our findings.

Each chapter refers to a series of summary tables that provide an easily readable abstract of each research study. In order not to interfere with the flow of the text, these tables are contained in the Appendix. The tables summarize the population, age distribution, and relevant findings of each study, including the reported statistics. The tables are not always uniform due to variations in the reporting styles of many authors and journals. At appropriate locations in the text, we summarize the research findings and organizational implications. Also included are suggested areas for future research. We hope this will serve as a guide for researchers interested in this important area of organizational concern. The book concludes with a detailed bibliography of articles, books, and government documents on the aging work force.

A Brief Note on Statistics and Research Design

We have written this book for the academic researcher, government official, and manager in a policymaking position. The litmus test for this book will be the ability of researchers to use our summaries and future research recommendations to further their own search for knowledge and understanding of the older worker. For the nonacademic audience we will have failed if the information and recommendations do not help in meeting the challenges presented by an aging work force.

In order to interpret the contents of this book, an understanding of several basic principles of statistics and research methodology is required. To aid in the interpretation of the contents of this book, in this section we briefly define some statistical terms and discuss research methodology. Most of our academic readers will be very familiar with this discussion and will prefer to proceed to Part II.

Much of the research we have reported has been correlational in nature. That is, the investigator has attempted to determine whether age is related to some other variable but is unable to place any causality to that relationship. A correlation can be either positive or negative, with positive indicating that as age increases, the other variable also increases. A negative correlation would have indicated that as age increased, the other variable of interest decreased in intensity, or vice versa. The statistical symbol for a correlation is "r". The r (or correlation) found to exist is, in and of itself, of limited value since its significance can be a function of the size of the population used for the investigation.

In addition to correlation analysis, much of the research has employed multiple regression analysis. In these studies, the investigator has sought to determine the degree to which a series of variables, for example, age, sex, and marital status, predict variation in a dependent variable. The symbol used to report regression results is "R." If the dependent variable in our example above was pay satisfaction, then a large R would indicate that age, sex, and marital status were good predictors of variation in pay satisfaction. Generally it is R^2 that is reported, which indicates the percentage of variation in the dependent variable that is explained by the other variable(s).

Multiple regression analysis permits the investigator to hold all but one of the predictor variables constant and assess the degree to which the remaining variable explains change in the dependent variable. This is particularly useful in studying a variable such as age. Hence, in our example above, the investigator would hold sex and marital status constant and attempt to determine the degree to which changes in age affected the dependent variable of pay satisfaction. Unfortunately, this type of analysis was seldom conducted and constitutes a major limitation of the findings presented in this report. We will be proposing a series of studies employing more sophisticated statistical techniques.

In addition, we frequently refer to the level of statistical significance. Crano and Brewer (1973: 20) state: "Statistical 'significance' is achieved when the probability is so low as to render the chance explanation implausible." We have set the appropriate level of significance at $p < .05$ or better. This signifies a relationship in which the probability that the results are incorrect is no more than five out of one hundred or less.

There are also several research design issues of which the reader will wish to be aware. One is the internal validity of a study. This involves the question of whether the variables chosen by the investigator are appropriate for consideration or whether some other variable or set of variables not considered by the investigator could better explain his or her results. In addition, much of the research reported here has involved narrowly defined populations of subjects—for example, employees in one organization, or college sophomores. This raises the concern that we as scientists have as to our ability to generalize the findings beyond the population under study. This also constitutes a major limitation in the studies reported here.

Finally, only a handful of studies have been longitudinal panel studies; that is, studies that have examined work behavior over time. Certainly, if one were to adequately study the aging process, it would be most important to follow individuals through their work careers. Unfortunately, due to the time, expense, and difficulty in conducting longitudinal investigations, they rarely occur in organizational settings.

NOTES

1. Exec. Order No. 11141, 3 C.F.R. § 112 (1974) and 41 C.F.R. § 1-12. 1000 to 1.-12. 1003 (1975).

2. 29 U.S.C. § 621-34 [1970 & Supp IV (1974)], as amended by Age Discrimination in Employment Act Amendments of 1978, Pub. L. No. 95-256, 92 Stat, 189 (1978).

3. Senate Report No. 95-493, 95th Cong. 2nd Sess., reprinted in (1978) U.S. Code Cong. and Admin. News 976.

4. Ibid.

5. 29 U.S.C. § 623.

6. 29 U.S.C. § 631 (1967). Amended 1978 Pub. L. No. 95-256, 92 Stat. 189 (1978).

7. 29 U.S.C. § 623 (a).

8. 29 U.S.C. § 623 (b).

9. 29 U.S.C. § 623 (c).

10. 29 U.S.C. § 623 (f), as amended. See Marshall v. Westinghouse Electric Corp., 576 F. 558 (5th Cir. 1978); Usery v. Tamiami Trails Tours, Inc., 531 F. 2d 224 (9th Cir. 1976); Hodgson v. Greyhound Lines, Inc. 449 F. 2d 224 (7th Cir. 1974); and Brennan v. Greyhound Lines, Inc. 419 U.S. 1122 (1974); also, United Airlines, Inc. v. McMann, 434 U.S. 192 (1977); Marshall v. Hawaiian Tel. Co., 575 F. 2d 763 (9th Cir. 1978); Thompson v. Chrysler Corp. 569 F. 2d 989 (6th Cir. 1978); and Currier v. Bell Helicopter Textron, Div. of Textron, Inc., 567 F. 2d 1307 (5th Cir. 1978).

11. 29 U.S.C. § 623 (f) (1).

12. See, for example, Burwell v. Eastern Airlines, Inc., 633 F. 2d 361, 370 n.15 (4th Cir. 1980); EEOC v. City of St. Paul, 500 F. Supp. 1135, 1146 (D. Minn. 1980); also, 29 C.F.R. § 1625(a), 46 Fed. Reg. 47,727 (1981).

13. See, for example, Hodgson v. Greyhound Lines, Inc. 499 F. 2d 859 (7th Cir. 1974), Cert. denied, 419 U.S. 1122 (1975). Another version of this "rationale basis" test requires that safety be the essence of the particular business involved. See, e.g., Usery v. Tamiani Trail Tours, Inc., 531 F. 2d 224 (5th Cir. 1976).

14. See, for example, Smallwood v. United Airlines, Inc., 26 FEP Cases 1376, 1379n. 7 (4th Cir. 1981), where the court stated that "economic considerations cannot be the basis for a BFOQ—precisely those considerations were among the basis of the Act."

15. See, for example, EEOC v. County of Allegheny, 26 FEP Cases 1087, 1091 (W.D. Pa. 1981).

16. See, for example, Price v. Maryland Casulaty Co., 561 F. 2d 609 (5th Cir. 1971); Mastie v. Great Lakes Steel Corp., 424 F. Supp. 1299 (E.D. Mich. 1976).
17. 29 U.S.C § 623 (f) (2), as amended.
18. See, for example, Sexton v. Beatrice Foods Co., 30 F. 2d 478, 486 (7th Cir. 1980); Brennan v. Taft Broadcasting, 500 F. 2d 212, 217 (5th Cir. 1974).
19. See, for example, Hays v. Republic Steel Corp., 12 FEP Cases 1640 (N.D. Ala. 1979), modified, 531 F. 2d 1307 (5th Cir. 1976).
20. See, for example, Marshall v. Westinghouse Elec. Corp., 576 F. 2d 588 (5th Cir. 1978).
21. 29 U.S.C § 626 (d) (1976), as amended by Age Discrimination in Employment Act Amendments of 1978, Pub L. No. 95-256, § 4 (d) (1), 92 Stat. 189. Prior to July 1, 1979, the Secretary of Labor was responsible for enforcement of the ADEA. On July 1, 1974, enforcement responsibility was transferred to the EEOC, pursuant to Reorganization Plan No. 1 of 1978, 43 Fed. REg. 19,807 (1978).
22. 29 U.S.C. § 626 (d).
23. 29 U.S.C. § 626 (d).
24. See, for example, Kelly v. American Standard, Inc., 640 F. 2d 974 (9th Cir. 1981).
25. See, for example, Wehr v. Burroughs Corp., 619 F. 2d 276 (3rd Cir. 1980).
26. See, for example, Kelly v. American Standard, Inc., 69 F. 2d at 980.
27. See, for example, Cova v. Coca Cola Bottling Co. of St. Louis, 574 F. 2d 958 (8th Cir. 1978).
28. 29 U.S.C. § § 211(b), 216, 217.
29. See "Age Discrimination in Employment Suits: A Practical Guide," 81 W. Virg. L. REv. 503 (1979).
30. For a discussion of the Fifth Circuit's effect on burden-of-proof issues in ADEA cases, see Edelman and Siegler, Federal Age Discrimination in Employment: Slowing Down the Gold Watch, pp. 182–193 (1978).
31. Lindsey v. Southwestern Bell Telephone Co., 546 F. 2d 1123, 1124 (5th Cir. 1977); Wilson v. Sealtest Foods Division of Kraftee Corporation. 501 F. 2d 84, 86 (5th Cir. 1974).
32. 411 U.S. 792, 802, 93 S. Ct. 1817, 1824, 362 L. Ed 2d 668–678 (1973).
33. See, for example, Williams v. General Motors Corp., 656 F. 2d 120 (5th Cir. 1981); McCuen v. Home Ins. Co., 633 F. 2d 1150 (5th Cir. 1981).
34. See, for example, Sutton v. Atlantic Richfield, 646 F. 2d 407 (9th Cir. 1981); Loeb v. Textron, 600 F. 2d 1003, 1013 (1st Cir. 1979).
35. United States v. Wiggins, 39 U.S. (14 Pet) 334, 347, 10 L. Ed. 481, 488 (1840); Marshall v. Goodyear Tire & Rubber Co., 554 F. 2d 730, 735 (5th Cir. 1977).
36. Marshall v. Goodyear Tire & Rubber Co., 554 F. 2d at 735.
37. Laugesen v. Anaconda Co., 510 F. 2d 301, 312 (6th Cir. 1975). For a slightly different version of the prima facie formulation, see Cova in Coco-Cola Bottling Company of St. Louis, Inc., 574 F. 2d 958, 959 (8th Cir. 1978).
38. See, for example, Texas Dept. of Community Affairs v. Burdine, 450 U.S. 248, 253–254 (1981) (Title VII).
39. See, for example, Douglas v. Anderson, 27 FEP Cases 47,50 (9th Cir. 1981).
40. Hodgson v. Sugar Cane Growers, 5 FEP 1136 (D.C. Fla. 1973); Buchholz v. Symons Manuf. Co., 445 F. Supp. 706 (E.D. Wis. 1978).
41. Hodgson v. First Federal Savings and Loan Assoc., 455 F. 2d 818, 821–822. Use of statistical evidence showing that for more than one year all 35 individuals hired by defendant as tellers were younger than 40, while defendant's interview notes read

"too old for teller," where protected persons were interviewed, and defendant specified to employment agency that only teller trainees between the ages of 21 and 24 were sought; also, Mistretta v. Sandia Corp., 15 FEP 1690 (D. Ct. N.M. 1977)—proof of discriminatory conduct through use of statistical evidence showing salary and layoff policies of employer to be age-biased.

42. Marshall v. Goodyear Tire and Rubber Co., 554 F. 2d 730.

43. O'Connell v. Ford Motor Co., 11 FEP 1471 (E.D. Mich. 1975).

44. Hodgson v. First Fed. Savings and Loan Assoc. 455 F. 2d 818, 822–823; see, generally, Edelman and Siegler, supra at pp. 185–186.

45. Moore v. Sears, Roebuck and Co., 464 F. Supp. 357, (E.D. Georgia 1979).

46. Bittar v. Air Canada, 512 F. 2d 58L (5th Cir. 1975); Hodgson v. First Federal Savings and Loan Association, 455 F. 2d 818, 822 (5th Cir. 1972); also, Zell v. United States, 472 F. Supp. 356, 359 (E.D. Pa. 1979).

47. Price v. Maryland Gas Co., 561 F. 2d 609 (5th Cir. 1977); Rodriguez v. Taylor, 569 F. 2d 1231, 1239 (3rd Cir. 1977).

48. See, for example, Smith v. University of North Carolina, 632 F. 2d 316, 337 (4th Cir. 1980).

49. McDonnell-Douglas Corp. v. Green, 411 U.S. at 802 (Title VII).

50. See, for example, Laugesen v. Anaconda Co., 510 F. 2d 201; Mastie v. Great Lakes Steel Corp., 424 F. Supp. 1299, 1321–1322 (E.D. Mich. 1976); 29 C.F.R. § 860. 103 (c).

PART I

Characteristics of
the Older Worker

An important prerequisite for designing personnel systems compatible with the changing demographic composition of the work force is a general understanding of the characteristics of the older worker. Part I examines those characteristics that would seem potentially to influence organizational effectiveness. In this regard, two major categories are examined: (a) psychological characteristics (Chapter 2), including values, needs, attitudes, and intentions; and (b) work behaviors (Chapter 3), including performance, turnover, absenteeism, and accidents. Chapter 3 concludes with a summary that integrates the findings with regard to psychological characteristics and work behaviors. In addition, suggestions for integrative research are presented.

The discussion that follows is the result of an exhaustive literature search. With the exception of studies of overall job satisfaction and its dimensions, an attempt was made to locate all studies in which age-related differences were reported, regardless of whether age was a focal variable. This approach was taken because of the limited research directly focusing on age differences. But for overall job satisfaction and its dimensions, only those studies in which age was a major focal variable are reported. Here, a sufficient number of studies were methodologically superior to those where age was included for purposes of control. For each of the specific factors discussed, the factor is first defined and its importance to the manager discussed. Next, empirical research is presented. This discussion is supported by tables summarizing the studies examining age-related differences. Then, potential explanations of findings are offered. Finally, the section concludes with a discussion of managerial implications, when appropriate, and future research issues.

CHAPTER 2

PSYCHOLOGICAL CHARACTERISTICS OF THE OLDER WORKER

Values

Values are "basic convictions that a specific mode of conduct or end-state is personally or socially preferable to an opposite or converse mode of conduct or end-state of existence" (Rokeach, 1973). Put more simply, values represent a person's ideas as to what is right, good, or desirable. Being global in nature, values are more basic than attitudes: a person may have thousands of attitudes and only several dozen values. Values are learned and relatively stable; however, they are not fixed and can change very slowly.

IMPORTANCE OF VALUES

Values are important in that they may help explain job attitudes. Several models of the value-attitude relationship have been set forth. First, values have been viewed as direct determinants of attitudes (Fishbein, 1967). For example, Kidron (1978) implied this relationship when he found a significant positive association between the value orientation of belief in the Protestant work ethic and moral commitment to the organization. Values, likewise, have been treated as antecedents of job involvement (Rabinowitz and Hall, 1977). Second, values have been treated as moderators of the job characteristics/employee response relationship. That is, it has been suggested that employees will respond differently to a given job situation depending on their value orientations. For example, a number of studies have examined the moderating effects of the Protestant work ethic on the relationship between job scope and employee responses with varying results (White, 1978).

Older workers are thought to be more work-oriented than younger workers. Three arguments have been set forth explaining this phenomenon (Cherrington, 1977). First, the different kinds of experiences associated with growing older change one's perspective and frame of reference. Second, older workers have experienced a different set of historical events, including the Great Depression and World War II, which would have a strong influence on work values. Third, older workers have been exposed to different kinds of training and socialization pressures than younger workers.

REVIEW OF EMPIRICAL RESEARCH

Despite the widespread belief that older and younger workers hold significantly different value systems, there has been very limited research in this area. In fact, the popular press espoused the existence of a "generation gap" during the 1960s, while the empirical studies that do exist regarding age and values were not published until the 1970s.

At least fourteen work-related values have been identified, and five studies have empirically tested age differences, all employing cross-sectional analyses (see Table A-1, Appendix). Our discussion will first focus on the belief in the Protestant work ethic, as this particular value has been found to be related to work attitudes.

Age differences in belief in the Protestant work ethic have been examined in three studies with mixed results. Using Blood's (1969) pro-Protestant ethic measure, Aldag and Brief (1977) found that older workers adhered more strongly to the Protestant work ethic than younger workers in three separate samples, including manufacturing operatives, janitorial and food service workers, and police officers. On the other hand, in a study of union leaders, managers, and blue and white collar employees, Buchholz (1978) found stronger adherence to the work ethic among younger workers than among older workers. The discrepancy in results may be attributed in part to the use of different measures in the two studies. While Blood's (1969) scale emphasized the concept of hard work, Buchholz's scale stressed the notion of independence.

Further support for the positive association between age and belief in the work ethic is provided by Cherrington et al.'s (1979) study of 3053 subjects in diverse occupations. In a multiple regression controlling for sex, income, seniority, and occupational level, older age was the strongest predictor ($\Delta R^2 = .088$) of the moral importance of work. While Cherrington et al. suggested both cohort and age explanations, their methodology does not allow them to draw conclusions in this regard.

The function and meaning of work were examined by Vecchio's (1980) replication of Morse and Weiss's (1955) earlier work. In a sample of 1099 full-time employed males, the central issue was the desire to work as assessed by the following question: "If you were to get enough money to live as comfortably as you would like for the rest of your life, would you continue to work or would you stop working?" With the exception of the 45 to 54-year-old age category, all age groups expressed a stronger preference to discontinue working relative to the Morse and Weiss sample. Moreover, a discriminant analysis revealed age and job satisfaction to be the most important predictors of desire to continue working, with older workers having a stronger desire to discontinue working than younger workers.

In addition to the Protestant work ethic, Cherrington et al. compared responses of older and younger workers on a number of other work values. They found that older workers placed less emphasis than younger workers on the importance of money, the importance of friends over work, and the acceptability of welfare as an alternative to work. On the other hand, older workers valued pride in craftsmanship to a greater extent than younger workers. Finally, upward striving was not related to age.

Other values examined by Buchholz were the organizational belief system (that is, the belief that success in the organization is more dependent on the ability to get along and "play the game" than it is on individual productivity); the humanistic belief system (that work is a fundamental way in which people fulfill themselves); the leisure ethic (that human fulfillment can only be found in leisure activities); and Marxist-related beliefs (that work does not allow people to fulfill themselves as creative individuals but mainly benefits the ownership classes). No significant age differences were found with regard to the organizational belief system, the humanistic belief system, and the leisure ethic. However, young people under 30 were more committed to Marxist-related beliefs than older workers.

Age differences in commitment to the values of ecosystem distrust, intrinsic reward, self-expression, pride in work, and extrinsic reward were studied by Taylor and Thompson (1976) based on a sample of 1058 subjects employed in diverse occupations in government, hospital, and private sales and service organizations. Older workers were found to place less emphasis than younger workers on self-expression (including the opportunity to learn and to make independent decisions), extrinsic rewards (that is, attachment to money as a reward for working hard on the job), and intrinsic rewards (that is, preference for intrinsic over extrinsic job characteristics). However, no significant age differences were found in the value placed on pride in work (as exemplified by contemporary workers' competence and pride in their work) and ecosystem distrust (that is, distrust of people, things, and institutions in one's environment). Finally, with regard to ecosystem distrust, a significant interaction effect with age and occupational classification was found. This means that ecosystem distrust increases with age for blue collar workers but not for managerial, professional, technical, or clerical workers.

Finally, a recent longitudinal study found that occupational experiences have an influence on the development of occupational reward values (Mortimer and Lorence, 1979). This study suggests that the values people hold may change depending on their organizational experiences.

SUMMARY, IMPLICATIONS, AND FUTURE RESEARCH ISSUES

Research examining age and work values is sparse. For only one value—belief in the work ethic—are there sufficient studies to begin to draw any conclusions, but here results were mixed. Moreover, the existing studies did not examine the plausibility of the generational or cohort explanation of differences in values which is alluded to in the literature. However, the studies point out that demographic characteristics as a whole are relatively poor predictors of values. For example, in Cherrington et al.'s study, the largest amount of variance in values explained by age, education, seniority, occupational status level, sex, and income was 9 percent.

Clearly, value differences between age groups is an area needing further research. In particular, more study of age differences in belief in the Protestant work ethic is warranted. Moreover, if values do indeed affect attitudes and behaviors, a greater understanding of the value-formation process is called for. Toward this end, longitudinal studies examining the relative influence on value development of organizational factors versus individual characteristics could be undertaken.

Need Importance and Preferred Job Characteristics

A need is an internal state that makes certain outcomes, or job characteristics, appear attractive (Robbins, 1979). A basic premise of most motivation theories is that people engage in activities to

satisfy needs. From an organizational perspective, rewarding effective performance with outcomes that satisfy needs reinforces desired
performance. Hence, identifying needs that are important to the
employee is crucial to motivating effective performance. Clearly, if
there are age differences in need importance, the process of identifying those needs would thus be aided.

IMPORTANCE OF NEEDS

The relationship between age and need importance using Maslow's
(1954) need classification scheme has been examined in several
studies. In a study of 1916 managers at all levels in the organizational
hierarchy, Porter (1963) found that the importance of needs for security and affiliation increased with age, while the importance of self-
actualization decreased. However, no age differences were found for
the importance of needs for esteem and autonomy. Hall and Mansfield
(1975) reported similar findings for security and affiliation needs in a
sample of research scientists and engineers in 1967, but not in 1969.
However, in contrast to Porter (1963), esteem needs became more
important with age. The significant correlations between age and
need importance were generally weak, with age explaining no more
than 4 percent of the variance. According to Hall and Mansfield, the
lack of significant relationships in 1969 demonstrated that changes in
the environmental conditions and differential treatment based on age
between 1967 and 1969 had a stronger impact than age on need
importance. Specifically, in 1967 younger employees were in high
demand and older workers felt less organizational support, but in
1969, when budgets and staffs were cut, the younger workers were
laid off first.

Further evidence of the importance of the need for security to the
older worker was found in a study of female paraprofessional employees (Holley et al., 1978). When asked to respond to a series of
questions relating to their reasons for accepting employment, older
workers reported wages and job security to be significantly more
important than did younger workers.

Growth need, or higher-order need strength has been examined in a
number of studies as an individual difference that would affect an
employee's reaction to job characteristics (see White, 1978, for a
review). This need is equivalent to Maslow's self-actualization need
plus the intrinsic component of Maslow's esteem needs. Various
researchers have suggested that employees with high growth need
strength would respond more positively (be more satisfied, motivated,
and the like) to an enriched job than employees with low growth need
strength (Hackman and Lawler, 1971). In fact, Wanous (1974) found

that higher-order need strength had a stronger moderating effect on employee responses to job characteristics than either Protestant work ethic or rural/urban background. However, a number of studies have failed to replicate these earlier results (White, 1978); hence, it is difficult to make a definite statement as to the importance of higher-order need strength as a moderator of an individual's response to an enriched job. On the other hand, the importance of growth need strength as an independent predictor of job performance was assessed in a recent study, and findings indicated that there was a strong positive relationship between growth need strength and performance for older (57+) workers, but not for younger (less than 47 years) workers (Holley et al., 1978). In conclusion, growth need strength is not only a much researched variable, but a potentially important one for understanding individual behavior in organizations.

Seven studies were identified involving ten samples that examined age differences in growth need strength (see Table A-2, Appendix). In four instances, older workers were found to have lower growth need strength than younger workers (Aldag and Brief, 1977; Cook and Wall, 1980; Evans et al., 1979; Hackman and Oldham, 1976), while in six samples no significant differences emerged (Aldag and Brief, 1977; Alderfer and Guzzo, 1979; Holley et al., 1978; Warr et al., 1979). The highest explained variance in growth need strength was 8.4 percent ($r = .299$) (Cook and Wall, 1980), indicating that the association is not strong. All the studies except Aldag and Brief's (1977) police officer sample offered directional support for the negative relationship. Hence, there is weak support for the existence of age-related differences in growth need strength.

PREFERRED JOB CHARACTERISTICS

Preferences for job characteristics as a function of age for blue and white collar samples were examined by Wright and Hamilton (1978) using data from the 1972-73 Quality of Employment Survey in an attempt to explain increasing job satisfaction with age. Table 2.1, reprinted from their article, allows us to assess the importance of very specific job characteristics and, consequently, gives us information in a more useful form than global measures, such as growth need strength. At the same time, items are categorized according to four factors: (a) enrichment, self-actualization, and job freedom; (b) extrinsic factors;[1] (c) diminished capabilities; and (d) interpersonal factors. Hence, the relative importance of the different categories for the older worker can be assessed. As Wright and Hamilton do not report tests of significance, it must be emphasized that all interpretations are highly tentative. In particular, because of the extremely small sample size of the 16-19 and 60+ groups, only very large differences between these and other groups would be significant.[2] In the absence of rigorous studies of preferences for job characteristics related to age, the Wright and Hamilton tables are presented here primarily for their descriptive value.

In general, no important differences by age emerged in the value people attached to fulfilling, meaningful and enriching work. In fact, for white collar workers of all age categories, intrinsic job characteristics as a group were more important than extrinsic factors. Having enough authority to do the work was the most important job characteristic for white collar workers over 50 years and increased in importance with age in both the white and blue collar samples. Developing abilities and having interesting work were rated very important by more than 70 percent of all white collar workers in all age groups. However, the importance of these two factors declined with age for blue collar workers.

For the over-50 blue collar workers, extrinsic factors were rated relatively more importance than intrinsic aspects, with good pay, security, and fringe benefits rated as very important by more than 70 percent of the 50–59 group, and authority being the only intrinsic factor rated by more than 70 percent as being very important. For both blue and white collar workers, consistent with Porter (1963) and Hall and Mansfield (1975), security, fringe benefits, and working hours tended to increase in importance with age. Younger workers, on the other hand, attached greater importance to opportunities for promotion. Finally, the importance of pay was fairly constant across all age categories for white collar workers. For blue collar workers, pay importance increased through age 40–49 and then dipped for the 50–59 group, increasing in importance for the 60+ group.

Some interesting differences are apparent with regard to resource support ("diminished capabilities") and interpersonal factors. Older workers attached a great deal more importance to receiving help and assistance on the job. For the over-60 blue collar worker, of 23 items, the one item rated most highly was having enough help and equipment to do the job. These results are consistent with the notion of declining capacity for work accompanying old age. Finally, the importance of having friendly supervisors and co-workers taking an interest increased with age for both white and blue collar workers.

Because of the small number of subjects in the 60+ groups, it is with a great deal of caution that we point out the existence of sharp differences between the 50–59 and the 60+ groups. In all, 10 to 23 job

TABLE 2.1 Percentage Rating Selected Job Characteristics as "Very Important" By Age and Social Class (Economically Active Males, 16-64)

Job Characteristics	16-19	20-29	30-39	40-49	50-59	60+
Age			*a. White-Collar*			
N*	13	121	151	132	75	18
Enrichment, Self-Actualization & Job Freedom						
Develop abilities	61.5	83.5	76.0	68.9	79.7	76.5
Work interesting	100.0	77.7	73.5	75.0	75.7	83.3
Do best things	61.5	54.5	59.9	56.9	50.0	76.5
Problem hard enough	0.0	68.6	66.0	55.4	51.4	77.8
Have freedom	61.5	62.8	60.5	55.4	60.8	76.5
Enough authority	50.0	66.1	73.3	64.6	82.4	94.4
Extrinsic Factors						
Good promotion	61.5	72.7	66.0	50.4	57.3	58.8
Good pay	38.5	51.2	59.9	52.8	59.5	76.5
Good security	15.4	49.6	58.0	51.6	56.8	77.8
Good fringe	38.5	38.7	51.3	44.5	45.9	61.1
Good hours	15.4	18.2	20.7	37.0	33.8	55.6
Promotion fair	23.1	70.4	64.9	55.9	20.0	66.7

38

"Diminished Capabilities"

Enough help	30.8	50.4	60.0	59.2	70.3	66.7
No excessive work	15.4	10.7	8.8	9.8	9.3	25.0
Enough time	38.5	29.7	34.2	41.5	43.2	77.8
Supervisor helpful	38.5	37.2	43.4	48.8	42.3	55.6
Co-workers helpful	15.4	34.7	46.2	53.1	47.3	60.0

Interpersonal

Make friends	15.4	33.9	31.7	40.6	45.3	50.0
Co-workers friendly	76.9	62.8	70.0	67.7	79.7	61.1
Co-workers take interest	0.0	18.2	24.1	41.4	28.4	50.0
Supervisor friendly	0.0	34.5	32.0	40.3	38.0	77.8
Co-workers friendly	53.8	33.9	38.7	50.0	36.5	44.4

*N's shown are for the total sample. Missing data were omitted on an item-by-item basis.

Source: From James D. Wright and Richard F. Hamilton, "Work Satisfaction and Age: Some Evidence for the 'Job Change' Hypothesis." *Social Forces*, 1978, 56, pp. 1140-1158. Copyright © The University of North Carolina Press. Reprinted by permission.

TABLE 2.1 Percentage Rating Selected Job Characteristics as "Very Important" By Age and Social Class (Economically Active Males, 16-64)

b. Blue-Collar

	Age					
N*	16-19 42	20-29 217	30-39 106	40-49 108	50-59 95	60+ 24
Enrichment, Self-Actualization and Job Freedom						
Develop abilities	59.5	74.4	69.9	71.0	51.1	54.5
Work interesting	64.3	76.0	72.1	71.0	59.6	47.6
Do best things	52.4	52.1	58.4	61.7	58.1	75.0
Problem hard enough	7.1	24.6	26.7	25.5	23.1	55.0
See results	54.8	61.1	63.7	61.7	53.8	54.5
Have freedom	50.5	48.6	41.6	54.6	53.3	45.5
Enough authority	42.9	59.8	57.4	62.0	73.4	81.0
Extrinsic Factors						
Good promotion	52.4	71.0	73.5	47.1	38.0	42.9
Good pay	59.5	68.2	78.6	82.2	75.3	81.8
Good security	42.9	66.4	69.3	78.8	80.9	81.0

Good fringe	50.0	53.3	67.6	73.6	71.3	76.2
Good hours	40.5	49.3	46.5	54.2	64.5	77.3
Promotion fair	54.8	65.0	68.3	55.8	46.2	60.0
"Diminished Capabilities"						
Enough help	73.8	68.2	75.2	79.4	77.4	95.5
No excessive work	16.7	17.3	17.8	24.8	34.8	36.4
Enough time	45.2	53.5	56.0	58.3	59.6	77.3
Supervisor helpful	38.1	49.5	56.6	54.7	61.3	81.8
Co-workers helpful	50.0	50.5	56.0	48.6	64.5	77.3
Interpersonal						
Make friends	38.1	43.7	42.2	44.8	48.9	36.4
Co-workers friendly	73.8	68.5	64.4	64.5	63.0	66.7
Co-workers take interest	19.0	31.9	23.7	32.4	48.9	52.4
Supervisor friendly	47.6	47.5	48.0	51.9	56.4	81.8
Co-workers friendly	57.1	57.1	53.5	56.0	58.1	57.1

*N's shown are for the total sample. Missing data were omitted on an item-by-item basis.

Source: From James D. Wright and Richard F. Hamilton, "Work Satisfaction and Age: Some Evidence for the 'Job Change' Hypothesis." *Social Forces*, 1978, 56, pp. 1140-1158. Copyright © The University of North Carolina Press. Reprinted by permission.

characteristics were rated by more than 70 percent of the 60+ subjects as very important as compared to 5 of 23 for the 50–59 group. In fact, in the white collar group, for six items there was a difference between these two age groups of more than 20 percent of the number of subjects rating that item very important. Clearly, it is important to note that findings for the 50–59 age group will not necessarily be generalizable to those over age 60. Particularly in view of the recent national legislation raising the mandatory retirement age, it is also important that future research be undertaken to determine the extent to which these differences do exist.

SUMMARY, IMPLICATIONS, AND FUTURE RESEARCH ISSUES

In general, Wright and Hamilton's study is consistent with Porter's (1963) and Hall and Mansfield's (1975) findings that security and affiliation needs increase in importance with age. However, these need importance and job preference research findings are not consistent with the work values studies on the importance of extrinsic rewards (Cherrington et al., 1979; Taylor and Thompson, 1976) and of friends (Cherrington et al., 1979). The use of different measures may account in part for the inconsistent results.

According to Wright and Hamilton, it would appear that age-related differences in job preferences and need importance are not generational or cohort differences. First, there are only modest age-related differences in what people regard as important in their work. Moreover, values relating to the enrichment and meaningfulness of work, which were thought to be of great importance to the young, showed minimal age differences.

Another possible explanation is that changes in preferences are simply a function of psychological aging; that is, standards and expectations decline as people age. This explanation is ruled out because the evidence showed to the contrary—that for the most part expectations remain constant with age, and that in some cases there appears to be an escalation of demands. An alternate aging phenomenon that is consistent with the findings is a life-cycle/career stage explanation. According to this explanation, both extra-work and work factors will have an influence on preferences for job characteristics, and the age differences that do exist reflect changes in the pattern of need as one moves through the life cycle. For example, one extra-work factor that would affect preferences for fringe benefits and job security would be the increased financial responsibilities associated with having a family. Consistent with Mortimer and Lorence (1979), the nature of the work experience would seem to account for at least some of the differences found between white and blue collar workers—for example, those noted for developing abilities and having interesting work. Finally, according to this explanation, as workers move through the life cycle, they typically move into "better" jobs—better paying, offering more autonomy and responsibility—and this accounts for the increased satisfaction with age.

In view of the absence of research, further research on age-related differences in job preferences is needed. It might be possible to rely on already existing data sets, such as the 1972-73 and 1977 Quality of Employment Surveys or the National Longitudinal Surveys, for preliminary analyses. However, even larger samples than that in the Quality of Employment Survey may be necessary in order to explore differences in the 60+, as compared to the 50–59 age group. Identifying causes of age-related differences in job preferences will require longitudinal as well as cross-sectional data.

Attitudes

Attitudes may be defined as "learned predispositions to respond to social objects in a specific manner" (Jabes, 1978). The values that people hold explain their attitudes and sometimes their behavior (Rokeach, 1973). Because attitudes may affect job behavior, employee attitudes are a relevant concern of organizations. By finding ways to encourage the development of attitudes leading to work behaviors congruent with organizational goal attainment, managers can influence organizational effectiveness.

In this section, research results concern the relationship between age and work attitudes are presented. Job satisfaction, job involvement, internal work motivation, and organizational commitment are the specific work attitudes that will be examined.

JOB SATISFACTION

Job satisfaction is "a postive or pleasurable emotional state resulting from the appraisal of one's job or job experience" (Locke, 1976). The three major causal models of job satisfaction are similar in that they specify that an individual's satisfaction is dependent on an interaction between the person and environment; however, they differ in delineating which internal processes determine the reaction (Locke, 1976). One prominent theory argues that job satisfaction is a function of the discrepancy between what an individual expects from his or her work environment and what he or she attains (for example,

McClelland et al., 1953). According to a second theory, need fulfillment is the key determinant of job satisfaction; that is, job satisfaction results from the fulfillment of an individual's needs (for example, Porter, 1962). Finally, it has been argued that it is not the discrepancy between what a person attains and what the person needs or expects that influences job satisfaction, but rather the discrepancy between what a person attains and what the person values or wants. Moreover, job satisfaction also reflects the importance of what is wanted (Locke, 1969). Hence, an individual's expectations, needs, and desires have variously been viewed as having a causal connection with job satisfaction.

Job satisfaction has been studied in a global sense. However, as the job situation is quite complex and has multiple dimensions, job attitudes are likewise complex. Hence, measures of satisfaction have been developed that attempt to assess satisfaction with specific job dimensions. Typical job facets that have been studied include: (a) work itself, (b) pay, (c) promotion, (d) recognition, (e) benefits, (f) supervision, (g) co-workers, (h) working conditions, and (i) company and management.

Importance of Overall Job Satisfaction. Overall job satisfaction, as well as satisfaction with different job facets, are relevant workplace concerns because of the consequences of satisfaction and dissatisfaction. Our attention is first directed to some consequences of overall job satisfaction.

First, people who express high overall job satisfaction are less likely to leave the organization and more likely to attend work, so long as they are able to (Mobley, Griffeth, et al., 1979; Porter and Steers, 1973; Price, 1977; Steers and Rhodes, 1978), than those expressing low job satisfaction. Because the amount of variance in turnover and absenteeism accounted for by job satisfaction is generally low, it has been suggested that the relationship between the variables is indirect (Mobley, Griffeth, et al., 1979; Steers and Rhodes, 1978).

Second, while the theory that "satisfaction causes performance" is not supported by research (Brayfield and Crockett, 1955; Herzberg et al., 1957; Vroom 1964), satisfaction may contribute to productivity in several ways. A company with satisfied employees may become known as a good place to work; hence, job applicants will be attracted to the company. The company, in turn, will be able to select highly qualified personnel (Quinn, et al., 1974). Moreover, satisfaction may improve group or organizational productivity through teamwork and communication.

Finally, some evidence suggests that job satisfaction is related to life satisfaction, self-confidence, physical health and longevity, and employee mental health (Locke, 1976). Naturally, these potential consequences are of great concern to the employee. Moreover, they could have an indirect organizational impact.

Importance of Job Satisfaction Dimensions. The dimensions of job satisfaction should be of concern to organizations because of their association with certain work behaviors. The dimensions of job satisfaction that are examined in this book—work itself, pay, promotions, supervision, and co-workers—have been found to be negatively associated with turnover, although there is stronger support for the first three factors (Mobley, Griffeth, et al., 1979; Porter and Steers, 1973; Price, 1977). On the other hand, the relationship of the facets of job satisfaction with absenteeism, similarly to that found for overall satisfaction, is more tenuous. Occasional studies have reported inverse relationships, however, and of the five dimensions, there is the strongest support for an inverse relationship between satisfaction with work itself and absenteeism (Rhodes and Steers, 1978). It seems plausible that the relationship between absence and the facets of job satisfaction is indirect and moderated, as in the case of overall satisfaction. In conclusion, as various dimensions of satisfaction are associated with withdrawal behavior, the organization should be concerned with age-related differences.

Review of Empirical Research—Overall Job Satisfaction. There is overwhelming evidence that overall job satisfaction is positively associated with age (see Table A-3, Appendix). That is, older employees in general report greater satisfaction with their jobs than do younger employees. While earlier studies reported a U-shaped relationship (Herzberg et al., 1957), post-Herzberg et al. studies have reported a linear increasing relationship between age and both overall and facet satisfaction (Gibson and Klein, 1970; Hulin and Smith, 1965; Hunt and Saul, 1975; Weaver, 1978).

The positive linear relationship between age and overall satisfaction appears to hold at least up to age 60. However, there is conflicting evidence, along with limited information, for the period after age 60. Saleh and Otis (1964) found that satisfaction increased through age 59 and decreased in the 60–65 period. Using a retrospective methodology of questionable validity, they asked two groups of subjects—one 50–59 years old, and the other 60–65 years old—to remember past feelings and anticipate future feelings. The decrease in satisfaction in the preretirement period may have been influenced by the fact that the organization in which the study was conducted had mandatory retirement at age 65. On the other hand, Staines and Quinn (1979), as shown in Table 2.2, found that the age 65+ workers reported higher levels of satisfaction than any other age group in each of three years. In other studies finding a positive age-satisfaction relationship, the over-60 workers are included in other age categories in describing the sample and/or in data analysis (Aldag and Brief, 1975; Gibson and Klein, 1970; Hunt and Saul, 1975; Weaver, 1978, 1980). Hence, these studies fail to shed light on the 60+ age group.

The relationship between age and job satisfaction holds for diverse representative household samples (Glenn et al., 1977; Near et al., 1978; Staines and Quinn, 1979; Weaver, 1980), as well as organization-specific samples (Gibson and Klein, 1970; Siassi et al., 1975). Moreover, the relationship holds for white collar (Hunt and Saul, 1975) and blue collar workers (Aldag and Brief, 1975; Gibson and Klein, 1970; Siassi et al., 1975; Stagner, 1975). In bivariate analysis, satisfaction of both male and female employees increases with age. However, multivariate studies, including other demographic and work-related factors along with age as predictors, report a consistent positive association for males, while positive results are less consistently reported for females (Glenn et al., 1977; Hunt and Saul, 1975; Weaver, 1978).

Table 2.2 shows trends in the age-satisfaction relationship based on data derived from the 1969 Survey of Working Conditions and the 1973 and 1977 Quality of Employment Surveys. First, corroborating the previous discussion, for each time period, older workers are more satisfied with their jobs than younger workers, and the relationship increases linearly. Second, there was a significant decline in overall satisfaction between 1969 and 1977 for all age groups, with the exception of those under 21. Weaver's (1980) study showed no change in the level of job satisfaction as measured by a single-item scale over the period 1972 to 1978. Staines and Quinn (1979) likewise reported that no change in levels of job satisfaction occurred when they used a single-item measure rather than the composite scale reported in Table 2.2. They concluded that a single-item measure was less sensitive to changes because the question was so general.

Age is quite frequently correlated with other variables, which are in turn related to job satisfaction. In particular, age is generally positively related to tenure, occupational level, and income, while it is negatively associated with educational level. Consequently, the relationship found between age and satisfaction could be due to these other factors. In view of the above, the nature of the age-satisfaction relationship can be better understood through an examination of multivariate studies. These studies will be discussed according to two major categories: (a) those that dealt with the relative influence of age and tenure; and (b) those that examined other demographic and organizational variables.

TABLE 2.2 Overall Job Satisfaction Index by Age

Age	1969		1973		1977	
	Number of Respondents	Mean Job Satisfaction	Number of Respondents	Mean Job Satisfaction	Number of Respondents	Mean Job Satisfaction
Under 21	97	-40	173	-42	203	-41
21-29	333	-21	568	-26	594	-49
30-44	489	5	634	11	759	-20
45-54	340	12	422	11	389	-4
55-64	210	19	248	17	271	-2
65 or older	55	23	41	63	45	11

Note: The overall job satisfaction index is an equally weighted combination of the general satisfaction and the specific satisfaction values transformed to a mean of zero and a standard deviation of 87 in 1959. Negative figures indicate deviations below the 1969 mean. Because significance indicators are not provided, the reader should note that some subpopulations are very small and have unstable means.

1. Number of respondents in 1973 and 1977 was weighted to provide comparability with 1969 data.

Source: From "American Workers Evaluate the Quality of their Jobs," by G.L. Staines and R. P. Quinn, *Monthly Labor Review*, 1979, 102, 3-32.

Three studies examined the relationships between age, tenure, and overall satisfaction (Gibson and Klein, 1970; Hunt and Saul, 1975; Siassi et al., 1975). Gibson and Klein (1970) examined the relationships between age, tenure, and overall satisfaction in two blue collar samples, one predominantly female and the other all male. In both samples, overall satisfaction increased with age across all tenure levels, while overall satisfaction decreased with tenure for all age categories. According to Gibson and Klein, the previous findings of a U-shaped relationship between age-tenure and satisfaction could be explained by the preponderance of short-tenured people who are young and long-tenured people who are older. Gibson and Klein concluded that the age-satisfaction relationship was in part a function of the psychological aging process rather than movement to a better job. In controlling for tenure, they had in effect controlled for job level and income factors, both of which are primarily associated with tenure in blue collar samples. They explained the age-satisfaction relationship in terms of changing needs, a mellowing process, and changing cognitive structures associated with age. Empirical research finding different predictors of overall satisfaction for older than younger people is cited by Gibson and Klein as support for the suggested change in cognitive structure.

Hunt and Saul (1975), in a survey of Australian white collar employees, found sex differences in the relationship between age, tenure, and job satisfaction. In the female sample, age was not a significant predictor of satisfaction, while tenure was positively associated with job satisfaction. In the male sample, multiple regression analyses revealed that both age and tenure were positively associated with job satisfaction, although age had a stronger influence. The existence of sex differences in needs, expectations, and work experiences is tentatively offered by Hunt and Saul as an explanation for the discrepant findings.

Siassi et al. (1975), in a sample of 558 blue collar workers, reported that workers over 40 years old had higher levels of job satisfaction than those under 40 regardless of the length of time workers had been on the job. They suggested that coping capacity increases with age, perhaps as a result of greater stability, ego strength, or the like.

In a probability sample similar in demographic composition to national probability samples, Near et al. (1978) examined the relationship between age, occupational level, and overall satisfaction. Univariate analyses revealed that occupational level and age were the strongest predictors of job satisfaction ($E^2 = .08$ and $.07$, respectively) among 18 variables. Moreover, when the effects of occupation were controlled, age remained a significant predictor of satisfaction.

Aging and cohort explanations of age differences in job satisfaction were examined systematically in two separate studies with varying results (Glenn et al., 1977; O'Brien and Dowling, 1981). The aging explanation that they examined was that the rewards associated with growing older (including higher income, more responsible jobs) increase job satisfaction. That is, many workers as they age move into more challenging work with higher income, which leads to greater job satisfaction. The cohort explanation was the tendency for older workers to have less formal education on the average than young adults. Education has a negative effect on job satisfaction because as education increases, so do one's expectations, such that a person may become dissatisfied with performing routine tasks. Both studies employed cross-sectional methodology and statistical control to isolate causal explanations of age-related differences.

In Glenn et al.'s study based on General Social Survey data for 1972, 1973, and 1974, age was positively related to satisfaction for both males and females while controlling for reward variables (an aging explanation). The reward variables included occupational prestige, family income, authority, and autonomy. Moreover, the age-satisfaction relationship was further upheld when education (a cohort explanation) was added as a control variable. For males, there was a slight reduction in the variance explained by age when reward variables were added, while there was virtually no change in explained variance for females. The authors concluded that the extrinsic rewards associated with age explained at least in part of the relationship for males but not for females, and that education was of rather minor importance in the age-satisfaction relationship, if valid at all.

The relative influence of a number of aging and cohort variables on job satisfaction was examined by O'Brien and Dowling (1981) based on an Australian household sample with 1383 subjects. Variables associated with aging included skill utilization, influence, variety, and income. In addition to education, they considered desired skill utilization, desired influence, and desired variety as variables associated with cohort membership. It should be pointed out that such a classification is somewhat arbitrary, as age differences in these variables could just as likely be accounted for as a result of aging. Similar to Glenn et al.'s findings, they reported that neither cohort nor aging variables alone accounted for the positive association between age and job satisfaction. However, for male samples the correlation became nonsignificant when partialing out the joint effects of aging and cohort variables. While the partial correlation for the total sample and for females remained statistically significant, the amount of explained variance was negligible. They conclude that the positive age-job satisfaction relationship results from both cohort and aging effects, specifically the decreasing differences between perceived and desired job attributes.

Similar to Glenn et al.'s study, Weaver's (1978) research was based on the General Social Survey data for 1972, 1973, and 1974. Weaver included marital status and religious intensity in the analysis, in addition to the control variables appearing in Glenn et al. In both the male and female samples, age was a significant predictor, while controlling for all the other variables, in one out of three years. Therefore, in contrast to Hunt and Saul (1975), Weaver did not find support for the existence of sex-related differences in the age-satisfaction relationship.

Review of Empirical Research—Dimensions of Job Satisfaction. Age-related differences in satisfaction with work itself, promotions, supervision, and co-workers are summarized in this section. However, pay satisfaction studies are summarized later in the discussion on compensation (pp. 134-138).

Empirical evidence strongly supports the existence of a positive association between age and satisfaction with work itself (see Table A-4, Appendix). Moreover, based on scant evidence, the relationship, at least up to age 60, appears to be linear rather than curvilinear (Hunt and Saul, 1975; Hulin and Smith, 1965; Schwab and Heneman, 1977a). Older workers in household samples (Muchinsky, 1978) as well as organization-specific samples report greater satisfaction with the work itself than younger workers. The relationship holds for both blue and white collar males. Results are mixed, however, with regard to females; there is some evidence that the relationship holds for female white collar workers (Hunt and Saul, 1975) but not for female blue collar workers (Hulin and Smith, 1965; Schwab and Heneman, 1977a). However, the number of studies is insufficient to draw firm conclusions. Age and satisfaction with work itself are positively related even when controlling for tenure (Gibson and Klein, 1970; Hunt and Saul, 1975). Finally, multivariate studies examining a large number of independent and, in some cases, dependent variables have consistently reported that age was a significant predictor of satisfaction with work itself (Herman et al., 1975; Hom, 1979; James and Jones, 1980; Newman, 1975).

Results have been mixed with regard to the relationship between age and satisfaction with promotion (see Table A-5, Appendix). The few studies finding a significant relationship report that older workers are *less* satisfied with promotions than younger workers (Hunt and Saul, 1975; Muchinsky, 1978). It would seem likely that the relationship between age and satisfaction with promotion would be highly organization-specific, depending on the promotion policies of the firm and the available opportunities for promotion. In fact, Newman (1975) found that satisfaction with promotion opportunities was explained to a great extent by differences between work groups. Age differences in opportunities for promotion, of course, would be influenced by the demographic composition of the work force.

Satisfaction with supervision does not appear to be related to age (see Table A-6, Appendix). In fact, only 4 of 13 analyses reported a significant association between age and this variable. Two reported a positive relationship (Gibson and Klein, 1970; Newman, 1975), while Hunt and Saul (1975) found a U-shaped relationship in their sample of male white collar workers.

Finally, there are few significant relationships reported for age and satisfaction with co-workers (see Table A-7, Appendix). Furthermore, the results are mixed, with Muchinsky (1978) finding that employees over 50 were less satisfied than employees in other age groups, Gibson and Klein (1970) and Newman (1975) finding a positive relationship, and Hunt and Saul (1975) reporting a U-shaped relationship for males.

Summary, Implications, and Future Research Issues. There is strong evidence supporting both a positive association between age and overall job satisfaction and satisfaction with work itself. These relationships are found in both bivariate and multivariate studies. In several studies, age has been found to be negatively associated with satisfaction with promotions, but the preponderance of studies have reported nonsignificant differences. Finally, there is almost no evidence in support of age-related differences in satisfaction with supervision and co-workers.

In view of the absence of age-related differences in satisfaction with pay, promotions, supervision, and co-workers, it would seem that the increase in overall job satisfaction associated with age is in large part a reflection of the increase in satisfaction with the nature of the job. There is mixed support for this view. Schwab and Heneman (1977a) reported a positive association between age and intrinsic satisfaction, controlling for experience, for female ($r_p = .19$, $p < .05$) and male ($r_p = .26$, $p < .05$) blue collar operatives, while the relationship between age and extrinsic satisfaction was nonsignificant for both samples. On the other hand, Arvey and Dewhirst (1979), in a sample of 291 scientists and engineeers, reported exactly opposite results, with age being positively associated with extrinsic satisfaction ($F = 3.20$, $p < .04$), while it was unrelated to intrinsic satisfaction ($F = 1.16$, $p < .31$). Finally, according to Andrisani et al. (1978), subjects in the National Longitudinal Survey who were highly satisfied in their jobs were more likely to report intrinsic (as opposed to extrinsic) rewards as their most preferred job aspect.

The lack of relationship between age and extrinsic satisfaction is understandable, in that extrinsic outcomes are under the control of the organization (Schwab and Heneman, 1977a). Because of this, it would be expected that organizations would differ in their administration of pay and promotion policies. Moreover, co-worker relations, supervision, and opportunities for promotion may vary from one work group to another (Herman et al., 1975; Newman, 1975). Hence, there is no reason to expect that age and satisfaction with pay, promotions, co-workers, and supervision would be related in a consistent manner across organizations.

Explaining the positive association between age and satisfaction with intrinsic rewards is more difficult. Three major explanations have been offered with regard to the increase in overall satisfaction, and these would apply equally to intrinsic satisfaction. Wright and Hamilton (1978) dubbed these: (a) the cohort explanation, or the Lordstown hypothesis; (b) the aging explanation, or the "grinding down" hypothesis; and (c) the life-cycle explanation, or the "job change" hypothesis (which is also an aging explanation).

The argument for the cohort explanation is simply that younger workers have a different value set than older workers. Among these values are a willingness to question authority, a reduction in materialism, and a demand for fulfilling and enriching work (Wright and Hamilton, 1978). These values are seen to arise in part because of the higher educational level of younger workers (O'Brien and Dowling, 1981).

The contradiction in the needs of the system and the values of the workers are seen to account for the dissatisfaction of the younger workers. As was noted earlier, there is in fact little empirical evidence supporting generational differences in values. Differences in preferences and needs between older and younger workers appear to be related more to life-cycle development than to cohort differences. However, in the absence of evidence derived from longitudinal studies with an individual level of analysis, the cohort explanation cannot be eliminated as a plausible theory.

The second possibility is that needs, preferences, and expectations are lowered with age. In this case, greater satisfaction could result without any objective change in the job situation. Salvendy and Pilitsis's (1971) study on the effects of paced work on men of different ages provides some support for this explanation. They found that younger men had the highest physiological efficiency and reported the most satisfaction when they could set their own work pace. On the other hand, older workers were equally satisfied with paced (as compared to unpaced) work and were more efficient when on paced work. Glenn et al.'s (1977) study provides further support for this view, in that age and satisfaction were found to be related even when controlling for occupation. However, it is possible that the occupation variable in their study was not specific enough to measure qualitative occupational differences.

Finally, the life-cycle explanation holds that the greater satisfaction of older workers may result from progression in a career to a "better" job and from changes in expectations and needs associated with life-cycle development. Supporting this, Stagner (1975) noted that in one manufacturing site, the percentage of blue collar workers on line assembly declined as a function of age. The increase in satisfaction accompanying age may reflect the success of discontented older workers in transferring off the line to jobs more congruent with their preferences. Phillips et al. (1978) suggested that the high satisfaction associated with age could be explained by the similarity of the older worker's preferences for job structural attributes and their perceptions of what the job is offering. In their sample, however, they did not find the typical age-satisfaction relationship ($r = 10$, n.s.). Moreover, perceived job congruency was similar for the old and young group. At the same time, they did find a high positive association between satisfaction and job congruency ($r = .42$, $p < .001$). These results, while not actually confirming their explanation, are consistent with it.

It could well be that no one cause predominates in explaining job satisfaction. Rather, as suggested by O'Brien and Dowling (1981), each explanation in part may play a role in the increased job satisfaction of older workers.

Further research is needed to determine the extent to which each of the suggested explanations does indeed account for age-related differences in job satisfaction. Needless to say, longitudinal panel studies similar to the National Longitudinal Survey (Andrisani et al., 1978) would provide important information with regard to changes in job satisfaction with age. In future studies, special attention should be directed to changes in job satisfaction of the over-60 worker. Of particular interest is the effect of mandatory retirement at 70 on job satisfaction.

JOB INVOLVEMENT

Job involvement refers to "the degree to which a person is identified psychologically with his work, or the importance of work in his total self-image" (Lodahl and Kejner, 1965). The job-involved person is affected to a great extent by the whole job situation, including the work itself, co-workers, and so forth. Work is extremely important to his or her psychological life. The non-job-involved person, on the other hand, places primary emphasis on his or her off-job activities. Work is not so important to the identity of the non-job-involved person.

Having employees who are involved in their jobs is important to organizations for several reasons. First, the job-involved person is less likely to leave the organization (Rabinowitz and Hall, 1977). Furthermore, high job involvement is associated with high job satisfaction, and in particular with satisfaction with work itself, supervision, and people (Rabinowitz and Hall, 1977). Finally, there is limited support for a negative relationship between job involvement and absenteeism (Rabinowitz and Hall, 1977). Interestingly, studies have generally shown no relationship between job performance and involvement (Rabinowitz and Hall, 1977), although task success has been found to lead to job involvement (Bray et al., 1974; Hall and Nougaim, 1968).

Review of Empirical Research. The majority of studies examining job involvement have adapted scale items originally used in Lodahl and Kejner's (1965) study. Sample items in this scale include the following: "The major satisfaction in my life comes from my job." "I live, eat, and breathe my job." "I am very much involved personally in my work." Another measure that taps involvement is Dubin's (1956) central life interest scale.

The relationship between age and job involvement has been examined in a number of studies (see Table A-8, Appendix). In a recent review of the literature, Rabinowitz and Hall (1977) found seven bivariate studies involving nine samples which examined the age-involvement relationship (Gurin et al., 1960; Hall and Mansfield, 1975; Jones et al., 1975; Lodahl and Kejner, 1965; Mannheim, 1975; Schuler, 1975; Schwyhart and Smith, 1972). In six of the nine studies, a significant positive correlation between age and job involvement was reported.

Since Rabinowitz and Hall's (1977) review, eleven additional studies examining the age-job involvement relationship have been located. Seven of these studies were primarily bivariate in nature. Four single-sample studies found a positive association between age and job involvement (Blumberg, 1980; Hammer et al., 1981; James and Jones, 1980; Stevens et al., 1978). In addition, Aldag and Brief (1977) found that older workers were more involved in their jobs than younger workers in three out of four separate samples. Reitz and Jewell (1979) tested the relationship between job involvement and age for industrial workers in six different countries, including the United States, Turkey, Mexico, Yugoslavia, Thailand, and Japan. Job involvement and age were positively related for all samples except the Yugoslavian group of industrial workers. Finally, Warr et al. (1979), as part of a study developing work attitude scales, found a nonsignificant relationship between work involvement and age in a sample of 590 British male manual workers. In general, there is consistent support for a positive bivariate association between age and job involvement.

The age-job involvement relationship was examined in four multivariate studies. The relative influence of organizational structure variables versus personal characteristics on employee job attitudes was the focus of two studies (Herman et al., 1975; Newman, 1975). The other two studies focused on the relationship between job involvement and personal-demographic, personal-psychological, and situational characteristics (Rabinowitz et al., 1977; Saal, 1978). Three studies found support for the older worker being more job involved than the younger worker (Herman et al., 1975; Newman, 1975; Saal, 1978). However, in all three instances, other factors, including job situation (Saal, 1978), psychological (Saal, 1978) and organization structure characteristics (Herman et al., 1975; Newman, 1975) were more important than demographic characteristics in explaining job involvement. In the Rabinowitz et al. (1977) study, although age was significantly related to job involvement in bivariate correlation analysis, age was a nonsignificant predictor when controlling for psychological characteristics and job scope.

Summary, Implications, and Future Research Issues. In 19 out of 25 cases, bivariate correlations between age and job involvement were significant, with a median r of .29. It appears, then, that age is related, albeit weakly, to job involvement. Interpretation of this relationship, however, is not simple. All the studies that have been performed have been cross-sectional in nature and reflect both age and cohort effects (Palmore, 1978). We cannot say whether the relationship between age and job involvement is simply the result of the aging process or the historical situation of an age group. Moreover, age is frequently correlated with other variables, such as length of service and job level, which have been found to be related to job involvement (Rabinowitz and Hall, 1977). Hence, the possibility of a spurious relationship exists. Studies have been conducted in a multivariate framework, with mixed results. Three out of four multivariate studies find support for the older worker being more job involved, with age being an important demographic predictor. However, characteristics of the job situation and psychological characteristics of the worker appear to be more important influences on job involvement than age.

Future research should focus on identifying causal factors regarding the age-involvement relationship. Longitudinal panel studies that include variables representing age and cohort effects are needed.

INTERNAL WORK MOTIVATION

Internal work motivation may be defined as the degree to which the employee "is motivated to perform well on the job because of some subjective rewards or feelings that he or she expects to receive as a result of performing well" (Lawler, 1969). From a managerial standpoint, employees with high internal work motivation would not require close supervision, thus making the supervisor's job easier.

Internal work motivation has been found to be associated with other factors that are beneficial to the employee and the organization. First, people who report high internal work motivation are generally more satisfied with their jobs (Warr et al., 1979). Second, there is some indication that internal work motivation is positively associated with employee mental health (Warr et al., 1979).

Review of Empirical Research. Three studies involving six samples were found that examined the relationship between age and internal work motivation (see Table A-9, Appendix). Populations from which samples were drawn included scientists and engineers (Hall and Mansfield, 1975), government correctional officers (Aldag and Brief, 1977), police officers (Aldag and Brief, 1977), and manufacturing operatives (Aldag and Brief, 1977; Warr et al., 1979). A positive association was found between age and internal work motivation in all samples except one (correctional officers). It must be emphasized, however, that the relationship was weak, with no more than 7 percent of the variation in motivation being explained by age. This would suggest that other factors, either singly or in concert, are more important than age in explaining internal work motivation.

Summary, Implications, and Future Research Issues. As with the findings on job satisfaction, internal work motivation has been found to be consistently related to age. In view of the fact that all the reported studies were cross-sectional and bivariate in nature, they give no information as to causality. Future research should be designed to address this question. Some specific causal explanations that could be explored are suggested later in the job satisfaction discussion. For example: Is increased internal motivation a function of the aging process, or are the higher levels of reported internal work motivation simply a reflection of increased levels of job responsibility as the employee progresses in his or her career?

ORGANIZATIONAL COMMITMENT

The concept of organizational commitment relates to the relative strength of an individual's identification with and involvement in an organization. According to Porter et al. (1974), a highly committed member has a strong belief in and acceptance of the organization's goals and values, is willing to exert effort on behalf of the organization, and has a strong desire to remain in the organization.

Having committed employees is important to organizations for several reasons. First, recent findings indicate that commitment is associated with lower absenteeism (Mowday et al., 1979; Steers, 1977). Moreover, commitment is a better predictor of turnover than is job satisfaction (Koch and Steers, 1978; Mowday et al., 1979; Porter et al., 1974). Finally, several studies suggest that highly committed employees may perform better than less committed ones (Mowday et al., 1979; Porter et al., 1974; Steers, 1977).

Review of Empirical Research. Eighteen studies have been identified which examined the relationship between age and organizational commitment (see Table A-10, Appendix). Populations in which the age-commitment relationship has been examined include three samples of research scientists and engineers (Lee, 1971; Sheldon, 1971; Steers, 1977) and five hospital samples (Aldag and Brief, 1977; Jamal, 1981; Kidron, 1978; Steers, 1977; Welsch and LaVan, 1981). Other samples include police officers (Aldag and Brief, 1977), mental health employees (Hrebiniak, 1974; Michaels and Spector, 1982), insurance company employees (Bluedorn, 1982; Kidron, 1978), personnel specialists (Kidron, 1978), federal government supervisors (Stevens et al., 1978), nonfaculty university employees (Morris and Steers, 1980), state government employees (Morris and Sherman, 1981), nonsupervisory employees in an employee-owned firm (Hammer et al., 1981), accountants (Arnold and Feldman, 1982), bus company managers and employees (Angle and Perry, 1981), employees in a service-oriented business (Martin, 1980), and manufacturing employees (Cook and Wall, 1980). Hence, diverse samples have been studied.

Results of seventeen bivariate analyses have found older workers to be more committed to the organization than younger workers (Aldag and Brief, 1977; Angle and Perry, 1981; Arnold and Feldman, 1982; Bluedorn, 1982; Cook and Wall, 1980; Hammer et al., 1981; Hrebiniak, 1974; Jamal, 1981; Kidron, 1978; Lee, 1971; Morris and Sherman, 1981; Michaels and Spector, 1982; Morris and Steers, 1980; Sheldon, 1971; Stevens et al., 1978; Welsch and LaVan, 1981). However, in four analyses, differences in commitment between older and younger workers were not significant (Aldag and Brief, 1977; Kidron, 1978; Martin, 1980; Sheldon, 1971).

Results of multivariate studies are less conclusive, with five analyses supporting a positive relationship (Bluedorn, 1982; Michaels and Spector, 1982; Morris and Sherman, 1981; Steers, 1977; Stevens et al., 1978), and six finding nonsignificant results (Bluedorn, 1982; Lee, 1971; Steers, 1977; Stevens et al., 1978). These results suggest that age and commitment may be related as a result of their association with a third variable.

A possible confounding variable in examining the age-commitment relationship may be tenure. A theoretical explanation for the relationship between age and commitment has been offered by Sheldon (1971). According to Sheldon, as one's investment in the organization increases, so does one's commitment. Growing older increases one's investment in several ways. As the individual ages, he or she is bound more tightly to the organization, for example through pension plans and seniority rights. Furthermore, opportunities for interorganizational mobility are reduced with age, as other organizations are reluctant to provide incentives necessary to lure away the older worker. At the same time, however, it seems that Sheldon's arguments could be used equally well to explain a positive association between tenure and commitment.

Summary, Implications, and Future Research Issues. While bivariate studies support a positive relationship between age and organizational commitment, results of multivariate studies only weakly support such a relationship. Hence, it is possible that the relationship found in bivariate studies is spurious. It will be the task of future research to examine the relationship between age and commitment while controlling for other potentially important variables, such as tenure.

Turnover Intention

Behavioral intentions are an important link between attitudes and behaviors (Fishbein, 1967). Recently, a number of studies have examined the role of intentions in predicting turnover. These studies have reported a consistent positive relationship between intentions to leave the organization and subsequent turnover (Mobley, Griffeth, et al., 1979). Moreover, intentions have been found to be a better predictor of turnover than job satisfaction (Mobley, Griffeth, et al., 1979). With these facts in mind, it seems important to understand the relationship between age and turnover intention.

The age-turnover intentions relationship has been examined in thirteen studies (see Table A-11, Appendix). It should be noted that in several cases, the populations that have been sampled have demographic characteristics representative of the U.S. labor force, lending confidence in the generalizability of results. Both bivariate (Arnold and Feldman, 1982; Jamal, 1981; Martin, 1979; Martin and Hunt, 1980; Miller et al., 1979; Mobley et al., 1978; Rousseau, 1978; Waters et al., 1976) and multivariate (Arnold and Feldman, 1982; Gupta and Beehr, 1979; Martin, 1979; Mobley et al., 1978) analyses have supported a consistent negative relationship between age and turnover intention. Of 23 analyses, only six found nonsignificant relationships (Bluedorn, 1982; Evans et al., 1979; Martin and Hunt, 1980), and two showed positive relationships (Michaels and Spector, 1982; Zey-Ferrell, 1982). The narrow (5-year) age range of the sample may have been responsible for the nonsignificant findings in the Evans et al. study. There is strong evidence, therefore, suggesting that older workers are less likely to have an intention of leaving the organization than younger workers.

Implications of the age-turnover intention relationship are similar to those for age and turnover. These are discussed, along with future research issues, in Chapter 3.

Conclusions

Psychological characteristics of the older worker have been examined in considerable detail. More than sixty empirical studies were reviewed. Important findings are highlighted below:

- The existence of generational differences in values between older and younger workers is not clearly supported by the literature. More research is needed with regard to the value-formation process and age-related differences in values.

- Differences do exist in the needs and preferences of older and younger workers. In particular, older workers have greater needs for security and affiliation and lower needs for self-actualization than do younger workers. These differences appear to be related to career stage and life-cycle influences, as opposed to cohort membership.
- Older workers have consistently expressed greater overall satisfaction than younger workers. There is some indication that satisfaction with work itself (also consistently higher for older workers) is the major influence on the higher levels of expressed job satisfaction.
- There are no consistent differences found between older and younger workers with regard to satisfaction with pay (see Chapter 6), promotion, supervision, and co-workers. Some evidence suggests that organization-specific factors are more important in explaining these facets of job satisfaction than individual difference variables.
- Older workers report higher levels of internal work motivation and job involvement than younger workers. No empirical research was found that explained these relations.
- Although age and organizational commitment have been found to be positively related, the lack of consistency in multivariate studies suggests that the relationship is spurious. More research is needed in this regard.
- Older workers are less likely than younger workers to have the intention of leaving the organization.

While there is considerable evidence showing the existence of age-related differences in psychological characteristics, the major weakness of the research is that it does not enable us to understand *why* these relationships exist. In fact, only two studies attempted to statistically separate cohort from aging influences (Glenn et al., 1977; O'Brien and Dowling, 1981). The major task of future research is to identify relevant causal factors associated with age-related differences.

NOTES

1. Preferences for extrinsic factors are discussed in greater detail in Chapter 6.

2. Approximate sampling errors of differences between two percentages depend on the sample size and the magnitude of the percentages involved (Quinn and Shepard, 1974). As an example, for two subsamples with at least 100 subjects in each, if percentages ranged between 35 percent of 65 percent, there would have to be at least a 15 percent difference for the percentages to be significantly different at the .05 level.

CHAPTER 3

WORK BEHAVIORS OF THE OLDER WORKER

Job Performance

A major concern associated with raising the mandatory retirement age and with the projected aging of the work force is work performance of older employees. The concern stems from a widespread belief that work performance declines as age increases (Britton and Thomas, 1973; Rosen and Jerdee, 1976a, 1976b; Haefner, 1977; Rosen and Jerdee, 1977; Craft et al., 1979). The question is, however, whether the negative attitudes toward the older worker (which are discussed more fully in Chapter 4) are well founded. In an attempt to answer that question, the research studies of the age-job performance relationship are examined.

REVIEW OF EMPIRICAL RESEARCH

As shown in Table B-1 in the Appendix, 28 empirical studies of the age-performance relationship, conducted over the past 30 years, were located. Essentially bivariate in nature, these studies sampled a variety of workers ranging from production to managerial, engineering, scientific, and professional workers. The two largest groups sampled, however, consisted of industrial production workers and scholar-scientists. With sample sizes ranging from 45 to more than 10,000, the samples generally represented the adult worker ranging in age from 25 years to 60 and above.

In very general terms, the research findings provide mixed results on the relationship between age and performance. First, there were a considerable number of studies showing a nonsignificant relationship

(Arvey and Mussio, 1973; Bowers, 1952; Breen and Spaeth, 1960; Chown, 1972; Greenberg, 1961; King, 1956; Klores, 1966; Kutscher and Walker, 1960; Maher, 1955; Schwab and Heneman, 1977b; Smith, 1953). Several studies also showed some older workers' performance to be better in terms of accuracy and steadiness of work output and output level (Eisenberg, 1980; Holley et al., 1978; Maher, 1955; Kutscher and Walker, 1960). Finally, there was evidence that performance declined with age (Clay, 1956; Cole, 1979; Dalton and Thompson, 1971; Dennis, 1954, 1968; Eisenberg, 1980; Greenberg, 1961; Lehman, 1953; Mark, 1956, 1957; Mathews and Cobb, 1974; Pelz and Andrews, 1966; Roe, 1965; Stumpf and Rabinowitz, 1981; Walker, 1964).

Nonsignificant relationships between age and performance were not quite as prevalent as were findings of decreases in performance with age. Studies reporting nonsignificant relationships included samples of blue collar employees (Breen and Spaeth, 1960; Bowers, 1952; King, 1956; Schwab and Heneman, 1977b), female production workers (Mark, 1956), clerical workers (Arvey and Mussio, 1973; Greenberg, 1961; Kutscher and Walker, 1960; Smith, 1953), male supervisors (Maher, 1955), and a group of professional, supervisory, and clerical employees (Klores, 1966).

Performance was found to increase with age in four instances. Maher's (1955) study of salespersons and Holley et al.'s (1978) study of paraprofessionals found older workers to be better performers than younger workers. Moreover, older clerical workers were found to be more accurate and have greater steadiness of output, with performance declining only for workers 65 and older (Kutscher and Walker, 1960). Finally, older examiners and materials handlers in a garment manufacturing plant had higher productivity based on their piece rate earnings (Eisenberg, 1980). In this same study, however, there was a moderate decline in piece rate earnings for older sewing machine operators. The reported differences between these jobs were that the examiner and materials handling jobs required more skill, whereas the sewing machine operator job required speed.

Decreases in performance with age were reported in fifteen studies. Clay (1956) reported a slight decline in performance after age 50 for printers, Mark (1956) reported a drop in productivity after age 55 for male production workers, Greenberg (1961) reported a slow decrease in performance for factory workers beginning after age 44, Walker (1964) reported a slight performance decline for mail sorters who were 55–59 years old, and Mathews and Cobb (1974) found a negative correlation between age and performance for air traffic controllers. Cleveland and Landy (1981) found that older ratees (ages 45–65) received lower ratings than younger ratees (21–44) on two out of eight performance dimensions—self-development and interpersonal skills. In addition, as noted earlier, the productivity of sewing machine operators in Eisenberg's (1980) study declined after age 54.

The balance of the studies showing a decline in performance revealed essentially an inverted U-relationship between age and performance for scholars, engineers, and scientists (Cole, 1979; Dalton and Thompson, 1971; Dennis, 1954, 1968; Lehman, 1953; Pelz and Andrews, 1966; Roe, 1965). Peaking of performance occurred in the 30s in Lehman's (1953) study of the bibliographies of more than 10,000 individuals in the sciences, in medicine, surgery, and related fields, and in philosophy, music, art, and literature. However, in a longitudinal study of scholars and scientists who lived to age 79, Dennis (1968) found relatively high productivity during the age decades of the 60s and 70s. For the men in the sciences, for example, from 17 to 32 percent and from 13 to 21 percent of their total works were completed while in their 60s and 70s, respectively.

Double-peaking, or a saddle-shaped curve, was also found for scientists (Pelz and Andrews, 1966). Some explanations given for the trough between the peaks were that the mid-40s are when people may not take on risky new assignments because of heavy family financial needs or when they may experience a midlife crisis and consequently performance declined for a time.

Peaking also varied between fields (Dennis, 1954, 1968; Lehman, 1953) and within fields (Cole, 1979; Dennis, 1968; Pelz and Andrews, 1966; Roe, 1965). For Lehman (1953), peaking occurred earlier in the abstract sciences such as mathematics and later in empirically based disciplines such as biology. Dennis (1968) proposed that the earlier decline in productivity in the arts occurred because art, music, and literature reflected individual creativity, while a greater period of training and accumulation of data enabled the scholar and scientist to make contributions in later years.

To investigate within-field differences, Cole (1979) studied a sample of mathematicians longitudinally. He found that strong publishers remained strong throughout their lifetimes while younger, weak publishers shifted over time to become nonpublishers. Cole interpreted his results to suggest that the shift by the weak publishers might have occurred because their early work had gone unrecognized, while that of the early strong publishers had received recognition. Rather similarly, Pelz and Andrews (1966) suggested that the research climate, in addition to motivation and self-reliance, might help reduce the decline in performance with age.

Finally, the effect of experience was examined in three studies (Kutscher and Walker, 1960; Mathews and Cobb, 1974; Schwab and Heneman, 1977b). In two of the studies, experience moderated the age-performance relationship (Kutscher and Walker, 1960; Schwab and Heneman, 1977b). In the first instance, for the more experienced (more than 9 months) clerical workers only, the average rates of output for six age groups (covering ages from less than 25 to 65 and above) were almost the same. In the second study, when controlling for experience, the partial correlation between age and performance was .04 for piece rate workers. But in the third study (Mathews and Cobb, 1974), the negative correlation between age and performance for air traffic controllers declined only from –.44 to –.35 when controlling for experience. Actually, in this occupation one would expect performance to be more of a function of experience than it is because of cumulative stress effects.

SUMMARY, IMPLICATIONS, AND FUTURE RESEARCH ISSUES

The evidence on the age-performance relationship is clearly mixed, but strong evidence is also absent to support the generally held negative belief about older worker performance. It is possible that level of motivation, self-reliance, and recognition, plus the workplace climate itself, may influence performance with age. It also seems plausible that age differences in performance depend on the nature of the demands of the job. Support for this view is provided by studies in the gerontology literature of the relationship between age and skill and abilities (see Chapter 4 for additional discussion). Examples of abilities and skills that have been found to decline with age include speed of movement, problem solving, perception, and memory, as well as hearing and vision (Birren and Schaie, 1977; Poon, 1980).

Questions are being raised, however, about whether the decline of some of the abilities and skills are pure age effects (Birren et al., 1980; Cunningham, 1980; Fozard, 1980; Giambra and Arenberg, 1980; Layton, 1975). For example, speed of behavior is believed to be affected by changes in the central nervous system, although an alternative consideration might be that the structure of the nervous system is a function of its activity level (Birren et al., 1980). In addition, to what extent is slowing learned or a habit? Suggestive of these possibilities are findings such as older active individuals being less slow in responding than inactive persons (Birren and Renner, 1977).

Practice may reduce the memory performance deficit, increase intellectual capacity, and effect compensatory changes which prevent a decline in some component of behavior or performance (Birren and Renner, 1977; Fozard, 1980; Willis and Baltes, 1980). Combining the behavioral, biological, and physiological sciences in a longitudinal design will help isolate the pure age effects (Birren and Schaie, 1977; Poon, 1980).

Two limitations in the age and performance literature were the use primarily of bivariate analyses and cross-sectional data. Multivariate analyses would make it possible to delineate more clearly the effects of variances such as experience, motivation, and workplace climate. Cross-sectional studies obscure the heterogeneity within age groups and do not allow for observations of change over time, assessments of generational effects, or of the "survivor" phenomenon effect (U.S. Dept. of Labor, 1979). The survivor phenomenon (that is, the possibility that older workers remaining in organizations are not representative) can take two forms. Survivors may consist of those whose performance continues to be acceptable, others having transferred or retired, or it is possible that older worker groups comprise individuals whose performance has declined but whom organizations retain until retirement.

Absenteeism

The cost of employee absenteeism to organizations in the United States has been estimated at $26.4 billion per year (Steers and Rhodes, 1978). This figure is derived from estimates of the number of work days lost each year at an estimated cost of $66 per day per absent employee (Mirvis and Lawler, 1977). These costs include lost productivity, downtime, fringe benefits paid to the missing worker, replacement work force costs, and unabsorbed fixed costs. In view of the high costs associated with absenteeism, understanding its causes is an important workplace concern.

REVIEW OF EMPIRICAL RESEARCH

The relationship between age and absenteeism has been examined in thirty studies, with mixed results. As the age-absence relationship is in part a function of absence-type and gender, the studies will be discussed according to two absence types, avoidable and unavoidable absence, and the gender of the sample (see Tables B-2 and B-3 in the Appendix). Casual, voluntary, unsanctioned, and frequent absences were classified as avoidable, while sickness, involuntary, sanctioned, and time-lost absences were classified as unavoidable (Nicholson et al., 1977). A summary of bivariate studies included in Tables B-2 and B-3 appears in Table 3.1.

As the table demonstrates, avoidable absence has generally been found to be inversely related to age, with this tendency being more distinct for males than females. However, for male samples non-significant relationships occur almost as frequently. For males, both direct and nonsignificant relationships between age and unavoidable absences are common. For females, nonsignificant relationships predominate on unavoidable absence, but direct relationships are also reported. These results suggest that older men are less likely to be absent on a casual basis than younger men, but more likely to be absent for sickness reasons. For women, there is weak support for a similar pattern, but the results are more ambiguous.

Multivariate studies of age and avoidable absence generally report either negative relationships (Froggatt, 1970; Martin, 1971; Nicholson and Goodge, 1976; Nicholson et al., 1977; Rousseau, 1978) or nonsignificant relationships (Froggatt, 1970; Hammer et al., 1981; Nicholson et al., 1977) for male, female, and mixed samples. Tenure (Froggatt, 1970; Nicholson and Goodge, 1976; Nicholson et al., 1977), overtime (Martin, 1971), and travel distance (Martin, 1971) are the variables that have been controlled for in these studies. In addition, Rousseau (1978) examined the relative influence of characteristics of individuals, positions, and departments on attitudes and behaviors. Results of canonical correlation analysis indicated that individual characteristics, particularly age, sex, and the need for clarity, were the best predictors of attitudes and behaviors, and of absenteeism in particular. However, departmental and positional characteristics were also important predictors of attitudes and behaviors.

Much less conclusive are the results of multivariate studies of unavoidable absence and age. For male samples, positive (Martin, 1971) and nonsignificant (Constas and Vichas, 1980; Nicholson et al., 1977; Watson, 1981) relationships have been reported. For females, studies have found positive (Martin, 1971), negative (Constas and Vichas, 1980), inverted-U (Nicholson and Goodge, 1976), and nonsignificant (Nicholson et al., 1977; Watson, 1981) relationships. Finally, mixed-gender samples are fairly consistent in reporting negative relationships (Garrison and Muchinsky, 1977; Hammer et al., 1981; Johns, 1978; Spencer and Steers, 1980; Watson, 1981), although positive (Garrison and Muchinsky, 1977) and nonsignifi-

TABLE 3.1 Nature of Relationship between Age and Different Absence
Types for Male, Female, and Mixed Samples (bivariate
analyses)

Sex	Positive	Negative	U-Curve	Inverted-U	Zero
Avoidable Absence					
Male	4	21	2	1	15
Female	2	5	-	2	2
Mixed	-	4	-	-	2
Unavoidable Absence					
Male	7	3	1	-	12
Female	3	-	-	-	13
Mixed	2	4	-	-	1

Note: Cell totals show the number of samples for which each type of relationship between the variables have been reported. This does not equal the number of
studies as some studies have been based on multiple samples.

cant relationships (Flanagan et al., 1974; Watson, 1981) have also
been found.

The inclusion of a greater variety of predictor variables with age in
multivariate studies of unavoidable absence (as compared to studies
of avoidable absence) may account in part for the discrepant results.
Moreover, much variation exists between studies in terms of the number and kinds of variables that have been included. While Nicholson
and Goodge (1976) and Nicholson et al. (1977) controlled for just
one variable—tenure—Watson (1981) included twelve variables
along with age in a multiple regression analysis. The variables that
have been controlled for most frequently are tenure (Garrison and
Muchinsky, 1977; Martin, 1971; Nicholson and Goodge, 1976;
Nicholson et al., 1977; Spencer and Steers, 1980; Watson, 1981)
and sex (Constas and Vichas, 1980; Flanagan et al. 1974; Johns,
1978; Spencer and Steers, 1980; Watson, 1981). Personal-demographic characteristics, including marital status (Constas and Vichas,
1980; Watson, 1981) and number of dependents (Constas and Vichas,
1980; Garrison and Muchinsky, 1977; Watson, 1981), have also
received some attention. In addition, job satisfaction variables (Garrison and Muchinsky, 1977; Watson, 1981) and leadership and task
variables (Johns, 1978) have been included in several studies.

Nicholson and Goodge (1976) found age to be the most salient biographical predictor of unsanctioned absenteeism among female blue collar workers when controlling for length of service. Using three different measures of unsanctioned absenteeism, they found that older workers were less likely to be absent than both middle-aged and young workers. Moreover, middle-age females had significantly more sickness absences than either the older or younger employees.

Nicholson et al.'s (1977) study of absenteeism among blue collar workers in sixteen organizations representing four industries is the most comprehensive study to date of the age-absence relationship. Examining both age and tenure in isolation using part correlation analysis, Nicholson et al. found that only age remained a viable predictor of absence. In addition to correlational analysis, they examined differences in absence rates between age groups. Findings indicated that male employees under the age of 26 were more absence-prone, while men over 46 were least, using an avoidable absence measure. However, three different types of relationships emerged between age and the time-lost index. For female sewing machine operators, women under 26 and over 46 had relatively low absence rates, while those between 26 and 35 had high absence rates. For the three male groups, a U-curve emerged for the continuous process workers, while no discernible pattern was found for bus company and foundry workers. Although Nicholson et al. found support for the trends indicated in prior studies, because of organizational and industry differences, they concluded that both organization-specific and industry-specific factors seemed to exert considerable influence over the association between age and absence.

SUMMARY, IMPLICATIONS, AND FUTURE RESEARCH ISSUES

The fact that age and absence *are* related is not nearly so important as understanding *why* they are related. For each of the major findings, an attempt is made to identify the physiological and psychological determinants of absence which are associated with aging.

The finding with the greatest empirical support is that older male employees generally have lower rates of avoidable absence than younger male employees. The avoidable absence measure is viewed as an indicator of attendance motivation and reflects attitude toward work. Citing Chown (1962) and Neugarten (1963), Nicholson et al. (1977) explained this finding as a function of increasing stability and the need for regularity which are associated with age.

The higher rates of unavoidable absence among older male workers that have been found in some instances may be associated with several factors. First, the relationship may be a function of deteriorating health and the onset of chronic illness associated with aging. Second, older workers when injured usually have a longer recovery period than younger workers. The lack of consistency in the results for male samples may be explainable in part by the nature of the work. Extremely severe and arduous work may affect one's health over time (Powell, 1973). The increasing incapacity associated with age may in turn have a more profound effect on arduous work in terms of meeting job demands and, consequently, may influence absence due to illness and accidents. Since women are less likely to engage in severe work, the differential findings with regard to males and females on unavoidable absence provide further support for the above explanation.

Male-female differences in age-absence trends may be explained in large part by differences in levels of domestic responsibility or in the centrality of the work role (Isambert-Jamati, 1962). The frequently found inverted-U relationship for women with regard to unavoidable absence, for example, may be a reflection of the woman's traditional role in caring for sick children and of her own susceptibility to illness as a result of exposure.

In terms of future research needs to increase our understanding of the age-absence relationship, the *why* of the relationship should be explored more thoroughly. First, there needs to be study of the effect of work conditions and job demands on individual health, physical functioning, and the aging process. Second, the nature of the age-absence relationship for women should be explored further. A life-cycle approach might be taken here, with the development of composite predictors reflecting levels of family responsibility (age, marital status, number and age of dependents, and so forth). Finally, empirical research should be directed toward verification of the psychological factors that have been implied to be associated with age and avoidable absence.

Turnover

Employee turnover has been of considerable concern to management practitioners, behavioral scientists, and personnel researchers. The primary focus has been on voluntary turnover—that is, turnover that is initiated by the employee rather than the organization. Our attention, likewise, is directed toward voluntary turnover.

IMPORTANCE OF TURNOVER

Employee turnover has potentially detrimental consequences to the organization. Costs of turnover include those associated with the recruitment, replacement, and training of personnel (Mirvis and Lawler, 1977). Additionally, work quality and quantity may suffer if there are large numbers of inexperienced workers on the job as a result of high turnover. Productivity problems are further exacerbated if the people who leave the organization are high performers rather than low performers.

On the other hand, employee turnover is also important from the standpoint of having potentially positive consequences for the organization (Dalton and Todor, 1979). For example, there is evidence that turnover *increases* organizational effectiveness because of the relationship between mobility and innovation (Grusky, 1960). Mobility encourages innovation by bringing new ideas into the organization. Innovation, in turn, is related to effectiveness. Therefore, in the case of either positive or negative consequences, turnover is an important area of management concern.

REVIEW OF EMPIRICAL RESEARCH

In reviewing the literature of the relationship between age and turnover, we relied on Mobley, Griffeth, et al. (1979) and Porter and Steers (1973) as primary sources. In addition, a literature search was made to update these earlier reviews. In all, 28 separate studies were found which examined the relationship between turnover and age (see Table B-4, Appendix).

All three major literature reviews have reported a consistent inverse relationship between age and turnover. Of the eight studies reviewed by Porter and Steers (1973),[1] six reported a negative relationship between age and turnover (Bassett, 1967; Farris, 1971; Fleishman and Berniger, 1960; Ley, 1966; Minor, 1958; Robinson, 1972). In one study, a negative relationship existed for female employees, while no relationship was found for male employees (Shott et al., 1963).

The eighth study reported by Steers and Porter found that older workers were more likely to terminate employment during the training period than were younger workers. However, after the end of the training period, younger workers were more likely than older workers to leave the organization (Downs, 1967). According to Downs, since older workers are more likely to stay with the organization once trained, it is important that the organization pay particular attention to the critical induction period and that training methods be devised that take into account learning problems of older workers.

Mobley, Griffeth, et al. (1979) identified five studies which found an inverse bivariate relationship between age and turnover (Mangione, 1973; Marsh and Mannari, 1977; Mobley et al., 1978; Porter et al., 1974; Waters et al., 1976).[2] However, results were mixed when age was treated as one of a number of predictor variables, with one study finding a negative relationship (Mangione, 1973) and two studies finding a nonsignificant relationship (Mobley et al., 1978; Waters et al., 1976).

In reviewing the literature since the Mobley, Griffeth, et al. (1979) article, fourteen studies were found examining the age-turnover relationship. Neither the bivariate nor the multivariate results of these studies were nearly as conclusive as the prior ones. Eight studies reported significant negative bivariate relationships between turnover and age (Arnold and Feldman, 1982; Bluedorn, 1978; Katz, 1978; Miller et al., 1979; Sheridan and Vredenburgh, 1978; Stumpf and Dawley, 1981; Taylor and Weiss, 1972; Williams et al., 1979), while six studies reported nonsignificant relationships (Koch and Rhodes, 1981; Michaels and Spector, 1982; Mobley, Hand, et al., 1979; Spencer and Steers, 1980, Stumpf and Dawley, 1981; Wanous et al., 1979). However, as the Mobley, Hand, et al. (1979) study was concerned with young marine corps recruits with a standard deviation in age of only 1.52 years, the lack of association may be attributed to a restriction of range problem on the age variable. Of seven studies using multivariate techniques, Bluedorn (1982), Gupta and Beehr (1979), Miller et al. (1979), and Stumpf and Dawley (1981) found age to be a significant negative predictor of turnover. Moreover, four multivariate studies reported only indirect relationships between age and turnover (Arnold and Feldman, 1982; Martin, 1980; Michaels and Spector, 1982; Mobley et al., 1978).

SUMMARY, IMPLICATIONS, AND FUTURE RESEARCH ISSUES

In summary, existing evidence clearly suggests that older workers are less likely to leave an organization than younger workers, with 25 out of 31 bivariate analyses finding a negative relationship. However, the relationship is not strong, with a median r of −.25; hence, age accounts for only 6 percent of the variance in turnover. Furthermore, multivariate results are inconsistent with five studies reporting a negative relationship, six reporting a nonsignificant relationship, and three finding indirect age-turnover effects.

Mobley et al.'s (1978) conceptual model is useful for understanding the relationship between age and turnover (see Figure 3.1). This model has some research support (Arnold and Feldman, 1982; Miller

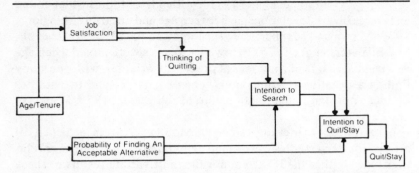

Source: From W. H. Mobley, S. O. Horner, and A. T. Hollingsworth, "An Evaluation of Precursors of Hospital Employee Turnover," **Journal of Applied Psychology**, 1978, **63**, pp. 408-414. Copyright © by the American Psychological Association, Inc. Reprinted by permission.

Figure 3.1: The Mobley, Horner, and Hollingsworth Turnover Model

et al., 1979; Michaels and Spector, 1982; Mobley et al., 1978). According to the model, older/longer-tenured workers are less likely to leave the organization for two reasons: (1) they are more satisfied with their jobs; and (2) they believe that there is a low probability of finding an acceptable alternative. The relatively low correlation that has been found between age and turnover is explained by this model. That is, in that the relationship between age and turnover is not a direct one, but rather indirect with several intermediate linkages, a low correlation would be expected. For example, the model in Figure 3.1 shows "job satisfaction" and "thinking of quitting" to be among the intermediate linkages between age and turnover.

The Mobley et al. (1978) model makes a contribution in that it gives insight into why older workers in general are more likely to stay with an organization than are younger workers. However, some important questions are left unanswered with regard to the turnover behavior of older workers.

First, in future studies of the voluntary turnover of older workers, it would be well to examine the relationship between job performance and turnover. This would give us some important information as to whether the low turnover of older workers is positive or negative from an organizational viewpoint.

Second, the consistent positive association between job satisfaction and age needs to be more fully understood. This was discussed in greater detail earlier in the attitudes section. However, with regard to turnover in particular, we need to identify age differences in the causes of job satisfaction that are, in turn, related to turnover. It may well be that we need to reconceptualize our independent predictors of turnover. Rather than looking at a number of demographic characteristics as predictors, we might identify precursors of turnover as they relate to career stage and life cycle (Greenhalgh, 1980). In this regard, there is now developing a body of literature exploring causes of occupational and career change in midlife (Neapolitan, 1980; Thomas, 1980; Thomas and Robbins, 1979), and it is important to integrate the results of these studies in model-building efforts to understand employee turnover. Moreover, a composite variable reflecting career stage and life cycle and based on age, sex, marital status, number and age of dependents, organizational tenure, job tenure, and job level might aid in future research. Such a variable could be used to assess the moderating effects of career stage/life cycle on factors associated with turnover.

Third, if the probability of finding an acceptable alternative is indeed related to the turnover decision, it would seem important to understand what factors contribute to an individual's estimation of that probability. Several examples can be cited that demonstrate the salience of understanding this variable. First, if perceptions of discrimination based on age have entered as a major factor for the older worker, then as organizations modify their hiring practices, older workers may modify their probability estimate. Hence, the age-turnover relationship may not remain stable over time. Second, if an employee factors his or her substandard performance into the probability estimate, this has implications for the type of individual who is staying with the organization.

Finally, it is important in future studies that the components of turnover be made explicit. This has rarely been done in past studies. Moreover, in view of the recent national legislation raising the mandatory retirement age, it seems important that nonmandatory retirement be treated separately from other forms of voluntary turnover. A recent study of the propensity to retire among older executives found that job characteristics and attitudes were generally unimportant predictors of the propensity to retire (Eden and Jacobson, 1976); this finding is in contrast to those on the turnover behavior. If retirees have in the past been included in voluntary turnover measures, this may offer an explanation for the relatively weak attitude-turnover relationship.

If the relationship between age and turnover does hold in the future, both positive or negative consequences could result depending on the nature of the organization and its previous rate of turnover. For example, we might expect that with the large number of older workers in the work force who have a greater tendency to remain with an organization, the upward mobility of younger members will be frustrated. Moreover, there will be less ability to bring "new blood" into the organization from outside at upper job levels. In organizations where innovation is essential to effectiveness, the consequences could be detrimental. On the other hand, if an organization had previously been experiencing extremely high rates of turnover that had been negatively influencing effectiveness, then the shift in the age composition of the work force may have the positive effect of bringing about stability. Of course, the scenario would be completely different if the age-turnover relationship changed. Clearly, then, the implications may vary widely depending on the situation.

Workplace Accidents

Research related to workplace accidents is discussed in this section. Before turning our attention to the review of the literature, we address the question: Why should the practicing manager be concerned with industrial accidents?

IMPORTANCE OF INDUSTRIAL ACCIDENTS

During 1977, 5.3 million industrial accidents occurred in the United States. These accidents resulted in 2.7 million lost work days (U.S. Department of Labor, 1978). There are numerous costs associated with industrial accidents, including those borne by the employer, the employee, and society. We shall focus on the employer costs of accidents.

A major cost to the employer associated with accidents is that related to compensation insurance. That is, worker's compensation insurance rates are in part influenced by the accident experience of the firm. Therefore, the greater the incidence of accidents, the higher the cost of compensation insurance.

In addition, there are a number of uninsured costs borne by the employer (Grimaldi and Simonds, 1975). These include: (a) wages paid for work time lost by insured workers; (b) wages to injured workers for non-work time other than that covered by compensation payments; (c) costs to repair and/or replace equipment damaged as a result of an accident; (d) wages for overtime work necessitated by interruption of the production process; (e) wages to supervisory personnel for accident-related matters; (f) extra wages resulting from decreased efficiency of the worker upon returning to the job; (g) costs of training a new worker to replace an injured one, as well as costs of lower initial productivity; (h) uninsured medical costs paid by the employer; (i) costs associated with investigating and processing accident reports; and (j) other unusual costs, such as loss of contracts due to inability to perform. From the standpoint of employer costs alone, industrial accidents are an important workplace concern.

REVIEW OF EMPIRICAL RESEARCH

The subject of age and accidents has received much attention in the literature. In all, 24 studies examining the relationship between age and accidents were located. In addition, there have been no less than nine articles reviewing the age-accident literature (Berkowitz, 1972; Hale and Hale, 1972; Heinrich, 1950; King and Speakman, 1953; McFarland, 1943; Surry, 1977; Tiffin and McCormick, 1952; Vernon, 1936). Factors that have been analyzed with respect to age-related differences include: accident frequency, duration of disability, fatalities caused by accidents, permanent disabilities, the nature of injuries, the causes of injuries, and accident proneness. These factors will each be discussed in turn.

Accident Frequency. In all, 21 studies spanning nearly 60 years examined the association between age and accident frequency (see Table B-5, Appendix). These studies report a number of different relationships between age and accident occurrence. The most frequently reported relationship was a negative one found in ten studies involving fifty samples (Barkin, 1933; Chelius, 1979; Hewes, 1921; Kossoris, 1940; Mann, 1944; Newbold, 1926/1964; Padley, 1947; Root, 1981; Sutherland et al., 1950; Van Zelst, 1954). Seven positive (Barrett et al., 1977; Griew, 1959; Klebba, 1941; Newbold, 1926/1964; Simonds and Shafai-Sahrai, 1977), four inverted-U (Barkin, 1933; Kossoris, 1948; Schulzinger, 1956; Surry, 1969), five U-shaped (Heinz, 1953; Kossoris, 1940; Mann, 1944; Padley, 1947; Vernon, 1945), and seven nonsignificant (Griew, 1959; Whitfield, 1954) relationships were also reported. (The number of cases does not equal the number of studies, as some studies reported results for more than one sample.)

Discrepancies in findings can be accounted for by the nature of the samples under study. For example, a negative or inverted-U relationship is generally found for samples based on a mass of data collected from many operations (Barkin, 1933; Chelius, 1979; Kossoris, 1940, 1948; Root, 1981; Schulzinger, 1956; Surry, 1969; Simonds and Shafai-Sahrai, 1977). One problem with these studies is that they do not deal with the issue of age differences in exposure to hazard and the influence of selection. In this regard, there is some evidence that older workers may selectively leave hazardous occupations so that only those who can meet the job demands remain in such lines of work (Powell, 1973).

On the other hand, mixed results are more likely to occur in single-plant samples (Barrett et al., 1977; Griew, 1959; Hewes, 1921; Kossoris, 1940; Mann, 1944; Vernon, 1945; Sutherland et al., 1950; Heinz, 1953; Whitfield, 1954; Van Zelst, 1954). Some of these single-plant studies give us insight into the nature of the age-accident relationship.

Both Newbold (1926/1964) and Van Zelst (1954) examined the relationship between age and accidents while controlling for experience. Newbold found that age was more important than experience in explaining accidents. However, a limitation of her study was that her sample included few absolutely new recruits. Van Zelst's (1954) study found lower rates of accidents for an older versus a younger group, both when the older and younger groups had the same experiences, and when the older group was less experienced than the younger group. Surry (1977) summarized other studies examining the influence of experience, and her conclusion was that experience was the critical factor in accident causation among new recruits. After the initial period of employment, however, experience was no longer relevant, although age remained important.

Griew (1959) found that fluctuations of accident rates with age were a function of the type of work studied. More specifically, older workers were particularly liable to incur accidents in jobs normally occupied by younger workers, such as electricians, millers, and grinders. According to Griew, the higher accident rate suggested that older workers were not able to meet the demands of the job successfully. As the major discrepancies between observed and expected accident frequency occurred in the 45–52 age group rather than 52+, he suggested that older workers begin to select out of these jobs prior to age 52. Powell's (1973) study provides further strength to Griew's argument, as he documented the turnover of older workers engaged in heavy work.

Barrett et al. (1977) investigated three information-processing capacities as predictors of accidents in a younger and an older group of drivers. They found a positive association between age and accident involvement. Moreover, younger drivers in the sample were found to be more effective on information-processing tasks and had faster motor-reaction times. Finally, multiple regression results for older drivers showed that complex reaction time and perceptual style measures were related to accident occurrence.

Duration of Disability. One indication of the severity of an accident is the duration of disability. Six studies were located that examined the relationship between age and duration of disability (see Table B-6, Appendix). These studies consistently reported that the average length of disability for older workers was greater than that for younger workers. However, there was some variation reported in the shape of the relationship. Four studies found that the length of disability increased with age (Barkin, 1933; Klebba, 1941; Kossoris, 1940; Stevens, 1929), while two studies found a U-shaped relationship, with average length of disability decreasing up to middle age and increasing sharply thereafter (Heinz, 1953; Kossoris, 1948).

Stevens (1929) examined the relationship between age and average length of disability by nature of injury. There was a strong positive association between age and duration of disability for each of the following injuries: (a) cuts, punctures, and lacerations ($r = .93$, $p < .01$); (b) bruises, contusions, and the like ($r = .86$, $p < .02$); (c) fractures, traumatic amputations, dislocations ($r = .73$, $p < .03$); (d) sprains and hernias ($r = .86$, $p < .02$); and (e) schedule losses ($r = .60$, $p < .02$). A nonsignificant relationship was found between age and duration of disability resulting from burns and scalds.

The explanation that is generally offered for the relationship between age and duration of disability is that with physiological changes associated with age that affect the body's healing powers, the older worker requires a longer period for recuperation (see Barkin, 1933).

Fatalities Caused by Accidents. Empirical research (see Table B-6, Appendix) strongly shows that death rates for accidents (that is, deaths per 1000 injuries) rise with advancing age (Barkin, 1933; Kossoris, 1940; Root, 1981). Furthermore, this relationship holds for both males and females (Kossoris, 1940). Statistics presented by Kossoris (1940) demonstrate the seriousness of the problem of deaths from accidents for the older worker. The death rate for the over-50 worker was twice that of the 21–25-year-old worker. Moreover, the over-60 death rate was three times that for the 21–25-year-old category.

Permanent Disability. Four studies were found that examined the relationship between age and permanent disability (see Table B-6, Appendix). Four studies (Barkin, 1933; Kossoris, 1940; Root, 1981; Surry, 1969) reported a positive association between advancing age and the proportion of injuries resulting in permanent disabilities. The relationship held regardless of whether the disability was total or partial (Barkin, 1933). The data presented by Barkin indicate that 25.3 percent of the injured workers in the 60–69 age group suffered a permanent disability as compared to only 14.5 percent of those under 20.

Klebba's (1941) study found a positive association between age and disabilities resulting from industrial injuries accumulating over the lifetime of the individuals. Hence, the study does not give information as to the older worker's susceptibility to incurring a permanent disability, as do the other studies. On the basis of the first three studies, however, we can conclude that when an older worker is injured, that injury is more likely to result in a permanent disability.

Nature of Injuries. Some age-related differences have been found with regard to the nature of the injury incurred on the job (see Table B-6, Appendix). First, cuts and lacerations and crushing injuries were found to decrease in proportion with age (Barkin, 1933; King, 1955). Moreover, older workers were less likely to incur burns than were younger workers (Barkin, 1933). Explaining these findings as the result of greater care on the part of the older worker, Barkin (1933:328) stated that the older worker "is not impelled to the restlessness common to youth." Moreover, Barkin attributed the first-mentioned finding to the greater proficiency that accompanies experience.

Both King (1955) and Barkin (1933) found a greater liability on the part of older workers to incur bruises. Finally, both Padley (1947) and Barkin found that dislocations and fractures increased with age, while King found no significant differences among age groups. According to Barkin, the increased tendency toward dislocations and fractures results from the increasing brittleness of the bone structure associated with the physiological deterioration of aging.

Causes of Injury. In an analysis of nearly 2000 accidents to agricultural workers, King (1955) found that there were some age-related differences in the causes of injury (see Table B-6, Appendix). Older workers were most likely to be injured due to falling from heights, slipping and tripping, and being hit by falling or moving objects. On the other hand, younger workers were more likely to incur injury by being caught in machines and from starting engines. Also, the proportion of injuries resulting from mishaps with hand tools and from continued activity decreased with age. No significant age differences were found for a number of other causes.

King suggested that the sensorimotor slowing that accompanies aging might account for all the categories of injury that increase with age. For the decreases in injuries from mishaps with hand tools and continued activity, King hypothesized that greater experience and refinement of skill in using tools, as well as greater care, were contributing factors.

Because strength had been shown in other studies to decline with age, King found it difficult to explain the absence of age variation in injuries from the lifting or moving of heavy objects. He suggested that perhaps older workers were avoiding the heaviest jobs to some extent, as was observed by Richardson (1953) in another sample.

Accident Proneness. Younger workers were found to be disproportionately represented among the accident prone (Smiley, 1955; Wolff, 1950) (see Table B-6). Whitfield's (1954) study of male coal miners identified some important differences between young and old accident-prone workers. That is, young accident-prone workers showed deficiencies in perception and cognition, while older accident-prone workers were deficient in motor response performance. This study is noteworthy in that it is one of the earlier studies that empirically linked accident behavior on the part of the older worker with sensorimotor performance.

SUMMARY, IMPLICATIONS, AND FUTURE RESEARCH ISSUES

Studies based on massed data generally report that older workers are less likely to incur accidents than younger workers. However, the mixed results obtained when samples are drawn from single plants or narrow occupational groups serve as a caution to making blanket generalizations about age-related differences in accident occurrence. In fact, the evidence suggests that there are different determinants of accident occurrence in younger and older workers. While inexperience and a possible lack of caution seem to be associated with accidents among the younger workers, the decline in physiological functioning, such as sensorimotor response, is more salient for the older worker. Age-related differences reported in the nature and causes of injuries also suggest differential causation for older and younger workers. Finally, at least one explanation for the negative association between age and accidents is that older workers who are less physically capable of meeting job demands leave physically demanding and hazardous jobs, and the higher accident occurrence among younger workers merely reflects their greater exposure to hazard. At this point, however, it must be stressed that as there have been only a few studies that have explored causal factors connected with age differences in accident behavior, these implications are presented tentatively.

Greater confidence can be placed in findings examining the relationship between age and accident severity. That is, once injured, the duration of disability is longer as one ages. Moreover, injuries to older workers are more likely to result in death or permanent disability than are injuries to younger workers. Therefore, accidents to older workers tend to have more serious consequences.

As the work force ages, there may be greater pressure placed on the older worker to perform jobs with physical demands beyond his or her capability. If such were to occur, a change in the general pattern of relationships between age and accidents could come about. In view of the findings with regard to age and accident severity, the negative consequences would be enormous.

In order to circumvent such a possibility, a careful study of jobs needs to be undertaken in organizations in terms of the physical demands to be met for successful and accident-free performance. Moreover, individual workers should be tested not only upon entry into the job, but also periodically, in order to determine the degree to which they meet the demands. Although there may be general age-related patterns with regard to capability, organizations under the law would not be permitted to exclude workers from jobs based on age. Rather, each individual must be considered in terms of his or her own capability to perform the job in a safe manner. It would also be important for organizations to assess the extent to which retraining can be used to develop safe behavior as opposed to a job transfer strategy. By taking advantage of modern technological advances, job redesign strategies might be employed to engineer the job to fit the person (see Murrell, 1965; Rey, 1965). Finally, career paths that consider the physical capabilities of workers at various career stages need to be developed (see Abrams, 1965).

In spite of the extensive research regarding age and accidents, there are still questions left unanswered. With regard to the older worker, the relationship between physiological functioning and accident liability needs to be explored further. Moreover, occupations need to be assessed in terms of their physical requirements.

Conclusions

Behaviors of the older worker have been examined in considerable detail. Some important findings are highlighted below.

- The performance of older workers is not necessarily either better or worse than that of younger workers. Other factors such as level of motivation, self-reliance, recognition, workplace climate, experience, and job demands may influence performance with age. Multivariate longitudinal studies are needed to delineate the effects of these other factors, as well as age, on performance.

- Older workers are less likely than younger workers to leave an organization. Preliminary evidence suggests that higher overall job satisfaction and a lower estimate of the probability of finding an acceptable alternative account for these findings.

- Older males generally have lower rates of avoidable absence than younger male employees. Moreover, in some instances older males have been found to have higher rates of unavoidable absence. More research is needed to understand why these relationships exist.

- Older workers have generally been found to have lower rates of accidents than younger workers. Future research needs to be directed toward explaining this relationship. Important differences exist in causes of accidents for older and younger workers.

- Older workers, once injured, take longer to recuperate from accidents than younger workers and are more likely to have fatal accidents or to suffer a permanent disability.

In general, research indicates that the job attitudes and work behaviors of older workers are in general congruent with effective organizational functioning. However, it must be emphasized that age-related differences seldom account for more than 10 percent of the variance in any particular attitude or behavior. Hence, personnel decisions should be based on individual differences rather than age differences per se.

The need for longitudinal panel studies using multivariate techniques has emerged over and over again in our discussion. Without such studies, we cannot explain the age-related differences that have been found. Moreover, differing explanations will have significantly different implications for managing an aging work force.

Ideally, future research should include all the dependent variables discussed in these two chapters, so that interrelationships among the variables may be explored. Moreover, the research should be based on causative models that are now possible to develop as a result of this extensive literature review. On the basis of the small amount of variance for which age can account, it is recommended that model-building efforts be built around the concepts of career stage and life-cycle development.

NOTES

1. Porter and Steers (1973) included in their review a ninth turnover study, Stone and Athelstan (1969). As the dependent variable in this study was tenure, not turnover, we did not include it in our review.

2. Hellriegel and White (1973) found a nonsignificant relationship between age and turnover. However, the Hellriegel and White study did not directly test the age-turnover relationship; rather, the authors examined the moderating effects of age on the attitude-turnover relationship. Another study (Federico et al., 1976) was not covered here because it dealt with tenure rather than turnover.

PART II

Staffing, Career Planning and Development

Part II is concerned with age and the functional areas of human resource management. Chapter 4 focuses on the selection and performance evaluation of the older worker, topics associated with staffing an organization. Chapter 5 examines age as it relates to career stages and learning, training, and preretirement program outcomes.

PART II

CHAPTER 4

STAFFING

In Chapter 1, we noted that the aging work force has serious implications for the organizational decision-making process related to such actions as screening, selection, placement, and training. In staffing organizations, the basic concern is making employment decisions in a nondiscriminatory manner. The process of deriving nondiscriminatory practices began in regard to selecting minorities and women; the aging work force intensifies the need for continuing that effort, particularly because of the prevailing beliefs about older workers' capabilities.

Because negative beliefs about older workers' capabilities can most directly affect staffing decisions, the literature on attitudes toward the older worker is discussed first. Included in this discussion is a summary of the literature on older persons' abilities and skills in order to examine the accuracy of some beliefs about older workers. Finally, assessment and evaluation methods are examined, in addition to person-job matching strategies associated with the staffing process.

Older Worker Abilities: Beliefs and Reality

The holding of negative attitudes toward the older worker has been confirmed in some recent studies (see Table C-1, Appendix). The findings reflect the attitudes of subjects who were managers (Haefner, 1977), employment interviewers (Britton and Thomas, 1973), *Harvard Business Review* subscribers (Rosen and Jerdee, 1977), and both undergraduate business and MBA students (Craft et al., 1979; Rosen and Jerdee, 1976a, 1976b).

Job-related beliefs about older workers are generally associated with their ability to meet job demands and with training. In terms of job demands, the older worker is frequently perceived to be lacking in creativity, less able to cope with stress (Rosen and Jerdee, 1977), and lower in performance (Britton and Thomas, 1973; Rosen and Jerdee, 1976b). Some perceptions associated with training are that the older worker is less interested in developing (Rosen and Jerdee, 1976a), more resistant to change (Rosen and Jerdee, 1977), and more difficult to train (Britton and Thomas, 1973).

The empirical literature on abilities and skills provides some support for such beliefs about the older worker, as reported in two recent collections of summaries of the literature. The collections are the *Handbook of the Psychology of Aging,* edited by Birren and Schaie (1977), and *Aging in the 1980's: Psychological Issues,* edited by Poon (1980). Speed of behavior and memory in particular were identified as the "two behavioral processes most consistently found to decline with age" (Birren and Williams, 1980:201; Welford, 1977). Age-related decrements were also reported for processes such as perception (Layton, 1975), hearing (Corso, 1977), and vision (Fozard et al., 1977). However, there were some specific findings, as well as methodological problems associated with the studies of abilities and skills, suggesting the possibility of other than the aging process as an explanation for the declines.

The methodological problems included the use of cross-sectional designs (noted in, for example, Arenberg and Robertson-Tchabo, 1977; Layton, 1975), generalization from laboratory experiments (Goldstein, 1980; Laufer and Fowler, 1971; Poon, 1980), the absence of other potential explanatory variables (Haberlandt, 1973; Willis and Baltes, 1980), and subject dropout in longitudinal designs (Botwinick, 1977). The cross-sectional design problem was mentioned with regard to the interpretation of the learning research (Arenberg and Robertson-Tchabo, 1977). Of course, laboratory experiments are essentially cross-sectional in nature, and a large portion of the abilities and skills data were derived from laboratory experiments (Birren and Schaie, 1977; Goldstein, 1980; Poon, 1980). The perceptual and cognitive data in particular were based on laboratory experiments (Goldstein, 1980; Laufer and Fowler, 1971; Poon, 1980). Generalization of these laboratory findings to real work situations was felt to be tenuous also because of the difficulty of including experimental treatments that were significant for job success. Therefore, interactions between age and experimental treatment or success of the intervention were suggested, calling for a more complex interpretation of the results (Poon, 1980).

The problems of not including an important explanatory variable and subject dropout were cited as producing inaccurate research results. One example of a potential explanatory variable that was not examined in the studies of intelligence was education level; therefore, the rising educational level of the general population might have biased findings against the older worker (Haberlandt, 1973). Subject dropout was identified as possibly producing results in longitudinal studies that inaccurately showed high performance for older workers because only those subjects who were performing well were willing to continue participating in the study (Botwinick, 1977).

In order to more fully (but briefly) present the most relevant age-related findings associated with abilities and skills, the literature as reviewed in the two volumes is summarized specifically for speed of behavior, memory, perception, and cognition. A number of explanations for the decline in speed of behavior were offered by Birren and Williams (1980). First, central nervous system changes have been shown to be a major contributor to slowing with age (Stern et al., 1980). But it has also been proposed that level of activity or having practiced may affect the central nervous system structure, and therefore that activity may prevent a decline in rate of responding (Birren and Renner, 1977). Birren and Renner also suggested that reaction time could be an individual effect, with some individuals having a faster reaction time throughout life. Finally, another partial explanation of slowing with age is cautiousness, which could be either learned or a behavior set (Birren et al., 1980). As a learned trait, it would have been reinforced over time as an outcome of having responded quickly but incorrectly. Based on these considerations, it becomes apparent that the effect of aging on speed of behavior is not clear. According to Birren et al. (1980: 302): "There remains a continuous discussion of the extent to which an older subject must be slow, wants to be slow, or has a set to be slow."

Slowing memory was also attributed to neural system changes. Therefore, as with speed of behavior, the neural system structure may adapt to the level of activity of the system (Birren et al., 1980). In any case, there is some preliminary evidence that practice reduces memory decline with age (Fozard, 1980). At the same time, increased forgetfulness with age was found to occur in the retrieval of information rather than during storage (Arenberg and Robertson-Tchabo, 1977; Craik, 1977). Although retrieval can be aided by mnemonic aids, it has been shown that adults are less likely to use them, even though they are able to use them effectively (Fozard, 1980). Finally, attention deficits and poor health have also been identified as helpful for explaining some of the age decrement (Craik, 1977; Cunningham, 1980).

General support was found in the literature for an age-related perception decrement (Layton, 1975). However, cross-sectional designs made it difficult to determine whether the decline was an aging or a generational (cohort) effect. In addition, health had typically not been controlled in the studies; therefore, it was not clear what its effect was (Layton, 1975).

Cognition is, of course, affected by memory and perceptual skills. Hence, intellectual functions involving memory and/or perceptual-manipulative skills might be expected to show a decline with age (Baugher, 1978; Botwinick, 1977; Green and Reimanis, 1970; Willis and Baltes, 1980). It appears, however, that the verbal, abstracting qualities did not decline. Nevertheless, factors such as cross-sectional design limitations and subject dropout also raised questions about these findings (Willis and Baltes, 1980). Willis and Baltes concluded that whether or not intellectual capacity remains at the same level through old age was "an open question."

The extent to which there is an aging effect on skills and abilities is, therefore, still unclear. It remains to be shown how factors such as education, health, level of activity, and expectations affect ability levels. It seems possible, for instance, that changed expectations about older worker capabilities on the part of the worker and others, in addition to activity or practice, may prevent or lessen declines. In any case, these findings reconfirm the importance of making staffing decisions on the older worker on an individual ability and skill basis.

Of concern, therefore, are findings of generalized negative beliefs about older workers which can lead to making nonindividualized staffing decisions. Haefner (1977) found that managers who made hiring decisions preferred a younger highly competent person (age 25) over an older highly competent person (age 55). There was also evidence that the older worker was viewed as less employable (Britton and Thomas, 1973; Rosen and Jerdee, 1976b) and less likely to receive retraining and promotion (Rosen and Jerdee, 1976a, 1977).

It would seem, though, that the publicity and discussion surrounding the Age Discrimination in Employment Act would have caused some perceptions about older workers to change. The results of the Craft et al. study may reflect such a change in that age seemed not "to be a central variable of overwhelming influence on the overall perception of the worker" (1979: 100). The subjects, 304 enrollees in an MBA executive development program, were asked to describe hypothetical persons in a 35-, 50-, 60-, and 70-year-old age group by checking 28 employment-related adjectives. The age groups were rated differently (χ^2 test, p $<$ .01) only on four of the 28 adjectives.

Regarding these four adjectives, the older worker was described less often as serious, ambitious, and strong, and more often as opinionated. However, signifcant differences between the age groups were not found for some important performance adjectives such as adaptable, capable, conscientious, creative, efficient, and "shows initiative."

In time, many perceptions of the older worker will undoubtedly change. Nevertheless, any remaining generalized negative beliefs can mean that many workers will be judged unfairly. Further research is therefore needed to determine the extent to which age stereotypes actually influence personnel decisions.

Assessment and Evaluation Methods

Various assessment and evaluation methods are believed to have the potential for objectifying the decision-making process and thus for insuring fair treatment of the older worker. Most common to this process are recruitment, testing, the interview, and performance appraisal. The literature in which age and these topics are considered is discussed in the following sections.

RECRUITMENT

There is very little evidence on applicant age as it relates to recruitment. In a recent review of the research on reactions to organizational recruiting, few studies were found in which the characteristics of applicants generally were examined (Rynes et al., 1980). Older subjects have not been included in organizational choice research, either, which has tended to be of college undergraduates (Wanous, 1977). Finally, a review of the realistic recruitment literature did not provide any age-of-applicant findings.

Two studies were located that examined age relative to sources of recruitment (Breaugh, 1981; Pursell and Torrence, 1980). In the Pursell and Torrence study of the job searches and reemployment of females seeking unemployment insurance, the older females (over 45 years) completed a significantly different job search from that of the younger females (45 years and younger). More specifically, the older females were more likely to apply directly to the employer for a job ($\chi^2 = 22.1$, p $<$ .01), while the younger females were more likely to seek out testing, job counseling, and suggested training, ask friends and relatives about jobs where they worked or elsewhere, check with the state employment service, use newspaper ads and union hiring halls, and take civil service examinations (χ^2s = 4.9 to 24.7, p $<$

.05). There were no significant differences, however, between age groups in the use of private employment services and community action organizations.

In the second study, univariate analysis of variance showed no significant source-of-recruitment differences for age, F(3,108) = .84, for subjects who were male and female research scientists working in an applied research organization (Breaugh, 1981). The mean age for these subjects was 36.4, but the age range itself was not specified. It is possible, therefore, that a restriction of range in the age variable accounts for the nonsignificant findings. Alternatively, the sources of of recruitment may not vary sufficiently for a particular professional occupation.

Obviously, research is needed to determine if recruiting practices have differential age effects, thereby depriving organizations of potentially valuable employees.

SELECTION TESTING

The concept of validity is critical to a discussion of selection testing, as well as to the interview and performance appraisal. Validity is of concern particularly because of the ADEA's prohibition of discrimination against employees in the 40–70 age range.

In the selection context, validity is the extent to which a test, for example, or the interview are indicators of successful performance on the job (Glueck, 1978). The level of validity is expressed as a correlation coefficient. It is important to add that validity coefficients can potentially differ between two subgroups. That is, a test may exhibit differential validity. With regard to age, a test may be valid for younger workers, but not equally valid for the older worker. Generally, there is little evidence to support differential validity (Campbell et al., 1973; Feild et al., 1977; Fox and Lefkovitz, 1974; Gael et al., 1975a, 1975b; Kirchner, 1975; Linn, 1978; O'Connor et al., 1975; Sandman and Urban, 1976; Schmidt et al., 1973), but a majority of the differential validity research has been on the sex and race variables.

Several empirical investigations having age implications for test validity were located (see Table C-2, Appendix). Arvey and Mussio (1973) examined the validity of five tests. They were the Minnesota Multimode Analogy Test, which taps basic reasoning ability; the Short Employment Tests (SET), which measure clerical aptitude, plus verbal and numerical skills; the Strong Vocational Interest Blank; the Gough adjective checklist; and a biographical inventory. The sample of 266 female clerical workers was divided into age groups, with comparisons made between the younger (<24 years old, n = 70) and the older group (>50 years, n = 67). There was no difference between these two groups in job performance, but the older group did not perform as well on the clerical aptitude test as the younger group. On the other hand, this test and the verbal skills test were reported as significantly valid for the older group (respectively, r = .47 and .25), but none of the tests were valid for the younger group. In addition, a significant difference (p < .01) between the correlation coefficients for the younger and older groups on the clerical aptitude test provided evidence for differential validity.

In two other studies, the relationship between test score and performance levels also differed for the younger and older participants (Salvendy, 1974). In the first study, the sample consisted of 181 British female manual operators. The older group (ages 36–58) earned lower scores on the Purdue Pegboard, the one-hole test, and a nonverbal intelligence test than did the younger operators (ages 15–35), but the older workers had significantly higher production performance (t = 2.34, p < .05). In the second study, the participants were female industrial operators from an American electromechanical factory. The younger operators (ages 19–22) had higher SRA verbal intelligence test scores than did the older operators (ages 23–48) (t = 2.40, p < .05), but the two groups had the same production performance. Although differential validity is suggested, the validity coefficients for these two studies were not reported.

Some evidence has been found in research conducted in England for the validity of "trainability tests" for selecting the young and old for jobs requiring semi-skilled manual labor (Robertson and Downs, 1979). The trainability test is described as a special form of work-sample test used to select people who do not have skills required by a job. The test includes "a structured and controlled learning period and the systematic observation of how things are done as well as what is done" (1979: 49). These results lend support to a conclusion reached in a work-sample test literature review that these tests are relatively more valid than other tests (Asher and Sciarrino, 1974).

Selection test bias on the basis of age appears to be a possibility unless confirmation of age group validity is obtained. There is, however, a potential problem in doing validity studies when using currently employed older workers (Arvey and Mussio, 1973). That is, this group may not be representative of older applicants in general because some older workers over time may have quit, or may have been fired or transferred. What is of concern again in this instance is the survivor phenomenon effect. Validity research, therefore, is needed using workers who are seeking employment.

SELECTION INTERVIEW

The research on the relationship between age and the selection interview is relatively limited. Arvey (1979) reviewed this literature to find only two age-related studies (Rosen and Jerdee, 1976a; Haefner, 1977). These studies of attitudes toward older workers were discussed earlier in this chapter in the Older Worker Abilities section. The studies on the attitudes toward older workers were conducted using primarily case histories or an in-basket (simulated decision-making exercises); therefore, the studies do not provide direct evidence for the differential effect of the interview itself (Arvey, 1979).

One other study was found in which an interview transcript was employed (Connor et al., 1978). The stimuli consisted of an interview transcript and a resumé with photographs attached of an old (60–70s) or young (20s) woman. The photographs were judged to be of average attractiveness and close to the stated age of the job applicant. In addition, to control for the effect of the particular characteristics of a single photograph, two photographs were used at each age level. The participants (86 male and 91 female introductory psychology class students) were not asked to select between applicants, but to evaluate how likely they would be to hire the single applicant. A nonsignificant age-by-hiring interaction was found based on multivariate analysis of variance (F = not reported).

It is important to reiterate that additional research of the interview relative to age is needed to establish whether interview decisions are unfair to the older worker. As an example, the relationship between the judgments of interviewers and the performance of those hired should be assessed to determine whether the judgments made on the basis of the interview are accurate and therefore valid.

Interview decisions should also be examined for adverse impact on older applicants. Have a proportionately smaller number of older applicants been selected relative to the younger applicant group? A finding of adverse impact would suggest that managers be sensitized to biases and stereotypes about older workers. An effort should be made to ensure that interviewers are asking questions that are free of age bias.

PERFORMANCE APPRAISAL

Interest in improving performance appraisal programs has been aroused by court decisions in recent age discrimination cases and by the New Uniform Guidelines, which became effective on September 25, 1978. The New Uniform Guidelines have implications for performance appraisal because it is defined as a test. At the same time, because the product of performance appraisal is used to make promotion, layoff, involuntary retirement, or discharge decisions, the reliability and fairness of various appraisal techniques have been called into question in many cases arising under the ADEA (Schuster and Miller, 1981, 1982).

Some court decisions which have pointed out the need for valid performance appraisals are Brito v. Zia Co. (1973), Rich v. Martin-Marietta (1977), Sarcini v. Missouri Railway Co. (1977) and Mistretta v. Sandia Corporation (1977). In ruling against Sandia, for instance, the judge concluded:

> The evidence presented [by Sandia] is not sufficient to prove or disprove the contention that at Sandia performance declines with age, but there is sufficient circumstantial evidence to indicate that age bias and age based policies appear throughout the performance rating process to the detriment of the protected age group.

But in a recent analysis of 21 ADEA cases in which the employer's past performance was called into question, Schuster and Miller (1982) concluded that formal performance evaluation procedures are not required as a matter of law for an employer to establish a nondiscriminatory personnel action successfully. That is, the courts have permitted less reliable sources of employee information to be used as conclusive evidence substantiating an employer's claim of nondiscriminatory decision making. Examples of informal performance evaluation procedures include the use of contemporaneously written notations, the irregular use of performance appraisal forms, and oral testimony uncorroborated by written documents by supervisory personnel. However, an employer who conducts periodic, well-designed performance appraisals and who makes personnel decisions based on the appraisal process improves considerably the likelihood of rebutting an ADEA claim.

In their analysis, Schuster and Miller cited an example of an employer who failed to maintain a formal and equitable performance evaluation system (Buchholz v. Symons Manufacturing Co., 1978). An employee who had been discharged was successful in an ADEA action when the employer could offer no objective documentation of performance evaluation to support the defense of "poor performance." In fact, it appeared that the employer's own defense was injured by two attempts to offer such documentation. The employer presented one evaluation that had been authored by a manager who stood to gain personally by the employee's departure. The second evaluation had not been written until after the employee's discharge. Such ill-conceived and potentially unfair appraisal methods are likely to produce frustrated employees and expensive litigation.

The type of personnel action also appears to dictate the nature of the proof required to substantiate a nondiscriminatory employer decision (Schuster and Miller, 1982). For instance, promotion and layoff-retirement decisions require an employer to demonstrate that an employee is not as qualified as others selected for the new position or selected to remain. In constrast, a discharge decision will not be upheld where an employee has performed at a minimally acceptable level. Thus, discharge decisions appear to require an expanded justification by the employer to establish that such decisions are made in a nondiscriminatory manner.

To assess the relationship between performance appraisal itself and age, and because performance of the older worker was discussed in Chapter 3, only specific performance appraisal differences will be examined here. Five such empirical studies were located (see Table C-3, Appendix). Four of them were field studies (Bass and Turner, 1973; Cleveland and Landy, 1981; Klores, 1966; Maher, 1955), and the other involved a simulated evaluation task (Schwab and Heneman, 1978).

The majority of the findings did not reveal significant age differences, yet there were some positive and negative age-specific results. In terms of ratee performance, there were no age differences among manufacturing supervisory employees on the basis of a forced choice or graphic rating scale (Maher, 1955); chemical research division professional, nonprofessional, supervisory, and clerical employees using a forced distribution rating scale (Klores, 1966); black full-time and black plus white part-time tellers using a graphic rating scale (Bass and Turner, 1973); secretaries in the simulated evaluation task for four performance dimensions, promotability, and salary (Schwab and Heneman, 1978); and exempt managerial employees in a manufacturing organization for ratings on six of eight performance dimensions (Cleveland and Landy, 1981). A positive relationship was reported for white full-time bank tellers on customer relations, new accounts, and alertness dimensions (r's > .25, p < .01) (Bass and Turner, 1973), but older managers (ages 45–65) were rated lower than middle-aged ratees (ages 35–44) on self-development and interpersonal skills ($t = 2.00$, p < .05) (Cleveland and Landy, 1981).

As for a rater effect, older secretaries were rated lower by older raters on job knowledge and responsibility, and on recommended salary increase (partial correlation coefficients = –.41 to –.52, p <

.05) (Schwab and Heneman, 1978). In the Cleveland and Landy (1981) study, a small rater age main effect for interpersonal skills was found in one sample ($R^2 = .01$, $F = 7.60$, $p < .05$), but the effect was not replicated in the second sample. In this same study, a small rater-age-by-ratee-age interaction was obtained for self-development and interpersonal skills ($R^2 < .03$, $F < 10.99$, $p < .05$); however, only 1 to 4 percent of the performance variance was accounted for by age.

A limitation to the interpretation of these findings generally is the absence of an assessment of the relationship between the rated performance and the actual performance; therefore, it cannot be determined whether the performance ratings reflect true performance, rater or ratee age, or other effects. One exception was the Bass and Turner (1973) study, in which the number of shortages and overages in balancing each day's transaction was included as an objective performance measure. In this instance, the common variance between the performance ratings and the objective measures ranged from .00 to .38 for the full- and part-time tellers. But for more fully understanding to what extent the supervisory ratings reflected actual performance or possible bias against an age group, it would have been helpful to find more extensive analyses of the two performance measures relative to age specifically.

In a very preliminary sense, ratee age appears to have less of an effect on performance ratings than attitudes about the older worker would suggest. Additional research needs to be performed, however, in which the effects of ratee, rater, and other factors are partialed out to identify any ratee age differences beyond true variance. Some other factors which can influence ratings are gender, race, and experience (Landy and Farr, 1980). Also, situational characteristics such as the age composition of the immediate work group may affect how older worker performance is perceived (Kirchner and Dunnette, 1954).

Person-Job Matching Strategies

For those workers who find themselves unable to carry out their job responsibilities because of changes in skills and abilities, some special person-job matching strategies can potentially facilitate continued utilization of remaining skills. There are two types of such strategies; one is what we will call placement, and the other is job redesign.

PLACEMENT

Placement involves matching individual capacities to the requirements of existing jobs. Such person-job matching systems are discussed because they have been developed and employed specifically for placing older workers (Koyl, 1974; Kuh, 1946). In this event, functional age rather than chronological age serves as the selection criterion (Batten, 1973).

Of the three systems we located, one was created during World War II for placing older job applicants in the Kaiser Shipyards (Kuh, 1946). In all, 25 environmental factors were used to analyze workers and jobs. Some of these factors were high and low temperature, vibration, noise, moving objects, cramped quarters, and high places.

Another person-job match system was developed by Hanman (1958) in Stockholm. On the basis of an 80-point physical demands analysis sheet, job and individual physical capacity were compared. This method was apparently implemented at the Aluminum Company of Canada, Ltd. (Koyl and Hanson, 1969), as well as by several insurance companies (McFarland, 1973).

Finally, the GULHEMP system was developed in the 1960s by Koyl and associates at de Havilland Aircraf, Ltd. in Toronto (Koyl, 1974; Meier and Kerr, 1976). In this system, minimum functional criteria for the performance of individual jobs were established for seven functional areas. The functional areas were general physique, upper extremities, lower extremities, hearing, eyesight, mentality and personality (the first letter of each producing the term GULHEMP). The areas were each defined on a five-point scale so that the person and job profiles could be compared for their match. This system was also adopted in 1970 by an Industrial Health Counseling Service in Portland, Maine (Batten, 1973; Meier and Kerr, 1976; Quirk and Skinner, 1973; Youry, 1975).

It appears that the GULHEMP system continues to be employed, since articles on its use appeared in the 1970s. However, the literature is essentially descriptive in nature; therefore, no validity data for the system relative to performance on the job were located, except for a reported reduction in sick leave in three large organizations that were utilizing the Maine services (Batten, 1973).

JOB DESIGN

Designing jobs to match the ability and needs of the older worker offers an alternative to matching the individual to fit the job. This strategy may be increasingly salient as compared to a job placement or transfer strategy as the work force ages and there is a potential shortage of younger persons to fit job requirements.

The relationship between age and job design has been treated from two perspectives. First, job design has been considered from the standpoint of the ability to meet the physical demands of a job as one ages. Second, age differences in reactions to task characteristics (for example, job complexity, task significance, and autonomy) have been examined. Each of these perspectives are discussed below.

Physical Demands of the Job. Redesigning jobs specifically to meet the presumed declining capacities of older workers has been undertaken rarely in the United States. In one survey of 500 companies employing 500 or more workers, only 8 percent of the 250 responding companies indicated that they had redesigned jobs affecting older workers (Abrams, 1965). Additionally, a survey of 49 plants that employed 67 percent of the employees in the Rochester (NY) area reported few experiences with job redesign for older workers (Abrams, 1965). Generally, when job engineering is done, it is usually implemented systematically and not just for the older worker. However, the older worker benefits as a result.

Perhaps the most expansive discussion on job redesign for the older worker is the report published by the Organization for Economic Cooperation and Development, entitled *Job Re-design and Occupational Training for Older Workers* (1965). This report examined in detail the need for job redesign in response to declining capabilities. The following excerpt from this report identifies features in the work situation which place strain on older workers:

(1) Age changes in physical work capacity are most likely to be reflected in the performance of older workers who are engaged on (sic):

    (a) Jobs which require occasional "bursts" of energy or effort which are higher than the maxima which the older worker has at his disposal.

    (b) Jobs in which demands on energy expenditure are so continuous that the older worker is prevented from taking the short recuperative rest-pauses he requires. These jobs are usually paced.

    (c) Jobs in which inadequate rest is permitted by the employer during the course of the day's work.

(2) Age changes in the worker's tolerance of environmental stresses are most likely to be reflected in older worker's performance on:

    (a) Jobs in excessively hot or humid workshops. If the work is heavy, this effect will be enhanced;

    (b) Jobs involving the risk of exposure to polluted atmospheres;

    (c) Jobs in very noisy workshops, especially if much listening is involved;

(d) Jobs at badly lighted work places, especially if work is visually demanding;

(e) Jobs at work places in which a glare source is present. Again, if the work is visually demanding, this effect will be enhanced.

(3) Age changes (pathological and normal) in the skeletal-musculature are most likely to have significance for:

(a) Jobs on equipment which is designed in such a way that prolonged stooping, bending, or stretching is called for;

(b) Jobs in which the worker has to support part of his own weight, or the weight of part of his equipment, for prolonged periods. This category will include many jobs which involve the prolonged use of unsupported hand tools, and those involving equipment the controls of which are placed in such a way that arms or legs must be outstretched, or otherwise not at rest, for prolonged periods;

(c) Jobs in "untidy" work places in which objects such as duck boards, coils of rope or wire, cartons, and components lie about and constitute hazards likely to cause tripping and falling accidents. Also in this category are workshops in which the arrangement of benches, tools, steps, ramps, hoists, and so on, is not orderly, or in which it is frequently subject to change.

(4) Age changes in a worker's capacity for organized perceptual-motor activity will be reflected mainly in jobs which involve:

(a) Severe visual or auditory demands. If poor lighting or excessive noise (respectively) are also involved, this effect will be enhanced;

(b) Fine discriminations, especially if the time available for making them is limited by the speed of work;

(c) Methods of conveying information or instructions which are unnecessarily complex, ambiguous or "unnatural." A good example of this type of job is one in which quantitative (that is, numerical) information is given in an indirect and non-numerical form, perhaps by means of a scalar indicator which must be "read." Another example involving the same principle would be a job in which purely qualitative information (perhaps about a direction or rate of change in a process) is given quantitatively in the form, perhaps, of a reading on a counter;

(d) Working to a degree of accuracy or precision which requires a very wide choice of action or delicacy of action. Associated with any form of speed-stress, this feature is likely to cause very substantial difficulty;

(e) The need to remember small amounts of information for very short periods of time while engaged in other activity. For example, the need to remember the last reading from a piece of equipment while making an adjustment to a control may place the older worker at a severe disadvantage.

(5) Any job, whatever additional features it displays, which forces him to adopt a speed of work not under his own control, will strain the capacities of the older worker. For example, most work at a conveyor belt will tend to affect the older worker in this way. Add to this "paced" type of work any other demand with which he cannot easily cope, and the older worker's difficulty will be very greatly increased [Clay, 1965: 26-28].

Case histories provide examples of how jobs have been redesigned for older workers and the effects of the redesign (Abrams, 1965; Heijbel, 1965). Redesign efforts have dealt with problems associated with jobs requiring standing for long periods of time, extreme physical exertion, heavy lifting, and constant walking (Abrams, 1965). In some instances, job redesign has resulted in a reduction in manpower requirements. For example, the reengineering of jobs held by older women in a spinach-trimming operation eased the fatigue associated with the job and reduced the number of women needed from 40 working 8 hours a day to 16 working 4 hours.

While numerous case histories of the effects of job redesign are available, rigorous research on the effects of job engineering on performance has yet to be undertaken. Clearly, this is an important area for future research. In this regard, field experiments employing an experimental and control group design with pre- and postmeasures should be utilized.

Job redesign to ease fatigue and strain associated with the physical demands of a job is a strategy that should be employed on a general basis for all jobs, regardless of whether the incumbents are older workers. In addition, in view of our discussion on age and abilities, it seems reasonable to make specific accommodation for individual capabilities on a person-by-person basis as workers age so that they may continue to perform their jobs. While the effects of job redesign are likely to be greater for the older worker, it is expected that improvements in health and performance may occur as well for younger workers. Other benefits may also result, such as reduced turnover, less absenteeism, and fewer accidents.

Reactions to Task Characteristics. Age differences in affective and behavioral reactions to task characteristics have been examined in four cross-sectional studies (Aldag and Brief, 1975; Gould, 1979a; Phillips et al., 1978; Rabinowitz and Hall, 1981). In addition, a fifth study focusing on responses to task characteristics associated with job longevity contributes to our understanding of age differences (Katz, 1978). These studies are briefly reviewed (see Table C-4, Appendix).

Aldag and Brief (1975) examined levels of general satisfaction and growth satisfaction as a function of task characteristics (that is, skill variety, task significance, task identity, autonomy, and feedback) and age in two separate samples. They found that older employees (those over 40) and younger employees (those under 40) in both samples were significantly *more* satisfied with higher levels of skill variety, autonomy, and feedback. For the manufacturing company sample, older employees showed little difference in growth or general satisfaction as a function of task significance and task identity. For the public sector service agency sample, older workers expressed greater growth satisfaction for jobs higher on task identity than those low on task identity, while younger workers reported greater growth satisfaction for jobs lower on task identity than those high on task identity. Hence, the pattern of age-related responses to task characteristics varied in each sample.

Using discriminant analysis, Phillips et al. (1978) found clear age differences in preferences for task attributes in a sample of blue collar workers in an automotive plant. Older workers (those over 47 years) preferred higher levels of attention, responsibility, and interest than younger workers (those under 47). On the other hand, older workers preferred lower levels of variety, task identity, independence, intrinsic motivation, interpersonal relations, clarity, and co-worker relations than younger workers. These results were upheld when controlling for education and seniority.

A major problem with both the Aldag and Brief (1975) and the Phillips et al. (1978) studies was the lack of a theoretical basis for categorizing age and older versus younger employees. In the following two studies, age categories were established based on career stage.

Gould (1979a) examined the moderating effects of career stage on the relationship between job complexity and job satisfaction plus job performance based on a sample of administrative and managerial public agency employees. In all multiple regression analyses, Gould controlled for salary, tenure, sex, level, and occupational group.

The career stages, theoretically derived from Super et al. (1957), were based on three age groupings, including: (a) the trial stage (ages 22–30); (b) the stabilization stage (31–44); and (c) the maintenance stage (ages 45–65). Job complexity, measured by a single-item scale, was defined as "the extent to which the job (1) lacks repetitiveness and routineness, (2) provides opportunities for exercising independent judgment, and (3) requires creativeness and originality in the performance of duties" (Gould, 1979a; 211).

Gould's findings indicated that job satisfaction was more strongly related to perceived job complexity in the trial stage than in either of the other two stages. That is, individuals under 30 responded more favorably to a complex job than did those between 30 and 44 or over 45 years. Moreover, no significant differences emerged in the job complexity-satisfaction relationship between the maintenance and stabilization stages. These results are consistent with earlier findings that high challenge during the early career was related to high levels of job satisfaction and involvement, and lower turnover (Berlew and Hall, 1966; Dunnette et al., 1973).

Career stage also moderated the relationship between job complexity and job performance (Gould, 1979a). Specifically, a significantly stronger positive relationship was reported between job complexity and job performance in the stabilization stage than in the trial stage. However, no differences in the strength of the complexity-performance relationships were found between the trial and maintenance stages and the stabilization and maintenance stages. These results are consistent with Super et al.'s (1957) conceptualization of the stabilization stage as that period of steady growth in one's career. In the stabilization stage, it is likely that the highest performers will be placed in the most complex jobs. On the other hand, during the trial stage—a period of learning, numerous job changes, and low job tenure—a strong relationship between job complexity and performance would not be expected. Similarly, in the maintenance stage, because the job that one holds may be more a function of one's past achievements, job complexity would not be as strongly related to performance as during the stabilization period.

Consistent with Gould's (1979a) study are the Rabinowitz and Hall (1981) results based on a sample of Canadian transport ministry employees. In this study, career stage, defined in terms of age, was found to moderate the relationship between job characteristics and job involvement. More specifically, job characteristics were more strongly and consistently related to job involvement in the early career stage (ages 21–35) than in either the midcareer (ages 36–50) or late career (ages 51+) stages. Two job characteristics, autonomy and task identity, were more strongly related to job involvement for the early-stage group than for the middle-stage group. Moreover, job involvement and task identity were more strongly related in the early- than in the late-stage group. Finally, no significant differences were found in correlations across stages in the relationships between job involvement and variety and feedback. In all analyses, the influence of job level was controlled for.

Finally, Katz (1978), based on a sample of 3085 employees in municipal, county, and state government in all job categories, reported that job longevity moderated the relationship between task dimensions and job satisfaction in a number of ways. First, for employees employed in a job less than 3 months, job satisfaction was not significantly related to amount of skill variety or autonomy, but was positively related to task significance. Second, the strongest relationships between task dimensions and job satisfaction were found for employees in the 4–36-month interval. After three years on a particular job, with progressively longer job longevity, correlations between task dimensions and job satisfaction became progressively weaker. For employees assigned to the same job for at least fifteen years, all of the correlations between task dimension and job satisfaction were significant and close to zero. Finally, when correlations between task dimensions and satisfaction by longevity categories were computed separately by age groups (less than 35 years, 35–50, and greater than 50), the pattern of results was similar to that discussed above, indicating that job longevity (not age) is the important moderator.

Recognizing the difficulty of explaining the correlational attenuation in the cross-sectional study, Katz speculates that people adapt to being in the same job over time by becoming indifferent to the task characteristics. This reaction has implications for both job redesign and job transfer. In terms of job redesign, it is possible that workers who have been in the same job for a considerable period of time may not be receptive to job redesign so long as they remain in the same formal position. On the other hand, the worker who has been on the job a year or two may be particularly receptive to job redesign. Moreover, periodic job changes appear to be a feasible method to reestablish the relationship between dimensions and job satisfaction.

In summary, all studies report significant age-related or job tenure-related differences in affective and behavioral responses to task characteristics. While the results appear to be divergent, there is consistency when similar age categories are used. In particular, both Gould (1979a) and Rabinowtiz and Hall (1981) report strong affective responses to task characteristics in the early career stage. Similarly, according to Katz (1978), employees responded more positively to "enriched" jobs during the early stages of job tenure (after 3 months and up to 36 months).

An issue that still needs resolution is the role of age versus job tenure as moderator of the reactions to task characteristics. Panel studies that follow employees over time would be particularly appropriate. In addition to job satisfaction and performance, motivation level should be explored. Moreover, future job design experiments should also examine differences in responses based on age, job tenure, and organizational tenure.

Summary, Implications, and Future Research Issues

The staffing-related methods have received very little research attention with respect to age. On the other hand, the studies that we found on attitudes towards older workers suggest a need for assessing whether these attitudes affect staffing decisions. If negative attitudes are reflected in decision making, then older workers are being judged unfairly. It is important, therefore, that organizations assess whether staffing decisions are being made in an unbiased manner.

Selection tests that have been validated for older workers can help make the selection decision more unbiased. The test validity studies generally showed that work-sample tests have potential validity, and that tests may be differentially valid for individual age groups. There is a need, however, for more validity studies, but it is also important to check for differential validity.

Because the interview is a standard selection tool, it in particular should be studied for its effects on the older applicant. It should be noted also that in terms of equal employment opportunity in general, the selection interview is expected to be placed under increasing scrutiny (Arvey, 1979). It would be prudent, therefore, to examine interview decisions for adverse impact not only on the basis of age, but for protected groups generally.

The person-job matching strategies have appeal for their consideration of individual differences in the placement process. Unfortunately, there is a dearth of evidence on the effects or outcomes either of matching the older worker to the job or redesigning jobs to fit the abilities and needs of the older worker. One wonders, of course, how age, job tenure, and organizational tenure are related to either the motivation for job redesign and subsequent job performance and satisfaction.

Future research should be directed generally toward assessing the accuracy and/or objectivity of staffing methods. The first question to be asked by management in particular is whether recruitment practices, selection tests, the selection interview, performance evaluations, and placement are having an adverse impact upon the older worker. That is, are a disproportionate number of older workers eliminated from consideration because of the decisions made specifically on the basis of individual staffing methods? Another important question of concern is whether the methods are valid and/or accurate in distinguishing between effective and ineffective future performers. When validating selection tests, for instance, studying workers who are seeking employment, rather than just currently employed workers, will control for a potential survivor phenomenon effect. Finally, panel studies are needed to examine the effects of job redesign on job satisfaction and performance relative to age, job tenure, and organizational tenure.

CHAPTER 5

CAREER PLANNING AND DEVELOPMENT

Career planning and development are potentially important to maintaining and improving the performance of an aging work force. Age is therefore examined in the following sections in terms of topics such as career stages, learning, and training.

A career has been defined as "a sequence of positions occupied by a person during the course of a life-time" (Super and Hall, 1978: 334). It involves advancement through an "identifiable path" (Hall, 1976: 2–3). Career planning consists of developing a plan for a career and a strategy for achieving that plan. Within an organization, it is the process of identifying and planning out the paths that one can or will follow, which involves decisions on occupation, job assignments, work activities, and developmental programs (Gutteridge, 1976). Career development is the process of gaining experience and learning new skills.

In general terms, many training and development programs are carried out in industry. Most medium-sized and large companies conduct their own programs (Glueck, 1978), and there are data to suggest that the number of companies offering training programs is increasing. Comparison of a 1967 Bureau of National Affair's (BNA) Personnel Policies Forum Survey with a survey conducted in 1975 shows a general increase (Miner, 1976). For instance, the number of companies offering supervisory training and management development programs rose from 47 to 72 percent for the former, and from 31 to 60 percent for the latter.

Surveys of career planning and development programs were recently reviewed by Super and Hall (1978) to identify current practices. They concluded that such programs were "growing up piecemeal." Many new activities were added apparently in response to employee requests, rather than as a result of long-range planning. Companies were typically found to be using some career planning in addition to assessment centers and job-posting, but a recent survey of some of the largest organizations in Chicago suggests that *formal* career development programs may not yet be that prevalent (Seybolt, 1979).

It appears that relatively less training, as well as career planning and development, is made available in organizations to older workers. There is a dearth of research on career planning and development activities in industry, and even less of it in terms of the older worker (Super and Hall, 1978). Our review of the literature on training, career planning and development focuses on career stages, the middle career stage, career planning intervention effectiveness, learning and post-training performance, and preretirement programs.

Career Stages

The various career stage theories have been combined by Hall (1976) into a composite model as shown in Figure 5.1 (Hall, 1976). The G.I.A.W. refers to Getting into the Adult World, S.D. to Settling Down, and B.O.O.M. to Becoming One's Own Man (Levinson et al., 1978). The Exploration, Establishment, Maintenance, and Decline stages were defined by Super (1957). Inherent to the model is a career stage/age relationship. There are, however, differences of opinion regarding this relationship (Rush et al., 1980). Some theorists believe that the relationship is affected more by such factors as individual differences and the ability to complete tasks in each stage than it is by age (Dalton et al., 1977; Gould, 1979b).

The relationship between age and career stage, based on the Levinson et al. model, was investigated in one study (Rush et al., 1980). The stages in the Levinson et al. model are Getting into the Adult World (ages 20–29), Settling Down (ages 30–34), Becoming One's Own Man (ages 35–39), and Midlife Transition (ages 40–45). Based on 759 public sector managerial, technical, and professional subjects with a mean age of 41, Rush et al. found a nonsignificant difference between career stage and age ($\chi^2 = 3.52$, df = 9, p = .94). Subject subsamples (male, female, and valid pattern group) also failed to produce a significant career stage/age difference. The "valid pattern group" consisted of 282 participants whose careers fit Levinson's career-stage sequence.

Rush et al. have suggested that the age-linking of career stages may not be appropriate because it does not allow for early or late career

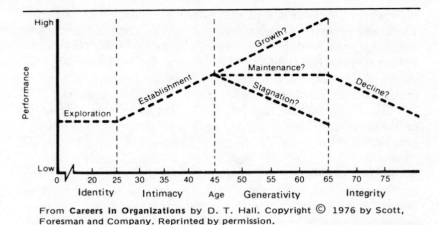

From **Careers in Organizations** by D. T. Hall. Copyright © 1976 by Scott, Foresman and Company. Reprinted by permission.

Figure 5.1: Stages in Career Development

starts. They cited the example of the young person who has held summer and part-time jobs as one who might be ready earlier for entering the G.I.A.W. stage.

Middle Career

To acquire a fuller understanding of how to manage the aging work force, it seems appropriate to examine what is known at the present time about the middle career stage, sometimes referred to as the midlife-crisis period. The previous discussion of older worker needs, values, and attitudes provides important preparatory information for assessing this career stage. Because these variables have been reviewed, the following section is limited to the literature associated specifically with (1) exploration and planning in midcareer and (2) midcareer changers.

EXPLORATION AND PLANNING IN MIDCAREER

There is evidence that workers at the midcareer stage have a need for growth (Alderfer and Guzzo, 1979) and a need for upward mobility (Rush et al., 1980). However, this is not very different from the needs of the workers in the earlier career stages (see Table D-1, Appendix). In the Alderfer and Guzzo study, the need for growth among 229 business students and participants in a management development course offered by a large organization was not significantly different between the Levinson et al. (1978) career stages ($F = 1.85$, $p < .10$). There was, however, a decreasing growth desire across career stages, except for a one-scale point increase from the Becoming One's Own Person stage to the Midlife Transition stage. These findings are only suggestive, however, of the need levels of workers in general, because the sample consisted only of people seeking development.

The need for upward mobility among the sample of 159 public sector managerial, technical, and professional workers was not significantly different either between the Levinson et al. (1978) career stages ($F = 1.51$, $p = .21$) (Rush et al., 1980). Of interest was the finding that the Midlife Transition Career Stage group (age 40–45) had lower job and career satisfaction than did those in the Getting Into the Adult World and Settling Down stages (age < 39). The need for upward mobility, combined with lower job and career satisfaction, suggests that career planning and development needs are not being met for those in the Midlife Transition career stage (age 40–45).

In another study of related interest, Gould (1979b) examined the relationship between extent of career planning and career stages. The career stages were operationally defined according to the age ranges associated with the stages proposed by Super (1957). They were: (1) exploration stage = ages 15–24, (2) trial stage = ages 25–30, (3) stabilization stage = ages 31–44, and (4) maintenance stage = ages 45–65. Gould hypothesized that career planning would be highest in the stabilization stage and lowest in the exploration and trial stages. Analysis of covariance, while controlling for tenure, showed a nonsignificant difference between career stages for this sample of 277 male and female municipal workers who were technicians, sales workers, professionals, and managers/administrators with a mean age of 38.5, $F(2,273) = .72$.

These findings, in combination with those on the need for growth and upward mobility, have potential positive implications for the older worker as an employee. Morrison (1977) suggested that career planning activity can mean that the worker is more adaptive.

The various findings noted above must be regarded as preliminary, however, until replications of the studies with other samples and longitudinal designs have been completed. With reference to career planning, research is also needed to identify what other factors may affect the level of planning activities of the older worker. For example, the extent of career planning may be affected by factors such as personal planning skills, self-esteem, past reinforcement for career planning, and the available opportunities in the career environment (Gould, 1979b).

Another phenomenon associated with the midcareer stage is obsolescence. The obsolescence of technical employees has received considerable attention (Kaufman, 1974; Thompson and Dalton, 1976). In a 1974 review of the literature on midcareer obsolescence, three employee characteristics were identified as associated with low obsolescence. The characteristics were high intellectual ability, high self-motivation, and personal flexibility (Kaufman, 1974). But Thompson and Dalton's research has led them to conclude that obsolescence also occurs because an organization is "out-of-date." An organization that is out-of-date was described as not responding to employee development needs, not engaging in adequate human resource planning, and not reducing barriers to movement within the organization (Thompson and Dalton, 1976).

A low level of organizational participation in development efforts was also identified as associated with high obsolescence by Shearer and Steger (1975). However, obsolescence was not linearly related to age ($r = .034$) for this cross-sectional study of 318 Air Force officers and 133 civilian Air Force employees. Obsolescence was found to decrease until the mid-thirties and increase thereafter.

MIDCAREER CHANGERS

Nine empirical studies are reviewed in which the motivations for midcareer change (Armstrong, 1981; Lawrence, 1980; Neapolitan, 1980; Snyder et al., 1978; Thomas, 1980) or career changers (Clopton, 1973; Gottfredson, 1977; Thomas and Robbins, 1979; Wiener and Vaitenas, 1977) were described (see Table D-2, Appendix). The studies were essentially retrospective or cross-sectional; thus, the data may not accurately reflect true explanations of the change. The majority of the samples studied represent either individuals who were students pursuing new careers (Armstrong, 1981; Clopton, 1973) or who were in technical, managerial, or professional careers (Neapolitan, 1980; Snyder et al., 1978; Thomas, 1980; Thomas and Robbins, 1979). There was one national sample studied, a 1-in-1000 sampling of the 1970 census data covering ages 21–70 (Gottfredson, 1977). Career changers were compared to non-career changers in four of the studies (Armstrong, 1981; Clopton, 1973; Neapolitan, 1980; Wiener and Vaitenas, 1977).

The motives for career change were found to be both intrinsic and extrinsic in nature. Intrinsic work motivation was cited as the reason for career change for two samples of managerial and professional types of employees (Neapolitan, 1980; Thomas, 1980). This motive was reflected in the rated importance of matching work values (48 percent) and "finding more meaningful work" (53 percent) in Thomas's study of 73 men between 34 and 54 years of age. In this same study, extrinsic factors were given to a lesser degree as reasons for making the change; that is, 11 percent specified salary and 13 percent specified greater security. In other samples, job dissatisfaction was the reason given for changing by enrollees in a community college (Armstrong, 1981), and obtaining more power and esteem was cited by professors who moved to take a department chair position (Snyder et al., 1978).

Career changers were described and compared to non-career changers in two studies (Clopton, 1973; Wiener and Vaitneas, 1977). Men who were pursuing an advanced degree to make the career change expressed greater self-esteem than did a sample of career persisters (Clopton, 1973). But in the Wiener and Vaitenas (1977) study of participants in a university career counseling program, the changers were lower in ascendancy and responsibility (scales from the Gordon Personality Inventory) and lower in dominance, endurance, and order (scales from the Edwards Personal Preference Survey). For the latter group of career changers, Wiener and Vaitenas suggested the presence of personality-work environment incongruity, according to Holland's (1973) theory of careers, and less task discipline. The differences in character between these two sets of career changers may reflect those who do and do not seek career counseling, with those who do feeling greater uncertainty about themselves because an actual career choice had not yet been made. Perhaps making the choice would produce personality-job congruence and/or higher task discipline (Wiener and Vaitenas, 1977).

Wiener and Vaitenas's (1977) study, in addition to Neapolitan's (1980) and Thomas's (1980), provide support for Holland's theory of personality-environment congruence. In Neapolitan's study, all 25 career changers reported congruence between their work orientations and the second occupations. Support for congruence was also found in the national census sample; that is, workers whose jobs were more congruent were more occupationally stable (Gottfredson, 1977). Contrary to these positive findings, Thomas and Robbins (1979) found little support for career changer movement into more congruent occupations. Among 61 male managerial, technical, and professional employee career changers, 39 percent moved into less congruent occupations while 43 percent moved into more congruent occupations. But whether the changer moved to a more or less congruent career, both groups found the second careers to be significantly more satisfying (Kolmogorov-Smirnov one-sample test, $p < .01$).

Two explanations were offered for these discrepant findings (Thomas and Robbins, 1979). One was potential error in identifying the work environments and in quantifying the degree of individual work orientation and occupation congruence. A second possible explanation was that there might have been differences in the level of work salience and a shift to more of a leisure orientation. Such individuals were thought to be able to move to incongruent occupations and yet be highly satisfied (Thomas and Robbins, 1979).

It may also be possible that some of Thomas and Robbins's sample were not voluntary career changers. The subjects in the Neapolitan, the Thomas, and the Wiener and Vaitenas studies were voluntary career changers. Involuntary career changers may be less likely to select a congruent occupation simply because less career exploration was completed and fewer employment options were available to them.

Research is therefore needed to explain career changes for voluntary and involuntary changers, as well as for those seeking and not seeking career counseling. In general, a more representative set of personal, organizational, and environmental factors need to be examined for their relative and interactive effects on the decision to change careers (Sonnenfeld and Kotter, 1982). Longitudinal designs are important for obtaining accurate data on the factors influencing actual career change.

Career Planning Intervention Effectiveness

Four empirical studies were located in which the effect of a career development seminar or workshop was examined (see Table D-3, Appendix). Although age was not specifically assessed, a fairly wide range of ages was represented in the samples.

One of the studies employed a relatively complex research design having three experimental career planning treatments and two control groups (Miller et al., 1973). The treatments were (1) completion of a forecasting questionnaire that focused on individual future work and changes in organizational needs, (2) forecasting questionnaire plus action planning, and (3) 1 and 2, plus career counseling discussions. For 450 research and development employees in three hierarchical levels (GS-11 and below, GS-12, and GS-13 and above) there was a significant difference in the number of self-development activities, $F(2,435) = 13.83$, $p < .001$. That is, career planning activity enhanced self-development activity at the lower hierarchical levels. There was a treatment effect, $F(4,435) = 2.44$, $p < .05$, for the increase in the number of courses taken ten months after the interventions. Miller et al. concluded that effective career planning requires more than simply forecasting and should include the perceived availability of action alternatives such as tuition rebates and times for longer-term self-development activities.

Of the remaining three studies, one employed a control group (Eng and Gottsdanker, 1979). The outcomes of a university career development program were examined, with subjects ranging in age from 25 to 59. The program consisted of ten 2-hour group sessions including assertiveness training and career planning, plus the use of exercises and tests. On the basis of career records, the authors found that a greater number of participants (40 percent) made career changes than did the control group (20 percent). The changes involved promotional transfers, job reclassifications, and the initiation of additional education.

As these studies reveal, little research has been completed to assess the effect of career planning interventions on the employed population. Longitudinal research is needed generally on the career planning and development process (Walsh, 1979), but particularly to learn how it affects the middle and late career stages. In addition, particular career planning methods need to be studied so that the relative effectiveness of specific methods can be identified.

Learning and Post-Training Performance

In view of changing technologies and the possibility of obsolescence, training becomes a potential tool for realizing a productive older work force. Of interest, therefore, is the evidence on the effect of training on performance for the older worker and, more basically, on the ability of the older worker to learn.

LEARNING PERFORMANCE

Studies on the ability of the older worker to learn go back to Thorndike's work of the 1920s. This research led to the conclusion that older persons could learn as well as younger persons, using the same materials and methods. The older person in this research was, however, somewhat younger (average age = 42, range = 35–50) than the older worker of today (Thorndike, 1928).

Floyd Ruch (1934) replicated some of Thorndike's research in the 1930s, except that he used three age groups: 12–17, 34–59, and 60–82. Ruch reported that the older group performed more poorly on a set of 33 tasks, but the differences were small and the group continued to learn well.

In a more recent review of the learning literature, Birren (1964) concluded that changes in learning ability with age were generally small. The differences that had appeared between age groups were believed to be related more to motivation level, physiological condition, attention, and perception than to learning capacity.

Five relatively recent studies of age related to learning were found (see Table D-4, Appendix). In three of them, there was support for the programmed-type training methodology (Dodd, 1967; Jamieson, 1969; Sieman, 1976). In Dodd's study (1967), successful learning occurred in a two-day period when teaching 13 open hearth personnel (ages 26–58) to be electric arc operators in a steel company. The training material consisted of a programmed handbook.

Siemen (1976) found no significant difference between 16–32 and 67–84-year-olds in their ability to learn new cognitive skills using programmed materials. There was, however, a considerable difference in the amount of time required to complete the program (a mean of 103 minutes for the older group and 45 minutes for the younger group).

In Jamieson's study (1969), the older worker learned as well as the younger worker, except when stress was applied. A different teaching method was used in teaching two groups of ten females to be sewing machine operators. One method was programmed in nature and the other was the traditional method that had previously been used. The traditional method consisted of a random presentation of information, and any deviation from the desired performance was scored as an error. Three subjects from the traditional group left, complaining of stress.

The positive findings for the use of programmed materials to teach the older worker coincides with Belbin's findings for what he calls the "discovery method." This method involves the presentation of tasks and problems to form "a path of exploration that allows the trainee to progress continuously" (Belbin, 1970: 57). Belbin has proposed that the method facilitates learning and minimizes stress for the older worker.

There is a fairly substantial amount of evidence to show that the older worker can continue to learn and learn well. Belbin's work with the "discovery method" and the support from recent studies suggest that a programmed teaching methodology facilitates older worker learning.

POST-TRAINING PERFORMANCE

In a recent review of the training literature pertaining to work situations, Goldstein (1980) concluded that little relevant data were available. Three studies of age related to post-training performance were found (Barber, 1965; Downs, 1967; Newsham, 1969). Barber assessed the performance of 140 male craftmen's mates one year after having completed retraining for one of four occupations. The subjects, ranging in age from 27 to 62 years, were trained using programmed instruction for spraygun operator, scaffolder, maintenance operator, and thermal insulator jobs. About 80 percent of the group were average and above average performers after one year in the new jobs. The 20 percent who were poor performers ranged in age from 28 to 55 years.

In a brief report of Newsham's study (1969) of British younger workers (< 35) and older workers (> 35) who received training of different types and of various lengths, the retention rate as time passed exceeded that of the younger workers. The retention rate three months after training showed the younger group to have less turnover, but at 24 months, the rate was greater than or equal to 57 percent for the older group and 42 percent for the younger group. Similar results were obtained in two United Kingdom public service organizations where a group of 800 workers in each were trained for outdoor and clerical jobs (Downs, 1967). During the six months after training, turnover was higher for those aged 35 and over, but after six months the trend reversed.

Based on these findings and in very tentative terms, it appears that the outcomes of training the older worker are better than when training the younger worker. Of course, additional research on a variety of skills training are needed. However, given the evidence on older workers' ability to learn, it seems that future studies will show post-training performance to be generally equal to that of the younger worker.

Preretirement Programs

Several review articles on preretirement programs were located. Hagerty (1973) prepared a bibliography through 1972, Kelleher and Quirk (1974) annotated the literature from 1965 to 1974, and Kasschau (1974) reviewed the empirical evidence.

It is not known exactly how many companies offer preretirement programs. A recent survey of employers who are members of the American Society of Personnel Administrators revealed that 36 percent of the respondent companies (n = 267) have programs (Bureau of National Affairs, 1980). In a survey of Fortune 500 companies, 29 percent of the 147 respondent companies had preretirement programs (Siegel and Rives, 1978). It was also estimated that about 60 percent of the responding companies would have a program by 1981.

Goals for offering preretirement programs include (1) to facilitate planning for retirement and (2) to promote adjustment to achieve satisfaction with retirement (Kasschau, 1974). Kasschau suggested that programs for achieving the first goal might be labeled retirement planning. To stimulate planning, the program would consist of information dissemination. This planning goal could be met essentially with the set of topics mentioned earlier as most common to preretirement programs (Kasschau, 1974).

The second goal—to promote adjustment in retirement—has been associated with changing attitudes toward retirement (Kasschau, 1974). Such programs might more appropriately be labeled retirement counseling. The content of a retirement counseling program would address feelings and fears about retirement.

Topics typically included in the programs are pensions, social security, financial planning, health, and leisure (Kasschau, 1974; Reich, 1977; Beveridge, 1980; Bureau of National Affairs, 1980). These topics were generally offered in 50–60 percent of the existing programs by the companies in the 1980 ASPA-BNA survey. Some of the specific topics that were identified were wills and inheritance, earning money after retirement, and organizations for retirees. Some of the less common topics mentioned were as follows. Of the companies, 20 percent offered tuition aid or other educational assistance for developing new interests or activities. In addition, 15 percent of the companies had "tapering off" programs wherein work time was gradually reduced as the individual approached retirement. Beyond the point of retirement, about half of the companies arranged for some employees to serve as consultants. Retirees were recalled for temporary assignments in 62 percent of the companies.

The content mentioned in terms of retirement counseling has usually not been found in programs (Kasschau, 1974; Siegel and Rives, 1978; Beveridge, 1980). On the basis of Siegel and Rives's survey of the Fortune 500 respondent companies, they noted that the programs contained little emphasis on dealing with the psychological problems of retirement. On the other hand, the ASPA-BNA survey did show that 48 percent of the programs covered the topic "mental/emotional aspects of retirement." The nature of the coverage, however, was not described; therefore it is possible that the focus was not on attitudes. Of course, organizations may prefer to refrain from dealing with feelings and fears about retirement to avoid intruding into employee's private realms (Reich, 1977).

The findings of preretirement program effectiveness studies were described by Kasschau (1974) and Morrow (1980) as inconclusive and/or contradictory. Kasschau attributed these findings to confusion over the program goals. She found that most programs are developed to accomplish the second objective of promoting adjustment in retirement, while the content is oriented to achieving the first (the planning) objective.

Some relatively recent studies of the effects of preretirement programs show the mixed results (Beveridge, 1980; Charles, 1971; Glamser, 1981; Lundgren, 1965; Morrow, 1980; O'Rourke and Friedman, 1972) (see Table D-5, Appendix). In Lundgren's study, for example, the retirees from companies that offered preretirement programs were more satisfied with retirement. The retirees represented former office and factory workers from thirteen companies, eleven of which reported having preretirement programs. The programs, however, varied and the content was not described.

Positive retiree attitude changes were also found among 368 individuals who had participated in Drake University's Pre-Retirement Planning program (Charles, 1971). On the basis of pre- and post-self-report questionnaires, self-pereceived personal competence and personal worth generally improved. The content of this program consisted of a weekly evening lecture, film, and discussion sessions on topics such as changing roles, leisure time activities, social security, and other financial aspects. It appears that the content was not what Kasschau identified as retirement counseling, but there was a positive attitude change.

In Morrow's (1980) survey of a stratified sample of employees age 50 and over at a midwestern university, participants in a retirement preparation program had a higher general attitude toward retirement than did nonparticipants ($t = -.168, p < .05$). It is not clear, however, that the difference between participant and nonparticipant attitudes was a program effect, because attitudes were not measured prior to program participation. In addition, the subjects had not yet retired; therefore, the program's effect on the actual retirement experience was absent.

Little or no change was reported, however, in two studies (Glamser, 1981; O'Rourke and Friedman, 1972). First, for two experimental groups and a control group, with a six-year postretirement program follow-up and after actual retirement, there was no significant difference between groups in life satisfaction, retirement attitude, and felt job deprivation (Glamser, 1981). The two experimental programs consisted of (1) what appeared to be traditional content with a group discussion format and (2) topical coverage in an individual briefing format. An important consideration in this study is whether the program should be expected to have such a long-term effect on adjustment and satisfaction (Glamser, 1981). In the O'Rourke and Friedman (1972) study, labor union members revealed relatively little attitude change. It was not completely clear what the content of this program was except that there were eight monthly discussion meetings with an expert instructor, and literature was distributed. Therefore, in both of these studies it is possible that the content of the programs was retirement planning rather than counseling, and thus positive changes in attitudes would not necessarily be expected.

On the basis of the information provided in general in the three studies, it is not clear to what extent the results can be explained by the presence or lack of a content-goal match. Therefore, evaluation research is needed to examine specific content relative to goals or outcomes. The research designs should include a control group. In addition, it is important to measure behavior before and after the program, because an attitude change does not necessarily mean that the participants have changed. Longitudinal studies with various treatment groups, and planned intermittent follow-up of the participants after retirement, would make a significant contribution to understanding the effects of preretirement programs.

Summary, Implications, and Future Research Issues

Organizations have been increasing what were already sizable training and development programs, but with limited offerings for the older worker. Formal career planning programs, however, appear to be fewer in number. There is also relatively little empirical evidence at the present time to serve as a basis for helping organizations to select optimal methods for maintaining and improving the performance of older workers. For this reason, the research findings can, in general, only be interpreted in very tentative terms.

The limited career planning, training and development offerings for the older worker and the preliminary evidence of the needs and attitudes of workers in the Midlife Transition Stage (ages 40–45), in addition to the reasons for career change, suggest that some career needs or aspirations are not being met at middle career and later. If additional studies with different subject samples support these findings, then it seems that discouragement, lowered performance, possibly obsolescence (as suggested by Thompson and Dalton, 1976), or turnover might be expected. Of course, multivariate and longitudinal studies are needed to examine how the needs, attitudes, and career planning and training programs interact and affect performance over time.

In addition to the implications that needs and attitudes have for older worker career planning and training, support for making the training available is also provided by the fairly substantial evidence of the older worker's continued ability to learn. In particular, the programmed teaching methodology, or "discovery method," has been shown to aid learning. The method is effective in part because it brings the pace of learning somewhat more under the control of the learner, thereby accommodating different learning patterns.

The transference of learning to the work setting has, however, not yet been sufficiently documented. More older worker training research has been completed in Europe. There is, in fact, a dearth of research on post-training performance in the United States. Nevertheless, on the basis of the evidence that is available, there is some cause to be optimistic about the outcomes of training the older worker, both in terms of performance and organization retention rates after training.

The lack of evidence for an age link to the career stages is not a particularly surprising finding because of the increasing preponderance of nontraditional career paths. The various career starts or late starts and career changes of women, as an example, would rather significantly counteract an age-career stage relationship.

Preretirement programs appear to be of a planning nature, although the goals and assessments of effectiveness may focus on satisfaction with retirement. That is, the content of the programs may not coincide with the intended goals of the program. It is important, therefore, for organizations to reconcile any preretirement program goal confusions, and to consider whether the content of the program coincides with its intended goals.

During the preretirement period, too, various methods are being employed for helping the older worker ease into retirement while potentially satisfying workers' needs for employment, and the organization's continuing or periodic needs for their expertise and skills. Studies of such programs are needed for identifying the effects of specific methods.

Future research needs on career planning, training and development of the older worker are extensive, but there are two major recurring needs. One is for program evaluation research with random assignment of subjects, a control group, pre- and postassessment, as well as assessment of performance in the program and of the effect of the program on post-training behavior. This type of research is needed to assess the relative outcomes or effectiveness of different career planning, training, and preretirement methods. It would be useful for organizations, for instance, to know more about the effects of various career planning methods on level of actual career planning, career change, job satisfaction, performance or obsolescence, and turnover.

The other research need is for multivariate and/or longitudinal designs. A longitudinal study would improve our understanding of the effects of career planning, training, and development processes. Multivariate research would make it possible to examine the interactions between variables and their effects on career change or level of career planning. Variables such as age, career stage, career planning skills, self-esteem, past reinforcement for career planning, and opportunity for career planning and training could be examined for their effects on career planning. To understand career change, the salience of work and various external and internal organization pressures could also be studied.

PART III

Compensation, Pensions, and Retirement

Compensation is the monetary reward paid by an organization to an employee for his or her efforts (Glueck, 1978). Glueck has noted that because employee compensation frequently equals 50 percent or more of the cash flow of an organization, it is one of the most important personnel functions. When compensation is considered in light of the management of human resources, it has been found to relate to the attraction, maintenance, and motivation of employees. The term compensation, as it is used in this book, is given a broad interpretation. Compensation is said to consist of five interrelated components: pay, legally required fringe benefits, employer-provided fringe benefits, employee services, and noneconomic rewards.

Pay is the money paid to employees in wages and salaries. Legally required fringe benefits (for example, social security, workers' compensation) are those mandated by government legislation, in contrast to those provided by the employer or bargained for under a collective bargaining agreement (for example, health insurance, pensions, vacations). Employee services (for example, cafeterias, employee discounts) are designed to build stronger bonds between the employer and employee by demonstrating the concern and interest of management in the employee's well-being. Finally, noneconomic rewards, such as promotions, status, and larger and more prestigious offices, have intrinsic values to employees.

This segment of the book examines the relationship between age and a series of compensation issues. In Chapter 6, we consider the relationship between age and earnings, followed by sections that examine compensation preferences, pay satisfaction, and pay for performance. Pensions, retirement preferences, and social security issues (Chapter 7) have also been included in this portion of the book, since income adequacy and the preference for work or retirement are interrelated. Finally, we examine retirement policies and practices in other industrialized countries.

CHAPTER 6

COMPENSATION

When employee earnings are considered in the broadest possible terms, older workers in the United States, Japan, Great Britain, and France earn more than younger workers (Suzuki, 1976). These relationships are presented in Figures 6.1 and 6.2. Moreover, in each of the four countries under consideration, older men earn more than older women. Although younger men and women (under age 25) earn approximately the same, by the age of 25 male earnings in all four countries exceed those of women. At their widest point, the earnings of Japanese males, followed by American males, far exceed their female age cohorts. The earnings spread in France and Great Britain is less significant.

In Japan and the United States, pay rises steeply for men until the ages of 49 and 44, respectively. Thereafter, earnings stabilize and eventually decline slightly. In France, the earnings curve of males are not as pronounced. In Great Britain, the male earnings curve is even less pronounced. The earnings of American women rise steadily until the age of 33, at which time they stabilize. The earnings of Japanese women slow at a very early age and eventually begin to decline. Male-female earnings differences become increasingly evident with age. In 1971, Japanese women (aged 18-19) earned 82 percent of the earnings of males in the same age group. At the same time, Japanese women aged 40-49 earned only 43 percent as much as men of the same age. In the United States, for the year 1972, women aged 16-19 earned 91 percent of male earning. At the same time, those aged 45-54 earned only 50 percent as much as their male counterparts. Although a portion of the spread between female and male earnings can be attributed to the interrupted labor force patterns of women (Suzuki, 1976), other factors such as employment discrimination and the structure of labor markets certainly play a role.

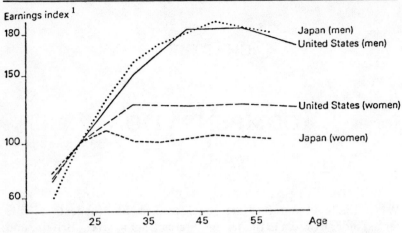

Note: From H. Suzuki, "Age, seniority and wages." International Labour Review, 1976, 113, 67-84.
1. 100 = Earnings of the 2-24 age group

Figure 6.1: Earnings Level by Age and Sex, United States and Japan

There is also an age-education interaction with respect to increased earnings. It is a well-known fact that individuals with more education earn more than those with less education. Suzuki (1976) has shown that individuals with the same level of education earn more as they age. Earnings growth is also influenced by age and occupation. Some workers' earnings level off sooner regardless of age because of their occupations. Other factors influencing earnings include nationality, race, and parents' status. However, within each of these groups, older workers tend to earn more.

At an organizational level, most human resource managers would like to design systems in which salaries bear a strong relationship to the level of difficulty, responsibility, and performance required. Pay and age are highly correlated in organizational settings because older or more "mature" workers tend to obtain the positions with greater difficulty and responsibility. One study has examined the relationship between employee salaries and maturity (age and experience).

Chandler et al. (1963) studied 6598 electronic computer programmers. The data were derived from an annual national survey of programmers for 1962. The authors found that age and experience were highly correlated ($r = .47$), as were age and salary ($r = .53$) and experience and salary ($r = .71$).[1] Age alone explained 28 percent of the variability in salary, while experience alone accounted for 51 per-

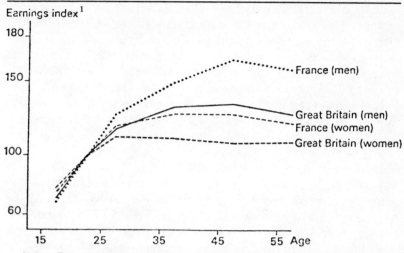

Note: From H. Suzuki, "Age, seniority and wages," International Labour Review, 1976, 113, 67-84.
1. 100 = Earnings of the 21-24 or 21-25 age group

Figure 6.2: Earnings by Age and Sex, Great Britain and France

cent of the variance. Multiple regression analysis using both age and experience resulted in a coefficient value of .74, thereby explaining 55 percent of the variability in pay, $F(2,6593) = 237.03$. This study's findings are limited, however, by the author's failure to control for salary differences across organizations and to hold experience constant while manipulating age.

Freeman (1979) has presented data supporting the proposition that the earnings of older men (aged 45-54) rise sharply relative to those of young men (aged 20-34). This differential was more pronounced for college graduates in the same age groupings than for high school graduates. The same result tended not to occur for women because of their relatively flat earnings curve.

In comparing male earnings data from 1968 and 1977, Freeman found a significant decline in the earnings of young workers vis-à-vis their older counterparts. This was particularly true for those with more education. Freeman then tested the proposition that the differences in wage increases for younger versus older workers could be explained by the sharp increase in the supply of younger workers which resulted from the post-World War II baby boom.

He found that when the level of economic activity is fixed (controlled), the size of the cohort (that is, the relative number of older to younger workers) has a demonstrable impact on male age-earnings profiles. This effect was far more significant for college-educated than high school-educated workers. The lower level of significance between older high school graduates and younger high school graduates is explained by the greater substitutability of high school-educated workers at all ages than is true of college-trained persons.

There are several implications for the management of organizations from the findings that the earnings of one age group (cohort) are significantly determined by the size of that group. This will be particularly important in the 1990s, when the number of entry-level workers is expected to decline. The large cohort presently working its way through the labor force may not enjoy the same earnings growth pattern as its predecessor group or the smaller one to follow. As the relative number of young workers declines in the 1990s and beyond, this group should enjoy relatively larger wage increases vis-à-vis their older counterparts. In addition, organizations may have to pay more to acquire these workers than they would have in the past. Hence, pay may become compressed, and the issue of equitable financial treatment will be brought to the forefront. Moreover, a prospective shortage of young workers, combined with the potential for higher than traditional wages, might cause organizations to consider the redesign of jobs in order to eliminate much of the work formerly conducted by younger, entry-level workers. This factor, combined with the likelihood of somewhat clogged career ladders caused by the bulge in the number of middle-age workers, might produce radically different changes in career paths. Whether older workers would accept and adjust to such a change would be strongly influenced by their abilities, characteristics, and needs.

SUMMARY AND IMPLICATIONS

The finding that older workers earn more than younger workers can hardly be considered a significant one, nor can the fact that earnings are influenced by education, nationality, race, parents' status, and a variety of other demographic factors. It has however been shown that as workers age, the male-female earnings differences increase. This has implications for society and for organizations. Human resource managers should expect continued environmental pressure (from government and women's rights organizations) to eradicate this situation.

The Freeman findings appear to have the greatest implications for researchers and human resource managers. If, as Freeman found, the earnings of one age group relative to another are influenced by the size of that group, then the expected decline in entry-level workers, combined with a relative excess of older, more mature workers, could set in motion a series of compensation-motivation problems. Researchers may find that organizational equity questions become of paramount importance.

Since it is projected that in the 1990s there will be relatively fewer young workers, organizations may expect to offer higher salaries in order to recruit entry-level employees. This development could lead to a series of related difficulties. For example, will organizations be able to maintain sufficiently high educational standards, or will they be required to settle for less qualified employees? What then will be the implications for organizational training? In addition, if young workers obtain higher than expected salaries, what motivational and equity factors must be considered with respect to both older and younger workers? Because of the size of the current group of young workers, they will probably earn less relative to their older counterparts, who are fewer in number. As the current group ages, they will tend to earn more relative to their younger peers, yet once again, because of their larger numbers vis-à-vis the new, young group, the pay differential might not be as great as they might have expected. Hence, organizations can expect a problem in creating equitable pay systems, as well as in using money to motivate workers.

Employee Compensation Preferences

Pay is only one of several forms of compensation. The research literature summarized in this section demonstrates that many workers would prefer less emphasis on pay and more on fringe benefits.

There are a growing number of organizations which permit employees to tailor their individual compensation programs to satisfy special needs. This approach, known as a cafeteria system, has been billed as one of the more important potential innovations associated with human resource management in recent years. Cafeteria systems provide each employee with a portion of the benefits allocation. Employees are permitted to select their own fringe benefits from the variety of options offered by the employer. Schuster (1968) has found that 75 percent of the employees in an aerospace firm would redistribute current compensation allocations. The findings in the next section clearly demonstrate that older workers and younger workers differ in their compensation preferences. These differences are summarized in Table E-1 (Appendix).

PAY VERSUS JOB SECURITY/FRINGE BENEFITS

Much of the compensation preferences research was conducted prior to 1975. In spite of this fact, and although many of the variables employed to explain employee preferences are intercorrelated, a consistent pattern of conclusions begins to emerge for some explanatory variables. In this section and the one that follows, studies examining age and compensation preferences are discussed along with variables that have been found to moderate this relationship.

Andrews and Henry (1964), in a study of 299 managers, found evidence suggesting that the cafeteria approach may have great appeal to older employees. These authors found strong statistical evidence to suggest that older workers would be willing to accept pay reductions in order to achieve increased job security ($\chi^2 < .10$), and even stronger evidence ($\chi^2 < .001$) that older workers preferred fringe benefits to pay. These results were supported by Gruenfeld (1967) in a study of 52 supervisors in 11 companies. Gruenfeld found statistically significant differences between older and younger supervisors on several compensation dimensions. Younger supervisors indicated a preference for higher wages ($p < .01$) and better fringe benefits ($p < .01$), while older supervisors preferred less job tension and more definite and regular work hours (both $p < .01$). Both younger and older supervisors differed with middle-aged supervisors in preference for job security. Middle-aged supervisors gave employment security the lowest preference score ($p < .05$). This latter findings can probably be explained by the balance between age, experience, and occupational mobility perceived by this group.

Schuster (1968), in a study of 325 aerospace workers, found that the most important feature of compensation programs among the older workers (aged 48-64) were medical insurance and retirement benefits. On the other hand, younger workers (aged 18-34) regarded retirement benefits as being least important, with base salary being most important. Interestingly, medical insurance was considered to be the most important feature of compensation plans by both middle-aged and older workers. Even among younger workers it was second.

However, Jurgenson (1948), in a study of 3723 applicants to a Minneapolis gas company during the period 1945-1947, found job security to be the most important job factor (among ten) for all workers except those under 20, where it was second most important. Pay was in the middle range for most workers, with fringe benefits consistently last. Other categories were advancement, company, coworkers, hours, supervisor, type of work, and working conditions. Although it might be presumed that the proximity of this research to the pre-World War II depression and the psychological effects of unemployment associated with that period might limit the generalizability of this study, such was not the case.

In a follow-up study to his own work, Jurgenson (1978) continued to collect data on gas company applicants. His sample of 56,621 applicants over a 30-year period indicates only limited changes in worker preferences. For male workers of all age groups, job security was the most important aspect of employment. This contrasted with females of all age groups who indicated that the type of work was the most critical aspect of employment. As workers age, female preferences tended to be more stable than males. As males age, pay and advancement became less important, while fringe benefits, the company, and the supervisor became more important. Similarly, pay was less important for older females, while fringe benefits became more important, except for the group over 55.

The findings of the Jurgenson studies are valuable because of their longitudinal character and the large population of workers. However, the results are potentially confounded by the use of job applicants rather than employed workers. Because most of the job applicants are likely to be unemployed, it should not be surprising that they would indicate that job security was their most important job preference.

Yet another study involving only fringe benefit preferences among unionized blue collar workers (Wagner and Bakerman, 1960) found that pensions were considered the most important fringe benefit by workers of all age groups. As would be expected, pensions became more important for older workers (38 percent in the 40-49 age group) than younger workers (29 percent in the 30-39 age groups). Group life and health insurance ranked second in preference for all age groups. Also noteworthy was the fact that the importance of income security benefits (supplemental unemployment benefits and guaranteed annual wages) declined steadily with age. This decline may be explained by the existence of seniority provisions in union contracts. As workers progress in age, so do their years of service. Since higher levels of seniority tend to increase one's employment security, the preference for such benefits should decline with age.

One of the largest studies to date was conducted by Nealey (1964a) and involved 1133 union workers. Nealey questioned workers on their preference for six compensation items: hospital insurance, a union shop, a 6 percent raise, three-week vacations, pensions, and a 37.5-hour work week. He found that preferences among these items shifted most dramatically for pensions. As Figure 6.3 demonstrates, employee preferences for pensions constitute a stable fifth among the six possible items for workers under 39 years of age. Thereafter, pref-

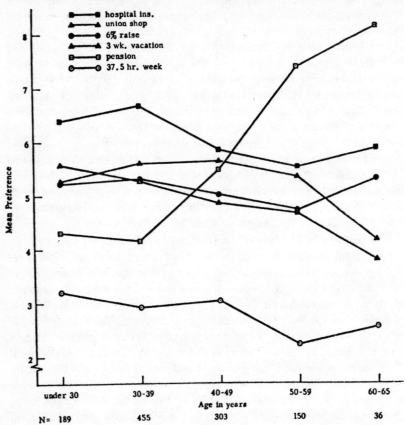

Figure 6.3: Benefit Preference by Age

Note: From S. M. Nealey, "Determining worker preferences among employees benefit programs." Journal of Applied Psychology, 1964, 48 2-12.

erences for pensions rose to third for the 40-49 age group and continued to rise until it became most important for the 50-59-year-old group. This finding supports Wagner and Bakerman's study for older workers but differs slightly with respect to younger-worker preferences.

Younger workers preferred medical insurance to all other compensation items in the Nealey research. For all groups of workers, pay was found to be the fourth most preferred compensation item, with the exception of the 60-65 age group, where it was third. Finally, although it might be suspected that older workers would prefer more time off from work, the results of the Nealey work showed just the opposite. Worker preferences for additional vacation time and the 37.5-hour work week declined with age. This finding differs from the Wagner and Bakerman study, which showed that workers in the 30-39 and 50-59 age brackets placed more emphasis on vacations, and that for all workers there was generally a slight rise in preference for vacation time associated with age.

One of the few recent studies, Crandall (1977) investigated the preferences of 128 managerial and nonmanagerial employees of a life insurance company. For the group aged 40 years or less, hospital and medical insurance ranked as the most important fringe benefit, while retirement benefits were far down the list of priorities. Older employees (aged 41-64) listed retirement benefits as being their number one concern and hospitalization insurance as second most important. Time off from the job ranked at the bottom of the preference list of older employees.

A later study (Crandall and Lundstrom, 1980) of 229 managerial and nonmanagerial life insurance company employees also found a preference by older employees (aged 38-64) for retirement benefits. Once again, hospital and medical insurance were the most preferred fringe benefit for employees 18-23 years of age and second most important for the 38-64 age group.

One caveat to the compensation preferences research should be noted. Nealey found that other personal characteristics dramatically shifted worker preferences for several types of compensation. Some of the personal characteristics that have been found to modify worker preferences include sex, marital status, number of dependents, education, and occupations. In the next section, these modifying variables are discussed.

FACTORS MODIFYING THE RELATIONSHIP BETWEEN AGE AND COMPENSATION PREFERENCES

The research designs employed in the pay preference studies severely restrict our ability to separate the individual influence of an array of explanatory variables. Therefore, determining whether age or some other factor contributes to a particular preference is confounded by these limitations. Some of the factors found to moderate the relationship between age and compensation preferences have been gender, marital status, number of dependents, salary, and occupation.

Jurgenson (1947) found important differences between male and female workers. Advancement, fringe benefits, and job security (all p

$<$ .01) were found to be more important to males than to females. In contrast, the type of work, the supervisor, working conditions, and co-workers were more important to females than males. These same findings held constant for the most recent Jurgenson (1978) study cited above. Chapman and Ottemann (1975) found no statistically significant sex differences, except for a male preference for dental insurance ($p <$ .01). Marital status dramatically shifted worker preference for hospital insurance and reduction in the work week (Nealey, 1964a). Married workers considered hospital insurance to be their most important benefit, whereas for unmarried workers it was the fifth most important item. Unmarried individuals preferred a reduction in the work week considerably more than married workers.[2]

In another study, Nealey (1964b) questioned 841 employees (635 males, 206 females) at six manufacturing plants. In that study of four compensation preferences (pensions, pay raises, sick leave, and vacation), the relationship between five employee characteristics (age, income, number of dependent children, type of job, and attitude) were examined. The results supported previous findings with respect to older worker preferences. That is, as workers age, their preference for pensions increased significantly. In addition, older workers were willing to forego pay raises and paid time off from work (sick leave and vacations). Although this relationship was true for all workers, it was more strongly pronounced among older males than older females.

The number of respondents' children also influenced employee responses (Nealey, 1964b). As the number of children increased from none to three or more, worker preferences for health insurance increased. At the same time, an increase in the number of children dramatically reduced preferences for pensions. Chapman and Ottemann (1975) found that employees with more dependents preferred dental coverage ($p <$ .01), while those with fewer dependents had a preference for increased pension coverage and shorter workday ($p <$ .01).

Differences in employee job preferences also tend to exist among applicants with different educational backgrounds and occupations.[3] Jurgenson (1978) found that college-educated male applicants placed greater emphasis on pay, type of work, and working conditions than those with less formal education. These same employees placed less emphasis on job security, co-workers, and hours. An important contrast was that those with a high school diploma or less considered job security the most critical job factor.

Similar distinctions were found when managerial and professional employees were compared with workers at lower organizational levels.

For male employees, the type of work and pay assumed greater importance for professional and managerial employees, whereas job security and co-workers were more critical to lower-level applicants. Chapman and Ottemann (1975) found differences in the preferences of operating, as compared to clerical employees. Operating employees had a statistically strong preference for dental coverage (p < .01), whereas clerical employees had a significant preference for additional time off (ten Fridays)[4] (p < .05). Contrary to this finding was the research of Lewellen and Lanser (1973) on 300 executives in seven corporations. They found no differences in the preferences of the executives by virtue of their age or their tax or income bracket. Across all groups there was a strong preference for postretirement income.

Nealey's (1964b) study produced additional moderating variables. Level of income was related to preferences for pension and pay. Employees with higher incomes had a preference for additional pension, while those with lower incomes preferred additional pay raises. Employees with more dependents exhibited a stronger preference for hospital insurance, while unfavorable employee attitudes were associated with a preference for higher pay. Unfortunately, none of the research has involved cross-tabulations between these worker characteristics and age vis-à-vis worker preferences. As will be discussed in a subsequent section, this limitation in the research should be addressed.

In a subsequent study of employee preferences among a set of compensation options, Nealey and Goodale (1967) studied 197 industrial workers. The purpose of this study was to assess preferences among options, all of which involved additional paid time from the job. Statistically significant differences were found between older workers aged 50-65 and younger workers aged 18-33 and 34-49 on three options. These were the desire for a four-day work week (preferred by younger workers, p < .05), preference for early retirement (preferred by older workers, p < .01), and five Fridays (preferred by younger workers, p < .01). Although older workers tended to prefer additional vacation time, sabbaticals, and pay increases, none of these differences was statistically significant. The Nealey and Goodale findings were supported by Jurgenson (1948), who found that hours of work became a less important issue for employees as they grew older.

Once again, personal characteristics appear to influence employee preferences on several compensation options. Married employees preferred early retirement (p < .05), while single employees differed on short workdays (p < .05). Female employees also preferred short workdays (p < .05), while male employees opted for pay increases (p < .05).

SUMMARY, IMPLICATIONS, AND FUTURE RESEARCH ISSUES

As workers age, their preferences for various types of compensation shift. Older workers prefer increased retirement, medical and life insurance benefits. At the same time, their preference for pay, additional vacations, and a shorter work week declines. It should be noted that this relationship can be modified by several personal characteristics including sex, marital status, number of dependents, type of work, income, and union membership. Health insurance appears to have equally strong appeal across all groups. The findings in this section strongly suggest a career stage/life-cycle explanation of preferences for compensation shifts similar to that suggested previously in chapter 2 for preferred job characteristics.

In 1957, Herzberg suggested that an employee's preference for pay was curvilinear. That is, wages are important for young workers but then steadily decline in importance until age 40, when they once again surge in importance with age. This position was criticized by Lawler (1971), who claimed that there was no evidence to support such a relationship, and that in fact the evidence ran to the contrary. Our review would seem to lend support for Lawler's argument while at the same time refuting Herzberg's position. The studies presented here would appear to lay the argument to rest. As workers age, their preference for fringe benefits increases, and they are willing to forego pay increases in order to acquire them.

These results strongly suggest that employees would prefer cafeteria-style benefits programs. As the number of different types of new fringe benefits increases (for example, prepaid legal insurance and dental insurance), worker preferences can be expected to become even more diverse. Thus, human resource managers would need to redesign benefits programs to permit more flexibility. It would be expected that better tailoring of employee pay and fringe benefits to individual needs would result in greater pay and job satisfaction, as well as increased organizational morale.

Unfortunately, some of the findings in this section are limited by defects in the manner in which the research was conducted. First, most of the studies used different preference items. Many do not contain some of the newer types of fringe benefits (for example, prepaid legal insurance and dental benefits). Moreover, since much of the research is dated, it is hard to know what the effect of inflation would be on these preferences. The research also does not subdivide employee preferences in a manner that permits closer examination of factors such as marital status, number of dependents, and level of income. Race and health are important factors not included in the research conducted to date. Moreover, there has been no attempt to examine the organizational implications of pay preferences; that is, whether or not pay preferences are related to pay satisfaction, job satisfaction, and performance.

Many of the studies have utilized somewhat narrowly defined samples. In others—for example, Nealey and Goodale (1967) and Wagner and Bakerman (1960)—findings differ in terms of preferences for time off. In addition, the findings on the preferences of older female workers are limited due to the small number of females involved in many of the studies.

A number of questions related to pay preferences should be investigated. The first involves the costs and practicability of cafeteria-style fringe benefit programs and worker preferences for them. Other studies could update and improve on the work cited in this report. Updated studies would permit an examination of the effect of inflation, include some of the newer types of fringe benefits, and would likely contain more female subjects. Improved studies would involve more categories of benefits for workers to choose from, permit more interaction variables to be considered, and involve broader samples of employees.

Pay Satisfaction

Pay satisfaction is an important issue for organizations because of the withdrawal (turnover) implications associated with higher levels of pay dissatisfaction. The research studies analyzed for this section have produced conflicting results. Table E-2 (Appendix) summarizes the eleven studies that have been reviewed. Five have found a relationship between age and pay satisfaction, while six have not.

STUDIES SHOWING A RELATIONSHIP BETWEEN AGE AND PAY SATISFACTION

Monczyka et al. (1977) found age to be correlated with pay satisfaction ($r = .20$, $p < .05$). Their study involved 354 employees in six organizations. These same investigators also found statistically significant ($p < .05$) correlations with pay satisfaction among six other individual and organizational variables. These were education (.09), organizational level (.13), salary level (.21), years in present job (.15), working conditions (.33) and nonmonetary rewards (.46). Education, organizational level, salary level, years in present job, and age were all found to be intercorrelated. Hence, it is difficult to be certain whether age or some other variable or groups of variables produce pay satisfaction. Even more interesting were the higher correlations between pay satisfaction and working conditions, and between pay satisfaction and noneconomic rewards.

Studies by Meltzer (1958), Gibson and Klein (1970), Oliver (1977), and Hulin and Smith (1965) support the Monczyka et al. (1977) findings. Meltzer studies 258 employees in diverse occupations in a manufacturing plant. Although 78 percent of his sample were age 45 or younger, he found statistically significant positive relationships for all groups between age and pay satisfaction (p < .05).

Similarly, Gibson and Klein, in their study of 385 predominantly female blue collar employees in a Southern plant and 1682 male blue collar workers in 18 plants, found statistically significant relationships between age and pay satisfaction. In this case, two-way analyses of variance produced F-statistics of 12.40 for the females and 3.57 for the males (p < .01 and p < .05, respectively). In the male sample, Gibson and Klein were able to control for experience, and this produced a correlation coefficient of .14 (p < .01). Oliver, in a study of 92 male life insurance agents, found pay satisfaction to be positively related to age and income.

Finally, Hulin and Smith found a positive relationship between age and pay satisfaction in their study of 195 male and 75 female electronics workers. Here, age and pay satisfaction were found to be related when controlling for job tenure and four other variables, but the significance level was not reported.

STUDIES SHOWING NO RELATIONSHIP
BETWEEN AGE AND PAY SATISFACTION

Studies that have found no relationship between age and pay satisfaction include Andrews and Henry (1964), Altimus and Tersine (1973), Hunt and Saul (1975), Schwab and Wallace (1974), Schwab and Heneman (1977b), and Muchinsky (1978). The Andrews and Henry study involved 299 managers in five firms. These investigators found no consistent trend for pay satisfaction to vary as a function of age. The same result occurred in Altimus and Tersine's research involving 63 male blue collar workers in a glass plant, although it appeared in this study that younger workers were less satisfied.

Three of the four other studies found evidence of a negative relationship. Hunt and Saul (1975) found a negative relationship between age and pay satisfaction for 579 of female workers and no relationship for 3338 males. In this case, the researchers were able to control for experience. Muchinsky (1978), in his study of 666 employees in diverse occupations in a public utility, found a negative monotonic (linear) relationship between age and pay satisfaction. Schwab and Heneman (1977b), in their study of 177 male and 96 female blue collar operatives, found no relationship between age and pay satisfaction. In this case, the researchers were also able to control for experience. Both Hunt and Saul (1975), and Schwab and Heneman (1977b) found no relationship between age and pay satisfaction when controlling for experience. These findings differ from those cited earlier by Gibson and Klein (1970), who did find a statistically significant relationship.

Finally, Schwab and Wallace (1974) appear to have conducted one of the most well-designed studies of age and pay satisfaction. Their study of 350 nonexempt employees in a manufacturing setting found no relationship between age and pay satisfaction when controlling for organizational level, wage level, piece rate, group rate, tenure, and sex. The generalizability of their findings are naturally limited by the inclusion of only nonexempt employees.

SUMMARY, IMPLICATIONS, AND FUTURE RESEARCH ISSUES

Since the eleven studies on pay satisfaction examined for this research have produced such diverse findings, it would be difficult to predict what course of action would be the most optimal for organizations. However, the better designed studies have found no relationship between age and pay satisfaction. The diverse results would suggest that the relationship between age and pay satisfaction depends on the particular organization, and organizational policies regarding pay.

Further evidence of the potential impact of organizational pay policies is indicated when factors such as occupation and job tenure are considered. One would presume that there might be differences for blue collar versus white collar workers. That was not the case here since studies on blue collar workers produced diverse results. It is also difficult to determine whether age or some other variable correlated with age is related to pay satisfaction, since one study controlled for experience and found a relationship, while two others controlled for job tenure and found no relationship.

Only one study (Schwab and Wallace, 1974) appears to have controlled for a sufficient number of organizational and personal variables. Therefore, additional well-designed studies of the relationship between age and pay satisfaction are required. Such studies should involve a large sample of employees across diverse levels of organizations and should control for a wide variety of personal, organizational, and pay systems administration variables (see, for example, Dyer and Thierault, 1976).

THE RELATIONSHIP BETWEEN AGE AND PAY FOR PERFORMANCE

This section examines the research on age as an influence on motivation to work for pay. The studies in this area have focused on the relative importance an employee places on pay.

In Lawler's (1971) review of the literature on employee motivation, he concluded that there is a negative relationship between age, performance, and the desire for pay. Two explanations are provided for this. First, older employees are paid more than younger ones, so their need for additional compensation is not as great. Second, the strength of needs changes over time. Lawler cites Porter's (1963) work, which found that as managers age, they place more emphasis on security and self-esteem.

Heneman (1973) tested Lawler's conclusions using an expectancy framework, thus permitting a direct examination of age and pay for performance relationship. According to the expectancy model, if the *valence* (perceived value) of pay decreases, it becomes ineffective as a reward. Individuals will not be motivated to obtain something they don't care about. In addition, Heneman also tested whether *instrumentality* (the belief that performance will lead to a reward) and *expectancy* (the belief that harder work will result in improved performance) are influenced by age.

Heneman's study employed an internal organizational mail questionnaire to 88 (64 male, 24 female) retail department store managers. Expectancy was measured using a 7-point scale in which the respondents were asked to indicate whether working harder would lead to higher performance. In all, 23 7-point valence and instrumentality measures were used.

Heneman found a significant, negative relationship between age and the valence of outcomes. This indicates that older managers placed less value on desirable outcomes of performance. In addition, older managers perceived less relationship between their performance (instrumentality) and achieving these outcomes. For the expectancy measure, there was a negative relationship for older males but not females. Thus, at least for the male managers, the perceived value of pay declines with age, as does the perception that harder work will result in improved performance. One possible explanation for this latter finding, unrelated to age, is based on job tenure. As a result of their organizational experience, those with additional tenure had become familiar with the imperfections of the pay-for-performance system and the dependency of one department on another.

Oliver (1977) also examined the valence and instrumentality of pay for workers of differing age. Again, age had a negative correlation with valence among 99 insurance agents (r < .40, p < .01). Instrumentality was also negatively related with age (r = −.34, p < .01).

Schwab (1973) investigated the impact of three pay systems (individual incentive, group incentive, and hourly wage) on 350 semi-skilled machine operators. A modified-paired comparison procedure was used. Schwab found a negative, but not statistically significant, relationship between age and instrumentality and valence perceptions.

SUMMARY, IMPLICATIONS, AND FUTURE RESEARCH ISSUES

It is difficult to make definitive conclusions based on so few studies. Yet the evidence from the studies on pay preferences and pay for performance suggests that pay is less important to older employees than it is to younger employees. Moreover, older workers are less likely to believe that an expanded level of performance will lead to greater rewards.

This is a fertile area for research. The small number of studies in relation to the importance of this topic make it a priority among the many research questions noted in this volume. Certainly, these studies should employ large samples, include diverse occupations, and consider organization pay policies.

If the previous findings continue to occur, it will have to be concluded that as the work force grows older, pay for performance will lose its effectiveness as a motivator. The implications for organizations will be severe, since most pride themselves on maintaining this relationship.

Conclusions

This chapter has considered the impact of age on a series of compensation issues, including overall earnings, pay preferences, pay satisfaction, and pay for performance. The following conclusions may be noted:

- Older workers earn more than younger workers. However, this relationship appears to be influenced by the size of the cohort group. Since the group addressed in this book is a large cohort preceded and followed by smaller cohorts, the extent to which this group will have relatively larger earnings than its younger counterpart is uncertain.

- As workers age, their preferences for various types of compensation shift. Older workers prefer increased retirement, medical and life insurance benefits. At the same time, their preference for pay and time away from work declines.
- There is mixed evidence on whether older workers are more or less satisfied with pay than younger workers. Other factors, such as organizational policies regarding pay, may be more important than age in determining pay satisfaction.
- Older workers are less likely to be motivated by pay for performance systems. Older workers place less value on pay and are less likely to view their efforts as leading to desirable outcomes than younger workers.

NOTES

1. Significance levels from this study were not reported.

2. In the Nealey (1964a) study, 1058 persons in his sample were married; only 75 were unmarried. It is quite likely that this distribution would be more balanced today.

3. These two variables tend to be intercorrelated; that is, professional and managerial employees dominate a college-educated group.

4. Ten Fridays is a fringe benefit that provides employees with five additional paid holidays, thereby giving them five extra three-day weekends.

CHAPTER 7

PENSIONS AND RETIREMENT

In this chapter the question of retirement and pensions are jointly discussed. The rationale for this is threefold. First, much of the literature ties the two subjects together. Second, retirement and pensions are uniquely related due to the fact that the quality of one's retirement years is tied to one's level of pension benefit and social security. Third, the willingness of workers to retire early or the need to work beyond traditional retirement years is in part a function of available income to the worker. The chapter begins with a summary of recent trends in pensions and continues with a brief discussion of the income replacement literature. This is followed by an in-depth review of the literature on the decision to retire and a survey of retirement policies in other industrialized countries. The chapter concludes with a discussion of social security and the policy issues confronting the future of the program.

Pension Plan Characteristics and Trends

The rapid increase in the incidence of retirement plans that began in the mid-1960s continued into the 1970s (Bell, 1975). This was largely due to increases in pension coverages of nonmanufacturing employees, particularly those in trade and services. Although at this place in the book we summarize the results of several recent government studies, the reader must bear in mind that pension coverage and actual receipt of a pension are distinctly different issues. Actual monies received by pension recipients are discussed in a subsequent section.

The percentage of all private nonfarm workers employed in establishments with employer contributions to a pension fund rose from 53 percent in 1966 to 65 percent in 1972. This increase coincided with the rise in actual retirement plan coverage from 26.3 million workers in 1966 to 29.7 million in 1970. Between 1968 and 1972, the incidence of retirement plans increased in all industries except transportation and public utilities. Although pension plans are more common in manufacturing, nonmanufacturing industries narrowed the differential. Office workers were more likely than non-office workers to have pension coverage, while unionized employers and those workers employed by large firms were more likely to be covered. Only 9 percent of the employees in unionized establishments were without retirement expenditures, compared with 48 percent in non-union groups (Bell, 1975).[1] Dyer and Schwab (1971), in a study of 17 manufacturing industries, have shown that 90 percent of the variability in pension plan coverage could be explained by unionization, firm size, and wage rates.

The Bureau of Labor Statistics (BLS) monitors pension plans and coverages regularly. In a recent analysis of changes in 131 pension plans during the period 1974-1978, BLS reported that a number of significant changes had occurred (Frumkin and Schmitt, 1979). In all, 62 plans (47 percent) had altered their eligibility requirements for normal retirement, while 94 (72 percent) had liberalized their normal retirement benefit formula by either improving the formula or by adopting a different type of formula. In 1978, 43 (33 percent) of all plans integrated the normal retirement benefit formula with social security. Normally, when this is done, pension benefits decrease as social security benefits increase. A total of 128 plans had early retirement provisions, of which 83 percent had disability retirement benefits and 75 percent provided death benefits for survivors (Frumkin and Schmitt, 1979).

Pension plans have been affected by recently enacted amendments to the Age Discrimination in Employment Act (ADEA). The 1978 amendments provided that benefit accrual will not be required past age 65, nor will employers be required to credit years of service to benefit accrual that occurred after the normal retirement age. Also, employers will not be required to increase the amount of benefits when an employee delays commencement of benefits due to later retirement (Namorsky, 1978).

SUMMARY AND IMPLICATIONS

As the work force ages, organizations can expect continued pressure to provide pension coverage for heretofore unprotected employees. To some extent, this may require employers to shift priorities within their compensation packages. It appears reasonable to presume that failure on the part of the business community to address this issue adequately will likely result in government intervention.

Retirement Income Levels

As workers approach retirement, a major concern is the quality of life following the end of their working years. This is particularly important since 15 percent of the elderly live below the poverty level. Only 12 percent of all Americans have incomes below the poverty level (Perspectives on Aging, 1979), yet one-fourth of the elderly are living at what is referred to as "near poor," that is, within 125 percent of the poverty line.

In a recent survey of retirees by Louis Harris and Associates (Employee Benefit Review, 1979a), 42 percent indicated that their incomes were insufficient to provide for an adequate standard of living. In general, the economic status of the aged is primarily dependent on four factors (Schulz and Carrin, 1972). The first is the worker's earnings-consumption pattern during his or her working life, thereby determining the extent to which personal savings are accumulated for the nonworking period. This is a factor largely controlled by the individual.

Other factors that determine a retiree's economic situation are frequently beyond the person's control or are only partially influenced by the individual. These factors are the distribution of workers' pay packages between current wages and private pensions, the age of retirement, and the extent to which society is willing to transfer income claims from workers to retirees via the tax benefit mechanism (Schulz and Carrin, 1972). The preferred allocation of workers' pay between current wages and private pensions was noted in a previous section on pay preferences. In that section, it was pointed out that as workers age, their preferences for various forms of compensation shift. Pension benefits and adequate health care are primary concerns of older workers. In this section, the issues of pension benefits and retirement income are discussed. As might be imagined, the problem of providing retirees with an adequate income has been exacerbated by the recent high rate of inflation.

One of the major issues associated with pensions and retirement for the human resource manager is the level of benefits needed by retirees to maintain preretirement living standards. Numerous variables must be considered when making these estimates. Schulz et al. (1979:31)

TABLE 7.1   Proportion of Median Male Workers With 30 Years of Service in Plans Maintaining Living Standards In Retirement (percentages)

Industry	Single Worker	Married Worker
Mining	3	5
Construction	13	27
Manufacturing	6	32
Transportation	12	35
Communications and utilities	13	68
Trade	9	23
Finance, insurance, and real estate	33	87
Service	3	22

Note: Based on 30 percent replacement of single workers and 45 percent replacement for married workers from social security. Assumes a replacement rate of 70 percent to maintain living standards in retirement.

have summarized many of these variables. They outline the process as being one in which a planner would need to account for pre- and postretirement differences in "taxes, savings rates, work-related expenses, discretionary consumption preferences and major budgetary constraints (for example, home financing, educational expenses for children, and health care)." Schulz et al. have stated that there is no precise estimate of replacement range, but that there is a general agreement that a 60-80 percent replacement rate measured against *gross* preretirement income would be necessary. Replacement income combines benefits paid by social security, as well as those derived from private pensions.

Although 30 million private wage and salary workers were covered by private pensions or deferred profit sharing (Yahalem, 1977), little is known about the adequacy of the benefits provided. Schulz et al. have examined this issue using 1974 Bureau of Labor Statistics (BLS) survey data. The BLS data upon which the study was based involved 1467 plans covering at least 100 employees. Following exclusions, 989 plans were analyzed. Data were analyzed under highly favorable conditions. Table 7.1 summarizes the results in terms of the 1974 proportion of male workers with 30 years of service covered by private pensions (plus social security) with a combined benefit level that realized a 70 percent replacement rate.

As seen from these results, few single males had combined social security and pension income equal to 70 percent of their preretirement earnings. The range was from 3 percent of the male employees with 30 years of pension plan coverage in mining and service to 33 percent in finance, insurance, and real estate. Married workers did considerably better. Here the range was more varied, from 5 percent in mining to 87 percent in finance, insurance, and real estate. Therefore, it is very clear that in order for an employee to maintain adequate living standards during retirement, supplemental economic resources will be needed.

It is important to stress that the Schulz et al. findings were presented under very favorable conditions. There were two important gaps in their research, which the authors acknowledge. The first is the assumption that workers will actually have 30 years of service. It is more likely that workers will have lengthy periods of noncoverage due to job shifts, layoffs, and the absence of early vesting. Moreover, both long periods without coverage and early retirement would have an adverse impact on social security and private pension replacement rates. Finally, the Schulz et al. research measures replacement rates at the point of retirement. During inflationary times, without cost-of-living adjustments, pension benefits can become insufficient.[2] In the next section, the effect of inflation on retirement income is discussed.

RETIREMENT INCOME AND INFLATION

One writer (Employee Benefit Review, 1979b:24) has pointed out the differential impact that inflation has on pensions and social security:

> "Inflation makes a mockery of fixed pensions. In contrast, when inflation rages, Social Security benefits become even more valuable."

This dichotomy results from the fact that social security is fully indexed to the Consumer Price Index, while most pension plans have no adjustments over time. Hence, workers who retired at age 65 would, by age 75, have their pension benefits reduced by 50 percent, assuming a modest annual rise in prices of 7 percent. At a 10 percent annual rate of inflation, each dollar of pension benefit would be worth 62¢ after only five years of retirement. In contrast, social security benefits tend to replace more of the income of lower as opposed to higher wage earners. As a result, the income loss due to inflation of lower paid workers will be less than that of higher paid workers (Employee Benefit Review, 1979b).

One possible solution to the problem of the declining value of pension benefits would be to add an automatic indexing option to employees' pensions. Under this system, each retiring employee would be provided with benefits that began at a lower level and increased over time. It has been suggested that benefits at age 65 be reduced by 20 percent, with increases of 3 percent per year (Employee Benefit Review, 1979b). There are three advantages to such automatic indexing mechanisms. The first is their ability to allow retirees to maintain preretirement levels of purchasing power during inflationary periods. In addition, those employees who elected not to choose the lower benefit option would be less likely to argue for pension supplements. Finally, the reduction in benefit levels is excellent documentation of the real cost of postretirement benefit adjustments.

A final point to be made in this section concerns the role of personal savings and other individual assets in offsetting the effect of inflation on pension benefits. Personal savings, moreover, are very important to the tens of millions of workers who do not have pension coverage, have inadequate coverage, or have coverage at a reduced level due to lack of service in a plan. Recent changes in the tax laws to encourage personal savings for retirement, especially through individual retirement accounts, are expected to stimulate more personal savings. One of the reasons why older americans are in a poor economic situation is that while average overall savings in the United States have not fluctuated greatly, the level of saving has not been sufficient to provide adequate funds in retirement (Schulz and Carrin, 1972).

SUMMARY, IMPLICATIONS, AND FUTURE RESEARCH ISSUES

The primary sources of income for retired workers are private pensions and social security. There is a general consensus that retirees must receive 60-80 percent of their preretirement income from these combined sources in order to maintain an adequate standard of living. The Schulz et al. research has shown that there is significant variability in the adequacy of retirement income across industries and by marital status. They estimated that 67-97 percent of the single workers with 30 years of service, and 13-95 percent of the married workers, were enrolled in private pension programs that provided insufficient social security and pension benefits.

The retirement income problem is further exacerbated by high rates of inflation. Although social security is indexed (adjusted) for inflation, most private pensions are not. Therefore, these plans quickly lose value during periods of high inflation of the type recently experienced.

The inadequacy of retirement income can be expected to impact on the management of human resources in at least three ways. First, the adequacy of potential retirement income will be a major determinant in workers' decisions to retire earlier or to work beyond the traditional retirement age of 65. In both cases, the data to be presented in the next section would seem to indicate that employees will continue to work if their retirement incomes are inadequate. Hence, organizations may find that more people continue to work not because they would prefer to do so, but because they feel compelled to do so by inadequate retirement income. This would mean that some workers might prefer to continue working at a time when the organization might prefer that they retire early or at the traditional age.

It may be expected that there will be increased pressures to provide additional revenues for pension programs. That is, the recent high levels of inflation and their impact on the private pension will result in costly changes in the benefit provisions of these plans. In this case, increased benefits and the indexing of benefits (adjusting for inflation) would provide additional retirement income but would also add significant costs to the organization. In an earlier section on compensation preferences, it was shown that as workers age, they prefer to adjust their compensation package to provide increased retirement income. Perhaps human resources managers should give this option serious consideration.

Finally, employer-sponsored preretirement counseling at earlier ages for employees may become more important. Counseling of this nature would involve encouraging employees to allocate a greater portion of their earnings to savings for retirement. Certainly a firm that converts its traditional compensation system to a cafeteria-style system would find employee counseling very beneficial.

There are several key issues worthy of future research. These include studies of the retirement income adequacy and experience of workers employed by individual companies rather than across all companies and industries. Included in such studies would be an assessment of employee satisfaction in retirement.

Another area in need of further investigation involves a determination of the adequacy of required retirement income. Earlier, it was stated that retirement income should be within a range of 60-80 percent of preretirement earnings. Research should be undertaken to measure more precisely the level of retirement income that is needed. This type of study should include an examination of retirees and the effect of inflation on the quality of their retirement years. Finally, studies of the costs of indexing pension plans would be most helpful for organizations contemplating such changes.

The Decision to Retire

As workers age and progress toward the end of their work careers, many factors potentially underlie the decision to retire earlier or later than scheduled. The effect of raising the mandatory retirement age to 70 years, along with prohibitions against discrimination based on age, have provided employees with greater flexibility than they have had in the past. At the same time, these changes have made the task of the organizational and human resource planner more difficult by lessening some of the certainty associated with age 65 retirement. Inflation also adds to the potential uncertainty associated with retirement planning and decision making because the decision to retire is influenced by financial security. To provide some perspective on the retirement process, the literature on the preferences for and determinants of retirement are examined.

Research concerning the factors influencing retirement spans the last 25 years (see Tables F-1 to F-4, Appendix). In the 24 cross-sectional and 10 longitudinal studies that we located, retirement (or the dependent variable representing retirement) was defined in a variety of ways. Basically, though, the dependent variable reflected either an anticipation of retirement or actual retirement, and the definitional variation appeared in the former when studying workers approaching retirement. Anticipatory or prospective data were used in eight of the 24 cross-sectional and in two of the 10 longitudinal studies. Retirement was studied in these instances in terms of preferred age of retirement (Rose and Mogey, 1972), planned retirement age (Hall and Johnson, 1980; Orbach, 1969; Usher, 1981), willingness to retire (Jacobson, 1972a, 1974), and preference for retirement (Jacobson and Eran, 1980). The results of such studies are, of course, suggestive, but cannot be fully relied on because circumstances eventually may have altered the determinants of actual retirement.

There were, however, 16 other cross-sectional studies that were conducted after actual retirement (for example, Pollman and Johnson, 1974; Parker and Dyer, 1976), thus providing a more accurate measure of retirement but only retrospective data on what factors affected the decision to retire. Retrospective data are suspect, as perceptions regarding decision making that are obtained after the decision to retire may be inaccurate as a result of intervening events and post hoc rationalization. A recent comparison of retrospective responses with longitudinal data derived from the National Longitudinal Study of men provided support for this concern (Parnes and Nestel, 1981). The optimal design for studying the determinants of retirement, therefore, is an analysis of longitudinal data, at the end of which retirement occurs.

In the 10 longitudinal studies (see Table 7.2), the populations reflect various panel studies such as the National Longitudinal Study (NLS) (Parnes and Nestel, 1975, 1981), the Study of Income Dynamics (Boskin, 1977), and the Cornell Study of Occupational Retirement (Streib and Schneider, 1971; Streib and Thompson, 1957). Other groups that were represented were the Michigan Civil Service (Schmitt and McCune, 1981) and auto workers (Barfield and Morgan, 1970; Burkhauser, 1979). The dependent variable in the preceding eight studies was actual retirement, but the two remaining longitudinal studies were prospective in nature, in that the dependent variables were defined as plans to retire early (Barfield and Morgan, 1978, using the University of Michigan Survey Research Center national cross-section data). The first eight longitudinal studies mentioned, therefore, will be the key to understanding retirement decision making.

In drawing together the literature on retirement decision making, several literature reviews were also located. An early one appeared in Riley and Foner's *Aging and Society* (1968) under a section entitled "The Retirement Decision." In the *Handbook of the Psychology of Aging* (1977) and the *Handbook of Aging and the Social Sciences* (1976), respectively, Chown and Sheppard provide a brief overview of the factors affecting retirement. More recently, Gordus (1980) discussed about a dozen studies related to "Choosing to Retire Early." The objective in the literature review that follows is to synthesize the studies included in the previous reviews and to expand on and update that collection. The summary is divided into the following sections: (a) individual demographic variables, (b) financial factors, (c) physiological and psychological variables, and (d) organizational variables. In the discussion of the research results, comparisons will be made between the longitudinal-actual retirement results and those from all other studies.

INDIVIDUAL DEMOGRAPHIC VARIABLES

Included in this category are age, dependents, education, gender, marital status, occupation, place of residence, race, and tenure. Table F-1 summarizes the research on these variables.

Age. There is some evidence in the age-retirement results that the older one is, the later one prefers to retire. This preference was found in two cross-sectional studies. The first study was of males from the Veterans Administration (VA) Normative Aging Study (Rose and Mogey, 1972), and the other involved Israeli male executives (Eden and Jacobson, 1976). In another recent cross-sectional study, how-

(text continued on page 155)

TABLE 7.2 Longitudinal Data Analysis of Studies of Retirement

Study	Population	N	Age	Dependent variables	Independent variables
Barfield and Morgan (1970)	Working plus retired UAW members 1963-1966	1090	59-64	Retirement status	Income from assets, education, time traveling to work, income earned by spouse, age at which home mortage will be paid, age of co-workers, place of residence of children, number of dependents, race, family income change during last year of employment, family pension, and social security income entitlement

Study	Sample	N	Age	Dependent variable	Independent variables
Barfield and Morgan (1978)	University of Michigan Survey Research Center national cross-section 10-year follow-up	486	35-64	Plans to retire early	Age, age free of mortgage payments, age free of responsibility for children, number of pensions expected, family income, sex/marital status/working wife, and ability to keep up with pace of work
Boskin (1977)	Married males in panel study of income dynamics, followed from 1968 to 1972	131	61-65 in 1968	Retirement— works less than quarter	Social security benefits, income from assets, net earnings, and hours ill (as estimate of health)
Burkhauser (1979)	Male auto workers, cross-sectional data and 2-year resurvey	761 326	59-64	Acceptance of early pension	Actuarial penalty for postponing pension, earnings, health, race, assets, age, and marital status
Ekerdt et al. (1976)	Males from VA normative aging study, followed for 10 years	1458	$T_1 = 25\text{-}55+$	Preferred age of retirement	Age cohorts

TABLE 7.2 Longitudinal Data Analysis of Studies of Retirement (continued)

Study	Population	N	Age	Dependent variables	Independent variables
Streib and Schneider (1971)	Cornell Study of Occupational Retirement followed from 1952 to 1958, from 259 organizations	1969	≥63 in 1952	Retirement status	Health, general satisfaction with life, age, income, feelings of usefulness, economic deprivation, marital status, type of industry, occupation, social class, education
	males	1486			
	females	483			
Streib and Thompson (1957)	Males from Cornell Study of Occupational Retirement employed in 1952 and recontacted in 1954 (sample contains a disproportionate number of professionals)	2007	64 in 1952	Retirement status	Health, job satisfaction, value of work, income, home ownership, and voluntary or compulsory retirement

| Parnes and Nestel (1975) | Males from National Longitudinal Study | 3817 | 50-64 | Actual retirement | Age, race, marital status, number of dependents (excluding wife), net assets, pension coverage and tenure, health, class of workers (private, government, or self-employed), work commitment, hourly earnings, and job satisfaction |
| Parnes and Nestel (1981) | Males from National Longitudinal Study who retired between 1967-1976 | 1047 | 55-69 | Actual retirement | Marital status; education; industry, class of worker, pension coverage, age, and occupation of preretirement job; and income per dependent in year preceding retirement |

TABLE 7.2 Longitudinal Data Analysis of Studies of Retirement (continued)

Study	Population	N	Age	Dependent variables	Independent variables
Schmitt and McCune (1981)	Michigan civil service employees with a 1-year follow-up	513 379	55>70	Retirement status	Race, age, marital status, job level, education, size of community lived in and length of time lived in, actual hourly wage, knowledge of existence of pension plan, adequacy of retirement income at 65, adequacy of early retirement income, number of dependents, needed retirement income, importance of adequate income, employed spouse, health, and job attitudes (feedback from others, motivating potential, job satisfaction, job involvement, and desire to work)

ever, preferences for retirement did not differ on the basis of age for Israeli physicians (Jacobson and Eran, 1980). In this instance, most respondents wanted to continue employment beyond retirement from their current employment; therefore, these results do not conflict with the preceding findings.

One longitudinal study, also based on subjects from the VA Normative Aging Study, provided some support for the cross-sectional results of an age and later retirement preference relationship (Ekerdt et al., 1976). In this study there was a shift over a 10-year period to a preference for later retirement for those age 50 and older at T_2 ($p < .01$). For those aged 35-44 at T_2, there was a decrease during the 10-year period to a preference for earlier retirement (ns). Some of this longitudinal shift, however, may be a survivor effect, in that 16 percent of the original sample had retired, died, or dropped out of the study. Nevertheless, the longitudinal data confirm an aging effect, albeit one limited to the older cohorts (Ekerdt et al., 1976).

In another longitudinal study, the proportion of the five-year NLS sample expressing an intention to retire prior to age 65 increased from 28 percent in 1966 to 38.5 percent in 1971 when they were 50-60 years of age (Parnes and Nestel, 1975). But because the intention to retire does not fully correspond with the preference for retirement, the later findings do not necessarily conflict with the Ekerdt et al. (1976) findings. In addition, a substantial increase in health problems over the five-year period for the NLS sample helped to explain the increase in the intent to retire early.

There is also some evidence that simply feeling younger may lower the preference for retirement, as suggested in the two cross-sectional studies of the relationship between subjective age and preference for retirement. The previously mentioned Israeli executives (Eden and Jacobson, 1976) and a sample of male British factory operatives (Jacobson, 1972b) who felt younger revealed less of a desire to retire.

Dependents. Four of the six studies of dependents and retirement indicate that there is an inverse relationship; that is, the greater the number of dependents, the lower the preference for retirement (Barfield and Morgan, 1970; Parnes and Nestel, 1975; Quinn, 1977; Schmitt et al., 1979). Parnes and Nestel (1975) did find a stronger negative relationship between number of dependents and expecting to retire early ($F = 3.33$, $p < .01$) than with actual retirement ($F = 1.64$, ns), but in the fifth study, Berman and Holtzman (1978) did not find a relationship between dependents and the decision to retire.

There is also the suggestion in the sixth study that a worker's perception of his or her family's preferences for retirement influences the decision to retire (Parker and Dyer, 1976). The subjects of this study, however, were naval officers, an occupation that would seem generally to have more appeal for single individuals. It is also possible that the determinants of retirement for this occupation may generally be somewhat different because these retirees are usually career changers rather than total retirees.

Education. All 10 studies that examined the relationship between educational level and retirement revealed that more education was associated with planning to retire or actually retiring later. The support for this relationship is particularly strong because this result was obtained in five longitudinal-actual retirement studies (Barfield and Morgan, 1970; Boskin, 1977; Parnes and Nestel, 1981; Schmitt and McCune, 1981; Streib and Schneider, 1971). There was also some confirmation that the relationship holds for men and women (Hall and Johnson, 1980; Streib and Schneider, 1971).

Gender. In two of the six studies in which gender-retirement relationships were examined, men planned to or were more likely to retire early (Jacobson, 1974; Usher, 1981). In Usher's (1981) study of workers in a private and public sector organization, women were more interested in working longer if alternative work options were available. In addition, female factory operatives in Jacobson's (1974) study expressed more willingness to continue working when positive social contacts existed in the workplace ($\chi^2 = 15.79$, p $<$ .001). Because Jacobson's sample was married and Usher's was 85 percent married, it is thought that these findings may reflect one or more of the following three factors: anticipatory widowhood, above-average motivation to work by women who chose to work later in life, and/or a search to enlarge one's social network in a mobile, transitory society (Jacobson, 1974).

A consistent relationship between gender and retirement possibly should not be expected, however, because marital status and other factors may moderate the relationship. For example, women may retire earlier when married and when their financial status is relatively secure (Barfield and Morgan, 1978). In addition, the married individual's retirement may depend on whether there is a working or nonworking spouse, as suggested in Schmitt et al's. (1979) study of Michigan civil service workers. Retirees in this instance were more likely to have a nonworking spouse.

The remaining four studies of the gender-retirement relationship continue to reveal variance in the findings. For Michigan civil service workers, women were more likely than men to retire (Schmitt et al., 1979; Schmitt and McCune, 1981), but marital status specifically did not help explain these findings, since the retirees did not differ from the nonretirees on this factor. Israeli physicians did not differ on the basis of gender in their preference for retirement (Jacobson and Eran, 1980), but these physicians also generally expressed a preference to work beyond retirement from their current jobs, thereby erasing the potential for gender and other factors to explain retirement from the current job.

Marital Status. The evidence on the relationship between marital status and retirement is mixed. This is also true if only the longitudinal-actual retirement results are considered (Burkhauser, 1979; Schmitt and McCune, 1981).

Of the eight studies providing findings on this relationship, four revealed that single people were more likely to retire or had plans to retire early (Barfield and Morgan, 1978; Belbin and Clark, 1970; Parnes and Nestel, 1975; Streib and Schneider, 1971). No relationship was found in three studies (Berman and Holtzman, 1978; Jacobson and Eran, 1980; Schmitt and McCune, 1981); however, in the Jacobson and Eran study of physicians, not finding a relationship can again be explained in part by the physicians' preference to continue working after retiring from their current jobs.

Married persons were also found to be more likely to retire or be planning to retire early in two studies (Barfield and Morgan, 1978; Burkhauser, 1979). In the Barfield and Morgan study, however, other factors appeared to moderate the relationship; that is, married women were more likely to retire early when there was a high family income, no mortgage payment, and no responsibility for children. In the Parker and Dyer (1976) study of naval officers (discussed previously under the Dependents factor), the wife's attitude as perceived by the husband helped to predict retirement.

Yet another factor that may help to explain the mixed marital status-retirement findings is whether the spouse is working or not working. In their study of Michigan civil service employees, Schmitt et al. (1979) found that retirees were more likely to have a nonworking spouse ($F = 6.15, p < .05$), thus making it possible for the couple to more fully share the retirement experience.

Occupation. Having a higher civil service job level (Schmitt and McCune, 1981) or higher perceived company rank (Rose and Mogey, 1972), as well as being a professional employee, were found to be related to later preferred or actual age of retirement. White men who were professional-managerial employees in the NLS 10-year follow-up were also more likely to retire early (46 percent) (Parnes and Nestel, 1981). For black men in the same study, the occupational group having the largest proportion retiring early were clerical and sales workers (50 percent). Planned retirement age did not differ by job class for a sample of United Auto Workers (UAW) (Orbach, 1969); however, the jobs of these workers did not differ as much as those found among the variety of subjects reflected in the other studies mentioned.

Two other factors that in some respects reflect job level have also been reported. First, the undesirability of the job among men from the Retirement History Study was positively related to earlier retirement (Quinn, 1977). Among British factory operatives, the more rigidly fixed the work pattern, the greater the willingness to retire (Jacobson, 1972b).

These findings provide some support for those in higher and more desirable occupations preferring later retirement. One would expect such a relationship, since job level is related to education level and, as noted earlier, education level is related to later retirement.

With reference to type of work, being self-employed was related to later retirement in one study (Hall and Johnson, 1980), and being a government worker meant earlier retirement for the NLS respondents (Parnes and Nestel, 1981). In the 10-year NLS data, 46 percent of the white and 36 percent of the black government workers retired early. It is expected that self-employed persons would retire later because they have a greater opportunity to adjust their hours downward prior to retirement (Parnes and Nestel, 1975). Moreover, it seems that government workers would to a greater extent be covered by pension plans, thereby enabling the worker to take earlier retirement and consider a second career.

Place of Residence. The evidence points to the tendency for residence in rural locations (Hall and Johnson, 1980) or in small communities (Schmitt et al., 1979; Schmitt and McCune, 1981) to be associated with earlier retirement. Among the Michigan civil service workers, for instance, retirees came from smaller communities ($F = 32.33$, $p < .05$). The only study found that shows rural and urban dwellers as being equally likely to retire was conducted in Connecticut (McKain, 1957). The author, however, acknowledged that the state was basically urban, which diminishes the significance of these findings.

Assuming that additional studies confirm the earlier retirement of those living in rural and smaller communities, answers to the following questions may help to explain the findings. One wonders, for instance, if rural-urban cost-of-living differentials help to account for the decision. Do smaller communities offer more or fewer opportunities for postretirement work and other activities that make earlier retirement more appealing? Also, do the people from rural and smaller communities differ from those in larger communities in terms of subjective age?

Race. Independently, race does not contribute much to explaining retirement. This was most clearly revealed in the five-year NLS sample in which the multiple classification analysis F-value dropped to .09 (ns) when controlling for other variables such as age, marital status, dependents, net assets, and expected retirement income (Parnes and Nestel, 1975). In the 10-year NLS sample, health surfaced as the reason for retirement for a greater proportion of black men (56 percent) than for white men (45 percent) (Parnes and Nestel, 1981). Race was not significant in distinguishing between Michigan civil service retirees and nonretirees (Schmitt et al., 1979; Schmitt and McCune, 1981). Finally, white male auto workers were more likely to take early retirement than were blacks ($\beta = .164$, $t = 3.05$; significance level was not provided) in a cross-sectional analysis, but the beta for race dropped to .109 in a two-year resurvey (Burkhauser, 1979).

Tenure. The three studies we found on the tenure-retirement relationship each provided different results (Jacobson and Eran, 1980; Rose and Mogey, 1972; Schmitt et al., 1979). In the Jacobson and Eran study of Israeli physicians, length of service was not related to preference for retirement. For the males in the VA Normative Aging Study, there was a small negative relationship between tenure and preferred age of retirement (partial $r = -.08$) (Rose and Mogey, 1972). Conversely, for the Michigan civil service employees, lower-tenured people were more likely to retire earlier ($F = .16.76$, $p < .05$) (Schmitt et al., 1979).

FINANCIAL FACTORS

Studies involving various financial factors are summarized in Table F-2 (Appendix). There is strong evidence of an association between expected pensions, social security income and net assets, and earlier retirement. More specifically, in 10 of 11 studies, expected pensions, social security, or retirement income were related to plans to retire early or to early retirement itself (Barfield and Morgan, 1970, 1978; Boskin, 1977; Hall and Johnson, 1980; Katona et al., 1969; Orbach, 1969; Pechman et al., 1968; Pollman, 1971; Quinn, 1977, 1981). Two of these studies were longitudinal, with an examination of actual retirement (Barfield and Morgan, 1970; Boskin, 1977). It was only in a study of male UAW machine, assembly, and utility workers where the retirees and nonretirees did not differ significantly with respect to retirement income (Pollman and Johnson, 1974).

In two of the three studies in which net assets were specifically examined, they were associated with a greater probability of retirement (Boskin, 1977; Burkhauser, 1979). In addition, in the five-year follow-up of the NLS sample, persons with $25,000 or more in assets, as well as those with none or negative assets, were more likely to retire (Parnes and Nestel, 1975). These three studies also had a longitudinal-actual retirement design.

When considering financial status more generally, there is also some support for its relationship to retirement. That is, adding a cluster of financial variables (for example, actual income, company retirement plan, expected early retirement income, and employed spouse) to demographic variables contributed significantly to explaining retirement status, $F (9, 125) = 3.32, p < .01$, for Michigan civil service workers (Schmitt and McCune, 1981). On the other hand, general financial status did not differ between UAW retirees and nonretirees in one instance (Berman and Holtzman, 1978) and was not related to preference for retirement among Israeli physicians (Jacobson and Eran, 1980). In this later study, however, there may not have been much variance in financial status for the physicians, and they also preferred generally to work beyond retirement; therefore, a financial status and preference for retirement relationship would be less likely.

The spouse's contribution to financial status also appears to affect the retirement decision. First, the probability of retirement was lower for males having spouses with greater earnings (Boskin, 1977). In addition, if the wife receives social security, the greater is the probability of early retirement (Hall and Johnson, 1980).

PHYSIOLOGICAL AND PSYCHOLOGICAL FACTORS

Included in this category are climate preference, desire for leisure, growth needs, health, job satisfaction, locus of control, self-esteem, and work commitment. Table F-3 (Appendix) summarizes the research on these variables, organized alphabetically by investigator for each factor.

Climate Preference. Only one study was located in which this factor was examined, and it appears to do little to help explain preferred age of retirement (Rose and Mogey, 1972). The zero-order correlation with preferred age of retirement was .16, but in a stepwise regression analysis of these cross-sectional data, preference for one's own climate accounted for only 1.5 percent of the preferred age of retirement variance, entering the equation third out of 27 variables.

Desire for Leisure. There was an increase from 1951 to 1963 in preference for leisure as a reason for retiring among retirees who were 65 years and older. The increase shifted from 3 percent to 17 percent among Old Age Survivor's Insurance (OASI) beneficiaries in the Survey of the Aged (Palmore, 1964). Beyond these data, preference for leisure was responsible for the early retirement of 22.6 percent of a sample of U.S. Civil Service retirees (Messer, 1969) and was the primary reason for early retirement among 19.49 percent of a group of male UAW retirees (Pollman, 1971).

Growth Needs. In the one study that included growth needs— which was one of ten motivational-psychological variables examined in a discriminant analysis—they, combined with skill variety, feedback from others, and extrinsic satisfaction, contributed significantly ($p < .05$) to retirement status (Schmitt et al., 1979). The growth needs discriminant function coefficient was $-.38$, clearly suggesting that growth needs were related to retirement among the Michigan civil service employees.

Health. The evidence that poor health is related to retirement is relatively strong (Barfield and Morgan, 1970; Burkhauser, 1979; Eden and Jacobson, 1976; Hall and Johnson, 1980; Jacobson, 1972b; Messer, 1969; Parnes, 1980; Parnes and Nestel, 1975, 1981; Pollman, 1971; Quinn, 1977, 1981; Streib and Schneider, 1971). These findings were derived in four instances from longitudinal-actual retirement data (Burkhauser, 1979; Parnes and Nestel, 1975, 1981; Streib and Schneider, 1971). In the Parnes and Nestel (1975) NLS data, for example, men with health problems were more likely to retire prior to age 65 than were men whose health did not affect their work ($F = 22.07$, $p < .01$).

Of the three studies showing a nonsignificant relationship (Jacobson and Eran, 1980; Schmitt and McCune, 1981; Stanford, 1971), the results of two of them warrant some qualification. That is, the dependent variables were preference for retirement (Jacobson and Eran, 1980) and retirement anticipation (Stanford, 1971), variables toward which someone in poor health would not be expected to have positive feelings. In the third study, however, the dependent variable was retirement status (Schmitt and McCune, 1981). In this instance, health added little to the canonical correlation beyond what the previously included demographic and financial variables did (Schmitt and McCune, 1981).

There was one study also in which men from the Panel Study of Income Dynamics were less likely to retire when having more hours ill during the year prior to retirement (Boskin, 1977), although Boskin noted that using the numbers of hours ill as a measure of health was open to question. For instance, being ill during a particular period does not necessarily signify long-term poor health.

Job Satisfaction. There is consistent support among the studies we located for a relationship between job dissatisfaction and preference for or actual retirement (Barfield and Morgan, 1970; Eden and Jacobson, 1976; Jacobson and Eran, 1980; Parnes and Nestel, 1975; Schmitt et al., 1979; Schmitt and McCune, 1981; Streib and Thompson, 1957). In the five-year follow-up of the NLS sample, for instance, the less satisfied were more likely to retire ($F = 9.41$, $p < .01$) (Parnes and Nestel, 1975). Moreover, job satisfaction combined with other job attitudes, such as job involvement, feedback from others, and motivating potential, added significantly to the prediction of retirement status even when entered into the discriminant analysis after the demographic, financial, and health variables (Schmitt and McCune, 1981).

Locus of Control and Self-Esteem. These two variables were both examined in the Schmitt et al. (1979) cross-sectional study of Michigan civil service workers. Neither one was found to be significantly related to early retirement.

Work Commitment. Work commitment, included in one study, was significantly related to retirement (Parnes and Nestel, 1975). As one would expect, the greater the work commitment, the less likely were men in the NLS sample to retire ($F = 13.49$, $p < .01$).

ORGANIZATIONAL VARIABLES

The organizational factors that were studied relative to retirement are summarized in Table F-4 (Appendix). The factors are amount of work, autonomy, co-workers, job change, job strain, job tension/stress, pay/extrinsic rewards, performance, pressure to retire, and promotions.

Amount of Work. In the two studies of this factor's relationship to retirement, the direction of the relationship differed. For the national and UAW samples studied by Barfield and Morgan (1970), amount of work was positively related to the decision to retire, while for Israeli executives there was somewhat of a negative correlation ($r = -.12$, ns) (Eden and Jacobson, 1976). It would seem that variables such as nature of the work itself, job satisfaction, and work commitment would be important possible moderators of this relationship and may help explain the findings in these studies.

Autonomy. There is some consistent support for lower autonomy being associated with retirement (Jacobson, 1972b; Quinn, 1977; Schmitt et al., 1979). This finding has some generalizability also because the samples are relatively diverse, including British factory operatives (Jacobson, 1972b), men from the Retirement History Study (Quinn, 1977), and Michigan civil service workers (Schmitt et al., 1979).

Co-workers. Peer relations were not found to be related to the desire for retirement ($r = .09$, ns) among Israeli executives (Eden and Jacobson, 1976) or male British factory operatives (Jacobson, 1974). On the other hand, female British factory operatives whose real friends were workmates were more reluctant to retire than when friends were outside of work ($\chi^2 = 15.79$, $p < .001$) (Jacobson, 1974).

Job Change. We found one study in which both recent ($\chi^2 = 18.18$, $p < .001$) and expected job change ($\chi^2 = 4.89$, $p < .05$) was greater for early retirees (Pollman and Johnson, 1974). For these UAW machine, assembly, and utility workers, monthly income did not differ significantly between retirees and nonretirees; therefore, income did not help influence early retirement. It is possible, of course, that job change or the expectation of a change could suggest to the worker that organizationally retirement would be timely (Pollman and Johnson, 1974).

Job Strain and Job Tension/Stress. In terms of job strain, first of all, there is evidence that for British factory operatives, the level of strain was associated with a greater willingness to retire at the pensionable age ($\chi^2 =$ not provided, $V = .368$, $p < .001$) and the belief that retirement should occur before the pensionable age ($V = .195$, $p < .05$) (Jacobson, 1972b). For job tension and stress, Israeli executives (Eden and Jacobson, 1976) and physicians (Jacobson and Eran, 1980) with more job tension and stress showed more preference for retirement. For the physicians specifically, as noted under the Job Satisfaction factor in Table F-3 (Appendix), a combination of more stress, less satisfaction, and a lower evaluation of medical competence strengthened the prediction of preference for retirement beyond what the instrumentality perceptions did.

Pay/Extrinsic Rewards. In five studies, greater earnings were associated with later probability of retirement (Barfield and Morgan, 1978; Boskin, 1977; Burkhauser, 1979; Parnes and Nestel, 1981; Rose and Mogey, 1972), while in one study a nonsignificant relationship was found (Parnes and Nestel, 1975). Four of the studies reporting a greater earnings/later retirement relationship were longitudinal, thereby strengthening these results (Barfield and Morgan, 1978; Boskin, 1977; Burkhauser, 1979; Parnes and Nestel, 1981). In addition, the recent findings by Parnes and Nestel (1981) of a greater earnings/ later retirement relationship runs counter to the earlier (1975) nonsignificant results, since the subjects in each were men from the National Longitudinal Study.

The importance of conducting multivariate assessments was affirmed in the Rose and Mogey (1972) analysis. The simple correlation of pay with retirement was .17, but the partial regression correlation fell to .03 because of pay's bivariate relationship with education (r = .47). Pay, therefore, was suppressed in the analysis.

In the remaining study, the independent effect of pay was not assessed (Eden and Jacobson, 1976). Extrinsic rewards, including working conditions, pay, and status, were found to be nonsignificantly related to the desire for retirement.

Greater earnings or pay is, therefore, fairly strongly associated with later retirement. Pay may, however, serve as a proxie for education and occupation. These three variables can also be considered part of a social class factor, suggesting that social class is related to later retirement (Parnes et al., 1970; Rose and Mogey, 1972).

Performance. Performance, as reported by the respondents, was negatively related to the desire to leave work among Israeli executives (Eden and Jacobson, 1976), to a lower preference for retirement among physicians (Jacobson and Eran, 1980), and to early retirement among automobile and agricultural implement workers (Katona et al., 1969). As noted by Eden and Jacobson (1976), if the self-reported performance in the above studies accurately reflects actual performance, this suggests that early retirement serves to eliminate what may be or could become "problem" employees. Of course, studies of actual performance relative to retirement are needed to verify the above findings.

Pressure to Retire. Pressure to retire was examined in a cross-sectional study of a national sample plus UAW members (Barfield and Morgan, 1970). Perceived and actual pressure from the union was related to the decision to retire.

Promotions. In the one study we located in which promotions were assessed relative to retirement, the relationship was negative for Israeli male executives (Eden and Jacobson, 1976). That is, the greater the number of previous promotions in the present organization, the less the desire to retire (r = 0.14, p < .05).

SUMMARY AND IMPLICATIONS

Of the studies on the factors influencing retirement, many were cross-sectional in nature, thereby providing either suspect prospective or retrospective data and findings. However, to the extent that these results are consistent and also confirmed in the longitudinal retirement studies, some summary generalizations are suggested.

The factors for which the evidence was strongest for explaining an employee's willingness to continue working or to retire were financial status, as represented by expected pensions, social security income, and net assets; education; and job satisfaction. For education and job satisfaction, the higher the amount, the lower the likelihood that the employee preferred retirement or actually retired. For financial status, those with higher status were more likely to retire early. There was also fairly consistent evidence that poorer health and lower pay were related to earlier retirement.

There were also other factors for which there was some tentative evidence of a relationship to retirement. Among the individual demographic variables specifically, feeling younger, having more dependents, having a high-level or more desirable occupation, and being self-employed were associated with a lower preference for or later retirement, while living in a rural or small community was related to early retirement. For the physiological and psychological factors, employees with a desire for leisure, greater growth needs, and a lower work commitment were more likely to retire. Finally, for the organizational factors there was some evidence that less autonomy; recent and/or expected job change; more job strain, tension, and stress; lower self-rated performance; fewer previous promotions; and pressure to retire were all related to a greater preference for or likelihood of retirement.

Inconsistent or mixed results were found for gender and marital status relative to retirement. For the gender-retirement relationship, it appears that the behavior of women varies more. To begin with, women who are married may be financially more secure or have a spouse who is retiring early and therefore may retire early. On the other hand, married women may be late career-starters who find they enjoy work or anticipate early widowhood, and for these reasons may prefer later retirement. Then, of course, there is the single woman who could be financially secure because of a full working career and thus prefers to retire early, while another could be financially insecure because of a divorce and a short working career and therefore prefers to retire later. Some of these same considerations would also help explain why marital status could be expected to have an inconsistent relationship with retirement. In addition, the wife's earnings and eligibility for social security under her own work record could delay or advance, respectively, the husband's retirement.

When considering the findings in general, one group of retirement determinants suggests that early retirement is more likely to occur for those whose work experience was less satisfactory. These factors are lower pay and job satisfaction; less autonomy; more job strain, tension, and stress; and unmet growth needs. But these factors are also to some extent an outcome of education and one's resultant occupational level. Therefore, one way to encourage workers to delay retirement is to provide additional education, and thus to improve the desirability and level of their jobs (Pollman and Johnson, 1974). Of course, to the extent that higher job level would improve financial status, the likelihood of retiring early could again increase. On the other hand, possibly a higher job level would moderate the financial status/early retirement relationship (Schmitt and McCune, 1981). Health and, to a lesser extent, the spouse are more unpredictable influences. Health, however, may be more of a factor also in the lower occupations with less education (Jaffe, 1972), because this is where more health risks are expected.

To fully assess the relative effects of the various factors associated with the retirement decision, future research should be inclusive of the variables identified in this review. In addition, a longitudinal panel study design is required for explaining actual retirement. Also, intraorganizational longitudinal studies of retirement are suggested, because none have been completed and these findings would be particularly valuable to human resource planners. Such studies would allow for the comparison of employees at different occupational levels who have been influenced by the same organizational factors. This methodology would therefore provide the clearest possible indications of the decision to retire. Finally, as Rose and Mogey (1972) have suggested, model-building should continue with the goal of reflecting the interactive effects and correlates of the independent variables associated with the decision to retire.

Retirement Policies Abroad

Nearly all industrialized countries are struggling with problems associated with retirement and income replacement. In addition, no consensus has developed as to the appropriate age for retirement, or

TABLE 7.3   Life Expectancy at Birth in Thirteen Industrialized Countries

Country	Year of Determination[1]	Sex Male	Sex Female
Belgium	1972	67.79	74.21
Canada	1972	69.34	76.36
East Germany	1976	68.82	74.42
France	1976	69.20	77.20
Great Britain	1970	67.8	73.8
Japan	1976	72.15	77.35
Norway	1977	72.12	78.42
People's Republic of China	1975	60.7	64.4
Soviet Union	1972	64.00	74.00
Sweden	1976	72.10	77.75
Switzerland	1977	71.8	76.22
United States	1975	68.7	76.5
West Germany	1977	68.61	75.21

1. Year of determination refers to the last available date for which data were available in each country.

Source: World Almanac and Book of Facts, 1982. New York: Newspaper Enterprise Association, 1981.

whether employees should be required to retire as a matter of law or social policy.

Certainly this issue is influenced by the life expectancy of individuals in each country. Table 7.3 summarizes life expectancy at birth for the populations in twelve industrialized countries. As indicated in the table, male life expectancy ranges from 60.7 years in the People's Republic of China to over 72 years in Japan, Sweden, and Norway. Female life expectancy at birth is shown to range from 64.4 years in the People's Republic of China to 78.4 years in Norway.

This section reviews retirement developments in eleven industrial countries—Canada, Great Britain, Sweden, Norway, the Soviet Union, France, Japan, Switzerland, West Germany, Belgium, and the People's Republic of China. One limitation to this section must be noted: The search for international documents was limited to English language publications.

CANADA

In 1978, the Canadian Council on Social Development, a private research group, issued a position paper on retirement age and income following examination of the country's census data. In their statement, they concluded that the opportunity for Canadians over age 65 to continue working rarely existed. This was because of the widespread use of compulsory retirement policies. In addition, the council found that only 40 percent of the Canadian labor force was covered by private pensions, with less than 10 percent of the labor force being eligible for a full pension. This latter point was particularly important, since Canadian government pension planning assumes that it is sufficient to provide only a reasonable minimum income through government programs and to leave the question of additional income to the private pension system and private savings (Collins and Brown, 1978).

Canada's government retirement pension plan consists of two parts. One component is the Old Age Security Pension (U.S. Dept. of Health and Human services, 1980). This is a flat sum to which a person is entitled if he or she has resided in Canada for 40 years since age 18. The second component is the Canada Pension Plan or the Quebec Pension Plan. Full benefits are provided to a worker at 65 if his or her income (from working) is below a set figure. If the person is earning more, the benefit is reduced. People over 70, however, are entitled to the full benefit regardless of how much they earn. Further financial assistance is provided to retired Canadians in the form of property tax grants, sales tax grants, and heating grants (each up to a maximum figure) (Allen, 1971). These are based on housing costs, consumption figures, and heating bills.

The council also made a series of recommendations to facilitate more freedom of choice by workers. These included adopting pension programs to allow more flexible retirement between ages 60 and 70, discouraging compulsory retirement, developing manpower programs to allow a worker of retirement age to continue working, implementing programs to update the educational skills of older workers to match technological changes, implementing preretirement education programs, and developing volunteer programs for the retired. Finally, it was recommended that Canadians be permitted to obtain their government pension after a maximum of 45 years in the labor force, or at 65 years of age, whichever came first (Collins and Brown, 1978).

GREAT BRITAIN

Great Britain's government pension plans are supported by employee contributions and taxes (U.S. Dept. of Health and Human Services, 1980). In 1971 there were approximately 8.9 million citizens over retirement age. Approximately 80 percent received National

Insurance Retirement pensions. Females are eligible upon reaching age 60, and males at age 65. An earnings rule is applied for the subsequent five years. A retiree must earn less than a specified amount or work fewer than twelve hours. Work-related expenses (transportation, uniforms) are deducted from earnings before they are applied to the test. Approximately 1.8 million retirees are affected by this earnings rule. Benefits are decreased proportionately to the amount earned above this stated level. Pensions average about 25-40 percent of a worker's take-home pay. Levels of payment do not include an automatic cost-of-living adjustment. Instead, they are periodically reviewed and raised by Parliament.

Great Britain also has a social insurance program, with 2.3 million Britons receiving supplementary pensions. Males 65 or over and women 60 or over who are not engaged in full-time employment and who are below a determined poverty level are entitled to the supplement. An additional benefit is free prescription drugs. Since 1975, the government has instituted occupational pensions funded by either employers or state reserves. To be eligible, a worker must average 50 contributions a year.

Although Britons can work after age 60 (females) or 65 (males), many find it difficult to obtain employment. Belbin and Clark (1970) compared 1961 and 1966 British Census data and found that on the average, retirement for the male population of Great Britain remained at age 65, and that workers showed no signs of developing a trend toward early retirement. Moreover, the investigators found that age 65 was becoming more rigidly adhered to as a retirement age than it was in 1961. The reason cited was the increasing number of persons employed in large organizations where a fixed retirement age is a matter of policy. In addition, some organizations may also be disposed to retain employees (even when their effectiveness is declining) who are approaching the retirement age out of a concern for good industrial relations.

SWEDEN

The Swedish national pension programs are built on two principles. First, persons whose capacity for work has been permanently reduced shall be able to receive disability pensions before the normal pensionable age. Second, anyone who is entitled to an old-age pension from the national pension program shall have the right to decide (with certain restrictions) when they prefer to begin drawing an old-age pension.

The Swedes have a two-tiered pension system composed of a basic Universal National Pension and a Supplementary Pension (U.S. Dept. of Health and Human Services, 1980; Helmers and Hyden, 1968; Rosenthal, 1967). The Universal National Pension provides coverage for all Swedish nationals (resident and nonresident) and all resident aliens covered by reciprocity agreements. Single employees receive 95 percent of a monthly adjusted (to the cost of living index) base, and married couples receive 155 percent thereof. Some individuals are also eligible for a 33 percent supplement to the base. The central government pays for more than half the cost from their general funds. Employers and self-employed individuals are required to contribute 8.3 percent of their payroll.

The Supplementary Pension is compulsory for all employees. Self-employed individuals may apply for exemption, but only some 10 percent have selected that option. The eligibility requirement is three years of coverage for Swedish citizens and resident aliens. The benefit is 60 percent of the difference between the average earnings of a worker's 15 best years and the base amount under the Universal National Pension. Employers and self-employed individuals are the sole contributors to this plan. They must contribute 11.75 percent of wages earned between the base amount and 7.5 times the base.

In 1976, the eligible age for full benefits was lowered from 67 to 65 (Tracy, 1979a). Retirement can be taken as early as 60 (if there was 10 years of coverage after age 45). The benefits are reduced, however, by .5 percent a month unless the worker is unemployed at 60 with no opportunities to find a job, at which point he or she receives full benefits. Benefits may also be deferred up to age 70, with an increase of 7.2 percent a month. Less than .5 percent of all pensioners do this. For those that do, however, the full benefit from both plans is two-thirds of the average earnings from their best 15 years. Sweden permits their pensioners to continue working with no loss of benefits. This encourages older workers to remain in the work force longer.

NORWAY

The system in Norway is similar to the social security system in Sweden. It is two-tiered, with a universal program that covers all residents and a secondary, earnings-related portion covering workers who have earned over a base figure for three years (National Council, 1974).

The universal pension is a base amount, adjusted once or twice a year by price levels. The eligibility for full benefits requires 40 years of coverage. Single persons are entitled to 100 percent of the base and a married couple to 150 percent of the base. Benefits are reduced proportionally as coverage time falls below 40 years to the minimum requirement of three years (Vig, 1973).

The earnings-based pension is calculated using the same base. The formula is eight times the base plus one-third of the average pension-earning income over the base amount. This results in benefits that are 8-12 times the base amount.

These programs are funded by residents and employers. An assessment of 4.4 percent on all taxable income is paid as part of the national tax that goes into the pension fund. Employees also contribute 5 percent of their pension-producing income. Self-employed persons contribute an additional 9.9 percent of their pension-producing income. Employers are required to pay in 12.3-16.5 percent of their pension-producing payroll, depending on the region (U.S. Dept. of Health and Human Services, 1980). The maximum earnings limit for calculating the contribution is 12 times the base.

In 1973, Norway lowered its retirement age from 70 to 67, for both males and females. Pensioners can continue working, but the total of earnings and benefits has a ceiling of 80 percent of former earnings until age 70. After 70 there is no limit. This partial pension scheme is the predominate choice (Tracy, 1979b; National Council, 1974). In addition to the high level of payments, pensioners receive a 9 percent increase on their full pension benefits for each year they are deferred (up to three years).

THE SOVIET UNION

Between 1941 and 1976, the number of pensioners in the Soviet Union increased 150-fold, from 0.2 to 30 million (Zakharov and Tsivilyou, 1978). All pensioners are covered under a single state pension system. There are no local supplements. The normal eligibility requirements for men are the attainment of age 60, and 25 years of work. For women, the requirements are age 55 and 20 years of service. Exceptions are made for workers in hazardous jobs and for women with five or more children. Age and work history requirements may be lowered from five (as for lumbermen and oilmen) to ten (as for underground miners) years. Location also creates exceptions. Workers in Siberia, for example, can retire at 55 (men) or 50 (women) (Babzhin, 1971; U.S. Dept. of Health and Human Services, 1980).

Benefits range from 50 to 100 percent of average earnings. A person has the choice of using the last year or any consecutive five from the last ten as the base. The percentage depends on the level of the average, with lower incomes receiving a higher percentage. The average benefit is 65 percent (Babzhin, 1971; Zakharov and Tsivilyou, 1978). Pensioners from dangerous occupations receive an additional 5 percent above the schedule. Bonuses are also given for periods of uninterrupted work and for the presence of a family. If a pensioner has worked fewer than the years described above (but for a minimum of five years), he or she is still entitled to a pension, but it is reduced proportionally by the length of service.

The pension plan is partially financed by a tax on employers of from 4.4 to 9.0 percent of payroll. The government pays the remainder of the cost, which is approximately 50 percent.

The Soviet Union tries to encourage pensioners to continue working by making work less demanding and more economically attractive. Laws exist to protect their positions in the work force. They are also entitled to greater benefits, such as longer rest breaks and more vacation time (Social security news, 1980).

If a pensioner continues working, his or her benefits are reduced 0-50 percent. Again, this variance is due to occupation and location. Agricultural and manual workers receive no deduction, while engineers and technicians receive a 50 percent reduction (Solovieu, 1980; Lykova, 1967).

Although only about 25 percent of men over 60 and women over 55 continue to work, the trend is toward increased labor force participation. In 1969, only 17.4 percent of all pensioners were working; by 1975, the number rose to 24.2 percent, and in 1979 it stood at 27.8 percent (Social security news, 1980).

FRANCE

The old-age pension system in France consists of a social insurance system and mandatory private pensions. All employed citizens are covered (U.S. Dept of Health and Human Services, 1980).

The normal retirement age is 65, with the requirement of 37.5 years of service for full benefits. The age 65 requirement may be lowered (1) due to disability, (2) if the worker is a woman with three children, or (3) if the worker is in an arduous occupation. If retirement is deferred, a premium of 5 percent per year of deferment is added to the benefit.

If an employee is laid off at age 60, there is a plan to pay up to 70 percent of his or her earnings. The pensioner must have been under social insurance for ten years and have had either one year of continuous employment or two cumulative years during the last five. The benefit terminates when a pensioner reaches 65. In 1977, a similar supplement was enacted for volunteer retirees between 60 and 65.

Again, the supplement, which guarantees 70 percent of one's last gross earnings, terminates when the pensioner reaches 65 or resumes working (Social security news, 1980).

The old-age pension benefit at age 65 is 25 percent of the average earnings of the individual's best ten years. Hence, retirement is not necessary. Moreover, if a person is unable to work due to his or her physical condition and the nature of the job, the proportion is increased to 50 percent (LaRoque, 1969). The private pension system provides additional benefits when a worker does retire.

The social insurance system is funded solely by employees and their employers. Employees are taxed 4.7 percent of their earnings. Employers contribute 8.2 percent of their payroll costs. Despite the liberalization of the disability qualification permitting early retirement and the increase in private pension plans, there has been no decrease in retirement age (Tracy, 1979b). For both men and women, it has remained stable at around 65.

JAPAN

Japanese society is growing older at a rate unprecedented in the industrial world. Although the United Nations defines an "aged country" to be one in which the ratio of those over age 65 to the entire population is 7 percent or more, the Japanese are already beyond this point. In 1965, 7 million Japanese (7 percent) were over 65 years of age. In 1977, the number reached 9 million (7.8 percent), and the projections are for continued growth—1995, 17 million (13 percent) and 2015, 26 million (20 percent). In addition to the percentage of persons over 65, the Japanese also have a unique system of early retirement.

Japan has the earliest mandatory retirement age (55) of all the industrialized countries (Kii, 1979). However, a majority of Japanese workers continue to participate in the labor force beyond that age. This is due to several factors. The first is that while mandatory retirement is at age 55, the government-sponsored old-age pension does not become available until age 60. Although employees receive from their employer a lump sum benefit upon retirement, the labor unions have claimed that it is inadequate to sustain workers until age 60. Because of labor shortages and the already high level of labor force participation by older persons, the government has taken steps to encourage the hiring or continued employment of older workers. Under the Older Workers Employment Promotion Law, 6 percent of a company's work force should be 55 or older. Grants are given to firms that hire unemployed older workers. If a worker is age 45-55, the firm receives 60-80 percent of his or her wages for the first six months, and 50-66 percent of their wages for the second six months. If a worker is over 55, the firm receives 60-80 percent of their wages for one year, and 50-66 percent for the next six months (International Federation on Ageing, 1980a).

The size of the company is a major factor in setting the retirement age. In 1973, a mandatory retirement age of 60 was more frequent among small and medium-sized companies than among large companies. This situation enables smaller companies to supplement their labor forces with employees who have retired at an earlier age from larger firms (Kii, 1979). In addition, many companies with mandatory retirement have permitted employees to extend their working years. Here again, smaller companies were more likely to take advantage of this than larger firms. Larger companies extended the retirement age by an average of 1.6 years over age 55, while smaller firms extended it an average of 4.9 years beyond 55.

The Japanese have implemented later retirement by using two novel techniques: a reemployment system, and an extension-of-employment system. The reemployment system, which is used more often by larger companies than smaller ones, enables management to retire workers who have reached the retirement age, and then subsequently rehire them. A 1970 Ministry of Labor survey found that 76 percent of the companies having this system reemployed only those retirees who were approved by management, whereas 21 percent reemployed anyone who wanted to work (Kii, 1979). When the retired were reemployed, both their positions and their incomes were normally reduced, even though the content of their work generally did not change. Of the reemployed, 54 percent received less than one-half the income they had earned before retirement, and less than 7.5 percent realized earnings higher than before retirement.

The extension of employment, which is preferred by smaller firms, enables certain workers who have reached retirement age to continue to work without retiring. As with the reemployment system, the majority of companies using this system only allow those workers who are approved by management to continue to work. These workers also find their positions and salaries reduced, although such reductions are made by a smaller proportion of the companies using this system than by those who reemploy retirees. Hence, this system provides for more favorable treatment of the employee.

The reason for this more favorable treatment under the extension-of-employment system is that companies use it for positions that are more difficult to fill. This is one reason why it is preferred by smaller companies. Larger companies tend to find it easier to replace workers.

In addition to these systems, the Japanese maintain computerized employment services and talent banks to shift workers into new jobs. The country's traditions and institutions afford the flexibility of both early retirement and retraining of middle-aged and older workers who desire second careers after retirement (Stewart, 1974). Employers have benefited because voluntary extension of the retirement age has enabled companies to reduce the costs of retaining workers without obtaining a legislative extension of the retirement age.

The government social security system is not yet mature. Only 22 percent of the Japanese people over 60 are receiving benefits from this program. Another 59 percent receive benefits from noncontributory pensions and special war pensions (Palmore, 1980). The social security system consists of two pension funds. One provides coverage for working citizens, while a second is for those not covered under the former plan and who make voluntary contributions (International Federation on Ageing, 1980c).

The employee pension retirement age is 55 for women and 60 for men. A minimum of 20 years of coverage is required for full benefits. Pensioners may work and receive benefits, but the payments are reduced. Those 60-64 get a reduction if they earn over a ceiling. If a person is working after age 64, the benefit is reduced a flat 20 percent. The benefit is calculated by multiplying the years of coverage (with a maximum of 35) times a base figure. An adjustment for earnings level and rising wage levels is made by adding 1 percent of the revalued average monthly earnings to this. Funding is provided by equal contributions from employer and employee. Men contribute 4.55 percent of their wages, and women 3.65 percent (U.S. Dept of Health and Human Services, 1980).

The program of voluntary coverage is funded by a standard contribution from individuals. If a person is classified as low income, the government will subsidize the payment. Benefits are calculated by multiplying a base times years of contribution. There is a minimum level of benefits for pensioners 70 or older.

Because only a relatively small number of Japanese receive government pensions, a large percentage (81 percent of the 60-64 group and 46.7 percent of those 65 and over) continue to work (Palmore, 1980).

FEDERAL REPUBLIC OF GERMANY (WEST GERMANY)

The normal retirement-eligibility age in West Germany is 65, with 15 years of coverage. In 1973, the country instituted a flexible system permitting early retirement at age 63 with a long service record (35 years of credits). Since then, there has been a shift toward early retirement. In 1973, 81-91 percent of the new pensioners were 65. This dropped to 33 percent in 1976. Between 1960 and 1976, the percentage of new pensioners aged 60-64 rose from 6 percent to 61 percent for men (Tracy, 1979a).

This was not entirely due to the long service provision. Workers are also permitted to retire from age 60 on, with full benefits, if they have been unemployed one year within the last 18 months. The pension will be reduced if work is resumed, and eliminated entirely if wages go beyond a ceiling. The proportion of early retirements strongly reflects the economic trends. High unemployment leads to early retirement. To offset this trend, the government encourages firms to recruit and hire unemployed older workers (45 and over) by offering grants from 50 to 80 percent of the older workers' wage (International Federation on Ageing, 1980a). The trend in early retirement among women does not reflect the variation in economic activity. Women may retire at 60 if they have 15 years of contributions, with 15 in the last 20. This allowance disregards employment status.

The new provisions in 1973 also permitted deferred payments to age 67, with an increase of .6 percent a month. In spite of this, the trend is still toward early retirement (Palmore, 1980).

Employees and employers each contribute 9 percent of wages to the pension fund. There is a maximum level of earnings for determining contribution. If an individual falls below a minimum, the employer is assessed the full 18 percent. A unique characteristic of the West German plan is that credits toward years of coverage can be made, without contribution, for periods of study, training, extended illness, or maternity leave (U.S. Dept. of Health and Human Services, 1980).

Self-employed workers are compelled to contribute 18 percent of their earnings. Nonworking individuals (for example, housewives) may receive coverage by making vountary contributions of a flat amount.

Benefits are figured by taking 1.5 percent of assessed wages and multiplying it by the years of coverage. Assessed wages are adjusted to the rising cost of living by taking the ratio of the individual's average earnings as compared to the national average and multiplying it by a base that reflects the current level.

SWITZERLAND

Switzerland considers its state social security system as merely a base for retirement income. It has, therefore, a very low replacement rate of earnings, bringing the pensioner only to a subsistence level. Retirement policies rely on two other sources of income for pensioners. These are a mandatory private pension program that operates to maintain a person's standard of living, and personal savings, which raise the pensioner above this level (Villars, 1979a).

All employed workers (regardless of nationality) are required to enroll. Nationals abroad and self-employed individuals do so voluntarily. An amount of 8.4 percent of wages, equally divided between employee and employer, is contributed to the state fund. Self-employed individuals must pay 7.8-9.4 percent of their earnings. Unemployed persons who wish to have or continue coverage in the plan contribute from whatever income they receive according to a schedule. The government must still subsidize 14 percent of the cost.

Retirement age is 62 for women and 65 for men. Payments may be postponed up to five years. Benefit increases are tied to actuarial value. To receive full benefits, a pensioner must have made a contribution every year since turning 20. For every missing year, the benefits are reduced. The minimum vesting contribution for a Swiss national is one year, and for an alien ten years (U.S. Dept. of Health and Human Services, 1980).

Benefits are calculated to a base that is reviewed and adjusted every three years or when there has been an eight-point increase in the price index. A variable portion is added, based on earnings. Retirement is not necessary.

The bulk of retirees' income is derived from private pensions made mandatory by a Constitutional Amendment approved in 1972. All public and private employees over age 25 and earning more than a base amount are covered. Approximately 300,000 blue and white collar workers are ineligible. Partial vesting occurs after five years of coverage. One is fully vested after 30 years (U.S. Dept. of Health, Education and Welfare, 1978).

When the private pension is combined with the state social security plan, the objective is to have the sum of two payments equal 80 percent of the final three years' average earnings. If the state plan meets that amount, no additional pension is paid. More commonly, the private pension provides supplementary coverage to reach 80 percent.

BELGIUM

In formulating its retirement policy, Belgium had to face the same problem as Great Britain—high unemployment among the young.

Therefore, the first striking characteristics of Belgium's plan is the strict rule against continued employment after retirement age. The only approval given is for small-scale farmers and nurserymen, vocational instructors of miners, and persons still under a public contract (even the last group is restricted as to the number of hours they can work and the amoung of money they can earn). In most cases, the government must be notified.

The normal retirement age is 60 for women and 65 for men. Early retirement may be taken with a 5 percent reduction per year in benefits. Single pensioners receive 60 percent of their average lifetime earnings, adjusted for wage and price changes. A married couple receives 75 percent. To receive full pension benefits, a man must have worked 45 years and a woman 40 years. Partial pensions are paid to those with shorter work histories (U.S. Dept. of Health and Human Services, 1980).

Employed and self-employed persons are covered. The insured person contributes 6 percent of his or her carnings. Employers contribute 8 percent of payroll. Earnings have a maximum level for calculating contributions and benefits.

In 1978, Belgium created a prepension plan to encourage older workers to leave the work force and make room for younger workers. If a woman 55 or older or a man 60 or older is discharged or steps down to be replaced by a younger person with no job, the retiree receives the regular unemployment benefit plus one-half the difference between the benefit and his or her last earnings (up to a maximum) until they reach statutory retirement age.

PEOPLE'S REPUBLIC OF CHINA

Despite the radical changes in China's social environment, the ancient value of filial piety continues to thrive. Family elders still control the lives, money, and property of their offspring.

This family structure is especially strong in the rural areas of China, the farming communes. Married children and grandchildren often live in the homes of their elders. All earnings are handed over to their control. The pressure for offspring to remain and care for their parents makes the need for public assistance virtually nonexistent on the communes. Any support given to aged workers is based on need. There is no retirement age for commune workers; the elderly and disabled are simply moved to less strenuous (and lower-paying) tasks as long as they can work (Treas, 1979).

Urban industrial workers are covered by social security. The ancient traditions are not as strong, although many extended families still live together. Funding is provided solely by government-owned firms. Each organization pays 10-20 percent of its payroll.

The general retirement age is 60 for men and 50-55 for women. As in many countries, China permits earlier retirement for workers employed in physically demanding jobs. Each firm encourages or discourages workers from retiring, depending on the skills of the individual and the availability of a replacement.

Retirement is necessary for the receipt of social security benefits. Benefits range from 50-70 percent of the last wage, depending on years of coverage. The minimum time for vesting is five years of continuous coverage. The maximum used for calculating benefits is 20 years for men and 15 years for women (U.S. Dept. of Health and Human Services, 1980).

SUMMARY, IMPLICATIONS, AND FUTURE RESEARCH ISSUES

Although data on foreign countries appear in English-speaking journals infrequently, it is clear that other countries have developed retirement and income replacement systems that provide greater flexibility to the employees and firms than those in the United States. In response to labor shortages in several countries, particularly Japan and the Soviet Union, incentives have been developed to encourage older workers to continue their employment beyond the usual working years. In other countries, such as Belgium, older workers are encouraged to retire early in order to create employment opportunities for younger workers. In other countries, phased retirement is encouraged.

The implications for human resource managers in the United States are clear. The fixed retirement of many older employees wastes valuable talent—skills that have been expensive to instill and develop. More flexible programs of phased work and retirement, including part-time employment opportunities, would permit firms to recapture this expertise.

Just as the enactment of the Age Discrimination in Employment Act and the raising of the mandatory retirement age to 70 years were the result of political and social pressures, human resource managers can expect such pressures to influence other retirement policies. Therefore, organizations should begin immediately to study the feasibility of other retirement options.

We recommend research designed to identify innovative company retirement programs in the United States, to evaluate their effectiveness and establish the determinants of their effectiveness. Finally, up-to-date studies of retirement policies in other industrial countries, involving experts in each country, should be commissioned and maintained. These studies would examine the effectiveness of the retirement policies of many countries and would provide valuable information for employers in the United States, as well as for American employers operating facilities overseas.

Social Security

SOURCES OF THE PRESENT PROBLEM

Social Security was established during the Depression to provide a minimum income for those who retire. Today, the Social Security program consists of three parts: (1) Old Age and Survivor's Insurance, which provides an income to retired workers and their dependents or survivors; (2) Disability Insurance, which supports disabled workers and their dependents; and (3) Medicare, providing hospital insurance coverage for the elderly.

There are over 35 million recipients of Social Security benefits. The expenditures on benefits comprise 22 percent of the total federal budget (U.S. House of Representatives, 1980a).

Cox and Wooten (1978) report that Social Security has become the sole source of income for many retirees. In all, 50 percent of all retired couples and 75 percent of all retired single workers receive 50 percent or more of their retirement income from the Social Security program. Moreover, one in three single workers and one out of seven retired couples receive 90 percent of their retirement income from Social Security.

In a recent survey sponsored by Johnson and Higgins, an employee benefit consulting and actuarial firm (Personnel Administration, 1979), 42 percent of the current employees surveyed responded that they had "hardly any confidence at all" that Social Security will pay the benefits to which they are entitled. Nearly the same number (41 percent) strongly questioned whether future generations would be willing to pay higher taxes for Social Security.

The Social Security benefit structure is set up on a pay-as-you-go basis, with reserves of less than one year's expected benefits payout. Thus the taxes paid by the present workers and employers are supporting the present population of retired persons. Nothing is being saved for future retirement. This system worked up through the 1960s, when the size of the labor force was increasing and the level of wages rising in order to support a growing retired population that was receiving larger benefits. These trends are no longer occurring. The Old Age and Survivors' Insurance program is in serious trouble. A series of factors, including lower birth rates, high unemployment, declining productivity, the 1972 Social Security Amendments, the trend toward early retirement, and increased longevity are frequently identified as the sources of the difficulty.

The birthrate has dropped to an average of 1.8 children per woman from a high of 3.7 (Morrison, 1981). There will eventually be a decrease in the number of persons entering the work force, resulting in fewer workers paying taxes to support the retired ones.

In 1972, Congress amended the Social Security Act to include an automatic benefit adjustment tied to changes in the Consumer Price Index. No corresponding tax rate increase was included. At that time, wages were increasing twice as fast as prices. Unfortunately, when inflation reached double digit levels in the late 1970s, wages did not grow at the same previous rate (Van Gorkom, 1976). (When wages are not keeping up with inflation, benefits are increasing faster than revenues.) High unemployment and increases in productivity further compounded this problem by adversely affecting the flow of funds into the program.

The trend toward early retirement and the increased longevity of the American people also put the future of the Social Security system in jeopardy. In 1955, 90 percent of the work force worked through age 64. By 1961, one-third of all workers retired before 65. In 1977, 60 percent of retiring workers were under 65 (U.S. House of Representatives, 1980b). The early retiree received a decreased benefit (as much as 80 percent of his full benefit at 62), but he or she receives benefits for a longer period and stops paying into the program that much sooner. In 1940, once one reached 65, the average life expectancy was to 77.8. In 1978, the life expectancy had increased 3.3 years to 81.1, an average of 3.3 more years of benefits for each retiree (Morrison, 1981).

SOCIAL SECURITY POLICY OPTIONS

The reserves in the Old Age and Survivors' Insurance Fund have become dangerously low in recent years. Many short-term remedies have been suggested, such as payroll tax hikes and interfund borrowing, but these are all temporary solutions. Even more dramatic changes are expected in the future. Indeed, the system may require radical changes if it is to survive into the next century.

There will be an intense acceleration of numbers in the 65 and older population around 2025. At that time, the baby boom children (those born during the all-time high birthrate of 3.7) will be ready to retire. The population 65 and older will jump from the present 11 percent to between 18 and 23 percent (Morrison, 1981). Under the present population structure, there are five workers for every retiree. Depending on future fertility rates, this number could range from 1.7 to 3.4 workers retired over 65 by the year 2040. Even under the most optimistic assumption that there will be a spurt in population growth shortly after the turn of the century, payroll taxes will not be enough; they are not enough now.

Richard Schweiker, Secretary of Health and Human Services (U.S. House of Representatives, 1981; U.S. Senate, 1981), has proposed the plan of the Reagan Administration. One objective is to discourage early retirement; that is, to encourage people to work beyond 65. Schweiker proposed to phase out the earnings test for those 65 and older. Presently, those over 65 are discouraged from continuing work. They receive a dollar deduction in benefits for every two dollars they earn over $6000. President Reagan's plan was to raise the minimum earnings and eventually abolish the test by 1986. The elderly would then be able to collect and still be contributing to the fund.

Kaplan (1976) proposed a plan to increase the eligible retirement age. This would be done slowly and with advance notice. The standard retirement age would be increased two months a year starting in 2005. If the delayed retirement credit was maintained as it is (relative to age 65), but the early retirement penalty moved with the increasing retirement age, the system would have a new equilibrium in 2018. Thus, a 68-year-old retiree would receive the same relative benefits then as a 68-year-old today. A 65-year-old in 2028 would only receive the benefit equivalent of a 62-year-old today. The House of Representatives Select Committee on Aging (1980b) also listed this proposal in their recommendations. They state that people are living longer, healthier lives, and that delaying retirement will keep workers contributing longer and collecting less.

The Ford Administration pointed out the flaw in the 1972 indexing method. Benefits were automatically adjusted for inflation after the earnings used to determine the base benefit had risen with inflation. Also, the total wage base used to collect the taxes was not increasing to meet the increased benefits adjusted from the inflation rate. The administration proposed to lower the replacement rates (initial benefits as a percentage of preretirement earnings). Although not enacted (no one wants to be the one that decreases benefits), the proposal is still considered an alternative (Kaplan, 1976; U.S. House of Representatives, 1980b; U.S. Senate, 1981). It becomes a stronger alternative as more and more retirees are receiving benefits greater than their working earnings.

The Social Security Advisory Board has recommended taxing half of the Social Security benefits (U.S. House of Representative, 1980b). Under the current system, employers' contributions are not taxed. Therefore, the board felt that they could be taxed to the recipients. The Congressional Budget Office estimated revenues of $39 billion for the first five years. It would mainly affect the high-benefit recipients, approximately 10.6 million returns.

No decision has been reached on what action to take. The uncertainties of fertility rates and inflation keep us from knowing the severity of the problems ahead, yet some changes appear to be inevitable.

CONTINUING EMPLOYMENT AND SOCIAL SECURITY

It has been suggested that the structure of the Social Security system provides a disincentive for older workers to continue to work. This disincentive is alleged to be the result of the early retirement option and the earnings test (Bixby, 1976). The early retirement option provides reduced benefits to those workers who elect to take advantage of it, while the earnings test reduces Social Security benefits by 50 percent on earned income—a one dollar benefit reduction for every two dollars earned.[3] A series of proposals have been considered which would modify this system, but none has been implemented to date.

The Advisory Council on Social Security (1975) has considered a series of proposals to improve the incentive for older workers to continue their employment (Bixby, 1976). Several of the proposals considered were for raising the earnings to one dollar for every three dollars earned. Other proposals which might increase the labor force participation rates of older workers included a refund of Social Security taxes for those over 65, a lowering from 72 to 70 of the age at which the earnings test no longer applies, and a shift from age 65 to 68 of the time for normal retirement with full benefits, and from 62 to 65 of the starting date for actuarially reduced benefits. While this report does not attempt to consider the merits of each proposal, we have examined retirement policies in other industrialized countries and discovered that those countries exhibit much greater flexibility and innovation in retirement policies, many in response to the income needs of the elderly and to offset manpower shortages.[4]

Conclusions

In this chapter we have examined private pension coverage; demographic, psychological, medical, and organizational factors influencing the decision to retire; retirement policies in other industrialized countries; and policy issues affecting the future of the social security system. The following conclusions may be drawn:

- Large segments of the American work force are employed in industries with no employer-provided pension coverage.
- Many employees who are covered by pension programs will never receive their pension, as insufficient job tenure will interfere with the vesting provisions of the program.
- As demonstrated by Table 7.1, many pension programs do not provide adequate replacement income. This will make personal savings and individual retirement planning of increased importance.
- Under present conditions, inflation erodes private pension coverage while raising the benefits of Social Security recipients, since unlike most pensions, Social Security is indexed.
- Several factors appear to influence individual retirement decision making. Financial problems and poor health were related to earlier retirement, while higher amounts of education and job satisfaction were associated with later retirement.
- Most other industrialized countries exhibit far more flexibility and innovation in retirement policy than the United States. Many countries provide opportunities for phased retirement or incentives for full-time employment beyond the normal retirement age.
- The Social Security system will require significant changes to insure it solvency as the ratio of active workers to retirees continues to decline. Maintaining employee confidence in the system will require difficult policy decisions. All of the present options under consideration—for example, raising the eligibility age, modification of the indexing provisions, and the taxing of benefits—will make other forms of income security (savings and private pensions) more important.
- Organizations sensitive to the needs of their employees will expand their efforts in the area of preretirement planning.

NOTES

1. In this study, the data may leave an inaccurate perception. Being employed by a company that allocates expenditures does not necessarily mean that one will receive a pension.

2. It should be noted that social security is presently indexed for inflation.

3. At the present time until age 72, the earnings of workers in excess of $3000 are taxed by the program at a rate of 5070.

4. See pp. 261-272.

CHAPTER 8

SUMMARY AND IMPLICATIONS

In this final chapter, we have condensed the findings of Chapters 2 through 7 to provide an integrated summary of our findings. In providing this summary, we have purposefully reduced the complexity of our presentation. Readers are therefore cautioned to refer to the appropriate sections of the main body of this book for a complete discussion of the issues. The following topics are discussed: (a) summary of findings, (b) organizational implications, (c) research method issues, and (d) future research needs.

Summary of Findings

CHARACTERISTICS OF THE OLDER WORKER

On the basis of existing research, we can say that the older worker has work attitudes and demonstrates work behaviors that are generally congruent with effective organizational functioning. Specifically, older workers are found to have higher levels of overall job satisfaction and are more satisfied with the nature of the job than younger workers. Moreover, older workers are more job-involved and internally motivated and less likely to have the intent of leaving. Also, there is some indication that with increasing age or perhaps tenure, one's commitment to an organization is strengthened.

With regard to work behaviors, existing research suggests that the performance of older workers varies relative to younger workers. Older male workers have lower rates of avoidable absence, but in some cases have higher rates of unavoidable absence than younger males. The latter finding may result from health problems associated with aging, or with longer recovery periods when injured. For women, an inverted-U relationship has been found in some instances between age and unavoidable absence. This may be a reflection of the role of caring for sick children. Older workers are less likely than younger workers to incur workplace accidents. This finding may reflect exposure to job hazard (Griew, 1959). Once injured, however, the older worker is disabled longer and is more likely to incur permanent disability or die from the injury, effects primarily associated with biological aging.

STAFFING, CAREER PLANNING AND DEVELOPMENT

There is a dearth of research on age in relation to recruitment, selection tests, the selection interview, performance appraisal, and person-job matching. On the basis of limited selection test validity research, there is evidence to suggest a differential validity for age groups. One form of work-sample test in particular is exhibiting validity for selecting the older worker. Because of the small number of studies of the age-selection interview and age-performance appraisal relationship, it is not clear whether negative attitudes are biasing the assessments or whether either method is a valid measure for the older worker.

Age does not appear to be related to career stage as the career-stage models imply. This finding may reflect the increasing frequency of nontraditional career paths. Career-change research reveals discrepant findings on the reasons for change. In addition, the effects of career-planning interventions are not clear because of limited program evaluation research.

A fairly substantial amount of evidence demonstrates that older workers continue to learn. Programmed teaching methodology shows promise for successfully facilitating older worker learning. Very little research, however, is available on organizational training performance and the post-training, on-the-job performance of the older worker. In very tentative terms, it appears that post-training performance levels (and tenure) are equal to or higher than those of the younger worker.

With reference to preretirement programs, there appears to be a discrepancy between the content and goals of these programs. The discrepancy may account for the inconsistent program outcomes.

COMPENSATION, PENSIONS, AND RETIREMENT

Several summary statements of age-related differences in the areas of compensation, pensions, and retirement must be made. Historically, the current group of older workers have earned significantly more money than their younger counterparts. The evidence discussed earlier seems to indicate that this differential can be explained, to a large extent, by the the differing size of the cohort groups. Due to the large size of the present group of young workers vis-à-vis the *next* group of young workers, which is much smaller, the earnings gap is likely to shrink. This may have an adverse effect on pay satisfaction for the older group.

Moreover, as workers age, their preferences for various types of compensation shift. Older workers prefer that their compensation packages provide greater retirement benefits. In order to obtain these benefits, older workers appear ready to forego a portion of their pay increases and time off.

At the present time, we have found conflicting evidence on the relationship between age and pay satisfaction. Moreover, no evidence is available on which to base judgments regarding the effectiveness of incentive systems or their ability to motivate older workers.

In the areas of pensions and retirement, an employee's decision to retire appears to be influenced most by three factors: financial status, education, and job satisfaction. Large numbers of workers do not have private pension coverage and must rely on Social Security and personal savings during their retirement years. In the case of those who enjoy both private pension coverage and Social Security, the evidence suggests that for most workers the combined income contribution from both sources will be inadequate at their date of retirement. The adequacy of retirement benefits may erode due to the effects of inflation. Although Social Security benefits are presently indexed for inflation, one must consider the extent to which employees will be willing to pay sizable tax increases to support the system.

Changes in the Social Security program, for example, on age of eligibility would greatly influence retirement practices. Other industrialized countries have permitted greated flexibility in their national retirement programs. Companies that have taken advantage of this flexibility have greatly benefited.

Organizational Implications

Although some consistent age-related differences in work attitudes and behaviors have been found, for several reasons the research provides little guidance in drawing implications for organizations. First, these differences account for a very small amount of the individual variance in attitudes and behavior. Second, the empirical research has not for the most part dealt with isolating whether the differences result from age, period, or cohort effects.

As was discussed in Chapter 2, work attitudes and behaviors are generally thought to be determined by an interaction between the individual and the environment. More specifically, to the extent that the organization rewards desired work behaviors with outcomes that either satisfy important needs or are attractive to the individual, the employee will be satisfied and thus motivated to repeat the rewarded behavior. There are age-relaged differences in needs and preferences; however, age is just one of the individual characteristics that shape needs and preferences. In fact, organizational experiences have been found to influence needs and preferences. Thus, organizational policies and practices are important determinants of work attitudes and behaviors because they not only determine the nature of the work environment but also, to some extent, influence individual needs and preferences.

Without isolating age, period, and cohort effects, it is impossible to determine the specific *causes* of age-related differences. And without knowing the causes, we cannot assume that the relationships found in the past will hold in the future. Therefore, we are cautious in drawing implications for organizations based on the existing research.

The implications touch all aspects of human resource management, including (a) personnel research; (b) organization and job design; (c) human resource planning and forecasting; (d) staffing; (e) training, career planning and development; and (f) compensation and fringe benefits.

PERSONNEL RESEARCH

Personnel research within organizations will be a particularly critical function in dealing with the uncertainties related to managing an aging work force. Personnel research will assist in finding solutions to problems and aid in evaluating the effectiveness of the personnel function. Finally, research will signal the need for changes in personnel policies and programs. Some specific types of personnel research which managers should implement are: (a) employee attitude surveys, (b) assessments of the differential effectiveness of training methods depending on age groups, and (c) assessments of career-planning methods.

Because knowledge of causes of age-related differences in job preferences, work attitudes, and work behaviors is limited, the human resource manager will periodically have to assess the needs and preferences of the employees in the organization, the degree to which these needs and preferences are being met, and the effect of discrepancies on work attitudes and behaviors. This assessment can be made through periodic organizational surveys, perhaps using survey feedback techniques and individual counseling sessions between employees and their immediate supervisor(s). Based on the feedback received, organizational policies and practices can be revised to reduce discrepancies. In this way, organizations will be able to adjust gradually to the changing character of the work force.

In view of the aging work force, training methods that have been used in the past may no longer be effective. It is important that training methods be assessed in terms of their differential validity according to age. On the basis of the results, training programs can be tailored for specific age groups in order to foster desirable outcomes.

As organizations implement career-planning programs to deal with some of the problems of an older work force, personnel research will need to be implemented to determine the effectiveness of the programs in bringing about desired outcomes. In particular, organizations may want to evaluate the effectiveness of career-planning methods in terms of forestalling obsolescence and the advent of the midlife crisis, and in maintaining high performance levels throughout one's career.

ORGANIZATION AND JOB DESIGN

The high premium placed by white collar workers of *all* age categories on fulfilling, meaningful, and enriching work, along with lower turnover rates of older workers and the importance of opportunities for advancement to younger workers, has some very specific implications for organizational development and job design strategies, as well as career pathing (see Hall, 1976; Porter et al., 1975). Organizations should examine whether the design of jobs and the organization itself provide ample opportunities for the advancement and growth of employees. Wasted human resource potential would have detrimental consequences for both the individual and the organization.

If a hierarchically structured organization with an inherent limit to opportunities cannot meet the needs of its employees, then perhaps alternative organizational arrangements are called for. Organizational redesign could be used to create a more organic, low-structured organization. This structure is most effective when individuals have relatively high skills that are widely distributed among them, and when individuals have high self-esteem and strong needs for achievement, autonomy, and self-realization (Porter et al., 1975). With rising educational levels, we would expect these types of individuals to predominate in organizations of the future, particularly those in high technology industries.

A change such as that mentioned above would also require that individual jobs be redesigned. What constitutes a "job" may need to be rethought. Rather than encouraging individuals to become more proficient at a very narrow skill, jobs and career paths might be envisioned such that they foster the development of mulitple skills. At the present time, the personnel practices of most organizations involve placing a person in a job area in which he or she performs well. As a means of recovering the organization's investment in the person, this seems logical and effective. However, the long-term result may be that the person becomes stagnant and incapable of adapting to new situations. In high technology industries, there is an increasing danger that technological change will lead to increased job obsolescence.

Much of this problem could be overcome by designing jobs which encompass multiple skills and functions such that learning may continue over a period of time. Job redesign in this manner might also be used to reduce the number of entry-level positions in organizations, and hence reduce the wage pressures identified in Chapter 6. Moreover, the practice of periodic job rotation, which would enable employees to move to new types of work requiring new learning, could be explored as a means of maintaining the flexibility of employees and encouraging the development of new skills.

Job redesign and career pathing are also indicated as strategies for solving problems associated with age-related differences in accident causation. As was pointed out in Chapter 2, as the work force ages, there may be greater pressure placed on older workers to perform jobs that make physical demands beyond their capability. Using modern technological advances, jobs may be redesigned such that the requirements for successful performance are not beyond the physical capacity of the aging worker. Moreover, career paths can be developed that consider the physical capabilities of workers at various career stages. These strategies will require that organizations study jobs carefully in order to determine the physical requirements for their successful and accident-free performance.

A most promising area for change to accommodate the "middle-age bulge" is the norm against downward movement in organizations (Hall, 1976). Admittedly, changing the norm will be difficult. There is some indication that moving into a lower-level job would be acceptable to older workers if the new job contained all the desired job changes. As another approach, rather than promotion being the only sign of one's success, movement and continual learning could be proposed as the success norm. In this manner, lateral movements would become more acceptable and valued.

There are several clear benefits to be gained from these practices. First, it gives the organization more flexibility in being able to move individuals up, down, and across, thus helping the organization to respond more effectively to internal and external needs. Another benefit is that inexperienced persons could work side-by-side with competent, experienced personnel and would thus benefit from the experienced person's years of service. It should be emphasized that these policies might apply to highly competent as well as less competent individuals.

It must be acknowledged that the proposals suggested here deviate considerably from the current practices of many organizations. However, these practices may be outmoded in dealing with the aging work force. It is necessary that current practices regarding organizational and job design be considered for their future feasibility.

HUMAN RESOURCE PLANNING AND FORECASTING

Human resource planning and forecasting will take on added importance in the future. This will be necessary to ensure an adequate supply of labor in entry-level positions, to monitor internal movements, and to reduce any uncertainty related to the wider range of retirement age.

Retirement practices will vary across organizations and between differing jobs within organizations. Through monitoring differences in retirement practices between jobs in an organization and monitoring employee health, potential retirement income, and job satisfaction (factors that have been found to be related to retirement), organizations may find it possible to predict employee attrition due to retirement. Organizations might find it beneficial, furthermore, to survey employees nearing retirement on a regular basis regarding their retirement intentions.

STAFFING

The major challenge facing organizations in making staffing decisions is that methods be used in an unbiased way. To the extent that older workers are unfairly eliminated from consideration for employment, promotion, and training to foster development, the organization misses an opportunity to utilize skills, and potentially helps to create a discouraged worker. At the same time, the New Uniform

Guidelines and recent court decisions require that organizations make assurances of organizational equal opportunity for the older worker.

Because of age-related differences in accident causation, a particularly important need in the area of selection and placement is the development of valid tests that can be used to determine the degree to which a worker is physically capable of meeting job demands. It is essential that individual workers be tested not only upon entry into the job, but also periodically.

TRAINING, CAREER PLANNING, AND DEVELOPMENT

Training may be necessary for those older workers in occupations with high rates of obsolescence, or in the case where a job-transfer strategy is indicated to relieve older workers from jobs beyond their physical capabilities. Organizations might also need to consider the possibility of retraining to develop safe job behaviors in view of declining physical capabilities. On the basis of the findings of older workers' ability to learn, there is some support for making training available to them. At the same time, it is important that organizations utilize training methods that have been found to be effective for the age group involved.

Career planning appears to be a promising activity in dealing with some of the potential problems of an aging work force. For example, career planning may help to circumvent technological obsolescence and the advent of the midcareer crisis. It may also facilitate both the maintenance of high performance levels throughout one's career and the career-change process. However, there is little information for making optimal program development decisions.

It is expected that preretirement programs will increasingly be instituted by organizations to ease the transition to retirement. These programs, including preretirement counseling, will be needed at earlier ages to prepare workers for the social, economic, and emotional impacts of retirement. The major preretirement program concern is achieving congruence between the content and goals of such programs. Evaluation research will undoubtedly produce evidence for selecting the most effective methods for achieving the desired preretirement program goals.

COMPENSATION, FRINGE BENEFITS, AND SERVICES

With a decline in supply and an increase in demand for entry-level workers, entry-level wages may be driven upward, and wage inequities between younger and older workers may result. Job redesign to reduce the number of entry-level jobs has been proposed as a potential way of dealing with this problem.

As the number of workers approaching retirement age increases, organizations will feel continued pressure to provide additional retirement benefits. One potentially satisfactory way to accomplish this, particularly in view of career-stage/life-cycle differences in pay preferences, would be through the institution of cafeteria-style fringe benefit plans.

Retirement policies and practices will become increasingly important. Optimal policies and practices will vary depending on the nature of the organization, the nature of the job, and the age composition of the work force. Companies in the United States could learn a great deal about their own potential for maximizing human resource utilization from European and Japanese experiences with phased retirement policies. Finally, the ability of organizations to manage their retirement policies will be affected by changes in the Social Security program, a factor over which they will have very little influence.

Research Method Issues

Throughout this book, we have attempted to point ou the limitations of the research studies. In this section, we will summarize the major limitations and recommend research methods to be used in future endeavors. Limitations were noted in the following areas: (a) the definition and operationalization of "age," (b) research design, (c) theoretical grounding, (d) statistical techniques, (e) populations and sample sizes, and (f) the reporting of results in articles.

DEFINITION AND OPERATIONALIZATION OF "AGE"

In nearly all studies, age was operationalized as chronological age. However, in most cases chronological age served implicitly as a proxy for various age-related phenomena. Only extremely infrequently was the concept of age defined explicitly in a study. For example, was age measuring psychological maturity, decline in physiological functioning, or personality rigidity? There are at least four kinds of age in addition to chronological age: (a) anatomical age, (b) physiological age, (c) psychological age, and (d) pathological age. It may well be that measures other than chronological age may make better proxies for these variables. It is recommended that future researchers be clear in defining which aspect of age they are studying and take care to operationalize the variable such that high construct validity results.

RESEARCH DESIGN ISSUES

The research design used almost exclusively was the cross-sectional design; that is, measures on variables are taken at one point in time. This design in many cases was inappropriate for drawing age-based conclusions because it does not permit the isolation of age, period, or cohort effects (Palmore, 1978).

The use of longitudinal panel studies (that is, measurements taken on the same group of subjects over a period of time) would enable the researcher to isolate age, period, and cohort effects. The longitudinal panel study would yield three measurable differences: (a) the longitudinal difference consisting of age and period effects, (b) the cross-sectional difference consisting of age and cohort effects, and (c) the time-lag difference consisting of the period effect minus the cohort effect (Palmore, 1978). Clearly, the use of the longitudinal panel study is called for in future research.

In assessing the effects of interventions, of training and preretirement programs as an example, incomplete designs were frequently used. Without a control group, for instance, it was difficult to determine whether changes taking place could be attributed to an intervention. It is recommended that future research for assessing the effectiveness of interventions incorporate research designs with treatment and control groups, pre- and postmeasures and, when feasible, the random assignment of subjects to conditions.

THEORETICAL GROUNDING

A major problem in much of the age-related research was that the empirical research was not grounded in theory. This was particularly true, and not at all unexpected, in cases where age was a minor variable, perhaps introduced for control purposes. However, this problem was also noted in some studies where age was the major independent variable of interest (for example, Aldag and Brief, 1977). There, the lack of theoretical grounding seemed to arise from a lack of integration across academic disciplines. In particular, organizational researchers did not appear to be grounded in the literature of the gerontology and psychology of human development. The lack of theory-based research perhaps contributed to the previously mentioned problem of the definition of age and the use of faulty research designs.

Future research efforts should be devoted to theory-building and theory-testing, with a major focus directed toward causal models of age-related differences. These models should be developed to incorporate all alternative causal explanations.

STATISTICAL TECHNIQUES

The following problems were noted with regard to statistical techniques: (a) the lack of significance testing and (b) the use of inappropriate techniques. A number of studies reported only descriptive statistics (for example, frequency distributions) and drew inferences based on these statistics. This is only appropriate when populations, rather than samples based on populations, are used.

In some instances, analysis of variance was performed based on a number of groups. However, the test statistic used provided limited information. It did not give any information as to the direction of differences. It simply meant that at least the mean response on one group is significantly different from that of another. In future research, it is recommended that appropriate multiple comparison testing procedures be used in conjunction with analysis of variance procedures.

Finally, many studies employed bivariate techniques when multivariate strategies, perhaps in conjunction with bivariate strategies, would have been more appropriate. The use of multivariate strategies allows the researcher to control for confounding variables, to examine the combined influence of several factors, and to identify interaction effects.

POPULATION AND SAMPLE SIZES

Several population and sample size issues need to be raised. First, research based on very narrowly defined populations suffers from the lack of generalizability of results outside that population. On the other hand, studies based on massed aggregated data may obscure causal explanations. Both kinds of studies, then, are necessary for purposes of internal and external validity. Finally, a major sample size problem identified in past research was that quite often there were an insufficient number of subjects in the older age categories, thus leading to problems of statistical conclusion validity.

REPORTING OF RESEARCH RESULTS

A problem of interpretation arose from the fact that quite frequently, research articles did not report the age characteristics of the sample. This was a major oversight in cases where age was the primary factor under consideration. When age characteristics were not reported, it was difficult to know whether a relationship held for all age groups or a restricted age range. Also, one did not know whether there was sufficient sample sizes in each age subgroup. In future reports, it is critical that age characteristics be noted, including mean, standard deviation, range, and number of employees in each subgroup.

Future Research Needs

Future research concerns that need to be addressed to better enable organizations to manage the aging work force are summarized below according to topical area.

CHARACTERISTICS OF THE OLDER WORKER

The most pressing need in this area is a large-scale study using both cross-sectional and longitudinal panel methodologies for the purposes of identifying causes and effects of age-related differences in work attitudes and behaviors. Examples of specific questions that need to be addressed in this study are:

- the relative influence of organizational factors versus individual characteristics on value development;
- the causes of age-related differences in work values—the importance of needs and of job characteristics;
- age differences in the causes of job dissatisfaction, which are in turn related to the components of turnover (voluntary and involuntary);
- an explanation of the underlying causal factors associated with age differences in perceptions of alternate job opportunities;
- the longitudinal effect of factors such as experience, rigidity, and the expectations of others regarding older worker performance;
- the age-absence relationship in terms of (a) the effect of work/job demands on individual health and physical functioning and the aging process, (b) composite predictors reflecting levels of family responsibility (a life-cycle approach) for women, and (c) the psychological factors affecting the age-avoidable absence relationship;
- the relationship between physiological functioning and accident liability, and an assessment of occupations in terms of their physical requirements.

STAFFING, CAREER PLANNING AND DEVELOPMENT

- the effects of various organizational recruiting practices relative to age;
- the validity of the interview and performance appraisal in terms of selection generally and also of age groups;
- the validity of person-job matching systems for the selection and placement of older workers;
- experimental studies on the outcomes of job redesign to meet age-related decline in physical capacity;
- the role of age versus job and tenure as moderators of reactions to task characteristics;
- the effects of level of career planning on factors such as personal planning skills, self-esteem, past reinforcement for career planning, and opportunities for career development;
- the effects of various work and extra-work factors on career change;
- the effects of the career planning and development process on workers in the middle and late career stages;
- the relative effectiveness of various career planning methods;
- the relative effectiveness of training methods for conveying to the older worker various types of knowledge and skills in terms of post-training behavior or performance;
- the effects of preretirement programs with different contents relative to the goals of the programs.

COMPENSATION, PENSIONS, AND RETIREMENT

- the forecasting of organizational manpower requirements to the year 2000 and beyond;
- the feasibility of job redesign for eliminating entry-level positions;
- the cost and practicability of cafeteria-style fringe benefit programs and worker preferences for them;
- updated studies on employee compensation preferences to assess the impact of inflation and recently developed fringe benefits (for example, prepaid dental and legal insurance, as well as preferences for pay increases and additional time off);
- the relationship between age and pay preferences to resolve the conflict that currently exists on this issue;
- the impact of incentive systems on the relative performance of older and younger workers;
- the measurement of and adequacy of retirement income considering the impact of inflation and Social Security indexation;

- continued model-building to delineate the interactive effects and correlates of the independent variables associated with the decision to retire;
- the identification and evaluation of the effectiveness of innovative, flexible company retirement programs in the United States;
- the retirement policies and programs in other industrialized countries;
- the factors affecting an employee's decision to retire or continue working.

To conclude, this book offers organizations and academic researchers some initial guidance for addressing the challenge of managing an aging work force. We hope our efforts will stimulate organizational planning and academic research in the directions suggested.

APPENDIX:
Summary Tables of Studies of Age in Relation to Work Variables

TABLE A-1 Studies of Age in Relation to Values

Factor-Investigator	Population	Age Characteristics	n	Statistical Technique	Results
Work ethic					
Aldag and Brief (1977)	manufacturing operatives	mean = 36 range = 18-64	131	correlation	positive (r = .305**, two-tailed)
	janitorial and food service workers in hospital	mean = 33 range = 18-60	129	correlation	positive (r = .333**, two-tailed)
	police officers	mean = 35 range = 21-36	75	correlation	positive (r = .204, p < .10, two-tailed)
Buchholz (1978)	union leaders, managers and blue and white collar employees	<29 = 169 30-49 = 339 50+ = 294	802	Student-Newman-Keuls multiple comparisons test	negative (p < .05)
Cherrington et al. (1979)	diverse occupations in 53 manufacturing companies	not given	3053	correlation	positive (r = .296)
				stepwise multiple regression	positive (ΔR^2 = .088, F = 143.625**)

Desire to work

Study	Sample	Age	N	Analysis	Results
Vecchio (1980)	employed, full time males representative of work force	21-34 = 425 35-44 = 246 45-54 = 244 55-64 = 157 65+ = 27	1099	t-test of % differences over time discriminant analysis	decrease in desire to work for every age group except 35-44 over time negative (strongest predictor, signif. level not reported)

Pride in craftsmanship

Study	Sample	Age	N	Analysis	Results
Cherrington et al. (1979)	diverse occupations in 53 manufacturing companies	not given	3053	correlation stepwise multiple regression	positive ($r = .156$) positive ($\Delta R^2 = .024$, $F = 41.474**$)
Taylor and Thompson (1976)	diverse occupations in government, hospital, and private sales and service organizations (male = 58%)	< 30 = 49.6% 30-39 = 16.7% 40-49 = 16.1% 50-64 = 18.0%	1058	one-way ANOVA	n.s. $F = 2.12$

(continued)

TABLE A-1 Studies of Age in Relation to Values (continued)

Factor-Investigator	Population	Age Characteristics	n	Statistical Technique	Results
Upward striving					
Cherrington et al. (1979)	diverse occupations in 53 manufacturing companies	not given	3053	correlation	n.s. (r = .012)
				stepwise multiple regression	n.s. $\Delta R^2 = .00$, F = .073)
Intrinsic rewards					
Taylor and Thompson (1976)	diverse occupations in government, hospital, and private sales and service organizations (male = 58%)	< 30 = 49.6% 30-39 = 16.7% 40-49 = 16.1% 50-64 = 18.0%	1058	one-way ANOVA	negative (F = 5.44**)
Importance of money (extrinsic rewards)					
Taylor and Thompson (1976)	diverse occupations in government, hospital, and private sales and service organizatoins (male = 58%)	< 30 = 49.6% 30-39 = 16.7% 40-49 = 16.1% 50-64 = 18.0%	1058	one-way ANOVA (no comparison testing of cell means)	negative (F = 10.92***)

| Cherrington et al. (1979) | diverse occupations in 53 manufacturing companies | not given | 3053 | correlation | significance level not reported ($r = -.075$) |
| | | | | stepwise multiple regression | negative ($\Delta R^2 = .008$, $F = 11.356**$) |

Importance of friends over work

| Cherrington et al. (1979) | diverse occupation in 53 manufacturing companies | not given | 3053 | correlation | significance level not reported ($r = -.059$) |
| | | | | stepwise multiple regression | negative ($\Delta R^2 = .005$, $F = 10.605**$) |

Acceptability of welfare

| Cherrington et al. (1979) | diverse occupations in 53 manufacturing companies | not given | 3053 | correlation | significance level not reported ($r = -.128$) |
| | | | | stepwise multiple regression | negative ($\Delta R^2 = .016$, $F = 29.745**$) |

(continued)

TABLE A-1 Studies of Age in Relation to Values (continued)

Factor-Investigator	Population	Age Characteristics	n	Statistical Technique	Results
Ecosystem distrust					
Taylor and Thompson (1976)	diverse occupations in government, hospital, and private sales and service organizations (male = 58%)	< 30 = 49.6% 30-39 = 16.7% 40-49 = 16.1% 50-64 = 18.0%	1058	one-way ANOVA	n.s. (F = 2.06)
				two-way ANOVA testing interaction between age and occupational status	positive (F = 3.55*)
Self-expression					
Taylor and Thompson (1976)	diverse occupations in government, hospital, and private sales and service organizations (male = 58%)	< 30 = 49.6% 30-39 = 16.7% 40-49 = 16.1% 50-64 = 18.0%	1058	one-way ANOVA	negative (F = 3.67**)

Organizational belief system

Buchholz (1978)	union leaders, managers, and blue and white collar employees	<29 = 169 30-49 = 339 50+ = 294	802	Student-Newman-Keuls multiple comparisons test	n.s.

Marxist-related beliefs

Buchholz (1978)	union leaders, managers, and blue and white collar employees	<29 = 169 30-49 = 339 50+ = 294	802	Student-Newman-Keuls multiple comparisons test	negative (p < .05)

Humanistic beliefs

Buchholz (1978)	union leaders, managers, and blue and white collar employees	<29 = 169 30-49 = 339 50+ = 294	802	Student-Newman-Keuls multiple comparisons test	n.s.

Leisure

Buchholz (1978)	union leaders, managers, and blue and white collar employees	<29 = 169 30-49 = 339 50+ = 294	802	Student-Newman-Keuls multiple comparisons test	n.s.

*p < .05
**p < .01
***p < .001

TABLE A-2 Studies of Age in Relation to Growth Need Strength

Investigator	Population	Age Characteristics	n	Statistical Technique	Results
Hackman and Oldham (1976)	Blue collar, white collar and professional employees in business organizations	not given	658	correlation	negative (r = -.15*)
Aldag and Brief (1977)	manufacturing operatives	range = 18-64 mean = 36	131	correlation	negative (r = -.217**)
	janitorial and food service workers in hospital	range = 18-60 mean = 33	129	correlation	n.s. (r = -.112)
	correctional officers and youth counselors	range = 21-64 mean = 41	104	correlation	n.s. (r = -.052)
	police officers	range = 21-56 mean = 35	75	correlation	n.s. (r = .023)
Holley et al. (1978)	female paraprofessional program assistants	mean = 51.1	326	mean difference tests high age = 57+ low age = <47	n.s. on six items

Study	Sample	Age	N	Method	Result
Alderfer and Guzzo (1979)	students and managers	18-22 = 104 23-27 = 42 28-32 = 32 33-35 = 16 36-39 = 14 40-45 = 9 46+ = 12	229	ANOVA	negative (F = 1.85, p < .10)
Evans et al. (1979)	supervisors and managers in auto assembly plant		81	correlation	negative (r = -.14*, two-tailed)
Warr et al. (1979)	male blue collar manufacturing employees	median = 40 range = 20-64	590	correlation	n.s. (r = -.09)
Cook and Wall (1980)	male blue collar manufacturing employees	median = 41 range = 20-64	260	correlation	negative (r = -.29***)

*p < .05
**p < .01
***p < .001

TABLE A-3   Studies of Age in Relation to Overall Job Satisfaction

Investigator	Population	Age Characteristics	n	Statististical Technique	Results
Handyside (1961)	male factory and office workers in five British firms	not given	730	median percentile technique	curvilinear (decreases to 35 and increases to 63), significance level not reported
	female factory and office workers	not given	270	median percentile technique	curvilinear (decreases to 23 and increases to 59), significance level not reported
Saleh and Otis (1964)	male managerial employees in organization with compulsory retirement age of 65	60-65	80	chi square	retrospective satisfaction increases to 50-59 and decreases in 60-65 period (p < .001)
	male managerial employees in organization with compulsory retirement age of 65	50-55	38	chi square	retrospective satisfaction increases to 50-59 and anticipated satisfaction decreases in 60-65 period (p < .001)

Study	Sample	Age	N	Analysis	Result
Gibson and Klein (1970)	blue collar employees of Southern U.S. plant—predom. female	<24, 25-39, 40+ not given	385	two-way ANOVA (no testing of all mean differences)	positive ($F = 12.11^{**}$)
	male blue collar manufacturing employees in 18 plants	<24, 25-39, 30-39, 40-49, 50+ not given	1682	two-way ANOVA (no testing of all mean differences)	positive ($F = 6.51^{**}$)
				partial correlation (controlling for tenure)	positive ($r_p = .25^{**}$)
Aldag and Brief (1975)	manufacturing operatives	range = 18-64 mean = 36	122	mean difference test	older workers more satisfied, $p < .05$
	public sector service agency employees	range = 21-64 mean = 41	99	mean difference test	n.s.
Hunt and Saul (1975)	male Australian white collar government employees	16-25 = 1,017; 26-35 = 790; 36-49 = 812; 50+ = 634	3338	multiple regression	positive linear ($B = .20^{*}$)
				correlation	positive (range of $r = .11^{*}$ to $.28^{*}$ for 5 tenure groups)
	female Australian white collar government employees	16-25 = 344; 26-35 = 107; 36+ = 99	579	multiple regression controlling for tenure	n.s.
				correlation	n.s. for 5 tenure groups

(continued)

TABLE A-3 Studies of Age in Relation to Overall Job Satisfaction (continued)

Investigator	Population	Age Characteristics	n	Statististical Technique	Results
Siassi et al. (1975)	male and female assembly workers (male = 75%)	<29 = 88 30-39 = 98 40-49 = 161 50-59 = 174 60+ = 37	558	chi square	workers over 30 more satisfied than under 30 ($p < .01$), satisfaction increases with age
				chi square controlling for tenure	workers over 40 more satisfied than under 40 (significance level not reported)
Stagner (1975)	male automobile assembly line workers	<29 = 51.5% 30+ = 48.4%	more than 200	chi square	positive ($p \leqslant .001$)
Glenn et al. (1977)	1972, 1973, 1974 representative sample of full-time employed white males	not given	1080	correlation	positive ($r^2 =$ .035***, .032***, .037*** for 1972, 1973, 1974)
				partial correlation with reward variables held constant	positive ($r^2 =$ .023**, .023**, .027*** for 1972, 1973, 1974)

		partial correlation with reward variables and education held constant	positive (r^2= .019***, .027**, .013* for 1972, 1973, and 1974
1972, 1973, 1974 representative sample of full-time employed females	not given	461	correlation	positive (r^2= .097***, .048** for 1972 and 1974)
			partial correlation with reward variables held constant	n.s. (r^2 = .004 for 1973); positive (r^2 = .094** and .050** for 1972 and 1974); n.s. (r^2 = .008 for 1973)
			partial correlation with reward variables and education held constant	positive (r^2= .062** and .048** for 1972 and 1974); n.s. (r^2 = .008 for 1973)
Near et al. (1978)	household probability sample in Buffalo representative of demographic characteristics of U.S.	not given	1041	one-way ANOVA	positive (E^2 = .07, F = 13.17**)
			multiple classification analysis for occupational level	unadjusted Eta = .29; adjusted Eta = .27

(continued)

213

TABLE A-3 Studies of Age in Relation to Overall Job Satisfaction (continued)

Investigator	Population	Age Characteristics	n	Statistical Technique	Results
Weaver (1978)	1972, 1973, 1974 representative samples of employed white males	not given	1232	correlation	positive linear (r = .193***, .179***, .193***, .188*** for 1972, 1973, 1974 and overall mean, respectively)
	1972, 1973, 1974 representative sample of full-time employed white males	not given	1232	multiple regression controlling for occupational prestige, family income, marital status, supervisory position, work, autonomy, religious intensity and education	positive linear (B = .131* for 1972; B = .129** for overall) n.s. (B = .125 and .130 for 1973 and 1974)
Weaver (1978)	1972, 1973, 1974 representative sample of full-time employed white females	not given	518	correlation	positive (r = .293***, .212**, and .190*** for 1972, 1974, and overall) n.s. (r = .066 for 1973)

				multiple regression	
Staines and Quinn (1979)	1969 national household sample of employed workers (Survey of Working Conditions)	< 21 = 97 21-29 = 333 30-44 = 489 55-64 = 210 65+ = 55	1969	not reported	positive (B = .242* and .182*** for 1972 and overall); n.s. (B = .131 and .173 for 1973 and 1974)
					(1) positively related to age in all 3 samples (significance level not reported)
	1973 national household sample of employed workers (Quality of Employment Survey)	< 21 = 173 21-29 = 568 30-44 = 634 45-54 = 422 55-64 = 248 65+ = 41	1455	not reported	(2) overall decrease in job satisfaction for older workers since 1969; no change for those under 21 (significance level not reported)
Staines and Quinn (1979) (continued)	1977 national household sample (Quality of Employment Survey)	< 21 = 203 21-29 = 594 30-44 = 759 45-54 = 389 55-64 = 271 65+ = 45		not reported	

(continued)

215

TABLE A-3 Studies of Age in Relation to Overall Job Satisfaction (continued)

Investigator	Population	Age Characteristics	n	Statististical Technique	Results
Weaver (1980)	representative sample of noninstitutionalized civilian population	18+	4709	Scheffe method for mean differences of age categories, <20, 20-29, 30-39, 40-49, 50+	(1) positive in each of 7 years—1972-1978 (significance level not reported)
					(2) positive in combining years (significance level not reported)
					(3) no improvement or worsening of job satisfaction for any age group across the 7-year period except 1972 versus 1974 < 20 age group

O'Brien and Dowling (1981)	1/2% household sample from Adelaide, Australia (male = 56%)	15-19 = 8.9% 20-24 = 16.2% 25-34 = 24.7% 35-44 = 21.6% 45-54 = 18.8% 55-59 = 6.3% 60+ = 3.5%	1383	correlation	positive (r = .14***); positive (r = .115***), male sample; positive (r = .193***), female sample
				one-way ANOVA	positive ($p < .01$)
				partial correlation controlling for aging variables	positive (r_p = .154***) positive (r_p = .099**), male sample positive (r_p = .224**), female sample
				partial correlation controlling for cohort variables	positive (r_p = .139***); positive (r_p = .135***), male sample; positive (r_p = .160***), female sample

(continued)

TABLE A-3 Studies of Age in Relation to Overall Job Satisfaction (continued)

Investigator	Population	Age Characteristics	n	Statististical Technique	Results
				partial correlation controlling for aging and cohort variables	positive ($r = .085^{**}$); n.s. ($r_p = .046$), male sample; positive ($r_p = .135^{**}$), female sample
					----

$^*p < .05$
$^{**}p < .01$
$^{***}p < .001$

TABLE A-4 Studies of Age in Relation To Satisfaction with Work Itself

Investigator	Population	Age Characteristics	n	Statistical Technique	Results
Hulin and Smith (1965)	male electronics workers in two plants	equal n from each age group	99 86	multiple regression controlling for tenure + 4 other variables	linear (B = .21 & .18) significance level not reported (overall R, p < .01)
	female electronics workers in two plants	equal n from each age group	35 40	multiple regression controlling for tenure + 4 other variables	linear (B = .05 & .03) significance level not reported (overall R, n.s.)
Gibson and Klein (1970)	blue collar employees of plant located in South—predominantly female	< 24 25-39 not 40+ given	385	two-way ANOVA (no testing of mean differences)	positive (F = 12.12**)
	male blue collar manufacturing employees in 18 plants	not given	1682	two-way ANOVA (no testing of mean differences)	positive (F = 4.68**)
				partial correlation controlling for tenure	positive (r_p = .18*)

TABLE A-4 Studies of Age in Relation to Satisfaction with Work Itself (continued)

Investigator	Population	Age Characteristics	n	Statistical Technique	Results
Altimus and Tersine (1973)	male blue collar employees in glass plant	<25 = 32 26-35 = 16 36+ = 15	63	Kruskal-Wallis one-way ANOVA Mann-Whitney U	significant ($p < .05$) <25 significantly less satisfied than other two groups ($p < .05$)
Herman et al. (1975)	non-unionized printing company employees	not given	392	canonical correlation	positive—older male workers who were primary wage earners were most satisfied with their work
				part canonical analysis controlling for organization structure influences	positive—older, poorly educated, married males were involved in their work and satisfied with it
Hunt and Saul (1975)	female Australian white collar government employees	16-25 = 344 26-35 = 107 36+ = 99	550	multiple regression controlling for experience	positive linear ($B = .15*$)

Study	Sample	Age	N	Analysis	Result
	male Australian white collar government employees	16-25 = 1017 26-35 = 790 36-49 = 812 50+ = 634	3253	multiple regression (controlling for experience)	positive linear ($p = .28$*)
Newman (1975)	insurance company employees at all hierarchical levels (male = 196)	not given	710	correlation discriminant analysis	positive ($r = .40$***) positive ($\chi^2 = .30$)
Schwab and Heneman (1977a)	female blue collar operatives	mean = 36.7 s.d. = 11.3	177	partial correlation controlling for experience correlation within 16 experience subgroups	n.s. ($r_p = .12$) n.s., proportion of positive r's = .69
	male blue collar operatives	mean = 33.4 s.d. = 13.4	96	partial correlation controlling for experience correlation within 10 experience subgroups	positive linear ($r = .32$**) positive (proportion of positive r's = 1.00**)
Muchinsky (1978)	employees in diverse occupations in public utility	18-29 = 246 30-39 = 156 40-49 = 168 50+ = 96	666	Scheffe's test on age categories	18-29 group less satisfied with work than other groups

(continued)

221

TABLE A-4 Studies of Age in Relation to Satisfaction with Work Itself (continued)

Investigator	Population	Age Characteristics	n	Statistical Technique	Results
Hom (1979)	part-time employees in stores, plants, and office of retail sales organization	not given	10003	canonical correlation	positive (canonical correlation = .45**); nonstudent, older or married part-time worker showed greater satisfaction with work
James and Jones (1980)	nonsupervisory employees in diverse work environments (male = 83.4%)	mean = 36.6	642	correlation two-stage least squares regression analysis controlling for educational level and three other variables	positive (r = .21**) positive (B = .13**)

*p < .05
**p < .01
****p < .001

TABLE A-5 Studies of Age in Relation To Satisfaction with Promotions

Investigator	Population	Age Characteristics	n	Statistical Technique	Results
Hulin and Smith (1965)	male electronics workers in two plants	equal n from each age group	99 86	multiple regression controlling for tenure + 4 other variables	(B = .00 & -.15, significance level not reported) (overall R, n.s. & p < .01)
	female electronics workers in two plants	equal n from each age group	35 40	multiple regression controlling for tenure + 4 other variables	(B = .05 and .01, significance level not reported) (overall R, n.s. and p < .05)
Altimus and Tersine (1973)	male blue collar employees in glass plant	<25 = 32 26-35 = 16 36+ = 15	63	Kruskal-Wallis one-way ANOVA	n.s.
				Mann-Whitney U	n.s.
Hunt and Saul (1975)	female Australian white collar government employees	16-25 = 344 26-35 = 107 36+ = 99	579	multiple regression controlling for experience	negative (B = -.19*)
	male Australian white collar government employees	16-25 = 1017 26-35 = 790 36-49 = 812 50+ = 634	3338	multiple regression controlling for experience	negative (B = -.21*)

(continued)

TABLE A-5 Studies of Age in Relation to Satisfaction with Promotions (continued)

Investigator	Population	Age Characteristics	n	Statistical Technique	Results
Newman (1975)	insurance company employees at all hierarchical levels (male = 196)	not given	710	correlation	n.s. (r = -.04)
Schwab and Heneman (1977a)	female blue collar operatives	mean = 36.7 s.d. = 11.3	177	partial correlation controlling for experience	n.s. (r_p = -.08)
				correlation within 16 experience subgroups	n.s. (proportion of positive r's = .50)

male blue collar operatives	mean = 33.4 s.d. = 13.4	96	partial correlation controlling for experience	n.s. ($r_p = .07$)
			correlation within 10 experience subgroups	n.s. (proportion of positive r's = .50)
Muchinsky (1978)	employees in diverse occupations in public utility	18-29 = 246 30-39 = 156 40-49 = 168 50+ = 96	666	Scheffe's test for post hoc analysis	negative monotonic relationship (significance level not reported)

*p < .05
**p < .01
***p < .001

TABLE A-6 Studies of Age in Relation to Satisfaction with Supervision

Investigator	Population	Age Characteristics	n	Statistical Technique	Results
Hulin and Smith (1965)	male electronic plant workers in two plants	equal n from each age group	99 86	multiple regression controlling for tenure + 4 other variables	(B = .13 and .28; significance level not reported) (overall R, n.s.)
	female electronic plant workers in two plants	equal n from each age group	35 40	multiple regression controlling for tenure + 4 other variables	(B = −.02 and −.31; significance level not reported) (overall R, n.s.)
Gibson and Klein (1970)	blue collar employees of Southern U.S. plant—predominantly female	24 25-39 40+ not given	385	two-way ANOVA (no testing of cell mean differences)	significant (positive) (F = 17.11**)
	male blue collar manufacturing employees in 18 plants	24 25-29 30-29 40-49 50+ not given	1682	two-way ANOVA (no testing of mean differences)	significant (positive) (F = 4.20*)
				partial correlation controlling for experience	positive (r_p = .20**)

Study	Sample	Age	N	Method	Result
Altimus and Tersine (1973)	male blue collar employees in glass plant	25 = 32 26-35 = 16 36+ = 15	63	Kruskal-Wallis one-way ANOVA	n.s.
				Mann-Whitney U	n.s.
Hunt and Saul (1975)	female Australian white collar government employees	16-25 = 344 26-35 = 107 36+ = 99	579	multiple regression controlling for experience	n.s.
	male Australian white collar government employees	16-25 = 1017 26-35 = 790 36-49 = 812 50+ = 634	3338	multiple regression controlling for experience	positive ($B = .11*$)
				multiple regression controlling for experience	curvilinear–U shaped ($R = .03*$)
Newman (1975)	insurance company employees at all hierarchical levels (male = 196)	not given	710	correlation	positive ($r = .12**$)
Schwab and Heneman (1977a)	female blue collar operatives	mean = 36.7 s.d. = 11.3	177	partial correlation controlling for experience	n.s. ($r_p = -08$)
				correlations within 16 experience subgroups	n.s. (proportion of positive r's = .55)

(continued)

TABLE A-6 Studies of Age in Relation to Satisfaction with Supervision (continued)

Investigator	Population	Age Characteristics	n	Statistical Technique	Results
Schwab and Heneman (1977a)	male blue collar operatives	mean = 33.4 s.d. = 13.4	96	partial correlation controlling for experience	n.s. (r_p = .11)
				correlation within 10 experience subgroups	n.s. (proportion of positive r's = .60)
Muchinsky (1978)	employees in diverse occupations in public utility	18-29 = 246 30-39 = 156 40-49 = 168 50+ = 96	666	Scheffe's test for post hoc analysis	n.s.

*p < .05
**p < .01
***p < .001

TABLE A-7 Studies of Age in Relation to Satisfaction with Co-Workers

Investigator	Population	Age Characteristics		n	Statistical Technique	Results
Hulin and Smith (1965)	male electronics workers in two plants	equal n from each age group		99 86	multiple regression controlling for tenure + 4 other variables	(B = .05 and .07, significance level not reported) (overal R, n.s.)
	female electronics workers in two plants	equal n from each age group		35 40	multiple regression controlling for tenure + 4 other variables	(B = .11 and –.20, significance level not reported) (overall R, n.s.)
Gibson and Klein (1970)	blue collar employees of Southern U.S. plant–predominantly female	24 25-39 40+	not given	385	two-way ANOVA (no testing of cell mean differences)	positive (F = 5.35**)
	male blue collar manufacturing employees in 18 plants	24 25-39 30-39 40-49 40+	not given	1682	two-way ANOVA (no testing of cell mean differences)	positive (F = 4.59**)
					partial correlation controlling for experience	positive (r = .09**)

(continued)

TABLE A-7 Studies of Age in Relation to Satisfaction with Co-Workers (continued)

Investigator	Population	Age Characteristics	n	Statistical Technique	Results
Altimus and Tersine (1973)	male blue collar employees in glass plant	25 = 32 26-35 = 16 36+ = 15	63	Kruskal-Wallis one-way ANOVA	n.s.
				Mann-Whitney U	n.s.
Hunt and Saul (1975)	female Australian white collar government employees	16-25 = 344 26-35 = 107 36+ = 99	579	multiple regression controlling for experience	n.s.
	male Australian white collar government employees	16-25 = 1017 26-35 = 79 36-49 = 812 50+ = 634	3338	multiple regression controlling for experience	positive (B = .10*)
				multiple regression controlling for experience	curvilinear U-shaped (Δ R = .03*)
Newman (1975)	insurance company employees at all hierarchical levels (male = 196)	not given	710	correlation	positive (r = .13**)

Study	Sample		N	Method	Result
Schwab and Heneman (1977a)	female blue collar operatives	mean = 36.7 s.d. = 11.3	177	partial correlation controlling for experience	n.s. (r = .06)
				correlation within 16 experience subgroups	n.s. (proportion of positive r's = .50)
	male blue collar operatives	mean = 33.4 s.d. = 13.4	96	partial correlation	n.s. (r = .07)
				correlation within 10 experience subgroups	n.s. (proportion of positive r's = .60)
Muchinsky (1978)	employees in diverse occupations in public utility	18-29 = 246 30-39 = 156 40-49 = 168 50+ = 96	666	Scheffe's test for post hoc analysis	50+ less satisfied than other groups

*p < .05
**p < .01
***p < .001

TABLE A-8 Studies of Age In Relation to Job Involvement

Investigator	Population	Age Characteristics	n	Statistical Technique	Results
Gurin et al. (1960)	employed males	21-34 = 292 35-44 = 237 45-54 = 208 55+ = 185	922	frequency distribution	n.s. (no significance testing)
Lodahl and Kejner (1965)	nursing personnel engineers	not given not given	137 70	correlation correlation	positive n.s.
Schwyhart and Smith (1972)	male middle managers	mean = 32.4 under 40	149	correlation	positive ($r = .18*$)
	male middle managers	mean = 34.6 under 40	50	correlation	n.s. ($r = .16$)
Hall and Mansfield (1975)	nonmanagerial scientists and engineers in 1967	20-34 = 103 35-49 = 151 50+ = 30	290	correlation	positive ($r = .29**$, two-tailed)
	nonmanagerial scientists and engineers in 1969	20-34 = 41 35-49 = 40 50+ = 8	90	correlation	positive ($r = .40**$)
Herman et al. (1975)	non-unionized printing company employees	not given	392	canonical correlation	positive ($r^2 = $ .08 of criterion variance), significance level not reported

Study	Sample	Age	N	Analysis	Result
Jones et al. (1975)	civil service and military engineering employees	mean = 38 range = 17-65	112	correlation	positive (r = .36**)
Newman (1975)	insurance company employees (male = 196)	not given	710	correlation	positive (r = .40***)
				discriminant analysis (6 age categories)	positive (significance level not reported)
Schuler (1975)	manufacturing employees at all job levels	not available	325	correlation	positive (r = .24, significance level not reported)
Mannheim (1975)	Israeli employed males at all job levels	not available	not available	not available	n.s.
Aldag and Brief (1977)	manufacturing operatives	range = 18-64, mean = 36	131	correlation	positive (r = .260**, two-tailed)
Aldag and Brief (1977)	janitorial and food service workers in hospital	range = 18-60 mean = 33	129	correlation	positive (r = .260**, two-tailed)
	correctional employees	range = 21-64 mean = 41	104	correlation	positive (r = .295***)
	police officers	range = 21-56 mean = 35	75	correlation	n.s. (r = .127)

(continued)

TABLE A-8 Studies of Age in Relation to Job Involvement (continued)

Investigator	Population	Age Characteristics	n	Statistical Technique	Results
Rabinowitz et al. (1977)	Canadian government employees in diverse occupations (male = 76%)	< 35 = 44% 36-50 = 37% 50+ = 19%	332	correlation	positive ($r = .30^{**}$), significance level not reported
				stepwise MR	n.s. ($F = 2.01$) (length of service one predictor)
Saal (1978)	blue and white collar manufacturing employees (diverse occupations) (male = 197)	mean = 41.3 s.d. = 13.0 range = 19-64	218	correlation	positive ($r = .34^{*}$).
				stepwise MR	positive $\Delta r^2 = .09$), significance level not reported
Stevens et al. (1978)	supervisors in federal government agencies (male = 84%)	not given	634	correlation	positive ($r = .177^{***}$)

Reitz and Jewell (1979)	Industrial workers in U.S. (male = 124)	not given	372	Spearman rank order correlation	positive (r = .21*)
	Turkey (male = 465)	not given	575		positive (r = .13*)
	Mexico (male = 315)	not given	487		positive (r = .27*)
	Yugoslavia (male = 242)	not given	478		n.s. (r = .08)
	Thailand (male = 158)	not given	254		positive (r = .16*)
	Japan (male = 519)	not given	716		positive (r = .35*)
Warr et al. (1979)	male blue collar manufacturing employees	median = 40 range = 20-64	590	correlation	n.s. (r = .04)
Blumberg (1980)	male coal miners	70% = 21-36 30% = 43-63	54	correlation	positive (r = .40***)
James and Jones (1980)	nonsupervisory employees in diverse work environments (male = 83.4%)	mean = 36.6	642	correlation	positive (r = .21***)
Hammer et al. (1981)	nonsupervisory employees in employee-owned firm	mean = 46.7	112	correlation	positive (r = .28**)

*p < .05
**p < .01
***p < .001

TABLE A-9   Studies of Age in Relation to Internal Work Motivation

Investigator	Population	Age Characteristics	n	Statistical Technique	Results
Hall and Mansfield (1973)	professional scientists and engineers in 1967	20-34 = 36% 35-49 = 52% 50+ = 10%	290	correlation one-way ANOVA	positive (r = .15*) positive (F = 3.11*)
	professional scientists and engineers in 1969	20-34 = 46% 35-49 = 44% 50+ = 9%	90	correlation one-way ANOVA	positive (r = .26*) positive (F = 4.64*)
Aldag and Brief (1977)	manufacturing operatives	range = 18-64 mean = 36	131	correlation	positive (r = -.159, p < .10)
	correctional officers and youth counselors	range = 21-64 mean = 41	104	correlation	n.s. (r = -.005)
	police officers	range = 21-56 mean = 35	75	correlation	positive (r = .235**)
Warr et al. (1979)	male blue collar manufacturing employees	median = 40 range = 20-64	590	correlation	positive (r = .17***)

*p < .05
**p < .01
***p < .001

TABLE A-10 Studies of Age In Relation to Organizational Commitment

Investigator	Population	Age Characteristics	n	Statistical Technique	Results
Lee (1971)	Public health service scientific	not given	170	stepwise multiple regression mean differences test	n.s. (4 analyses) positive (p < .01)
Sheldon (1971)	employees and supervisors, scientists and engineers	<40 = 63 40+ = 38	102	gamma test	positive (Gamma = .56) erratic
Hrebiniak (1974)	professional and nonprofessional mental health employees	not given	46	correlation	positive (r = .401***)
Steers (1977)	hospital employees, including administrators, registered nurses, LPNs, service and clerical employees	mean = 35	382	stepwise multiple regression	positive (B = .16, F = 19.07***) (tenure a competing variable)
	research scientists and engineers	mean = 38	119	stepwise multiple regression	n.s. (tenure a competing variable)

(continued)

TABLE A-10 Studies of Age in Relation to Organizational Commitment (continued)

Investigator	Population	Age Characteristics	n	Statistical Technique	Results
Aldag and Brief (1977)	janitorial and food service hospital workers	range = 18-60 mean = 33	129	correlation	positive ($r = .339**$, two-tailed)
	police officers	range = 21-56 mean = 35	75	correlation	n.s. ($r = .150$)
Kidron (1978)	insurance company clerical employees and supervisors (female = 70%)	mean = 25.7 s.d. = 10.3	237	correlation	positive (moral and calculative commitment) ($p < .05$)
	hospital employees, including female nurses, secretaries, supervisors, maintenance staff, housekeeping	mean = 36.6 s.d. = 13.3	75	correlation	positive (moral and calculative commitment) ($p < .05$)
	personnel specialists (male = 80%)	not given	41	correlation	n.s.
Stevens et al. (1978)	supervisors in federal government agencies (male = 84%)	not given	634	correlation	positive ($r = .117**$)
				multiple regression	n.s. ($B = .04$) positive ($B = .09*$)

Study	Sample	Age	N	Method	Result
Cook and Wall (1980)	male British blue collar manufacturing employees	median = 41 range = 20-64	260	correlation	positive (r = .28***)
Martin (1980)	service-oriented business organization's with diverse occupational characteristics (male = 34%)	not given	172	correlation	n.s. (r = −.14)
Morris and Steers (1980)	nonfaculty employees of U.S. university (male = 40%)	mean = 37.30 s.d. = 12.12	262	correlation	positive (r = .30***)
Angle and Perry (1981)	bus company employees and managers (male = 82%)	not given	1340	correlation	positive (r = .17***)
Hammer et al. (1981)	nonsupervisory employees in employee-owned firms	mean = 46.7	112	correlation	positive (r = .33***)
Jamal (1981)	Canadian hospital nurses (female = 97%)	mean = 31	440	correlation	positive (r = .15**)
Morris and Sherman (1981)	employees in diverse occupations in state government agency	mean = 33.16 s.d. = 8.47	506	correlation multiple regression	positive (r = .31***, two-tailed) positive (B = .11**)

(continued)

TABLE A-10 Studies of Age in Relation to Organizational Commitment (continued)

Investigator	Population	Age Characteristics	n	Statistical Technique	Results
Welsch and LaVan (1981)	professional, technical, and administrative employees in VA medical center	not given	141	correlation	positive ($r = .2812$***)
Arnold and Feldman (1982)	Canadian chartered accountants	mean = 37	654	correlation	positive ($r = .24$***)
Bluedorn (1982)	insurance company employees (female = 94%)	mean = 27.48 s.d. = 10.06	141	correlation multiple regression path analysis	positive ($r = .15$**) n.s. (B = −.07) positive (path coefficient = .12, $p < .05$)
Michaels and Spector (1982)	community mental health center employees	not given	112	correlation path analysis	positive ($r = .28$*) positive (path coefficient = .23)

*p < .05
**p < .01
***p < .001

TABLE A-11 Studies of Age In Relation to Turnover Intentions

Investigator	Population	Age Characteristics	n	Statistical Technique	Results
Waters et al. (1976)	nonsupervisory female clerical employees in insurance company	not given	105	correlation	negative (r = .27**)
Mobley et al. (1978)	service, technical, clerical and nursing service hospital employees	mean = 35.3 s.d. = 13.4	203	correlation	negative (r = -.36**)
				multiple regression (age-tenure composite)	negative (B = -.12*)
Evans et al. (1979)	supervisors and managers in auto assembly plant (male = 98%)	range = 30-35	343	correlation	n.s. (r = .06)
Gupta and Beehr (1979)	employees with occupational and demographic characteristics similar to national sample	not given	651	multiple regression with tenure included in analysis	negative (B = -.19**)

(continued)

TABLE A-11 Studies of Age in Relation to Turnover Intentions (continued)

Investigator	Population	Age Characteristics	n	Statistical Technique	Results
Martin (1979)	service-oriented business organizations with diverse occupational char. (male = 34%)	not given	177	correlation	negative $(r = -.30)$
Miller et al. (1979)	national guard members	mean = 28.61 s.d. = 6.34	235	multiple regression	negative $(B = -.25^*)$
				correlation	negative $(r = -.49^{**})$
		mean = 27.00 s.d. = 4.24	225	correlation	negative $(r = -.29^{**})$
Rousseau (1978)	employees in broadcasting firm (male = 35%)	range = 17-60 mean = 30	271	correlation	negative $(r = -.29^{**})$
Martin and Hunt (1980)	design bureau employees in state highway department	not given	80	correlation	negative $(r = -.26)$
				path analysis	n.s., direct effect
	construction bureau employees in state highway department	not given	239	correlation	n.s. $(r = -.04)$

242

Study	Sample		N	path analysis	n.s., direct or indirect effect
Jamal (1981)	Canadian hospital nurses (female = 97%)	mean = 31	440	correlation	negative (r = −.08*)
	manufacturing employees	mean = 35	383	correlation	negative (r = −.11**)
Arnold and Feldman (1982)	Canadian chartered accountants	mean = 37	654	correlation	negative (r = −.26***)
				hierarchical regression analyses	negative (B = −.13*)
Bluedorn (1982)	insurance company employees (female = 94%)	mean = 27.48 s.d. = 10.06	141	correlation	n.s. (r = −.15)
Michaels and Spector (1982)	community mental health center employees	not given	112	correlation	positive (r = .27*)
Zey-Ferrell (1982)	nonadministrative university faculty	not given	230	correlation	positive (r = .209***)
				stepwise multiple regression	entered 17th of 164 variables (R² = .045, significance level not reported)

*p < .05
**p < .01
***p < .001

TABLE B-1 Studies of Age in Relation to Performance

Investigator	Population	Age Characteristics	n	Statistical Technique	Results
Bowers (1952)	male and female industrial workers from a large corporation (unskilled up to minor executives)	18-76	3162	percentages	per performance appraisal ratings, performance was not related to age; new hires aged >45 up to 60 were appraised favorably.
Lehman (1953)	individuals in science; medicine, surgery, and related fields; philosphy; music; art; literature	lifetime	>10,000	frequencies	peak of creative achievement (outstanding works) occured most often during the 30s and fell off slowly; earlier decline in output for more recently born group; peaking occurred earlier in abstract disciplines (mathematics, theoretical physics) and later in empirically based disciplines (geology, biology)
Smith (1953)	male skilled, unskilled, and clerical workers	range = 18-76 (19% ≥ 60 47% ≥ 44)	903	frequencies and means	mean efficiency evaluations show little change with age (for the 18-44 age group up to the 45 group) and between occupational groups
Dennis (1954)	psychologists plus members of National Academy of Sciences	≥70	43 and 44, respectively	correlation	early in career, contributors continue to contribute until at least 70; psychologists reached maximum rate of publication in the 40s while NAS members reached it in the 30s

Maher (1955)	manufacturing: supervisory personnel	≥ 50 years = 87 ≤ 35 years = 114	201	frequencies and means	no significant differences for supervisory personnel per performance ratings
	sales personnel		129	correlations	older sales personnel were slightly better performers
Clay (1956)	male skilled printing workers	20 ≥ 60	63	means	a slight decline in performance with age from about ≥ 50 years; variability in performance increased with age, but older group contained best overall performers
King (1956)	female skilled sewing machinists	15-60	294	means and Tau-ranked correlations	production data showed older workers performed as well as other age groups with the exception of the peak performers, who were ages 27-31
Mark (1956)	male and female production workers in 8 manufacturing firms (footwear and men's clothing incentive workers)	<25-64	2200	output indices	no significant difference until age 55-64, when productivity dropped slightly for men (but not women)
Mark (1957)	male and female incentive production workers in 22 companies (footwear and wooden furniture)	25-65+	5100	output indices	on output data covering 4-12 weeks over a 2-year period, employees over 55 and under 25 produced less than those from 25-54

(continued)

TABLE B-1 Studies of Age in Relation to Performance (continued)

Investigator	Population	Age Characteristics	n	Statistical Technique	Results
Breen and Spaeth (1960)	male factory worker matched pairs from age groups: (1) 40-45 yrs and (2) 60-65 yrs, plus matched on place of work and occupation	see population information	132	means and variances	no significant differences in mean productivity or variance in production
Kutscher and Walker (1960)	incentive office workers in 5 federal agencies and 21 private companies (15% male)	<25 >65	6000	frequencies	on basis of output data covering periods of 4-13 weeks, output per manhour differences among age groups was essentially insignificant, but there was considerable output variation within age groups. older workers were more accurate and capable of steadier output; only workers ≥ 65 in footwear and furniture mfg. showed declines
Greenberg (1961)	Bureau of Labor Statistics study of factory and office workers	<25 >65	5594	frequencies	among office workers, no general decline in average performance; among factory workers, decline in performance after age 44, but decline was small in age group 45-54, larger in age group 55-64, and fairly significant for >65

Walker (1964)	mail sorters in U.S. Postal Service	<25>60	6000	frequencies	on basis of an Index of Performance (production score divided by the average production score of all workers aged 35-44 doing similar work in the city), older workers performed at a steadier rate, with less variation from week to week than workers in younger age groups except for a slight decrease for the 55-59 age group; little decline in performance to age 60, and only minor decline up to age 65
Roe (1965)	male research scientists from biological, physical, and social sciences	47-73	45	frequencies	based on complete bibliographies, men have continued to contribute to a high level; peak production of publications occurred anywhere from the first to the ninth 5-year period after receipt of Ph.D., with modes in the second and sixth 5-year periods
Klores (1966)	professional, nonprofessional, clerical, and supervisory employees in a chemical research division	not provided	>100	Kendal Tau correlations	age was not related to performance rating using forced distribution format
Pelz and Andrews (1966)	scientist-professors, scientists and engineers, plus government laboratory research personnel	<30>55	144 526	frequencies	pioneering discoveries were most likely to occur in late 30s and early 40s, plus another peak 10-15 years later

(continued)

247

TABLE B-1 Studies of Age in Relation to Performance (continued)

Investigator	Population	Age Characteristics	n	Statistical Technique	Results
Pelz and Andrews (1966)			641		the strongly motivated, especially those with strong self-reliance, resisted the normal erosion with age; suggestion that performance could vary with kind of research climate
Dennis (1968)	men of scholarship (from 1660-1900), sciences, and arts who lived to age ≥ 79	studied between ages 20-80	738	frequencies	output curve for those in arts rose earlier and declined earlier and more severely than for those in scholarship and sciences; scholars and scientists reached their peak in their 40s-60s
Dalton and Thompson (1971)	design and development engineers in six organizations	21>55	2500	frequencies	ratings of performance rose up to age 31-35, declined after age 36-40, but job complexity rose and fell in the same manner; more variability in ratings within age categories than between them
Chown (1972)	males and females in three occupational settings and two laboratory tasks	17-65	234	Tau, Spearman's rank order, and Pearson correlations	for the five separate investigations, correlations (r = .26 to .43) were smaller than those for rigidity and performance

Arvey and Mussio (1973)	female civil service clerical workers	age >50 = 67 and <24 = 70	137	t-test	on basis of supervisory ratings, no job performance difference between groups
Clemente (1973)	members of American Sociological Association in 1970; publications examined for 1940-1970	--	2205	regression	standardized partial coefficient = -.39; early publication activity related to subsequent productivity
Matthews and Cobb (1974)	journeymen air traffic controllers	<30>51	613	correlations, regression, and ANOVA	per performance appraisal ratings, age negatively related to performance when controlling for experience; partial $r = .35$
Schwab and Heneman (1977b)	piece rate employees (82% female)	25% <25, 25% >45, mean = 36.3	124	partial correlation coefficients	on work tasks requiring a fair amount of manual dexterity, older workers no more or less productive than younger after differences in experience taken into account ($r = .04$)
Holley et al. (1978)	females—Cooperative Extension service para-professional program assistants	mean = 51.1	362	means	performance ratings were higher for the > 57 age group than the < 47 group on every performance factor and job characteristic except "keeps personal files in order and up to date"

(continued)

TABLE B-1 Studies of Age in Relation to Performance (continued)

Investigator	Population	Age Characteristics	n	Statistical Technique	Results
Cole (1979)	male and female scientists in Ph.D.-granting institutions (random sample drawn from a 1969 American Council on Education study listing)	<35>60	not given	frequencies, means	on the basis of cross-sectional and longitudinal data, age has a slight curvilinear effect on the quality of published work; scientists >45 slightly less likely to publish high-quality research than those <45
Eisenberg (1980)	sewing machine operators, examiners and materials handlers in large garment manufacturing plant (73% female)	<25>65	171	Pearson correlations	for sewing machine operators (a speed job), examiners, and materials handlers, age related to piece rate earnings (r's = −.21, +.29, and +.48, respectively)

| Cleveland and Landy (1981) | exempt managerial employees from two divisions of a large manufacturing organization; two samples | 21-65 22-64 | 513 178 | canonical, correlation, t-tests | age generally accounted for only 1-4% of performance dimension variance; influence of age found in 2 out of 8 performance dimensions; older ratees (ages 45-65) received lower ratings than middle-aged (35-44) and younger ratees (21-34) on self-development and inter-personal skills |
| Stumpf and Rabinowitz (1981) | full-time business school faculty members of a large northwestern university | mean = 41.1 | 102 | correlations | $r = -.30$, $p < .01$; with age, research productivity (number of working papers written in past 3 years) declined; $r = .20$, $p < .05$; age related to positive peer performance assessments |

TABLE B-2 Studies of Age in Relation to Unavoidable Absence

Investigator	Population	Age Characteristics	n	Statistical Technique	Results
Buzzard and Shaw (1952)	British male workers in 28 industrial establishments	< 20 = 51 21-25 = 105 26-30 = 242 31-35 = 301 36-40 = 548 41-45 = 626 46-50 = 693 51-55 = 866 56-60 = 735 61+ = 579	4746	frequency distributions	positive: average days lost increase with age (no significance testing)
Kossoris (1948)	male industrial workers	< 20 = 78 20-24 = 464 25-29 = 1162 30-34 = 1966 35-39 = 1961 40-44 = 1980 45-49 = 2118 50-54 = 2545 55-59 = 2225 60-64 = 1378 65-69 = 505 70-74 = 126	16508	frequency distributions	negative to 60-64; increases slightly for 65-74 (no significance testing)

Study	Sample	Age distribution	N	Statistic	Findings
	female industrial workers	< 25 = 50 20-24 = 190 25-29 = 232 30-34 = 169 35-39 = 205 40-44 = 168 45-49 = 133 50-54 = 96 55-59 = 66	1309	frequency distribution	fairly stable: slight increase to age 39, then fluctuates (no significance testing)
Shepherd and Walker (1957)	British male iron and steel workers and engineering workers	< 20 = 56 25-34 = 366 35-44 = 442 45-54 = 428 55-64 = 201 65+ = 33	1526	cross-sectional frequency distribution	u-curve: % shift lost lowest for 35-44; higher for <25-34, and 45-54, highest for 55+ (no significance testing)
Tucker and Lotz (1957)	supervisory, office, clerical, trades, and manual employees in public utility	2/3 under age 35	10052	frequency distributions	positive (significance not reported)
Naylor and Vincent (1959)	female clerical workers	<31 >32 range = 18-58	220	chi square test	n.s.

(continued)

TABLE B-2 Studies of Age in Relation to Unavoidable Absence (continued)

Investigator	Population	Age Characteristics	n	Statistical Technique	Results
Baumgartel and Sobol (1959)	male blue collar workers	range = 18-60+	2487	Kendall's tau	n.s. (significance level not required)
	male white collar workers	range = 18-47	565	correlation	positive
	female white collar workers	range = 18-47	698		positive
	female blue collar workers	range = 18-47	148		positive
de la Mare and Sergean (1961)	male industrial workers	16-25 = 20 26-35 = 51 36-45 = 34 46-59 = 35	140	cross-sectional frequency distribution	positive (significance level not reported)
				longitudinal frequency distribution	positive (significance level not reported)
Sellett (1964)	female factory workers	<45 = 61% >45 = 39% range = 18-64	88	mean difference test	n.s. (two measures)

254

Cooper and Payne (1965)	British male manufacturing workers (three samples)	mean = 54.44 s.d. = 4.29	89	longitudinal frequency distribution	positive (two measures) (no significance testing)
		mean = 52.58 s.d. = 7.11	147	longitudinal frequency distribution	positive, n.s. (two measures) (no significance testing)
		mean = 58.06 s.d. = 4.80	156	longitudinal frequency distribution	positive, n.s. (two measures) (no significance testing)
Hill (1967)	British production workers	mean = 25 16-30 31-40 not 41-50 given 51-65	100	frequency distribution	positive (no significance testing)
Martin (1971)	British male light engineering workers	not given	44	chi square test	positive (p < .025)
	British female light engineering workers	not given	34	chi square test	positive (p < .05)

(continued)

TABLE B-2 Studies of Age in Relation to Unavoidable Absence (continued)

Investigator	Population	Age Characteristics	n	Statistical Technique	Results
Weaver and Holmes (1972)	female government employees	<30 not given 30-39 40-49 50-59	286	percentages/ age measured by decades	positive (no significance testing)
Flanagan et al. (1974)	industrial workers		group data	multiple regression	n.s.
Beatty and Beatty (1975)	Black female hard-core unemployed white collar	mean = 26.15 s.d. = 8.32	20	multiple regression	positive (p < .01) at 6 mos.; n.s. at 24 mos.
Nicholson and Goodge (1976)	British female blue collar food processing workers	low age not given mid age high age	303	correlation	n.s. (r = .01 and r = −.05, two measures)
Garrison and Muchinsky (1977)	white collar workers (females = 179)	mean = 34.75	195	correlation	positive (paid absence) (r = .17**) negative (unpaid absence) (r = .33**)

			N	Test	
Nicholson et al. (1977)	British female sewing machine operators (four samples)	not given	145 65 96 101	correlation	n.s. (r = .05) n.s. (r = .18) n.s. (r = -.03) n.s. (r = .12)
		not given	145 65 96 101	part correlation	n.s. (r_p = .05) n.s. (r_p = .21) n.s. (r_p = .11) n.s. (r_p = .12)
		< 19 19-25 26-35 not 36-45 given 46-55 > 55	407	Neuman-Keuls test	inverted-U (high absence, 26-35; low absence, >46)
	British male foundry workers (four samples)	not given	102 58 62 20	correlation	n.s. (r = -.08) n.s. (r = -.19) n.s. (r = .04) n.s. (r = .06)
			102 58 62 20	part correlation	n.s. (r_p = -.16) n.s. (r_p = -.15) n.s. (r_p = .14) n.s. (r_p = -.31)

(continued)

TABLE B-2 Studies of Age in Relation to Unavoidable Absence (continued)

Investigator	Population	Age Characteristics	n	Statistical Technique	Results
Nicholson et al. (1977)		< 19	242	Neuman-Keuls test	n.s.
		19-25			
		26-35 not			
		36-45 given			
		46-55			
		> 55			
	British male	not given	73	correlation	n.s. ($r = -.18$)
	continuous		61		n.s. ($r = -.07$)
	process workers		87		n.s. ($r = .08$)
	(four samples)		82		n.s. ($r = -.01$)
		not given	73	part correlation	n.s. ($r_p = -.16$)
			61		n.s. ($r_p = -.15$)
			87		n.s. ($r_p = -.16$)
			82		n.s. ($r_p = -.11$)
		< 19	303	Neuman-Keuls test	U-curve (high absence, <36, >56; low absence, 46-55)
		19-25			
		26-35 not			
		36-45 given			
		46-55			
		> 55			

Study	Sample	Age	N	Analysis	Results
Nicholson et al. (1977)	British male bus company workers (four samples)	not given	76	correlation	n.s. ($r = -.07$)
			63		n.s. ($r = .00$)
			58		n.s. ($r = .11$)
			73		n.s. ($r = .03$)
			76	part correlation	n.s. ($r_p = .08$)
			63	part correlation	n.s. ($r_p = -.11$)
			58	part correlation	n.s. ($r_p = .07$)
			73	part correlation	n.s. ($r_p = -.10$)
		< 19 19-25 26-35 not 36-45 given 46-55 > 55	270	Neuman-Keuls test	n.s.
Ilgen and Hollenbeck (1977)	female clerical workers	not given	166	correlation	n.s., negative ($r = -.06$, $-.20**$, and $-.23**$, three measures)
Johns (1978)	operative employees in manufacturing company (male = 76%)	not given	208	correlation subgroup analysis	negative ($r = -.12*$); age did not moderate relationship between absence and job attitudes and characteristics
				multiple regression	age was one of five best predictors (significance level not reported)

(continued)

TABLE B-2 Studies of Age in Relation to Unavoidable Absence (continued)

Investigator	Population	Age Characteristics	n	Statistical Technique	Results
Blumberg (1980)	male coal miners	21-36 = 70% 43-63 = 30%	54	Spearman correlation	negative (r = −.33**)
Constas and Vichas (1980)	hourly workers in American-based Puerto Rican electronics assembly plant (females = 86%)	mean = 32.54 s.d. = 7.65	50	multiple regression	negative (B = −.315*)
	skilled and semi-skilled employees in petrochemical company (male = 97%)	mean = 34.8 s.d. = 19.01	120	multiple regression	n.s. (B = −.064)
Spencer and Steers (1980)	clerical and service workers in hospital	mean = 37	200	correlation partial correlation	negative (r = −.17*) negative (r_p = −.23**)
Hammer et al. (1981)	nonsupervisory employees in employee-owned firm	mean = 46.7	112	correlation	n.s. (r = .06)
			96	hierarchical regression analysis	negative (B = −.0644, Δ R^2 = .04*)

Watson (1981)	production employees in small manufacturing firm	not given	116	correlation	negative (r = −.26*)
				multiple regression (full model with 13 variables)	n.s. (B = −.15)
				multiple regression (reduced model with 10 variables)	negative (B = −.24*)
				multiple regression (reduced model with 8 variables)	n.s. (B = −.16)
				multiple regression (female)	n.s. (B = −.13)
				multiple regression (male)	n.s. (B = −.05)
				stepwise regression	age was fourth variable to enter

TABLE B-3 Studies of Age In Relation to Avoidable Absence

Investigator	Population	Age Characteristics	n	Statistical Technique	Results
Tucker and Lotz (1957)	male supervisory, office, clerical, trades, and manual employees in public utility	2/3 under age 35	8752	frequency distribution	negative (significance tests not reported)
Baumgartel and Sobol (1959)	male blue collar workers	range = 18-60+	2428	Kendall's tau correlation	n.s. (significance level not reported)
	male white collar workers	range = 18-47	565	Kendall's tau correlation	positive (significance level not reported)
	female white collar workers	range = 18-47	698	Kendall's tau correlation	positive (significance level not reported)
	female blue collar workers	range = 18-47	148	Kendall's tau correlation	n.s. (significance level not reported)
de la Mare and Sergean (1961)	male industrial workers	16-25 = 20 26-35 = 51 36-45 = 34 46-59 = 35	140	cross-sectional (no significance testing)	curvilinear (decrease to 45; increase after 45)
				longitudinal frequency distribution	groups maintain frequency pattern over time

Study	Sample	Age	N	Method	Result
Isambert-Jamati (1962)	French male industrial workers	15-19 20-24 25-29 30-39 40-49 50-54 55-59 60-64 > 64 not given	4352	frequency distribution	inverted-U (significance level not reported)
	French female industrial workers		3967	frequency distribution	inverted-U (significance level not reported)
Sellett (1964)	female factory workers	< 45 = 61% > 45 = 39% range = 18-64	88	mean difference test	negative (p < .01)
Hammer et al. (1981)	nonsupervisory employees in employee-owned firm	mean = 46.7	112 96	correlation hierarchical regression	n.s. (r = -08) n.s. (B = -.0176) ΔR^2 = .00
Cooper and Payne (1965)	male manufacturing workers (three samples)	mean = 54.44 s.d. = 4.29	89	longitudinal frequency distribution	positive (two measures) (no significance testing)
		mean = 52.58 s.d. = 7.11	147	longitudinal frequency	n.s. (two samples) (no significance testing)
		mean = 58.06 s.d. = 4.80	156	longitudinal frequency distribution	positive, n.s. (two measures) (no significance testing)

(continued)

TABLE B-3 Studies of Age in Relation to Avoidable Absence (continued)

Investigator	Population	Age Characteristics	n	Statistical Technique	Results
Hill (1967)	British production workers (three samples)	mean = 25 16-30 31-40 not given 41-50 51-65	100	frequency distribution (no data presented)	negative (no significance testing)
Froggatt (1970)	British employees in light engineering company	not given	1500	multiple regression	negative (in 4 out of 8 study groups, including one female sample) (p < .05)
				curvilinear regression	cubic term significant in 1 of 8 samples
	British male employees in light engineering company	not given	140	multiple regression	negative (B = -.102***)
	British female employees in light engineering company	not given	83	multiple regression	n.s. (B = .027)
	British female government employees	not given	454	multiple regression	n.s. (B = -.033) negative (B = -.009*)
	male Northern Ireland government employees	not given	211	multiple regression	n.s., two samples (B = -.024 and +.001)

Martin (1971)	British male light engineering workers	not given	48	chi square test	negative (p < .05)
	British female light engineering workers	not given	42	chi square test	negative (p < .01)
Nicholson and Goodge (1976)	British female blue collar food processing workers	low age mid age high age not given	303	correlation	(r = -.01, -.05) negative (two measures)
Bernardin (1977)	male blue collar sales workers	mean = 23.8 mean = 22.97	57 52	correlation	negative (r = -.24 and -.34) (significance level not reported)
Ivancevich and McMahon (1977)	maintenance technicians in urban manufacturing co.	mean = 40.3	141	correlation	n.s. (r = -.12)
Nicholson et al. (1977)	British female sewing operatives (four samples)	not given	145	correlation	positive (r = .19* and r = .20*, two measures)
			65	correlation	n.s. (r = .15 and r = .12, two measures)
			96	correlation	negative (r = -.27* and r = -.30**, two measures)
			101	correlation	n.s. (r = -.12 and r = -.09, two measures)

(continued)

TABLE B-3 Studies of Age in Relation to Avoidable Absence (continued)

Investigator	Population	Age Characteristics	n	Statistical Technique	Results
Nicholson et al. (1977)		not given	145	part correlation	n.s. ($r_p = .14$ and $r_p = .12$, two measures)
			65	part correlation	n.s. ($r_p = .18$ and $r_p = .15$, two measures)
			96	part correlation	n.s., negative ($r_p = -.18$ and $r_p = -.23*$, two measures)
			101	part correlation	n.s. ($r_p = -.09$ and $r_p = -.04$, two measures)
		< 19 19-25 26-35 not 36-45 given 46-55 > 55	407	Neuman-Keuls test	n.s.
	British male foundry workers (four samples)	not given	102	correlation	negative ($r = -.34***$ and $r = -.33***$, two measures)
			58	correlation	negative ($r = -.37**$ and $r = -.34**$, two measures)

		N	Method	Result
		62	correlation	n.s. (r = -.11 and r = .17, two measures)
		20	correlation	n.s. (r = .19 and r = -.10, two measures) negative (r_p = -.28**)
	not given	102	part correlation	negative (r_p = -.28** and r_p = -.28**, two measures)
		58	part correlation	negative (r_p = -.29* and r_p = -.26*, two measures)
		62	part correlation	n.s. (r_p = -.05 and r_p = -.12, two measures)
		20	part correlation	negative, n.s. (r_p = -.51* and r_p = -.30, two measures)
	< 19 19-25 26-35 36-45 46-55 > 55 not given	242	Neuman-Keuls test	linear (high absence, <26; low absence, >46, two measures)
British male continuous process workers (four samples)	not given	73	correlation	negative, n.s. (r = -.25* and r = -.18, two measures)
		61	correlation	negative (r = -.48*** and r = -.43***, two measures)

(continued)

TABLE B-3 Studies of Age in Relation to Avoidable Absence (continued)

Investigator	Population	Age Characteristics	n	Statistical Technique	Results
Nicholson et al. (1977)		not given	87	correlation	n.s., negative ($r = -.17$ and $r = -.22$*, two measures)
			82	correlation	n.s. ($r = -.15$ and $r = -.10$, two measures)
			73	part correlation	negative, n.s. ($r_p = -.27$* and $r_p = -.18$, two measures)
			61	part correlation	negative ($r_p = -.34$** and $r_p = -.27$*)
			87	part correlation	n.s. ($r_p = -.14$ and $r_p = -.19$, two measures)
			82	part correlation	n.s. ($r_p = -.20$ and $r_p = -.05$, two measures)
		19 19-25 26-35 not 36-45 given 46-55 55	303	Neuman-Keuls test	linear (high absence, <26; low absence, >36, two measures)

(continued)

British male bus company workers (four samples)	not given	76	correlation	negative (r = -.47*** and r = -.48***, two measures)
		63	correlation	negative (r = -.41*** and r = -.46***, two measures)
		58	correlation	negative (r = -.38** and r = -.43***, two measures)
		73	correlation	negative (r = -.55*** and r = -.54***)
	not given	76	part correlation	n.s. (r_p = -.12 and r_p = -.16, two measures)
		63	part correlation	negative (r_p = -.33** and r_p = -.34**, two measures)
		58	part correlation	negative (r_p = -.45*** and r_p = -.46***, two measures)
		73	part correlation	negative (r_p = -.26* and r_p = -.26*, two measures)
	< 19 / 19-25 / 26-35 / 36-45 / 46-55 / > 55 not given	270	Neuman-Keuls test	linear (high absence, <26; low absence, >46 and >36, two measures)

TABLE B-3 Studies of Age in Relation to Avoidable Absence (continued)

Investigator	Population	Age Characteristics	n	Statistical Technique	Results
Johns (1978)	operative employees in manufacturing co. (male = 76%)	not given	208	correlation	negative (r = -.15*)
				subgroup analysis	age as moderator between absence and job attitudes and characteristics
				multiple regression	n.s. age was one of 5 best predictors (significance level not reported)

Rousseau (1978)	broadcasting company and employees (male = 35%)	mean = 30 range = 17–60	271	correlation	negative (r = –.27**)
Stumpf and Dawley (1981	bank tellers (1970–1976)	mean = 25.92 s.d. = 9.68	354	canonical correlation	negative (r = –.29, significance level not reported)
				correlation	n.s. (r = –.07)
	bank tellers (1977–1978)	mean = 25.10 s.d. = 8.55	242	correlation	negative (r = –.13*)

*p < .05
**p < .01
***p < .001

TABLE B-4 Studies of Age In Relation to Turnover

Investigator	Population	Age Characteristics	n	Statistical Technique	Results
Minor (1958)	female clerical workers	range 16-42 (at application)	440	Wherry-Gaylord test selection techniques using multiple predictors	negative (significance level not reported)
Fleishman and Berniger (1960)	female clerical workers	< 20 = 26 21-25 = 42 26-30 = 6 31-35 = 10 35+ = 36 (at application)	205	judgmental weighting using multiple predictors	negative (no significant individual factors)
Shott et al. (1963)	male office workers	not given	212	weighted application blank analysis	n.s.
	female office workers	not given older = 24+	349		negative (no significance testing for individual factors)
Ley (1966)	male factory workers	not given	200	mean difference test	negative (t = 2.68**)

Bassett (1967) (reported in Porter and Steers, 1973)	technicians and engineers	not available	200	not available	negative
Downs (1967)	public service organization employees (during training)	range = 20-60 <35 = 1203 35+ = 1036	2238	percentage loss	positive (no significance testing)
	public service organization employees (after training)				negative (no significance testing)
Farris (1971)	scientists and engineers in two organizations	not given	362	percentage test (% under 35 staying versus leaving)	negative (p < .05)
		categorical	203		negative (p < .05)
Robinson (1972)	female clerical workers	not given	200	weighted application blank; t-test; 20-25 and 30+	negative (p < .05)

(continued)

273

TABLE B-4 Studies of Age in Relation to Turnover (continued)

Investigator	Population	Age Characteristics	n	Statistical Technique	Results
Taylor and Weiss (1972)	discount store employees (female = 75%)	not given	475	mean difference test	negative (p < .01)
				discriminant analysis	discriminant weight = -.04 (8th largest weight of 11 variables)
Mangione (1973) (reported in Mobley, Griffeth, et al., 1979)	ISR diverse occupational sample	not available	294	chi square	negative (p < .001)
				multiple regression	negative (tenure in analysis)
Porter et al. (1974)	psychiatric technicians	not given	60	mean differences test	negative (p < .01)
Waters et al. (1976	female insurance company clerical workers	not given (at test admin.)	105	correlation	negative (r = -.25*)
				Wherry test selection	n.s.
Marsh and Mannari (1977)	Japanese electrical co. employees (male = 50%)	not given	1033	correlation	negative (r = -.22**)

Study	Sample	Age	N	Analysis	Result
Katz (1978)	public sector employees (male = 68%)	mean = 41	3085	correlation	negative (r = -.44**)
Mobley et al. (1978)	service, technical, clerical, and nursing service hospital employees	mean = 35.3, s.d. = 13.4 (at test admin.)	203	correlation	negative (r = -.22**)
				multiple regression	age-tenure composite n.s. (B = -.10)
Mowday et al. (1978)	female clerical employees in insurance office	mean = 27	157	stepwise regression	n.s. (B = -.09)
	female clerical employees in insurance office	mean = 27	157	stepwise regression	n.s. (did not enter stepwise solution)
Sheridan and Vredenburgh (1978)	female registered nurses, LPNs, and nurses aides	range = 19-65, mean = 34, s.d. = 11.31	216	correlation	r = -.19 (significance level not reported)
				multiple regression	n.s. (three analyses)
Gupta and Beehr (1979)	employees with occupational and demographic characteristics similar to national sample (male = 51%)	< 30 = 43% (at test admin)	615	multiple regression with tenure included in analysis	negative (B = -.28**)

(continued)

TABLE B-4 Studies of Age in Relation to Turnover (continued)

Investigator	Population	Age Characteristics	n	Statistical Technique	Results
Miller et al. (1979)	National Guard members	mean = 28.61 s.d. = 6.34	235	correlation	negative ($r = -.43$**, two-tailed)
		mean = 27.00 s.d. = 4.24	225	correlation	negative ($r = -.32$**, two-tailed)
Mobley, Hand, et al. (1979)	male Marine Corp recruits	mean = 18.85 s.d. = 1.52	1521	mean difference test	n.s.
				stepwise multiple regression	n.s. ($\Delta R^2 = .003$) (significance level not reported)
Wanous et al. (1979)	blue collar workers (male = 59%)	mean = 32.6 s.d. = 12.3	1736	part correlation	n.s. (voluntary turnover)($r_p = .07$)
				multiple regression	n.s. (voluntary turnover) ($\Delta R^2 = .004$)
				part correlation	n.s. (involuntary turnover) $r_p = -.03$)
				multiple regression	n.s. (involuntary turnover) ($\Delta R^2 = .002$)

Study	Sample	Age	N	Method	Result
Williams et al. (1979)	male and female unskilled service workers	< 30 = 47% > 30 = 53%	668	percentage differences in stayers and leavers	negative (p < .001)
Spencer and Steers (1980)	clerical and service workers in hospital	mean = 37	200	correlation partial correlation	n.s. ($r = -.06$) n.s. ($r_p = .02$)
Koch and Rhodes (1981)	female sewing machine operators	mean = 26-30	135	correlation hierarchical regression	n.s. ($r = -.04$) n.s. ($B = -.14$)
Stumpf and Dawley (1981)	bank tellers	mean = 25.92 s.d. = 9.68	354	correlation	negative, voluntary ($r = -.26$**) and involuntary ($r = -.21$**) turnover
				hierarchical regression	significant, voluntary ($\Delta R^2 = .051$**) and involuntary ($\Delta R^2 = .031$**) turnover
	bank tellers	mean = 25.10 s.d. = 8.55	242	correlation	n.s., voluntary ($r = -.11$) and negative, involuntary ($r = -.18$*)

(continued)

TABLE B-4 Studies of Age in Relation to Turnover (continued)

Investigator	Population	Age Characteristics	n	Statistical Technique	Results
Arnold and Feldman (1982)	Canadian chartered accountants	mean = 37	654	correlation	negative (r = -.22)
				hierarchical regression analysis	n.s.
Bluedorn (1982)	insurance company employees (female = 94%)	mean = 27.48 s.d. = 10.06	141	correlation	negative (r = -.24) (significance level not reported)
				path analysis	negative (path coefficient = -.20*)
Michaels and Spector (1982)	community mental health center employees	not given	112	correlation	nonsignificant (r = .00)
				path analysis	indirect relationship to turnover through organizational commitment and job satisfaction

*p < .05
**p < .01
**p < .001

TABLE B-5 Studies of Age in Relation to Accident Frequency

Investigator	Population	Age Characteristics	n (n accidents)	Statistical Technique	Results[1]
Hewes (1921)	male silk mill workers	< 15 to 65+ (small n in upper age groups)	2,891 (868)	frequency distribution	negative
	female silk mill workers	<15 to 65+ (small n in upper age)	1,819 (353)	frequency distribution	negative
Newbold (1926)	male factory workers in 22 industries	mean = 35-40	6,938	correlation	negative (24 out of 24) modal r = -.2
				partial correlation for length of service	negative (little change in age-accident relation)
	female factory workers in 22 industries	mean = 19-22	2,024	correlation	negative (13 out of 14 cases) modal r = -.2
Barkin (1933)	65 New York manufacturers	<20-65+	18,092 (282)	frequency distribution	negative
	four railroad repair shops	<20-65+	3,244 (66)	frequency distribution	negative curvilinear (increases to 31-34, then decreases)

(continued)

TABLE B-5 Studies of Age in Relation to Accident Frequency (continued)

Investigator	Population	Age Characteristics	n (n accidents)	Statistical Technique	Results [1]
Kossoris (1940)	male workers in two public utilities and two manufacturing companies (1937)	<21-60+	26,058 (634)	frequency distribution	<30 and 60+ had higher rates than those 30-55
	workers in Wisconsin during 1919-1938	18-65+	not reported	frequency distribution	negative 65+ < 45-64 < 20-44
	workers in Milwaukee during 1919-1938	<20-70+		frequency distribution	negative
Klebba (1941)	urban labor market in U.S.–employed workers, 1935-36	16+	784,717 (7,560)	frequency distribution	positive for injury causing disability of 7+ days (for total, and male and female subgroups)
Mann (1944)	male ordnance depot employees	17-60+	1,318 (792)	frequency distribution	negative
	female ordnance depot employees	17-60+	725 (219)	frequency distribution	curvilinear (decreases to 28-35, increases 35-45, 45-60)
Vernon (1945)	male coal-face workers	<20-60+	18,000	frequency distribution	curvilinear (decreases to 30-39, then rapidly increases with age)

Study	Population	Age	Sample size	Method	Finding
Padley (1947)	male workers in national health insurance population in Scotland	<20–60+	not reported	frequency distribution	negative
	single women workers in national health insurance population in Scotland	<20–60+	not reported	frequency distribution	curvilinear (decreases 30–44, increases sharply at 45+)
Kossoris (1948)	workers in 109 manufacturing plants	<20–74	17,800	frequency distribution	curvilinear for nondisabling injuries (increases to 25–29, then decreases steadily)
Sutherland et al. (1950)	male workers in two factories	15–55+	3,954	frequency distribution	negative (decreases with age in each factory)
	female workers in two factories	15–55+	331	frequency distribution	negative (decreases with age in each factory)
Heinz (1953)	production employees in Heinz plant	<24 = 200 25–34 = 460 35–44 = 620 45–54 = 440 55–64 = 280	2,000 (20)	frequency distribution	curvilinear (decreases to 45–54; increases for 55–64)
Whitfield (1954)	male coal miners	22–58+	1,384	comparison of observed and expected frequency of accidents by occupation within age groups	n.s.

(continued)

TABLE B-5 Studies of Age in Relation to Accident Frequency (continued)

Investigator	Population	Age Characteristics	n (n accidents)	Statistical Technique	Results[1]
Van Zelst (1954)	copper plant employees in operating division	not given	1,237	mean difference	negative (controlling for experience)
King (1955)	agricultural workers in Wales and England	15-80	(1,991)	frequency distribution	accident distribution between observed and expected not different except under−21 age group with lower proportion of accidents
Schulzinger (1956)	records of industrial accidents in general medical practice	15-75	(35,000)		accident rate peaks at 21, then decreases steadily with age
Griew (1959)	blue collar occupations in piston factory	21-28 = 460 29-36 = 657 37-44 = 758 45-52 = 717 53-60 = 510 61+ = 342	3,444 (268)	chi square	accident rate increases with age for electrician ($p < .05$); miller ($p < .05$); grinder ($p < .05$); these three jobs are ones in which younger workers are normally employed n.s. for turner, fitter (skilled and unskilled), inspector, laborer, and storekeeper

Surry (1969)	Canadian reported industrial accidents	<14-55+	not reported	frequency distribution	major discrepancies between observed and expected accident frequency occur in the 45-52 age group rather than 52, suggesting that selection occurs before the age of 52 is reached
Barrett et al. (1977)	utility company vehicle drivers	25-64	75	correlation	curvilinear; accident rate peaks at 20-25 and thereafter decreases (1) Positive relation between age and accidents ($r = .36**$) (2) Age positively correlated with information processing measures and reaction time measures
Simonds and Shafai-Sahrai (1977)	11 matched pairs of industrial firms	not reported	80-650 employees	Wilcox on matched pairs, signed rank test (bivariate)	Age positively realted to better saftey records ($p < .10$)
Chelius (1979)	U.S. injured employees 1948/49 and 1969/70 (Bureau of Labor Statistics)	not given	not given	multiple regression	positive relationship between increase in % of work force in 18-35 age group and increase in injury rates (i.e., decreases with age)

(continued)

TABLE B-5 Studies of Age in Relation to Accident Frequency (continued)

Investigator	Population	Age Characteristics	n (n accidents)	Statistical Technique	Results[1]
Root (1981)	1977 workers' compensation records from 30 states	16-65+	1 million	frequency distribution (work injury ratio)	negative (work injury ratio highest for ages 20-24 and lowest for those 65 and over)

$**p \leq .01$

1. Unless specifically indicated, reported results are not based on significance testing. Moreover, in many cases, significance testing is not necessary, as the results are based on population rather than sample data.

TABLE B-6 Studies of Age in Relation to Other Accident Variables

Factor Investigator	Population	Age Characteristics	(n accidents)	Statistical Technique	Results [1]
Duration of disability					
Stevens (1929)	male and female factory workers as reported to Bureau of Workmen's Compensation	<20-60+	(4,828)	tabled means	(1) average increase in length of disability to 50-59; then slight drop off at 60+, but *not* back to pre-50 level
				correlation	(2) positive for 5 of 6 types of injury (r = .90** for all injuries)
Barkin (1933)	New York State male employees with compensated accidents in 1929	not reported	(83,635)	frequency distribution	positive (average length of disability increased with age)
Kossoris (1940)	male workers in two public utilities and two manufacturing companies during 1937	<21-60+	(26,058)	tabled means	positive
	Wisconsin injured workers during 1927 and 1928	<18-65+	not reported	tabled means	positive

(continued)

TABLE B-6 Studies of Age in Relation to Other Accident Variables (continued)

Factor Investigator	Population	Age Characteristics	(n accidents)	Statistical Technique	Results[1]
Klebba (1941)	urban labor market in U.S.—employed workers	16-64	(784,717) (7,264)	tabled means	positive (for total, males and females)
Kossoris (1948)	workers in 109 manufacturing companies	20-74	17,800	tabled means	curvilinear (highest for 20-24; lowest 30-39; then high after 45)
Heinz (1953)	production employees in Heinz plants	<24 = 200 25-34 = 460 35-44 = 620 45-54 = 440 55-64 = 280	2,000 (200)	tabled means	curvilinear (decreases up to 45-54, increases sharply for 55-64)
Fatalities					
Barkin (1933)	mortality tables—U.S. and British	not given	not given	frequency distribution	death rates rise with increasing age, particularly after age 55
Kossoris (1940)	Wisconsin injured workers during 1919-1938	<18 to 71+	386,676	frequency distribution	positive (50+ death rate twice that of 21-25; 60+ three times thereof)
	New York injured workers, 1933-1937	<20–70+	345,663	frequency distribution	positive

	Age	N	Measure	Findings
female New York injured workers, 1933-1937	<20–70+	36,787	frequency distribution	positive (above 50 and above 60, average no. of deaths above that of younger workers)
Surry (1969)	Canadian industrial accident statistics	<20–70	not given	frequency distribution	fatality figures flat when expressed as fatalities/100,000 employees; when injured, however, older persons more likely to die
Root (1981)	1977 workers' compensation records from 30 states	16-65+	1 million	frequency distribution (work injury ratio)	positive (fatality ratios greater than 1.0 for 35-44, 55-64, and 65+ age groups and less than 1.0 for others)

Permanent disability

Barkin (1933)	New York State male employees with compensated accidents in 1929	<20–65+	(83,635)	frequency distribution	positive (% of permanent–total and partial–disability cases increased with advancing age)
Kossoris (1940)	Wisconsin injured workers, 1919-1938	<20-70+	386,676 (31,624)	frequency distribution	positive (permanent impairment per 1,000 injured increased with age)
	New York injured workers, 1933-1937	<20-70+	345,663 (85,727)	frequency distribution	positive (permanent impairment per 1,000 injuries increased with age)
Klebba (1941)	urban labor market in U.S.–employed workers	<16-64	784,717 (14,381)	frequency distribution	positive for total, male and female

(continued)

TABLE B-6 Studies of Age in Relation to Other Accident Variables (continued)

Factor Investigator	Population	Age Characteristics	(n accidents)	Statistical Technique	Results[1]
Root (1981)	1977 workers' compensation records from 30 states	16-65+	1 million	frequency distribution (work injury ratio)	positive (ratio highest for age group 35-64)
Nature of injuries Barkin (1933)	males compensated for temporary disability in Wisconsin—1927-1929	<13-82+	not reported	frequency distribution	(1) proportion of accidents due to crushing injuries, cuts, punctures, or lacerations declined with age (2) proportion with burns increased to age 30, then declined (3) decrease in bruises to 33, then increase after 33 (4) increase in proportion of dislocations and fractures with age

Padley (1947)	male workers in National Health insurance population in Scotland	$<20-60+$	not reported	frequency distribution	incidence of fractures U-shaped (20 and 60 greater liability than other age groups)
	single female workers in National Health insurance population in Scotland	$<20-60+$	not reported	frequency distribution	positive association between age and incidence of fractures
King (1955)	agricultural workers in Wales and England	not reported	(1991)	Whitfield's modification of Kendall's Tau	(1) miscellaneous injuries, bruises, and contusions increase with age ($p < .001$) (2) cuts and lacerations ($p < .001$), crushings ($p < .02$), decrease with age (3) no significant difference with regard to fractures, sprains and strains, hernias, misc.
	agricultural workers in Wales and England	not reported	(1991)	Whitfield's modification of Kendall's Tau	(1) falls from heights, slipping and tripping, and being hit by falling or moving object increases with age ($p < .001$ to $p < .004$) (2) injury from being caught in machine, inflicted by own tool, or from continued activity from starting engine decreases with age

(continued)

TABLE B-6 Studies of Age in Relation to Other Accident Variables (continued)

Factor Investigator	Population	Age Characteristics	(n accidents)	Statistical Technique	Results[1]
King (1955)					(3) n.s. for moving heavy objects, being knocked against or trod on, action of animals, or trapped (other than in machine)
Root (1981)	1977 workmens' compensation records from 30 states	16-65+	1 million	frequency distribution (work injury ratio)	(1) fractures, hernias, and heart attacks more frequent for older workers than for workers as a whole
					(2) cuts and lacerations, burns occurred less frequently with age
					(3) being struck by and against and caught in, under, or between things decreased with age
					(4) falls, particularly from the same level, increased with age

Accident proneness

Study	Population	Age	N	Method	Findings
Wolff (1950)	stamping plant factory workers	<30-60+	5,208 (14,825)	frequency distribution	(5) injuries associated with working surfaces increased with age (6) injuries associated with nonpower hand tools decreased with age
Whitfield (1954)	male coal miners	22-58+	1,384	correlation	negative relation between age and % of accident prone (does not control for proportion of work force in each age group) young accident-prone workers showed differences in perception and cognition, while older accident prone were deficient in motor response performance
Smiley (1955)	male factory employees	15-65+	187 (87)	frequency distribution	younger workers more likely to be accident prone than older workers (almost twice as many in the 26-35 age group for accident prone as compared to control group)

**p < .01

TABLE C-1 Studies of Attitudes Toward Older Workers

Investigator	Population	Age Characteristics	n	Statistical Technique	Results
Britton and Thomas (1973)	employment inter-viewers (41 males and 15 females)	range = 23-67	56	Friedman two-way ANOVA	the older worker (50+ years) was seen as being the most difficult to place during an economic recession, for an employer to train, and the slowest and least able to maintain production schedules (Friedman's statistic main effects due to age = 47.2; df = 3; $p < .001$)
Rosen and Jerdee (1976a)	business students (115 males and 27 females)	21-29	142	t-tests and chi-square	using an in-basket exercise, older workers were seen as (1) more resistant to change, (2) less likely to receive retraining, promotions, performance feedback; and less interested in developing, updating skills (p's $< .05$)
Rosen and Jerdee (1976b)	relators (n = 56); male and female undergraduate business students (n = 50)	18 to >53	106	t-test on means	on basis of an age stereotype questionnaire: (1) older workers perceived to be potentially less employable (p $< .01$) (2) perceived as less capable on creative, motivational, and productive job demands (p $< .01$) (3) perceived favorably on stability, quality, and reliability dimensions (p $< .01$)

Study	Subjects	Age	N	Statistic	Findings
Haefner (1977)	managers who could hire	not given	286	Tukey test	through assessments of hypothetical job candidates, found significant Age x Competence interaction ($p < .05$); younger highly competent person (age + 25) preferred over older highly competent person (age = 55); small difference in age preference for barely competent person
Rosen and Jerdee (1977)	Harvard Business Review subscribers	not given	1570	not given	on the basis of decisions to incidents, older employees seen as more resistant to change, less likely to receive opportunity for retraining or development, lacking in creativity, and unable to cope with stress
Craft et al. (1979)	enrollees in MBA development program	mean = 29	304	chi square	(1) age not a central variable on overall perception, but older worker described as less strong and ambitious and more opinionated ($p < .01$) (2) less willingness of manager(s) to hire 60 or 70-yr.-olds compared to 35 or 50-yr.-olds; if do hire older workers, conditions and qualifications attached to decision (3) manager(s) willing to hire older worker expressed no differences among age groups by type of reason given

TABLE C-2   Studies of Age in Relation to Selection Testing

Investigator	Population	Age Characteristics	n	Statistical Technique	Results
Arvey and Mussio (1973)	female civil service clerical workers	< 24 years = 70 > 50 years = 67	266	correlation	out of five tests, Short Employment Test Verbal and Clerical Aptitude were significantly valid for older employee group (r's = .25 and .47, respectively, p not given); none was valid for younger group
Salvendy—two studies (1974)	(1) British female operators in confectionary, electro-mechanical, and electronics industries (stratified random selection)	15-35 36-58	181	t-tests	older workers had signif. higher production (t = 2.34, p < .05) but earned lower, nonsignif. scores on the Purdue Pegboard, the One-Hole Test, and a nonverbal intelligence test

(2)	female industrial operators (stratified random selection) in an electro-mechanical factory (USA)	19-22 23-48	67	t-tests	younger operators had higher SRA verbal intelligence test scores (t = 2.40, p < .05) for the same production performance
Robertson and Downs (1979)	persons to be prepared for semi-skilled manual tasks	early 20s to late 50s	samples of 32-228	correlation	no difference in predictability of the "trainability test" for the young and old

TABLE C-3 Studies of Age in Relation to Performance Appraisal

Investigator	Population	n	Ratee Age	Statistical Technique	Results
Maher (1955)	ratees were manufacturing supervisory personnel	201	87 were > 50 years	frequencies and correlations	ratings on older supervisors compared favorably to those of younger ones using a forced choice and graphic rating scale except that older supervisors possibly unfairly rated down on promotability characteristics
Klores (1966)	professional, nonprofessional, clerical, and supervisory employees in a chemical research division	21 raters > 100 ratees	not provided	Kendall Tau correlations	in ratings completed during 4 years (1959-1962), rater or ratee age not related to performance ratings using forced distribution rating format
Bass and Turner (1973)	part-time and full-time tellers from a large metropolitan bank with branches; raters were their supervisors (n = 163)	244 190	not provided	correlations	r's = > .25, p < .01; on basis of a graphic rating scale, ratee age positively related to supervisory ratings for customer relations, new accounts, and alertness dimensions for white full-time tellers, but n.s. for black full-time tellers; no ratee age effect for part-time tellers

Schwab and Heneman (1978)	raters were personnel specialists, 2/3 male, mean age = 34.1, S.D. = 6.3	32	24 and 61	Multiple regression	partial r's: in an evaluation of written performance descriptions of four secretaries, no statistically significant main or interaction effects involving age and job experience of target secretary for the four performance dimensions, promotability, and salary increase
					age of participant rater positively related to recommended salary increase (r = .40, p < .05)
					age of participant rater by age of target interacted to influence job knowledge and responsibility performance dimensions and recommended salary increase (r's = −.41, 0.42, and −.52, respectively, p < .05); i.e., older participant raters gave older target secretaries lower evaluations

(continued)

TABLE C-3 Studies of Age in Relation to Performance Appraisal (continued)

Investigator	Population	n	Ratee Age	Statistical Technique	Results
Cleveland and Landy (1981)	ratees were exempt managerial employees from two divisions of a large manufacturing organization; raters were their supervisors; raters in			Canonical correlation, t-tests	influence of rater age and ratee age not found in ratings of six out of eight performance dimensions; in both samples, found influence of ratee age on ratings of self-development and inter-personal skills, being lower for older ratees (ages 45-65) than middle-aged ratees (35-44) ($t > 2.00$, $p < .05$); age generally accounted for only 1-4% of performance dimension variance, but it could not be determined whether small differences due to true performance differences or age bias: in sample 1, young raters gave higher ratings on interpersonal skills than did older raters ($t = 2.12$, $p < .05$), but ns rater effect in sample 2
	Sample 1: received extensive training on use of form ($n = 150$)	513	21-65		
	Sample 2: received only brief training session	178	22-64		

TABLE C-4 Studies of Age Differences in Reactions to Task Characteristics

Factor	Population	Age Characteristics	n	Statistical Technique	Results
Aldag and Brief (1975)	manufacturing company employees	mean = 36	122	not reported	(1) both younger (<40) and older (>40) employees significantly more satisfied (growth and general) with higher levels of variety, autonomy, and feedback
					(2) older employees (>40) showed little difference in growth and general satisfaction as a function of task significance and task identity
	public sector service agency	mean = 41 range = 21-64	99	not reported	(1) both younger (<40) and older (>40) employees significantly more satisfied (growth and general) with higher levels of variety, autonomy, and feedback
					(2) implies that both younger and older employees significantly more satisfied (growth and general) with higher levels of task significance
					(3) older employees responded more favorably (growth satisfaction) to jobs higher on task identity than those low on task identity, reverse true for younger employees

(continued)

TABLE C-4 Studies of Age Differences in Reactions to Task Characteristics (continued)

Factor	Population	Age Characteristics	n	Statistical Technique	Results
Katz (1978)	employees in municipal, county, and state government	not given	3085	correlation	job longevity moderates the relationship between task dimensions and job satisfaction as follows:
					(1) satisfaction of employees just beginning work on a job (3 mos.) not positively related to amount of skill variety (r = .02) or autonomy (r = .20). Only task significance and feedback positively associated with job satisfaction
					(2) strongest relationships between task dimensions and job satisfaction found for employees in 4-36-month interval
					(3) after 3 years, with progressively greater job longevity, correlations between task dimensions and job satisfaction progressively weaker
					(4) all task dimension-job satisfaction correlations insignificant and close to zero for employees assigned to the same job for at least 15 years

Phillips et al. (1978)	blue collar employees in automotive plant	mean = 46.7 range = 22-63	discriminant analysis	When correlations between task dimensions and satisfaction by longevity categories are computed separately by age groups (< 35, 35-50, > 50), the pattern of results is similar to above, indicating that longevity (and not age) is the important factor.

(1) older workers (>47) preferred higher levels of attention, responsibility, and interest than younger workers (<47)

(2) older workers preferred lower levels of variety, task identity, independence, intrinsic motivations, interpersonal relations, clarity, and co-worker relations than younger workers

analysis of covariance

highly significant difference between younger and older employees for composite of preference dimensions, $F(1,62) = p < .001$, when controlling for education and seniority

(continued)

301

TABLE C-4 Studies of Age Differences in Reactions to Task Characteristics (continued)

Factor	Population	Age Characteristics	n	Statistical Technique	Results
Gould (1979a)	administrative and managerial public agency employees	mean = 37	153	moderated multiple regression	(1) strongest positive relationship between job complexity and job satisfaction in the trial stage (< 30), as opposed to stabilization (30-44) and maintenance (45+) stages (controlling for salary, tenure, sex, level, and occupational group)
					(2) no significant difference in the job complexity-satisfaction relationship between maintenance and stabilization stages
					(3) job complexity interacts with career stage in predicting job performance (Δ R2 = .05)
					(4) stabilization stage had significantly stronger performance-job complexity relationship than did trial stage
					(5) no difference between trial and maintenance stage in job complexity-performance relationship

Rabinowitz and Hall (1981)	Canadian transport ministry employees (male = 76%)	not given	332	partial correlation	job characteristics more strongly and consistently related to job involvement in early career stage (ages 21-35) than in either middle (ages 36-50) or late (ages 51+) career stages
					(1) correlations between job involvement and autonomy and task identity significantly higher (p < .05) for early than for middle stage group
					(2) correlations between job involvement and task identity significantly higher (p < .05) in early than in late career group
					(3) no significant differences in correlations across stages on variety and feedback with job involvement

TABLE D-1 Studies of Age in Relation to Middle Career Stage

Investigator	Population	Age Characteristics	n	Statistical Technique	Results
Shearer and Steger (1975)	officers and civilians in the Air Force	officers mean = 34 civilians = 41	318 133	correlations	nonsignificant relationship between obsolescence and age (r = .034) high need achievement and organizational participation associated with low obsolescence
Thompson and Dalton (1976)	professionals in R&D organizations (5 large organs)	not provided	200		obsolescence reflects out-of-date organization rather than person
Alderfer and Guzzo (1979)	business students and participants in a mgmt. development course in a large organization (females = 82; males = 147)	not provided	229	F and t-tests	per Levinson et al., career stages, need for growth in job generally sloped downward, highest in Early Adult Transition, with increase of one scale point from Becoming One's Own Person stage to Midlife Transition; however, the mean Need for Growth in job between life-cycle stages not significantly different (F = 1.85, p < .10)

Gould (1979b)	municipal workers technicians, sales, professionals, managers/administrators; females and males	mean = 38.5 s.d. = 10.85	277	Anacova F-test	nonsignificant difference between super's career stages and career planning ($F = .72$; $df = 2/273$)
Rush et al. (1980)	public sector managerial, technical and professional 72% male and 28% female sampled population	mean = 41	759	means	per Levinson et al's (1978) Midlife Transition career stage (ages 40-45), job and career satisfaction lower than in stages 1 and 2
				discriminant function F-test	career satisfaction discriminated most between stages ($F = 14.61$, $p < .001$); nonsignificant difference between career stages on need for upward mobility ($F = 1.51$, $p = .212$)

TABLE D-2 Age in Relation to Mid-Career Change

Investigator	Population	n	Age	Statistical Technique	Results
Clopton (1973)	male career persisters and shifters, pursuing advanced degrees at five midwestern universities	20 20	31-52 32-53	not provided	persisters and shifters did not differ on childhood experiences or in family responsibilities, but shifters had experienced more personal counseling, and persisters less likely to have financial support for making a shift;
					for personality, per the California Psychological Inventory, Strong Vocational Interest Blank, and Rotter's Internal-External Scale, found two differences: shifters had greater self-esteem and thought more seriously about personal mortality
Gottfredson (1977)	1970 U.S. Census Bureau data which included retrospective data for 1965	1 in 1000 sample of population	21-70	Cohen's (1960) index of agreement	for workers aged 41-55 and using Holland's Occupational Classification, 25% of the men shifted from realistic to enterprising work; women moved most frequently between the enterprising and conventional or the realistic and conventional work; category-shifting occurred for about 10-14% of the sample
					workers whose jobs more consistent [per Holland's theory (1973)] also more occupationally stable

Study	Sample	N	Age	Method	Findings
Wiener and Vaitenas (1977)	participants in a career counseling program at a major university	experimental group = 45 control group = 66	mean = 35.5 35.4	discriminant function analysis	analysis conducted on (1) 15 scales of the Edwards Personal Preference Survey and (2) 8 scales of the Gordon Personal Inventory; on the EPPS scale, Endurance, Dominance, and Order (coefficients > −.43) important for differentiating between career changes and control groups; on the GPI, Responsibility and Ascendancy (coefficients > −.42, $p < .01$) had highest weights; therefore, career changers lower on Dominance, Ascendancy, Responsibility, Endurance, and Order
Snyder et al. (1978)	professors and department chairs at a northeastern university	268 45	not provided	t-tests for correlated samples	career leavers (movement from professor to department chair) agreed administrative role would lead to more power and esteem and less autonomy (differences significant at $p < .001$)
Thomas and Robbins (1979)	male managerial, technical, and professional changers who were referral sampled and had career changed in previous 2-5 years in New England	61	35-55	Kolmogorov-Smirnov one-sample test	Midcareer changers did not necessarily move to environments more congruent with personality; changers who moved to careers both more or less congruent with their personality significantly more satisfied with their new career ($p < .01$)

(continued)

TABLE D-2 Age in Relation to Mid-Career Change (continued)

Investigator	Population	n	Age	Statistical Technique	Results
Lawrence (1980)	male and female midlife career changers	10	35-55	frequencies	for three of ten cases, change was outcome of resolution of midlife crisis (one shifted from religious to a secular life); for the other seven, change was planned, noncrisis in form (e.g., the physics professor who shifted to a full-time job in the music world)
Neapolitan (1980)	career changers and nonchangers; professionals, managers, salespersons, semiprofessionals	25 25	30-50	frequencies	changers seeking greater intrinsic rewards and dissatisfied in first occupation; source of dissatisfaction was incongruence between individual work orientation and rewards of occupation

Thomas (1980)	male career changers, leaving professional and managerial careers	73	34-54	frequencies	most prevalent and important reason for making change was "a better fit for values and work" (48%) and "more meaningful work" (53%); 62% said second career very rewarding; motives for career change varied; therefore, developed a typology of career changers and the characteristics of the types differed
Armstrong (1981)	persons in school and previously enrolled at a community college	48 46	mean = 42.5	frequencies	job dissatisfaction major reason for seeking career change

TABLE D-3 Studies of Age in Relation to Career Planning Intervention Effectiveness

Investigator	Population	Age Characteristics	n	Statistical Technique	Results
Miller et al. (1973)	self-selected R&D employees from two major R&D labs (three experimental and two control groups)	mean = 37.1	450	ANOVA	at different hierarchical levels, (GS < 11, 12 and > 13), there was increased number of self-development activities, $F = 13.83$, $df = 2/435$, $p < .001$ career planning activity enhanced self-development activities only at lower hierarchical levels
Rubinton (1977)	community adult residents; 82% of completers were female	median age group = 27-36 $34\% \geqslant 48$ years	75	t-tests	after a career workshop, 77% decided to begin college training, to enter vocational training, to reenter college, to pursue high school equivalency, etc. (average of 69% completed the workshop); pre-and post-test on attitudes signified changes in "how and where to look for a job," confidence in decision making

Thornton (1978)	secretaries (self-selected)	not given (mean years experience = 11.5)	64	chi squares	after one-day career growth workshop, subsequent career planning actions greater for individuals with internal locus of control ($\chi^2 = 11.98$, $p < .01$)
Eng and Gottsdanker (1979)	university campus Career Development Program applicants (94% females)	range 25-29	not given	percentages	participants made some career changes, while 20% of a control group (n = 50) made changes

311

TABLE D-4 Studies of Age in Relation to Learning

Investigator	Population	Age Characteristics	n	Statistical Technique	Results
Dodd (1967)	technicians	range 26-58	13	percentages	older workers did as well as younger in two-day training program to prepare for new job requiring new technical knowledge
Jamieson (1969)	unemployed females, 10 control group and 10 experimental group subjects	range: 15-44	20	frequencies	no significant differences in performance in training between younger and older workers, but three older workers left control group, complaining of stress (where progress was prominently displayed and deviation from track scored as an error)
Stewart (1969)	male railroad workers	mean = 50 range = 41-60	60	percentages	trained men in clerical tasks which were complex and required high degree of accuracy: (1) set qualifying test scores had to be lowered to admit the men; *however*, 63% completed program successfully and were placed; 28% placed in other jobs, and 8% did not complete or were not placed in other jobs

Davis and Taylor (1975)	enrollees in senior community service project 60% female	60% over 65	880	percentages	(2) program proved to be economically feasible (3) very few untrainables training provided ability to take and perform community service jobs, e.g., homemaker service, thrift shop work, and home repair; 14% left for permanent employment; only 2% unfavorable terminations
Siemen (1976)	23 females, 7 males 20 females, 10 males	range: 67-84 16-32	30 30	means	using programmed materials, older subjects slower in completing material, but performance differences between young and old markedly reduced or nonexistent

TABLE D-5 Studies of the Effects of Pre-Retirement Programs

Investigator	Population	Age Characteristics	n	Statistical Technique	Results
Lundgren (1965)	male salaried and hourly retirees from 13 companies	<65	404	chi squares	retirees from companies having pre-retirement counseling programs tended to be more satisfied with retirement ($\chi^2 = 4.6$, ns, where χ^2 of 6.0 = $p < .05$)
Charles (1971)	male and female industrial, business, government, professional employees and community-at-large subjects	range = 45-72 mean = 57	368	chi squares	on basis of pre- and post-self-report questionnaires, found significant attitude changes reflecting general improvement in self-perceived personal competence and personal worth
O'Rourke and Friedman (1972)	small labor union members		not given		participant attitude changes not always in expected or desired directions, and magnitudes not great
Beveridge (1980)	male managers from seven organizations, randomly selected	6-7 mos. postretirement	185		life significance (self-acceptance, life purpose, and life interest or defined as worthwhileness) related to overall retirement satisfaction (r = .68), which has implications for preretirement programs, e.g., counseling on personal meaning of life

| Glamser (1981) | male semi-skilled workers in six plants of a glass container manufacturer located in one state | >60 in 1973, median = 62 | 132 in 1973, 110 in 1979 | means and chi squares | with 6-year follow-up, two experimental groups and a control group showed no significant difference in life satisfaction, retirement attitude, and felt job deprivation |
| Morrow (1981) | male and female employees— retirement program participants and nonparticipants—of a midwestern university | >50 | 269
62 | t-tests | participants had a higher general attitude toward retirement (t = −.168, p < .05) |

TABLE E-1 Studies of Age in Relation to Compensation Preferences

Investigator	Population	Age Characteristics	Statistical Technique	Results
Jurgenson (1947)	150 female 1189 male gas company applicants	< 25 = 415 25-29 = 344 30-34 = 182 35-39 = 119 40 or over = 88	rank order	no significant age differences detected
Jurgenson (1948)	378 female 3345 male gas company applicants	< 20 = 272 20-24 = 1171 25-29 = 842 30-34 = 452 35-39 = 253 40-44 = 128 45-49 = 77 50+ = 87	rank order	(1) job security most important overall characteristic; significantly more important than pay for all workers, including older ones (2) importance attached to supervisor increased with age (3) hours less important as workers get older
Wagner and Bakerman (1960)	600 union workers	< 30 30-39 40-49 50-59 60+	rank order	(1) pensions most important for all age groups (2) life and health second most important (3) people satisfied with fringe benefits as equivalent wage increases (4) importance of pensions increases with age; at 40-49, levels off

Author	Sample	Age groups	Method	Findings
Gruenfeld (1962)	52 male supervisors in 11 industrial companies	young = 17 middle = 17 old = 16	chi square	(1) young workers preferred money, $p < .01$ (2) older workers preferred more benefits, $p < .05$ (3) older and younger sought more job security; middle age less $p < .05$
Nealey (1964b)	635 males 206 females blue collar employees	< 30 30-39 40-49 50+	game board graphic presentation	(1) preference for pension increases with age; more dramatic for males than females (2) preference (males) for pay and sick leave fell steadily as age increased (3) vacation stable across all ages, then dropped off significantly for 50+ group
Nealey (1964a)	1133 union members	< 30 30-39 40-49 50-59 60-65	paired comparison graphic presentation	(1) preference for pensions rises sharply with age (2) medical insurance, initially first at 40-49 becomes second with age (3) preference for pay raises and time off do not vary significantly by age

(continued)

TABLE E-1 Studies of Age in Relation to Compensation Preferences (continued)

Investigator	Population	Age Characteristics	Statistical Technique	Results
Lahiri and Choudhuri (1966)	100 males in industrial plant 50 technical 50 nontechnical	25 26-30 31-35 36 and over	rank order	adequate earnings and job security key factors across all age categories
Nealey and Goodale (1967)	197 industrial workers 180 males 17 females	18-33 = 50 34-49 = 83 50-65 = 64	paired comparisons ANOVA	(1) older workers preferred early retirement, $p < .01$ (2) younger workers preferred 4-day week, $p < .05$ (3) younger workers preferred five Fridays, $p < .01$
Schuster (1968)	325 aerospace workers	18-34 34-48 48-64	paired comparisons	(1) older employees value medical plans, along with retirement—sick leave considered least important (2) older employers would improve their retirement and stock plans; decrease base salary, long-term disability, and sick leave

Study	Sample	Method	Findings
Chapman and Ottenman (1975)	N = 149 114 males 35 females utility employees 18-35 = 52 36-49 = 58 50-65 = 39	paired comparison ANOVA	(1) older workers preferred pension increases, $p < .01$ (2) younger workers preferred dental coverage, $p < .01$ and four-day week, $p < .05$
Lewellen and Lanser (1973)	300 executives in seven corporations N.A.	N.A.	(1) no preference results influenced by age, tax or income bracket (2) strong preference found for postretirement income
Crandall (1977)	128 managerial and nonmanagerial employees of life ins. co. < 25 = 48 26-30 = 26 31-40 = 22 41-49 = 12 50-64 = 10	rank order cross-tabulation	(1) retirement replaces hospital/medical insurance for 41 and older as number one comp. preference (2) retirement benefits increase in importance with age

Jurgenson (1978)	56,621 gas company applicants
	39,788 males
	16,833 females
	
	< 20 = 14127
	20-24 = 19644
	25-29 = 10475
	30-34 = 5269
	35-39 = 3250
	40-44 = 1722
	45-49 = 1070
	50-54 = 559
	over 55 = 381
		rank order	(1) job security most important preference for males—all groups, including older workers
			(2) less important with age (males)
			  (a) pay
			  (b) advancement
			(3) more important with age (males)
			  (a) fringe benefits
			  (b) company
			  (c) supervisor

(continued)

319

TABLE E-1 Studies of Age in Relation to Pay Satisfaction (continued)

Investigator	Population	Age Characteristics	Statistical Technique	Results
				(4) less important with age (females): pay (except over 55)
				(5) more important with age (females): benefits (except over 55)
Crandall and Lundstrom (1980)	229 managerial and nonmanagerial life ins. co. employees 80 males 149 females	17-22 23-27 28-34 35-64	rank order reallocation of compensation ANACONDA	retirement more important for older (38-64) than younger employees (18-23), where it was least important

TABLE E-2 Studies of Age in Relation to Pay Satisfaction

Investigator	Population	Age Characteristics	n	Statistical Technique	Results
Meltzer (1958)	employees in diverse occupations in manufacturing plant	<31 = 40% 31–45 = 38% 46–60 = 17% 61+ = 5%	258	mean differences satisfaction-dissatisfaction index	positive (p < .05 all groups)
Andrews and Henry (1964)	299 managers in 5 firms	median = 42.5	299	chi square	no consistent trend for pay satisfaction as a function of age, no relationship between age and pay comparisons; anticipation of large pay increments associated with younger workers Age: (1) less emphasis on merit, $\chi^2 > .10$ (2) greater willingness to take pay cut to get job security, $\chi^2 > .10$ (3) stray trend toward benefits instead of pay, $\chi^2 > .001$
Hulin and Smith (1965)	male electronics workers in two plants	equal n from each age group	99 86	multiple regression controlling for tenure + four other variables	B = -.09 and .35, significance level not reported (overall R, p < .01, both samples)

(continued)

TABLE E-2 Studies of Age in Relation to Pay Satisfaction (continued)

Investigator	Population	Age Characteristics	n	Statistical Technique	Results
Hunt and Saul (1975)	female Australian white collar government employees	16-25 = 344 26-35 = 107 36+ = 99 16-25 = 1017 26-35 = 790 36-49 = 812 50+ = 634		multiple regression (controlling for experience)	negative (B = -.14)
Schwab and Wallace (1974)	males nonexempt employees from a large manufacturing plant	n.a.	350	zero-order and partial correlations	n.s.
Monczyka et al. (1977)	354 employees 6 organizations	< 30 = 544 30-39 = 657 >39 = 257	1458	correlation	(1) age as well as several other variables correlated with pay satisfaction, $p < .05$ (2) note all these items inter-correlated, i.e., org. level, salary, tenure, with age (3) two other key factors with greater association to pay satisfaction, working conditions, nonmonetary rewards

Oliver (1977)	male life insurance agents		92	path analysis	pay satisfaction positively related to age and income and inversely related to job level
Schwab and Heneman (1977)	female blue collar operatives	mean = 36.7 s.d. = 11.3	177	partial correlation (controlling for experience) correlation within 16 experience groups	n.s. (r = -.05)
	male blue collar operatives	mean = 33.4 s.d. = 13.4	96	partial correlation (controlling for experience) correlation within 10 experience subgroups	n.s. (proportion of positive r's = .44)
					n.s. (proportion of positive r's = .40)
Muchinsky (1978)	employees in diverse occupations in public utility	18-29 = 246 30-39 = 156 40-49 = 168 50+ = 96	666	Scheffe's test for post hoc analysis	negative linear relationship (significance level not reported)

TABLE F-1 Studies of Relations Between Individual Demographic Variables and Retirement

Factor	Population	n	Age	Relations to Retirement
Age				
Eden and Jacobson (1976)	Israeli male executives from 13 organizations	179	50-75	$r = -.30$, $p < .01$; older age associated with less desire to retire
				$r = .22$, $p < .01$; feeling young associated with less desire to retire
Ekerdt et al. (1976)	males from VA Normative Aging Study	1458	T_1 range: 25-55+	ANOVA: longitudinally (over average of 10 years), a shift to preference for later retirement
Jacobson (1972b)	male British factory operatives from three medium-sized firms	145	55-64	chi square = $p < .05$, $V = .205$, older subjective age, more willing to retire
Jacobson and Eran (1980)	Israeli physicians females males	125 192	$50 \geqslant 65$	no difference in preferences for retirement per age; most preferred continued employment
Parnes and Nestel (1975)	National Longitudinal Study national sample, of which 9.4% retired between 1966-1971	3817	50-64 in 1971	multiple classification analysis; $F = 141.66$, $p < .01$; 60-64-year-olds had greater probability of retiring than those 50-59;
				proportion who expressed intention to retire prior to age 65 increased from 28% in 1966 to 38.5% in 1971

Rose and Mogey (1972)	males from VA Normative Aging Study	2000	various age groups	regression: age most important predictor, accounting for 8.1% of preferred retirement age variance; older people wish to retire later
Schmitt and McCune (1981)	Michigan civil service employees with more than 30 years service and with one-year follow-up	513 379	55-70	discriminant analysis: $r_c = .33$, $p < .05$ for demographic variables and retiree status (demographic variables = size of community, time in community, job level, education, age, sex, race, and marital status); retirees older than nonretirees
Stanford (1971)	army voluntary military retirees during 1967	729	—	older retirees more dubious about beginning second career—appears to reflect reluctance to give up one's occupational role
Dependents				
Barfield and Morgan (1970)	working plus retired UAW members	100	$< 59 \geqslant 64$	fewer dependents, more likely to retire
Berman and Holtzman (1978)	UAW workers and retirees	35 45	—	no relationship between number of at-home children and decision to retire
Parker and Dyer (1976)	male naval officers	702	—	in an expectancy model, perceived family attitudes or preference for retirement plus other variables predicted retirement 62.2% of the time

(continued)

TABLE F-1 Studies of Relations Between Individual Demographic Variables and Retirement (continued)

Factor	Population	n	Age	Relations to Retirement
Parnes and Nestel (1975)	National Longitudinal Study national sample, of which 9.4% retired between 1966-1971	3817	50-64 in 1971	multiple classification analysis, $F = 3.33$, $p < .01$; number of dependents inversely related to expecting to retire early $F = 1.64$, ns (number of dependents nonsignificantly related to actual retirement)
Quinn (1977)	married men from Retirement History Study	4354	58-63	regression: $t = 2.97$, $p < .01$; presence of dependents contributes to later retirement
Schmitt et al. (1979)	Michigan civil service retirees and nonretirees	250 422	$55 \leqslant 65$	discriminant analysis: retirees had fewer dependents, $F = 26.62$, $p < .05$
Education				
Barfield and Morgan (1970)	working plus retired UAW members	1090	$<59 > 64$	the greater the educational attainment, less likely to retire
Berman and Holtzman (1978)	UAW workers and retirees	35 45	–	retirees had fewer years of formal education
Boskin (1977)	married males in Panel Study of Income Dynamics, followed from 1968-1972	131	61-65 in 1968	regression: logit coefficient $= -.036$; with an increase in education level, modest lowering of probability of retirement

Author	Sample	N	Age	Findings
Hall and Johnson (1980)	Retirement History Study married men and women	1054 3557	58-63	regression: Logit coefficient = -.075, p < .01 for men; > -.068, p < .05 for women; more education associated with plans to retire later
Jaffee (1972)	national data from various government sources	—	—	labor force participation rates for older workers increase with education
Parnes and Nestel (1981)	National Longitudinal Study of men followed from 1966-1976	1047	55-69 in 1976	men with less than 12 years education more likely to retire early than those with more than 12 years
Rose and Mogey (1972)	males from VA Normative Aging Study	2000	various age groups	$r = .22$ between level of education and and later preferred retirement age regression: education accounted for 5.2% of preferred age of retirement variance
Schmitt et al. (1979)	Michigan civil service retirees and nonretirees	250 422	$55 \leqslant 65$	discriminant analysis: $F = 12.98$, $p < .05$; retirees have less education
Schmitt and McCune (1981)	Michigan civil service employes with more than 30 years service and with one-year follow-up	513 379	$55 > 70$	discriminant analysis: retirees have less education; see results for demographics under the age factor
Streib and Schneider (1971)	Cornell Study of Occupational Retirement, followed from 1952-1958	1969	> 63 in 1952	chi square: 158.21, $p < .001$ for men and 29.82, $p < .001$ for women; the more educated continue to work longer

(continued)

TABLE F-1 Studies of Relations Between Individual Demographic Variables and Retirement (continued)

Factor	Population	n	Age	Relations to Retirement
Gender				
Hall and Johnson (1980)	Retirement History Study married men and women	3557 1054	58-63 in 1969	regression: logit coefficient = .227, p < .10; males in rural locations retire earlier
Jacobson (1974)	British factory operatives married males and females	145 70	55-64 50-59	chi square = 15.79, p < .001; males more likely to retire early, particularly when females had positive social contacts in the workplace
				chi square = 7.32, p < .01; more males than females preferred to retire at the pensionable age;
Jacobson and Eran (1980)	Israeli physicians males and females	192 125	50 > 65	regression: no differences in preference for retirement
Schmitt et al. (1979)	Michigan civil service retirees and nonretirees	250 422	55 ≤ 65	discriminant analysis: F = 52.76, p < .05; retirees tend to be female
Schmitt and McCune (1981)	Michigan civil service employees with more than 30 years service and with one-year follow-up	513 379	55 > 70	discriminant analysis: females more likely to retire; see results under age factor for demographics

Study	Sample	N	Age	Findings
Usher (1981)	Workers from (1) private and (1) public sector organization; 84% were male, 85% married	333	mean age = 58.18	women more interested in extended alternative work lives (percentages not provided)
Marital Status Barfield and Morgan (1978)	10-year follow-up of University of Michigan Survey Research Center national cross-section	486	35-64	multiple classification analysis: single men much more likely to retire early; married women retire early when high family income, no mortgage payments, and no commitments to children
Belbin and Clark (1970)	1966 British census, mostly male	10% of group	55-74	married persons worked longer than singles, divorcees, and widows; singles had higher earlier retirement rate
Berman and Holtzman (1978)	UAW workers and retirees	35 45	–	no relationship to early retirement
Burkhauser (1979)	male auto workers, cross-sectional data and two-year resurvey	761 326	59-64	regression: married men more likely to take early retirement, but ns
Jacobson and Eran (1980)	Israeli physicians males and females	192 125	50 > 65	ns: marital status was nonsignificantly related to preference for retirement
Parker and Dyer (1976)	male naval officers	702	–	in an expectancy model, the perceptions of the wife's preference for retirement plus other variables predicted retirement 62.2% of the time

(continued)

TABLE F-1 Studies of Relations Between Individual Demographic Variables and Retirement (continued)

Factor	Population	n	Age	Relations to Retirement
Parnes and Nestel (1975)	National Longitudinal Study national sample, of which 9.4% retired between 1966 and 1971	3817	50-64 in 1971	multiple classification analysis: F = 3.42, p < .05; married men living with wives had lower probability of retiring than did nonmarried men
Schmitt et al. (1979)	Michigan civil service retirees and nonretirees	250 422	55 ≤ 65	discriminant analysis: F = 6.15, p < .05; retirees more likely to have a nonworking spouse
Schmitt and McCune (1981)	Michigan civil service employees with more than 30 years service and with a one-year follow-up	513 379	55 > 70	discriminant analysis: no difference in marital status; see results under age factor for demographics
Streib and Schneider (1971)	Cornell Study of Occupational Retirement, followed from 1952-1958	1969	> 63 in 1952	chi square > 29.82, p < .001; single women (43%) more willing to retire than married (24%)
Occupation				
Hall and Johnson (1980)	Retirement History Study married men and women	3557 1054	58-63	regression: logit coefficient < -.654, p < .01; self-employed plan to retire later

Jacobson (1972b)	male British factory operatives	145	55-64	chi square: $V = .306$, $p < .01$; the more rigidly fixed the work pattern, the higher the willingness to retire
Orbach (1969)	UAW Chrysler retirees	12220	–	specific job class not associated with decision to retire early
Parnes and Nestel (1975)	National Longitudinal Study national sample, of which 9.4% retired between 1966 and 1971	3817	50-64 in 1971	multiplication classification analysis; $F = .89$, ns; private, government, and the self-employed did not differ significantly in probability of retiring
Parnes and Nestel (1981)	National Longitudinal Study of men followed from 1976	1047	55-69 in 1976	among occupations, largest proportion retiring early for whites were professional-managerial workers (46%) and for blacks were clerical and sales workers (50%); largest proportion retiring early was the government worker for both blacks and whites
Quinn (1977)	married men from Retirement History Study	4354	58-63	regression: ns, but some evidence that undesirability of job related to early retirement decision, and poor health increases this relationship

(continued)

TABLE F-1 Studies of Relations Between Individual Demographic Variables and Retirement (continued)

Factor	Population	n	Age	Relations to Retirement
Rose and Mogey (1972)	males from VA Normative Aging Study	2000	various age groups	regression: $r = .21$; self-perceived company rank positively related to preferred age of retirement
Schmitt and McCune (1981)	Michigan civil service employees with more than 30 years service and one-year follow-up	513 379	55 > 70	discriminant analysis: see results for demographics under the age factor, but the civil service job level-retiree status univariate relationship was significant (level not provided); i.e., retirees had lower job level
Streib and Schneider (1971)	Cornell Study of Occupational Retirement urban aged from 259 organizations	1969	≥63	chi square: 167.24, $p < .001$ for men and 12.73, $p < .05$ for women; professional employees worked longer than did all the other occupational types (managers, white collar, unskilled, etc.)
Place of residence Hall and Johnson (1980)	Retirement History Study married men and women	3557 1054	58-63	regression: logit coefficient = .227, $p < .10$ for men; residence in rural locations associated with earlier retirement
McKain (1957)	males in Connecticut town and rural communities	553	65-74	rural and urban dwellers equally likely to retire

Study	Sample	N	Age	Findings
Schmitt et al. (1979)	Michigan civil service retirees and nonretirees	250 422	55 < 65	discriminant analysis: $F = 32.22$; $p < .05$; retirees come from smaller communities
Schmitt and McCune (1981)	Michigan civil service employees with more than 30 years service and one-year follow-up	513 379	55 > 70	discriminant analysis: retirees more likely to live in smaller communities (see results for demographics under the age factor)

Race

Study	Sample	N	Age	Findings
Burkhauser (1979)	male auto workers, cross-sectional data and two-year resurvey	761 326	59-64	regression: $B = .164$, $t = 3.05$, significance level not specified; whites more likely to take early retirement; $B = .109$ on resurvey
Parnes and Nestel (1975)	National Longitudinal Study national sample, of which 9.2% whites and 11.7% blacks retired between 1966 and 1971 white males black males	3817 2774 1043	50-64 in 1971	multiple classification analysis: $F = 0.09$, ns; controlling for other variables reduced the F value
Parnes and Nestel (1981)	National Longitudinal Study of men followed from 1966-1976	1047	55-69 in 1976	more black men (56%) than white men (45%) retire because of health
Schmitt et al. (1979)	Michigan civil service retirees and nonretirees	250 422	55 ≤ 65	discriminant analysis: $F = .44$, ns

(continued)

TABLE F-1 Studies of Relations Between Individual Demographic Variable and Retirement (continued)

Factor	Population	n	Age	Relations to Retirement
Schmitt and McCune (1981)	Michigan civil service employees with more than 30 years service and one-year follow-up	513 379	55 > 70	discriminant analysis: a few more retirees were nonwhite; sample included only a small number of nonwhites (see results for demographics under the age factor)
Tenure Jacobson and Eran (1980)	Israeli physicians males and females	192 125	50 > 65	regression: ns; length of service was not related to preferences for retirement
Rose and Mogey (1972)	males from VA Normative Aging Study	2000	various age groups	$r = -.10$; greater tenure related to a lower preferred age of retirement; regression: partial $r = -.08$
Schmitt et al. (1979)	Michigan civil service retirees and nonretirees	250 422	55 $\leqslant$ 65	discriminant analysis: $F = 16.76$, $p < .05$; less tenure, more likely to retire earlier

TABLE F-2 Studies of Relations Between Financial Factors and Retirement

Investigator	Population	n	Age	Relations with Retirement
Barfield and Morgan (1970)	working plus retired UAW members	1090	<59 >64	r was strongest for amount of expected pensions and annuity plus social security income in postretirement relative to plans to retire early; less important were asset level, preretirement savings, mortgage payment, and other debt obligations—ns; employment status of spouse related to plans to retire early
Barfield and Morgan (1978)	10-year follow-up of University of Michigan Survey Research Center national cross-section	486	35-64	multiple classification analysis: χ^2 = .049 (significance level not reported); number of pensions expected related to plans to retire early
Berman and Holtzman (1978)	UAW workers and retirees	35 45	—	no difference between retirees and nonretirees

(continued)

TABLE F-2 Studies of Relations Between Financial Factors and Retirement (continued)

Investigator	Population	n	Age	Relations with Retirement
Boskin (1977)	married males in Panel Study of Income Dynamics, followed from 1968 to 1972	131	61-65 in 1968	regression: logit coefficient = .893; the greater the social security benefits, the greater the probability of retirement
				coefficient = .132; the greater the income from net assets, the greater the probability of retirement
				coefficient = –2.048; the greater the net earnings, the lower the probability of retirement
				coefficient = –.225; the greater the spouse's earnings, the lower the probability of retirement
Burkhauser (1979)	male auto workers, cross-sectional data and two-year resurvey	761 326	59-64	regression: = .024, t = 8.42, significance level not reported; the greater the actuarial penalty for postponing acceptance of pension, the more likely were workers to take the pension; = .050 on resurvey
				= .0023, t = 2.33, significance level not reported; assets positively related to pension acceptance; = .0016 on resurvey

Hall and Johnson (1980)	Retirement History Study married men and women	3557 1054	58-63	regression: logit coefficient = 3.796, p < .001; spouse receiving social security increases probability of early retirement coefficients > .115, p < .001: for social security and expected annual private and government pensions related to probability of early retirement
Jacobson and Eran (1980)	Israeli physicians males and females	192 125	50 > 65	regression: ns; financial status not related to preference for retirement
Katona et al. (1969)	automobile and agricultural implement workers, retired and nonretired	1123	58-61	level of available retirement income related to early retirement decision
Orbach (1969)	UAW-Chrysler retirees	12220	—	availability of higher pensions facilitated earlier retirement

(continued)

TABLE F-2 Studies of Relations Between Financial Factors and Retirement (continued)

Investigator	Population	n	Age	Relations with Retirement
Parnes and Nestel (1975)	National Longitudinal Study sample, of which 9.4% retired between 1966 and 1971	3817	50-64 in 1971	multiple classification analysis: F = 2.92, p < .05; those having none or negative assets more likely to retire, with minimal differences between other asset categories
				F = 5.80, p < .01; likelihood of retirement increases with length of service for those eligible for private pensions
Parnes and Nestel (1981)	National Longitudinal study of men followed from 1966 to 1976	1047	55-69 in 1976	more white men having pension coverage retired early (46%) than did black men (39%)
Pechman et al. (1968)	International cross-section data from 19 countries—1960	—		regression: higher social security retirement benefits, lower labor force participation among the aged population
Pollman (1971)	male early UAW retirees	442	60-65	number one reason for early retirement was adequate retirement income; per 47.34% of group, poor health noted by 24.49%

Study	Sample	N	Age	Findings
Pollman and Johnson (1974)	male UAW skilled machine operators, assembly line, & utility class workers employees retirees	256 442	60-65	chi square: ns; retirement income not perceived differently by employees and retirees
Quinn (1977)	married men from Retirement History Study	4354	58-63	regression: eligibility for social security $(-.035, t = 3.32, p < .01$; for other pension $(-.048, t = 4.67, p < .01)$ or for both $(-.125, t = 7.06, p < .01)$ are related to early retirement decision
Quinn (1981)	self-employed males from Retirement History Study	836	58-63 in 1969	Regression: $= .129$, $t = 6.41$, significance level not reported; a two-year study revealed eligibility for social security positively related to self-reported retirement, but the whole R^2 was only .17
Schmitt et al. (1979)	Michigan civil service retirees and nonretirees	250 422	55-65	discriminant analysis: $F = 6.15$, $p < .05$; with nonworking spouse more likely to retire earlier
Schmitt and McCune (1981)	Michigan civil service employees with more than 30 years service and one-year follow-up	513 379	55>70	discriminant analysis: $F (9, 125) = 3.32$, $p < .01$; addition of financial variables to demographic variables contributes significantly to explaining retirement status $(r_c = .53)$, but expected early retirement income lower for retirees

TABLE F-3 Studies of Relations Between Physiological and Psychological Variables and Retirement

Factor	Population	n	Age	Relations with Retirement
Climate preference				
Rose and Mogey (1972)	males from VA Normative Aging Study	2000	various age groups	regression: preference for own climate accounted for 1.5% of preferred retirement age variance
				$r = .16$ for climate preference and preference for later retirement when controlling for health and geographic stability
Desire for leisure				
Messer (1969)	U.S. Civil Service early retirees	3299	55-60	22.6% retired to enjoy retirement while they still could
Palmore (1964)	1951 and 1963 Survey of Aged, of OASDI beneficiaries	—	—	among retirees > 65, reason for retiring on basis of preference for leisure increased from 3% in 1951 to 17% in 1963
Pollman (1971)	male UAW early retirees	442	60-65	19.49% gave wanting more free time as primary reason for retirement

Growth needs

Study	Sample	N	Age	Findings
Schmitt et al. (1979)	Michigan civil service retirees and nonretirees	250 422	55-65	discriminant analysis of 10 motivational-psychological variables on retirement status; coefficient = –.38 for growth needs; skill variety, feedback from others, and extrinsic satisfaction contributed significantly ($p < .05$) to the discriminant function; the greater the growth needs, the more likely to retire

Health

Study	Sample	N	Age	Findings
Barfield and Morgan (1970)	national sample of working and retired persons; working plus retired UAW members	1652 675 1090	35-59	those who assessed their health as poor or declining most likely to retire early, even when excluding those with poor health who were forced to retire
Burkhauser (1979)	male auto workers, cross-sectional data and two-year resurvey	761 326	59-64	regression: coefficient = .133, $t = 3.10$, significance level not reported; bad health positively related to pension acceptance; = .015 on resurvey
Boskin (1977)	married males in Panel Study of Income Dynamics, followed from 1968 to 1972	131	61-65 in 1968	regression: logit coefficient = –1.38; the greater the number of hours ill, the lower the probability of retirement
Eden and Jacobson (1976)	Israeli male executives from 13 organizations	179	50-75	$r = -.15$, $p < .05$; those who rated health low preferred to retire early

(continued)

TABLE F-3 Studies of Relations Between Physiological and Psychological Variables and Retirement (continued)

Factor	Population	n	Age	Relations with Retirement
Hall and Johnson (1980)	Retirement History Study married men and women	3557 1054	58-63	regression: logit coefficients $> .849$, $p < .01$; poor health related to early retirement
Jacobson (1972b)	male British factory operatives from three medium-sized firms	145	55-64	chi square: $V = .596$; $p < .001$; willingness to retire correlated closer with self-appraised health than with subjective age
Jacobson and Eran (1980)	Israeli physicians females males	125 192	50 > 65	regression: ns; self-rated state of health not related to preference for retirement
Messer (1969)	U.S. Civil Service early retirees	3299	55-60	13.6% retired for health or family reasons
Palmore (1964)	1951 and 1963 Survey of Aged, of OASDI beneficiaries	—	—	among retirees > 65, reason for retirement per health declined from 41% in 1951 to 35% in 1963
Parnes (1980)	National Longitudinal Study	5000	45-59 in 1966	20% of the employed versus 80% of retired reported severe physical and mental impairments

Study	Description	Sample	Age	Findings
Parnes and Nestel (1975)	National Longitudinal Study national sample, of which 9.4% retired between 1966 and 1971	3817	50-64 in 1971	multiple classification analysis: $F = 22.07$, $p < .01$; men with health problems more likely to retire prior to age 65 than those whose health did not affect work
Parnes and Nestel (1981)	National Longitudinal Study of men followed from 1966 to 1976	1047	55-69 in 1976	retirement because of poor health more common among unmarried white men (54%) than married men (41%), but slightly more common among married black men (53%) than unmarried (49%)
Pollman (1971)	male early UAW retirees	442	60-65	poor health noted by 24.49% as reason for early retirement
Quinn (1977)	married men from Retirement History Study	4354	58-63	regression: coefficient = $-.204$, $t = 20.71$, $p < .01$; health was single most important explanation of labor force status (retirement)
Quinn (1981)	self-employed males from Retirement History Study	836	58-63 in 1969	regression: $= .128$, $t = 6.51$, p not provided; health limitation positively related to self-reported status, but whole R^2 was only .17
Schmitt and McCune (1981)	Michigan civil service employees with more than 30 years service and one-year follow-up	513 379	55 > 70	discriminant analysis: health variables (general health, doctor visits, and illnesses) added nonsignificantly to the r_c following previously entered demographic and financial variables

(continued)

TABLE F-3 Studies of Relations Between Physiological and Psychological Variables and Retirement (continued)

Factor	Population	n	Age	Relations with Retirement
Stanford (1971)	military officers and enlisted men	729	≥20 years of active duty	chi square: statistics not provided; poor health was not significantly related to retirement anticipation
Streib and Schneider (1971)	Cornell Study of Occupational Retirement followed from 1952 to 1958	1969	>63 in 1952	chi square = 6.25, $p < .30$ for men and 15.39, $p < .01$ for women; older persons who retire tend to be less healthy than those who continue to work
Job satisfaction Barfield and Morgan (1970)	National sample of working and retired persons working plus retired UAW members	1652 675 1090	35-59	dissatisfaction related to decision to to retire
Eden and Jacobson (1976)	Israeli male executives from 13 organizations	179	50-75	$r = -.12$, $p < .05$; low job satisfaction related to being favorably disposed toward retirement
Jacobson and Eran (1980)	Israeli physicians males and females	192 125	50 > 65	$r = 0.14$, $p < .01$; job dissatisfaction correlated with the retirement preference index; prediction of preference for retirement by instrumentality perceptions stronger for those who were less satisfied, felt more work-related stress, and had a lower evaluation of medical competence

Messer (1969)	U.S. Civil Service early retires	3299	55-60	17.9% left because they were dissatisfied with work
Parnes and Nestel (1975)	National Longitudinal Study national sample, of which 9.4% retired between 1966 and 1971	3817	50-64 in 1971	multiple classification analysis: $F = 9.41$, $p < .01$; the less satisfied with work the greater the probability of retiring
Rose & Mogey (1972)	males from VA Normative Aging Study	2000	Various age groups	job satisfaction somewhat removed from age of preferred retirement; r's = .11, .08, .07, .05, and .02 for satisfaction with salary, initiative, pressure, opportunity for advancement, and supervisor, respectively; $r = .10$ between overall satisfaction and age of preferred retirement
		—	—	
Schmitt et al. (1979)	Michigan civil service retirees and nonretirees	250 422	55 < 65	discriminant analysis: $F = 4.74$, $p < .05$; retirees' jobs less intrinsically satisfying

(continued)

345

TABLE F-3 Studies of Relations Between Physiological and Psychological Variables and Retirement (continued)

Factor	Population	n	Age	Relations with Retirement
Job Satisfaction				
Schmitt and McCune (1981)	Michigan civil service employees with more than 30 years service and one-year follow-up	513 379	55 > 70	discriminant analysis: $F(5, 117) = 2.57$, $p < .05$; job attitudes (job satisfaction, job involvement, desire to work, feedback, and motivating potential) added significantly to prediction of retirement status following previously entered demographic, financial, and health variables ($r_c = .61$)
Streib and Thompson (1957)	male panel study employed in 1952 and recontacted in 1954	2007	64 in 1952	those who retired less satisfied with their jobs and less likely to regard work as an important value in itself

Locus of control Schmitt et al. (1979)	Michigan civil service retirees and nonretirees	250 422	55 < 65	discriminant analysis: $F = 1.00$, ns; locus of control not related to early retirement
Self-Esteem Schmitt et al. (1979)	Michigan civil service retirees and nonretirees	250 422	55-65	discriminant analysis: $F = 1.08$, ns; self-esteem not related to early retirement
Work commitment Parnes and Nestel (1975)	National Longitudinal Study national sample, of which 9.4% retired between 1966 and 1971	3817	50-64 in 1971	multiple classification analysis: $F = 13.49$. $p < .01$; the greater the work commitment, the less likely to retire

TABLE F-4   Studies of Relations Between Organizational Variables and Retirement

Factor	Population	n	Age	Relations with Retirement
Amount of work Barfield and Morgan (1970)	national sample of working and retired persons; working plus retired UAW members	1652 675 1090	35-59	positively related to decision to retire
Eden and Jacobson (1976)	Israeli male executives from 13 organizations	179	50-75	R = -.12, ns; number of hours worked per week negatively related to attitude toward retirement (which includes a desire to leave work element)
Autonomy Jacobson (1972b)	male British factory operatives from three medium-sized firms	145	55-64	chi square; V = .306, p < .01; the lower the autonomy, the greater the potential to be retirement-oriented
Quinn (1977)	married men from Retirement History Study	4354	58-63	regression: coefficient = -.014, t = 1.39, ns; low autonomy related to early retirement
Schmitt et al. (1979)	Michigan civil service retirees and nonretirees	250 422	55-65	discriminant analysis: F = 15.94, p < .05; retirees' jobs had less autonomy
Co-workers Eden and Jacobson (1976)	Israeli male executives from 13 organizations	179	50-75	r = .09, ns; peer relations not related to attitude toward retirement

Jacobson (1974)	British factory operatives males and females	145 70	55-64 50-59	chi square = 15.79, p < .001; women whose real friends were workmates more reluctant to retire than when friends were outside of work for men, ns
Job change Pollman and Johnson (1974)	male UAW skilled machine operators, assembly line, & utility class workers employees retirees	256 442	60-65	chi square = 18.175, p < .001; recent change in job greater for early retirees χ^2 = 4.885, p < .05; expected job change greater for early retirees than for those employed
Job strain Jacobson (1972b)	male British factory operatives from three medium-sized firms	145	55-64	chi square: V = .368, p < .001; strain (light, moderate, and heavy) positively related to willingness to retire at pensionable age V = .195, p < .05; the heavier the strain, the greater the belief that retirement should occur at age below the pensionable age
Job tension/stress Eden and Jacobson (1976)	Israeli male executives from 13 organizations	179	50-75	r = .13, p < .05; high job tension related to being favorably disposed toward retirement r = .13, p < .05; overload on job related to attitude toward retirement (including a desire to leave work element)

(continued)

TABLE F-4 Studies of Relations Between Organizational Variables and Retirement (continued)

Factor	Population	n	Age	Relations with Retirement
Jacobson and Eran (1980)	Israeli physicians females and males	125 192	50 > 65	r = .09, ns; job stress not significantly correlated with the retirement preference index, but the prediction of preference for retirement by instrumentality perceptions stronger for those who felt more work-related stress, less satisfied, and had lower evaluation of medical competence
Pay/extrinsic rewards Barfield and Morgan (1978)	10-year follow-up of University of Michigan Survey Research Center national cross-section	486	35-64	multiple classification analysis: low historical income experience leads to early retirement, is escape from frequent unemployment
Boskin (1977)	married males in Panel Study of Income Dynamics, followed from 1968 to 1972	131	61-65 in 1968	regression: logit coefficient = -2.048; the greater the net earnings, the lower the probability of retirement (education level variable included in regression)
Burkhauser (1979)	male auto workers, cross-sectional data and two-year resurvey	761 326	59-64	regression: = -.029, t = 5.10, significance level not reported; value of earnings stream in the present job negatively related to early pension acceptance, = -.022 on resurvey

Study	Sample	N	Age	Findings
Eden and Jacobson (1976)	Israeli male executives from 13 organizations	179	50-75	r = -.08, ns; extrinsic rewards (including working conditions, pay, and status) not correlated with attitudes toward retirement
Parnes and Nestel (1975)	National Longitudinal Study national sample, of which 9.4% retired between 1966 and 1971	3817	50-64 in 1971	multiple classification analysis: F = .98; ns; no relationship between average hourly earnings and the probability of retirement
Parnes and Nestel (1981)	National Longitudinal Study of men followed from 1966 to 1976	1047	45-59 in 1976	early retirement more common for men with income per dependent in year preceding retirement of < $2,000 than for those with > $2,000
Rose and Mogey (1972)	males from VA Normative Aging Study	2000	various age groups	r = .17; higher pay positively related to later preferred age of retirement regression: partial r = .03; pay was power indexed by education, which correlated with pay at r = .47
Performance				
Eden and Jacobson (1976)	Israeli male executives from 13 organizations	179	50-75	r = -.16, p .05; self-reported lower effectiveness negatively related to desire to leave work
Jacobson and Eran (1980)	Israeli physicians females males	125 192	50 > 65	regression: higher self-rated job competence related to less preference for retirement

(continued)

TABLE F-4 Studies of Relations Between Organizational Variables and Retirement (continued)

Factor	Population	n	Age	Relations with Retirement
Katona et al. (1969)	automobile and agricultural implement workers, retired and nonretired	1123	58-61	having difficulty keeping up with job and being unable to do anything about it was related to having retired
Pressure to retire Barfield and Morgan (1970)	national sample of working and retired persons; working plus retired UAW members	1652 675 1090	35-59	perceived and actual pressure from union positively related to decision to retire
Promotions Eden and Jacobson (1976)	Israeli male executives from 13 organizations	179	50-75	$R = -.14$, $p < .05$; the greater the number of previous promotions in the present organization, the less the desire to retire

REFERENCES

Aaron, H. *Outline of testimony of Henry Aaron before the Select Committee on Aging.* U.S. House of Representatives, May 20, 1981.

Abrams, A. J. Job engineering and job reassignment for the older worker. In *Job redesign and occupational training for older workers: International Management Seminar: Supplement to the final report.* Paris: Organisation for Economic Cooperation and Development, 1965.

Advisory Council on Social Security. *Reports of the Quadrennial Advisory Council.* Committee on Ways and Means, U.S. House of Representatives (94th Congress, 1st Session), 1975.

Age Discrimination in Employment Act of 1967, P.L. 90-202.

Aging and Work. EEOC reports increase in age discrimination complaints. Vol. 4(4), 1981.

Aldag, R. J., & Brief, A. P. Age and reactions to task characteristics. *Industrial Gerontology,* 1975, 2, 223-229.

Aldag, R. J., & Brief, A. P. Age, work values and employee reactions. *Industrial Gerontology,* 1977, 4, 192-197.

Alderfer, C. P., & Guzzo, R. A. Life experiences and adults' enduring strength of desires in organizations. *Administrative Science Quarterly,* 1979, 24, 347-361.

Allen, R. T. *Today is the first day of the rest of your life.* Toronto: McClelland & Stewart, 1971.

Altimus, C. A., & Tersine, R. J. Chronological age and job satisfaction: The young blue collar worker. *Academy of Management Journal,* 1973, 16, 53-66.

Andrews, I. R., & Henry, M. M. Management attitudes toward pay. *Industrial Relations,* 1964, 3, 29-39.

Andrisani, P. J., Appelbaum, E., Koppel, R., & Miljus, R. C. *Work attitudes and labor market experience: Evidence from the National Longitudinal Surveys.* New York: Praeger, 1978.

Angle, H. L., & Perry, J. I. An empirical assessment of organizational commitment and organizational effectiveness. *Administrative Science Quarterly,* 1981, 26, 1-14.

Arenberg, D., & Robertson-Tchabo, E. A. Learning and aging. In J. E. Birren & K. W. Schaie (Eds.), *Handbook of the psychology of aging.* New York: Van Nostrand Reinhold, 1977.

Armstrong, J. C. Decision behavior and outcome of midlife career changers. *The Vocational Guidance Quarterly,* 1981, 29, 205-211.

Arnold, H. J., & Feldman, D. C. A multivariate analysis of the determinants of job turnover. *Journal of Applied Psychology,* 1982, 67, 350-360.

Arvey, R. D. Unfair discrimination in the employment interview: Legal and psychological aspects. *Psychological Bulletin,* 1979, 86, 736-765.

Arvey, R. D., & Dewhirst, H. D. Relationship between diversity of interests, age, job satisfaction and job performance. *Journal of Occupational Psychology,* 1979, 52, 17-23.

Arvey, R. D., & Mussio, S. Test discrimination, job performance and age. *Industrial Gerontology,* 1973, 16, 22-29.

Asher, J. J., & Sciarrino, J. A. Realistic work sample tests: A review. *Personal Psychology,* 1974, 27, 519-534.

Babzhin, V. Accents on aging. *Public Welfare,* Jan. 1971.

Barber, J. W. Training the middle-age worker. In *Job redesign and occupational training for older workers.* Paris: Organisation for Economic Cooperation and Development, 1965.

Barfield, R., & Morgan, J. *Early retirement: The decision and the experience and a second look.* Ann Arbor: University of Michigan, Institute for Social Research, 1970.

Barfield, R., & Morgan, J. Trends in planned early retirement. *The Gerontologist,* 1978, 18(1), 13-18.

Barkin, S. *The older worker in industry.* Legislative Document No. 66 (State of New York), 1933, 17, 325-332.

Barrett, G. V., Mihal, W. L., Panek, P. E., Sterns, H. L., & Alexander, R. A. Information processing skills predictive of accident involvement for younger and older commercial drivers. *Industrial Gerontology,* 1977, 4, 173-182.

Bass, A. R., & Turner, J. N. Ethnic group differences in relationships among criteria of job performance. *Journal of Applied Psychology,* 1973, 57, 101-109.

Bassett, G. A. *A study of factors associated with turnover of exempt personnel.* Crotonville, NY: Behavioral Research Service, General Electric Company, 1967.

Batten, M. D. The industrial health counseling service: The application of a unique industrial health system. *Industrial Gerontology,* 1973, 19, 38-48.

Baugher, D. Is the older worker inherently incompetent? *Aging and Work,* 1978, 1, 243-250.

Baumgartel, H., & Sobol, R. Background and organizational factors in absenteeism. *Personnel Psychology,* 1959, 12, 431-443.

Beattie, W., Jr. Social policies and aging: A global perspective. *Lecture series: World perspectives and aging.* Institute on Aging, University of Washington, Oct. 16, 1980.

Beatty, R. W., & Beatty, J. R. Longitudinal study of absenteeism of hard-core unemployed. *Psychological Reports,* 1975, 36, 395-406.

Belbin, R. M. The discovery method in training older workers. In H. L. Sheppard (Ed.), *Toward an industrial gerontology.* Cambridge, MA: Schenkman, 1970.

Belbin, R. M., & Clark, F. L. The relationships between retirement patterns and work as revealed by the British census. *Industrial Gerontology,* 1970, 4, 12-26.

Bell, D. Prevalance of private retirement plans. *Monthly Labor Review,* 1975, 98(10), 17-20.

Berkowitz, M. Workmen's compensation and the older worker. *Industrial Gerontology,* 1972, 10, 1-13.

Berkowitz, M. The older worker's stake in worker's compensation. *Industrial Gerontology,* 1975, 2(1), 53-61.

Berlew, D. E., & Hall, D. T. The socialization of managers: Effects of expectations on performance. *Administrative Science Quarterly,* 1966, 11, 207-223.

Berman, H. J., & Holtzman, J. M. *Early retirement decisions: Factors differentiating retirees from non-retirees.* Paper presented at the 31st Annual Scientific Meeting of the Gerontological Society, Dallas, November 1978.

Bernardin, H. J. The relationship of personality variables to organizational withdrawal. *Personal Psychology,* 1977, 30, 17-27.

Beveridge, W. E. Retirement and life significance: A study of the adjustment to retirement of a sample of men at management level. *Human Relations,* 1980, 33, 69-78.

Birren, J. E. *The psychology of aging.* Englewood Cliffs, NJ: Prentice-Hall, 1964.

Birren, J. E., & Renner, V. J. Research on the psychology of aging: Principles and experimentation. In J. E. Birren & K. W. Schaie (Eds.), *Handbook of the psychology of aging.* New York: Van Nostrand Reinhold, 1977.

Birren, J. E., & Schaie, K. W. (Eds.). *Handbook of the psychology of aging.* New York: Van Nostrand Reinhold, 1977.

Birren, J. E., & Williams, M. V. (Eds.). Speed of behavior. In L. W. Poon (Ed.), *Aging in the 1980's: Psychological issues.* Washington, DC: American Psychological Association, 1980.

Birren, J. E., Woods, A. M., & Williams, M. V. Behavioral slowing with age: Causes, organization, and consequences. In L. W. Poon (Ed.), *Aging in the 1980's: Psychological issues.* Washington, DC: American Psychological Association, 1980.

Bixby, L. E. Retirement patterns in the United States: Research and policy interaction. *Social Security Bulletin,* 1976, 38, 3-19.

Blood, M. R. Work values and job satisfaction. *Journal of Applied Psychology,* 1969, 53, 456-459.

Bluedorn, A. C. A unified model of turnover from organizations. *Human Relations,* 1982, 35, 135-153.

Blumberg, M. Job switching in autonomous work groups: An exploratory study in a Pennsylvania coal mine. *Academy of Management Journal,* 1980, 23, 287-306.

Boskin, M. J. Social Security and retirement decisions. *Economic Inquiry,* 1977, 15, 1-25.

Botwinick, J. Intellectual abilities. In J. E. Birren & K. W. Schaie (Eds.), *Handbook of the psychology of aging.* New York: Van Nostrand Reinhold, 1977.

Bowers, W. H. An appraisal of worker characteristics as related to age. *Journal of Applied Psychology,* 1952, 36, 296-300.

Bratthall, K. Flexible retirement and the new Swedish partial-pension scheme. *Industrial Gerontology,* 1976, 3(2), 157-165.

Bray, D. W., Campbell, R. J., & Grant, D. L. *Formative years in business: A long-term AT&T study of managerial lives.* New York: John Wiley, 1974.

Brayfield, A. H., & Crockett, W. H. Employee attitudes and employee performance. *Psychological Bulletin,* 1955, 52, 396-424.

Breaugh, J. A. Relationships between recruiting sources and employee performance, absenteeism, and work attitudes. *Academy of Management Journal,* 1981, 24(1), 142-147.

Breen, L. Z., & Spaeth, J. L. Age and productivity among workers in four Chicago companies. *Journal of Gerontology,* 1960, 15, 68-70.

Brito v. Zia Company, 5 FEP 1207 (1973).

Britton, J. O., & Thomas, K. R. Age and sex as employment variables: Views of employment service interviewers. *Journal of Employment Counseling,* 1973, 10, 180-186.

Broberg, M., Melching, D. E., & Maeda, P. Planning for the elderly in Japan. *The Gerontologist,* 1975, 15, 242-247.

Buchholz v. Symons Manufacturing Co., 445 F. Supp. 706, E.D. WIS (1978).

Buchholz, R. A. An empirical study of contemporary beliefs about work in American society. *Journal of Applied Psychology,* 1978, 63, 219-227.

Bureau of National Affairs. *Retirement policies and programs.* ASPA-BNA Survey No. 39. Washington, DC: Author 1980.

Burkhauser, R. V. The pension acceptance decision of older men. *Journal of Human Resources,* 1979, 14, 63-75.

Buzzard, R. R., & Shaw, W. J. An analysis of absence under a scheme of paid sick leave. *British Journal of Industrial Medicine,* 1952, 9, 282-295.

Campbell, H. Group incentive schemes: The effect of lack of understanding and of group size. *Occupational Psychology,* 1951-1952, 25-26, 15-21.

Campbell, J., Crooks, L., Mahoney, M., & Rock, D. *An investigation of sources of bias in the prediction of job performance—a six-year study.* Princeton, NJ: Educational Testing Service, 1973.

Chandler, H. R., Foster, K., & McCornack, R. Age and experience as salary predictors. *Personnel Journal,* 1963, 42, 502-504.

Chapman, J. B., & Ottemann, R. Employee preference for various compensation and fringe benefit options. *Personnel Administrator,* 1975, 20(7), 31-36.

Charles, D. C. Effect of participation in a pre-retirement program. *Gerontologist,* 1971, 11(1), 24-28.

Chelius, J. R. Economic and demographic aspects of the occupational injury problem. *Quarterly Review of Economics and Business,* 1979, 19(2), 65-70.

Cherrington, D. J. The values of younger workers. *Business Horizons,* 1977, 20, 18-30.

Cherrington, D. J., Condie, S. J., & England, J. L. Age and work values. *Academy of Management Journal,* 1979, 22, 617-623.

Chown, S. M. Rigidity and age. In C. Tibbits & W. Donahue (Eds.), *Social and psychological aspects of aging.* New York: Columbia University Press, 1962.

Chown, S. M. The effect of flexibility-rigidity and age on adaptability in job performance. *Industrial Gerontology,* 1972, 12, 105-121.

Chown, S. M. Morale, careers, and personal potentials. In J. E. Birren & K. W. Schaie (Eds.), *Handbook of the psychology of aging.* New York: Van Nostrand Reinhold, 1977.

Clay, H. M. A study of performance in relation to age at two printing works. *Journal of Gerontology,* 1956, 11(4), 417-424.

Clay, H. M. Review of reports and discussions. In *Job redesign and occupational training for older workers: Final report.* Paris: Organisation for Economic Cooperation and Development, 1965.

Clemente, F. Early career determinants of research productivity. *American Journal of Sociology,* 1973, 79(2), 409-419.

Cleveland, J. N., & Landy, F. J. The influence of rater and ratee age on two performance judgments. *Personnel Psychology,* 1981, 34, 19-29.

Clopton, W. Personality and career change. *Industrial Gerontology,* 1973, 17, 9-17.

Cole, S. Age and scientific performance. *American Journal of Sociology,* 1979, 84, 958-977.

Collins, K., & Brown, J. Canada's retirement policies. *Aging and Work,* 1978, 1(3), 101-108.

Connor, C. L., Walsh, R. P., Litzelman, D. K., & Alvarez, M. G. Evaluation of job applicants: The effects of age versus success. *Journal of Gerontology,* 1978, 33, 246-252.

Constas, K., & Vichas, R. P. An interpretive policy-making model of absenteeism with reference to the marginal worker in overseas plants. *Journal of Management Studies,* 1980, 17, 149-163.

Cook, J., & Wall, T. New work attitude measures of trust, organizational commitment and personal need non-fulfillment. *Journal of Occupational Psychology,* 1980, 53, 39-52.

Cooper, R., & Payne, R. Age and absence: A longitudinal study in three firms. *Occupational Psychology,* 1965, 39, 31-43.

Corso, J. F. Auditory perception and communication. In J. E. Birren & K. W. Schaie (Eds.), *Handbook of the psychology of aging.* New York: Van Nostrand Reinhold, 1977.

Cox, S. R., & Wooten, P. R. The long run problems of financing the social security system. *American Journal of Economics and Sociology,* 1978, 37(4), 397-412.

Craft, J. A., Doctors, S. I., Shkop, Y. M., & Benecki, T. J. Simulated management perceptions, hiring decisions and age. *Aging and Work,* 1979, 2, 95-102.

Craik, F.I.M. Age differences in human memory. In J. E. Birren & K. W. Schaie (Eds.), *Handbook of the psychology of aging.* New York: Van Nostrand Reinhold, 1977.

Crandall, N. F. Age difference in compensation preference. *Industrial Gerontology,* 1977, 4(3), 159-166.

Crandall, N. F., & Lundstrom, A. B. Preferences for compensation options. *Journal of Business Research,* 1980, 8, 21-37.

Crano, W. D., & Brewer, M. B. *Principles of research in social psychology.* New York: McGraw-Hill, 1973.

Cunningham, W. R. Speed, age, and qualitative differences in cognitive functioning. In L. W. Poon (Ed.), *Aging in the 1980's: Psychological issues.* Washington, DC: American Psychological Association, 1980.

Dalton, G. W., & Thompson, P. H. Accelerating obsolescence of older engineers. *Harvard Business Review,* 1971, 49, 57-67.

Dalton, G. W., Thompson, P. H., & Price, R. L. The four stages of professional careers: A new look at performance by professionals. *Organizational Dynamics,* 1977, 19-42.

Dalton, D. R., & Todor, W. D. Turnover turned over: An expanded and positive perspective. *Academy of Management Review,* 1979, 4, 225-235.

Davis, D. L., & Taylor, W. The senior community service project: A manpower model for the older disadvantaged. *Industrial Gerontology,* 1975, 2, 122-134.

de la Mare, G., & Sergean, R. Two methods of studying changes in absence with age. *Occupational Psychology,* 1961, 35, 245-252.

Dennis, W. Predicting scientific productivity in later maturity from research of earlier decades. *Journal of Gerontology,* 1954, 9(4), 465-467.

Dennis, W. Creative productivity between the ages of 20 and 80. In B. L. Neugarten (Ed.), *Middle age and aging.* Chicago: University of Chicago Press, 1968.

Dodd, B. A study in adult retraining: The gas man. *Occupational Psychology,* 1967, 41, 143-153.

Downs, S. Labour turnover in two public service organizations. *Occupational Psychology,* 1967, 41, 137-142.

Dubin, R. Industrial workers' worlds: A study of the "central life interests" of industrial workers. *Social Problems,* 1956, 3, 131-142.

Dunnette, M. D., Arvey, R. D., & Banas, P. A. Why do they leave? *Personnel,* 1973, 3, 25-39.

Dyer, L., & Schwab, D. P. Private pension plan coverage in manufacturing: A cross-sectional study. *Industrial Gerontology,* 1971, 10, 21-28.

Dyer, L. D., & Theriault, R. The determinants of pay satisfaction. *Journal of Applied Psychology,* 1976, 61, 596-604.

Eden, D., & Jacobson, D. Propensity to retire among older executives. *Journal of Vocational Behavior,* 1976, 8, 145-154.

Eisenberg, J. Relationship between age and effects upon work: A study of older workers in the garment industry. *Dissertation Abstracts International,* 1980,

41(4A), 1982.

Ekerdt, D. J., Rose, C. L., Bosse, R., & Costa, P. T. Longitudinal change in preferred age of retirement. *Occupational Psychology,* 1976, 49(3), 161-169.

Employee Benefit Review. Attitudes toward pensions and retirement detailed in Harris study commissioned by Johnson & Higgins. Vol. 33, 1979. (a)

Employee Benefit Review. Inflation erodes pension benefit purchasing power. Vol. 33, 1979. (b)

Employee Benefit Review. Age 70 mandatory retirement: It became law and is now corporate policy, but will workers use it? Vol. 34, 1979. (c)

Eng, J. E., & Gottsdanker, J. S. Positive changes from a career development program. *Training and Development Journal,* January 1979, 33, 3-7.

Evans, M. G., Kiggundu, M. N., & House, R. J. A partial test and extension of the job characteristics model of motivation. *Organizational Behavior and Human Performance,* 1979, 24, 354-381.

Farris, G. F. A predictive study of turnover. *Personnel Psychology,* 1971, 24, 311-328.

Federico, J. M., Federico, P., & Lundquist, G. W. Predicting women's turnover as a function of extent of met salary expectations and biodemographic data. *Personnel Psychology,* 1976, 29, 559-566.

Feild, H. S., Bayley, G. A., & Bayley, S. M. Employment test validation for minority and nonminority production workers. *Personnel Psychology,* 1977, 30, 37-46.

Fishbein, M. Attitude and prediction of behavior. In M. Fishbein (Ed.), *Readings in attitude theory and measurement.* New York: John Wiley, 1967.

Flanagan, R. J., Strauss, G., & Ulman, L. Worker discontent and workplace behavior. *Industrial Relations,* 1974, 13, 101-123.

Fleishman, E. A., & Berniger, J. One way to reduce office turnover. *Personnel,* 1960, 37, 63-69.

Fox, H., & Lefkowitz, J. Differential validity: Ethnic group as a moderator in predicting job performance. *Personnel Psychology,* 1974, 27, 209-223.

Fozard, J. L. The time for remembering. In L. W. Poon (Ed.), *Aging in the 1980's: Psychological issues.* Washington, DC: American Psychological Association, 1980.

Fozard, J. L., Wolf, E., Bell, B., McFarland, R. A., & Podolsky, S. Visual perception and communication. In J. E. Birren & K. W. Schaie (Eds.), *Handbook of the psychology of aging.* New York: Van Nostrand Reinhold, 1977.

Freeman, R. B. The effect of demographic factors on age-earnings profiles. *Journal of Human Resources,* 1979, 14(3), 289-381.

Froggatt, P. Short-term absence from industry, I: Literature, definitions, data, and the effect of age and length of service. *British Journal of Industrial Medicine,* 1970, 27, 199-210.

Frumkin, R., & Schmitt, D. Pension improvements since 1974 reflect inflation, new U.S. law. *Monthly Labor Review,* 1979, 102(4), 32-37.

Gael, S., Grant, D. L., & Ritchie, R. J. Employment test validation for minority and nonminority clerks with work sample criteria. *Journal of Applied Psychology,* 1975, 60, 420-426. (a)

Gael, S., Grant, D. L., & Ritchie, R. J. Employment test validation for minority and nonminority telephone operators. *Journal of Applied Psychology,* 1975, 60, 411-419. (b)

Garrison, K. R., & Muchinsky, P. M. Attitudinal and biographical predictors of incidental absenteeism. *Journal of Vocational Behavior,* 1977, 10, 221-230.

Giambra, L. M., & Arenberg, D. Problem solving, concept learning, and age. In L. W. Poon (Ed.), *Aging in the 1980's: Psychological issues.* Washington, DC: American Psychological Association, 1980.

Gibson, J. L., & Klein, S. M. Employee attitudes a a function of age and length of service: A reconceptualization. *Academy of Management Journal,* 1970, 13, 411-425.

Glamser, F. D. The impact of preretirement programs on the retirement experience. *Journal of Gerontology,* 1981, 36, 244-250.

Glenn, N. D. Cohort analysts' futile quest: Statistical attempts to separate age, period, and cohort effects. *American Sociological Review,* 1976, 41, 900-904.

Glenn, N. D., Taylor, P. D., & Weaver, C. N. Age and job satisfaction among males and females: A multivariate multisurvey study. *Journal of Applied Psychology,* 1977, 62, 189-193.

Glueck, W. F. *Personnel: A diagnostic approach.* Dallas, TX: Business Publications, 1978.

Goldstein, I. L. Training in work organizations. In M. R. Rosenzweig and L. W. Porter (Eds.), *Annual review of psychology.* Palo Alto, CA: Annual Reviewers, 1980.

Gordus, J.P. *Leaving early: Perspectives and problems in current retirement practice and policy.* Kalamazoo, MI: W. E. Upjohn Institute for Employment Research, 1980.

Gottfredson, G. D. Career stability and redirection in adulthood. *Journal of Applied Psychology,* 1977, 62, 436-445.

Gould, S. Age, job complexity, satisfaction, and performance. *Journal of Vocational Behavior,* 1979, 14, 209-223. (a)

Gould, S. Characteristics of career planners in upwardly mobile occupations. *Academy of Management Journal,* 1979, 22(3), 539-550. (b)

Goulet, L. R., & Baltes, P. B. (Eds.). *Life-span developmental psychology: Research and theory.* New York: Academic Press, 1970.

Green, R. F., & Reimanis, G. The age-intelligence relationship: Longitudinal studies can mislead. *Industrial Gerontology,* 1970, 6, 1-16.

Greenberg, L. Productivity of older workers. *Gerontologist,* 1961, 1, 38-41.

Greenhalgh, L. A process model of organizational turnover: The relationship with job security as a case in point. *Academy of Management Review,* 1980, 5, 299-303.

Griew, S. Methodological problems in industrial aging research. *Occupational Psychology,* 1959, 33, 36-45.

Grimaldi, J., & Simonds, R. *Safety management.* Chicago: Irwin, 1975.

Gruenfeld, L. W. A study of the motivation of industrial supervisors. *Personnel Psychology,* 1967, 15, 303-314.

Grusky, O. Administrative succession in formal organizations. *Social Forces,* 1960, 39, 105-115.

Gupta, N., & Beehr, T. A. Job stress and employee behaviors. *Organizational Behavior and Human Performance,* 1979, 23, 373-387.

Gurin, G., Veroff, J., & Feld, S. *Americans view their mental health.* New York: Basic Books, 1960.

Gutteridge, T. Commentary: A comparison of perspectives. In L. Dyer (Eds.), *Careers in organizations: Individual planning and organizational development.* Ithaca, NY: Cornell University, 1976.

Haberlandt, K. F. Learning, memory and age. *Industrial Gerontology,* 1973, 19, 20-37.

Hackman, J. R., & Lawler, E. E. Employee reactions to job characteristics. *Journal of Applied Psychology,* 1971, 55, 259-286.

Hackman, J. R., & Oldham, G. R. Motivation through the design of work: Test of a theory. *Organizational Behavior and Human Performance,* 1976, 16, 250-279.

Haefner, J. E. Race, age, sex and competence as factors in employer selection of the disadvantaged. *Journal of Applied Psychology,* 1977, 62(2), 199-202.

Hagerty, K. V. *Retirement, a bibliography through 1972.* Chicago: University of Chicago, Industrial Relations Center, 1973.

Hale, A. R., & Hale, M. *A review of the industrial accident research literature.* London: National Institute of Industrial Psychology, 1972.

Hall, A., & Johnson, T. R. The determinants of planned retirement age. *Industrial and Labor Relations Review,* 1980, 33(2), 241-254.

Hall, D. T. *Careers in organizations.* Santa Monica, CA: Goodyear, 1976.

Hall, D. T., & Mansfield, R. Relationships of age and seniority with career variables of engineers and scientists. *Journal of Applied Psychology,* 1975, 60, 201-210.

Hall, D. T., & Nougaim, K. E. An examination of Maslow's need hierarchy in an organizational setting. *Organizational Behavior and Human Performance,* 1968, 3, 12-35.

Hall, J. L. *Making vocational choices: A theory of careers.* Englewood Cliffs, NJ: Prentice-Hall, 1973.

Hammer, T. H., Landau, J. C., & Stern, R. N. Absenteeism when workers have a voice: The case of employee ownership. *Journal of Applied Psychology,* 1981, 66, 561-573.

Handyside, J. D. Satisfactions and aspirations. *Journal of Occupational Psychology,* 1961, 35, 213-243.

Hanman, B. The evaluation of physical ability. *New England Journal of Medicine,* 1958, 258, 986-993.

Heijbel, C.J.A. Adjustment of middle-aged and older workers to highly mechanized work. In *Job redesign and occupational training for older workers: Final report.* Paris: Organisation for Economic Cooperation and Development, 1965.

Heinrich, H. W. *Industrial accident prevention.* New York: McGraw-Hill, 1950.

Heinz, C. H. Older worker productivity, accident proneness and sickness records. In *Proceedings of the second conference on the problem of making a living while growing old: Age barriers to employment.* Philadelphia: Temple University, 1953.

Hellriegel, D., & White, G. A. Turnover of professionals in public accounting: A comparative analysis. *Personnel Psychology,* 1973, 26, 239-249.

Helmers, D., & Hyden, S. O. *Modern trends in Swedish pension systems,* 1968.

Heneman, H. G. III. The relationship between age and motivation to perform on the job. *Industrial Gerontology,* 1973, 16, 30-36.

Herman, J. B., Dunham, R. B., & Hulin, C. L. Organizational structure, demographic characteristics, and employee responses. *Organizational Behavior and Human Performance,* 1975, 13, 206-232.

Herzberg, F. I., Mausner, B., Peterson, R. O., & Capwell, D. R. *Job attitudes: Review of research and opinion.* Pittsburgh: Psychological Service of Pittsburgh, 1957.

Hewes, A. Study of accident records in a textile mill. *Journal of Industrial Hygiene,* 1921, 3, 187-188, 194-195.

Hill, M. Who stays home? *New Society,* 1967, 9, 459-460.

Holland, J. L. *Making vocational choices: A theory of careers.* Englewood Cliffs, NJ: Prentice-Hall, 1973.

Holley, W. H. Jr., Feild, H. S., & Holley, B. B. Age and reactions to jobs: An empirical study of paraprofessional workers. *Aging and Work,* 1978, 1, 33-40.

Hom, P. W. Effects of job peripherality and personal characteristics on the job satisfaction of part-time workers. *Academy of Management Journal,* 1979, 22, 551-565.

Horlick, M. Switzerland: Compulsory private pensions. *Social Security Bulletin,* 1973, 36(10), 46-49.

Horlick, M. New private pension law in the Federal Republic of Germany. *Social Security Bulletin,* 1975, 38(7), 38-39; 56.

Hrebiniak, L. G. Effects of job level and participation on employee attitudes and perceptions of influence. *Academy of Management Journal,* 1974, 17, 649-662.

Hulin, C. L., & Smith, P. C. A linear model of job satisfaction. *Journal of Applied Psychology,* 1965, 4, 209-216.

Hunt, J. S., & Saul, P. N. The relationship of age, tenure, and job satisfaction in males and females. *Academy of Management Journal,* 1975, 18, 690-702.

Ilgen, D. R., & Hollenback, J. H. The role of job satisfaction in absence behavior. *Organizational Behavior and Human Performance,* 1977, 19, 148-161.

International Expert Group Meeting on Volunteer Support for the Elderly with Problems. *Eurosocial Reports* No. 16, Vienna, 1981.

International Federation on Ageing. *Employment for the elderly in other industrialized nations.* Washington, DC: Government Printing Office, 1980. (a)

International Federation on Ageing. *Flexible retirement in other industrialized countries.* Washington, DC: Government Printing Office, 1980. (b)

International Federation on Ageing. *The provision of retirement income in other industralized countries.* Washington, DC: Government Printing Office, 1980. (c)

Isambert-Jamati, V. Absenteeism among women workers in industry. *International Labour Review,* 1962, 85, 248-261.

Ivancevich, J. M., & McMahon, J. T. A study of task-goal attributes, higher order need strength and performance. *Academy of Management Journal,* 1977, 20, 552-563.

Jabes, J. *Individual processes in organization behavior.* Arlington Heights, IL: AHM, 1978.

Jacobson, D. Willingness to retire in the relation of job strain and type of work. *Industrial Gerontology,* 1972, 13, 65-74. (a)

Jacobson, D. Fatigue producing factors in industrial work and pre-retirement attitudes. *Occupational Psychology,* 1972, 46, 193-200. (b)

Jacobson, D. Rejection of the retiree role: A study of female industrial workers in their 50's. *Human Relations,* 1974, 27(5), 477-492.

Jacobson, D., & Eran, M. Expectancy theory components and non-expectancy moderators as predictors of physician's preference for retirement. *Journal of Occupational Psychology,* 1980, 53, 11-26.

Jaffe, A. J. The retirement dilemma. *Industrial Gerontology,* 1972, 14, 1-88.

Jamal, M. Shift work related to job attitudes, social participation and withdrawal behavior: A study of nurses and industrial workers. *Personnel Psychology,* 1981, 34, 535-547.

James, L. R., & Jones, A. P. Perceived job characteristics and job satisfaction: An examination of reciprocal causation. *Personnel Psychology,* 1980, 33, 97-135.

Jamieson, G. H. Age, speed, and accuracy: A study in industrial retraining. *Industrial Gerontology,* 1969, 8, 50-51.

Job redesign and occupational training for older workers: Supplement to the final report. Paris: Organisation for Economic Cooperation and Development, 1965.

Johns, G. Attitudinal and non-attitudinal predictors of two forms of absence from work. *Organizational Behavior and Human Performance,* 1978, 22, 431-444.

Johnston, D. F. The aging of the baby boom cohorts. *Statistical Reporter,* No. 76-9, March 1976, 161-165.

Jones, A. P., James, L. R., & Bruni, J. R. Perceived leadership behavior and employee confidence in the leader as moderated by job involvement. *Journal of Applied Psychology,* 1975, 60, 146-149.

Jurgenson, C. E. Selected factors which influence job preferences. *Journal of Applied Psychology,* 1947, 31, 553-563.

Jurgenson, C. E. What job applicants look for in a company. *Personnel Psychology,* 1948, 1, 433-445.

Jurgenson, C. E. Job preferences: What makes a job good or bad? *Journal of Applied Psychology,* 1978, 63, 267-276.

Kamerman, S. B. Community services for the aged: The view from eight countries. *Gerontologist,* 1976, 16, 529-537.

Kaplan, R. S. *Financial crisis in the Social Security System.* Washington, DC: American Enterprise Institute for Public Policy Research, Domestic Affairs Study 47, June 1976.

Kasschau, P. L. Reevaluation of the need for retirement preparation programs. *Industrial Gerontology,* 1974, 1(1), 42-59.

Kasschau, P. L. Retirement and the social system. *Industrial Gerontology,* 1976, 3, 11-24.

Katona, G., Morgan, J. N., & Barfield, R. E. Retirement in prospect and retrospect. In W. Donahue et al. (Eds.), *Trends in early retirement.* Ann Arbor: University of Michigan, 1969.

Katz, R. Job longevity as a situational factor in job satisfaction. *Administrative Science Quarterly,* 1978, 23, 204-223.

Katz, R. The influence of job longevity on employee reactions to task characteristics. *Human Relations,* 1980, 31, 703-725.

Kaufman, H. G. *Obsolescence and professional career development.* New York: American Management Association, 1974.

Kelleher, C. H., & Quirk, D. A. Age, functional capacity, and work: An annotated bibliography. *Industrial Gerontology,* 1973, 13, 80-98.

Kelleher, C. H., & Quirk, D. A. Preparation for retirement. *Industrial Gerontology,* 1974, 1(3), 49-73.

Kidron, A. Work values and organizational commitment. *Academy of Management Journal,* 1978, 21, 239-247.

Kii, T. Recent extension of retirement age in Japan. *The Gerontologist,* 1979, 19(5), 41-46.

King, H. F. An age-analysis of some agricultural accidents. *Occupational Psychology,* 1955, 29, 245-253.

King, H. F. An attempt to use production data in the study of age and performance. *Journal of Gerontology,* 1956, 11, 410-416.

King, H. F., & Speakman, D. Age and industrial accident rates. *British Journal of Industrial Medicine,* 1953, 10, 51-58.

Kirchner, W. K. Some questions about "Differential validity: Ethnic group as a moderator in predicting job performance." *Personnel Psychology,* 1975, 28, 341-344.

Kirchner, W. K., & Dunnette, M. D. Attitudes toward older workers. *Personnel Psychology,* 1954, 7, 257-265.

Klebba, J. Industrial injuries among the urban population as recorded in the National Health Survey. In *Public Health Report.* Washington, DC: Government Printing Office, 1941.

Klores, M. S. Rater bias in forced-distribution performance ratings. *Personnel Psychology,* 1966, 19, 411-421.

Koch, J. L., & Rhodes, S. R. Predictors of turnover of female factory workers. *Journal of Vocational Behavior,* 1981, 18, 145-161.

Koch, J. L, & Steers, R. M. Job attachment, satisfaction, and turnover among public sector employees. *Journal of Vocational Behavior,* 1978, 12, 119-128.

Kossoris, M. D. Absenteeism and injury experience of older workers. *Monthly Labor Review,* 1940, 51(10), 789-804.

Kossoris, M. D. Absenteeism and injury experience of older workers. *Monthly Labor Review,* 1948, 67(12), 16-19.

Koyl, L. F. *Employing the older workers: Matching the employee to the job.* Washington, DC: National Council on Aging, 1974.

Koyl, L. F., & Hanson, P. M. *Age, physical ability and work potential.* New York: National Council on Aging, 1969.

Kuh, C. Selective placement of older workers. *Journal of Gerontology,* 1946, 1(3), 313-318.

Kutscher, R. E., & Walker, J. F. Comparative job performance of office workers by age. *Monthly Labor Review,* 1960, 83(1), 39-43.

Lahiri, D. K., & Choudhuri, P. K. Perceived importance of job factors by technical and non-technical employees. *Personnel Psychology,* 1966, 19, 287-296.

Landy, F. J., & Farr, J. L. Performance rating. *Psychological Bulletin,* 1980, 87, 72-107.

Lantzev, M. The correlation between social security measures and labour problems in the USSR. *International Social Security Review,* 1978, 31(4), 472-477.

LaRoque, P. Social Security in France. In S. Jenkins (Ed.), *Social Security: An international perspective.* New York: Columbia University Press, 1969.

Laufer, A. C., & Fowler, W. M., Jr. Work potential of the aging. *Personnel Administration,* 1971, 34(2), 20-25.

Lawler, E. E. Job design and employee motivation. *Personnel Psychology,* 1969, 22, 426-435.

Lawler, E. E. III. *Pay and organizational effectiveness: A psychological view.* New York: McGraw-Hill, 1971.

Lawler, E. E. III, & Porter, L. W. Predicting managers' pay and their satisfaction with their pay. *Personnel Psychology,* 1966, 19, 363-373.

Lawrence, B. S. Midlife crisis: The myth of the midlife crisis. *Sloan Management Review,* 1980, 21(4), 35-47.

Layton, B. Perceptual noise and aging. *Psychological Bulletin,* 1975, 82(6), 875-883.

Lee, S. M. An empirical analysis of organizational identification. *Academy of Management Journal,* 1971, 14, 213-226.

Lehman, H. C. *Age and achievement.* Princeton, NJ: Princeton University Press, 1953.

Levinson, D. J., Darrow, C., Klein, E., Levinson, M., & McKee, B. *The seasons of a man's life.* New York: Knopf, 1978.

Lewellen, W. G., & Lanser, H. P. Executive pay preferences. *Harvard Business Review,* 1973, 51, 115-122.

Ley, R. Labour turnover as a function of worker differences, work environment, and authoritarianism of foremen. *Journal of Applied Psychology,* 1966, 50, 497-500.

Linn, R. L. Single group validity, differential validity, and differential prediction. *Journal of Applied Psychology,* 1978, 63, 507-512.

Liu, Y. Retirees and retirement programs in the People's Republic of China. *Industrial Gerontology*, 1974, 1(2), 72-81.

Locke, E. A. What is job satisfaction? *Organizational Behavior and Human Performance*, 1969, 4, 309-336.

Locke, E. A. The nature and causes of job satisfaction. In M. D. Dunnette (Ed.), *Handbook of industrial and organizational psychology*. Chicago: Rand McNally, 1976.

Lodahl, T. M., & Kejner, J. The definition and measurement of job involvement. *Journal of Applied Psychology*, 1965, 49, 24-33.

Lundgren, E. F. Needed—retirement counseling programs in business. *Personnel Journal*, 1965, 44(8), 432-436.

Lykova, L. *Social security in the USSR*. Moscow: Novasti Press Agency, 1967.

Maddox, G. L., & Wiley, J. Scope concepts and methods in the study of aging. In R. H. Binstock & E. Shanas (Eds.), *Handbook of aging and the social sciences*. New York: Van Nostrand Reinhold, 1976.

Maher, H. Age and performance of two work groups. *Journal of Gerontology*, 1955, 10, 448-451.

Mangione, T. W. Turnover—some psychological and demographic correlates. In R. P. Quinn & T. W. Mangione (Eds.), *The 1969-1970 survey of working conditions*. Ann Arbor: University of Michigan, Survey Research Center, 1973.

Mann, J. Analysis of 1009 consecutive accident cases at one ordnance depot. *Industrial Medicine*, 1944, 13, 368-374.

Mannheim, B. A comparative study of work centrality, job rewards and satisfaction. *Sociology of Work and Occupations*, 1975, 2, 79-102.

Mark, J. A. Measurement of job performance and age. *Monthly Labor Review*, 1956, 79(12), 1410-1414.

Mark, J. A. Comparative job performance by age. *Monthly Labor Review*, 1957, 80(12), 1467-1471.

Marsh, R. M., & Mannari, H. Organizational commitment and turnover: A predictive study. *Administrative Science Quarterly*, 1977, 22, 57-75.

Martin, J. Some aspects of absence in a light engineering factory. *Occupational Psychology*, 1971, 45, 77-91.

Martin, T. N., Jr. A contextual model of employee turnover intentions. *Academy of Management Journal*, 1979, 22, 313-324.

Martin, T. N. Modeling the turnover process. *Journal of Management Studies*, 1980, 17, 261-274.

Martin, T.N., & Hunt, J. G. Social influence and intent to leave: A path-analytic process model. *Personnel Psychology*, 1980, 33, 505-528.

Maslow, A. *Motivation and personality*. New York: Harper & Row, 1954.

Mathews, J. J., & Cobb, B. B. Relationships between age, ATC experience, and job ratings of terminal area traffic controllers. *Aerospace Medicine*, 1974, 45, 56-60.

McClelland, D. C., Atkinson, J. W., Clark, R. A., & Lowell, E. L. *The achievement motive*. New York: Appleton-Century-Crofts, 1953.

McFarland, R. A. The older worker in industry. *Harvard Business Review*, 1943, 21, 505-520.

McFarland, R. A. The need for functional age. Measurements in industrial gerontology. *Industrial Gerontology*, 1973, 19, 1-19.

McKain, W. C., Jr. Aging and rural life. In W. Donahue & C. Tibbetts (Eds.), *The new frontiers of aging*. Ann Arbor: University of Michigan Press, 1957.

Meier, E. L., & Kerr, E. A. Capabilities of middle-aged and older workers: A survey of the literature. *Industrial Gerontology*, 1976, 22, 147-156.

Meltzer, H. Age differences in work attitudes. *Journal of Gerontology,* 1958, 13, 74-81.

Messer, E. F. Thirty-eight years is a plenty. In W. Donahue et al. (Eds.), *Trends in early retirement.* Ann Arbor: University of Michigan Press, 1969.

Michaels, C. E., & Spector, P. E. Causes of employee turnover: A test of the Mobley, Griffeth, Hand, and Meglino model. *Journal of Applied Psychology,* 1982, 67, 53-59.

Michigan Survey Research Center. *Income and welfare in the U.S.* New York: McGraw-Hill, 1962.

Miller, H. E., Katerberg, R., & Hulin, C. L. Evaluation of the Mobley, Horner, & Hollingsworth model of employee turnover. *Journal of Applied Psychology,* 1979, 64, 509-517.

Miller, J. A., Bass, B. M., & Mihal, W. L. *An experiment to test methods of increasing self-development activities among research and development personnel.* Rochester, NY: University of Rochester, Management Research Center, 1973.

Miner, M. G. *Equal employment opportunity: Program and results.* Washington, DC: Bureau of National Affairs, 1976.

Minor, F. J. The prediction of turnover of clerical employees. *Personnel Psychology,* 1958, 11, 393-402.

Mirvis, P. H., & Lawler, E. E. III. Measuring the financial impact of employee attitudes. *Journal of Applied Psychology,* 1977, 62, 1-8.

Mistretta v. Sandia Corporation, 29 U.S.C.A., 621 (1977).

Mobley, W. H., Griffeth, R. W., Hand, H. H., & Meglino, B. M. Review and conceptual analysis of the employee turnover process. *Psychological Bulletin,* 1979, 86, 493-522.

Mobley, W. H., Hand, H. H., Baker, R. L., & Meglino, B. M. Conceptual and empirical analysis of military recruit training attrition. *Journal of Applied Psychology,* 1979, 64, 10-18.

Mobley, W. H., Horner, S. O., & Hollingsworth, A. T. An evaluation of precursors of hospital employee turnover. *Journal of Applied Psychology,* 1978, 63, 408-414.

Monczyka, R. M., Foster, L. W., Reif, W. E., & Newstrom, J. W. Pay satisfaction: Money is not the only answer. *Compensation Review,* 1977, 9(4), 22-28.

Morris, J. H., & Sherman, J. D. Generalizability of an organizational commitment model. *Academy of Management Journal,* 1981, 24, 512-526.

Morris, J. H., & Steers, R. M. Structural influences on organizational commitment. *Journal of Vocational Behavior,* 1980, 17, 50-57.

Morrison, P. A. *Demographic certainties and uncertainties in the future of Social Security.* Santa Monica, CA: The Rand Corporation, 1981.

Morrison, R. F. Career adaptivity: The effective adaptation of managers to changing role demands. *Journal of Applied Psychology,* 1977, 62, 549-558.

Morrow, P. C. Retirement preparation: A preventive approach to counseling the elderly. *Counseling and Values,* 1980, 24, 236-246.

Morse, N. C., & Weiss, R. S. The function and meaning of work and the job. *American Sociological Review,* 1955, 20, 191-198.

Mortimer, J. T., & Lorence, J. Work experience and occupational value socialization: A longitudinal study. *American Journal of Sociology,* 1979, 84, 1361-1385.

Mowday, R. T., Porter, L. W., & Stone, E. F. Employee characteristics as predictors of turnover among female clerical employees in two organizations. *Journal of Vocational Behavior,* 1978, 12, 321-332.

Mowday, R. T., Steers, R. M., & Porter, L. W. The measurement of organizational commitment. *Journal of Vocational Behavior,* 1979, 14, 224-247.

Muchinsky, P. M. Age and job facet satisfaction: A conceptual reconsideration. *Aging and Work,* 1978, 1, 175-179.

Murrell, K. F. H. Redesigning jobs for older workers. In *Job re-design and occupational training for older workers.* Paris: Organisation for Economic Cooperation and Development, 1965.

Namorsky, J. D. Impact of the 1978 ADEA amendments on employee benefit plans. *Employee Relations Law Journal,* 1978, 4, 173-184.

National Council for the Care of Elderly People. *Measures to assist elderly people in Norway.* Oslo, 1974.

Naylor, J. E., & Vincent, N. L. Predicting female absenteeism. *Personnel Psychology,* 1959, 12, 81-84.

Nealey, S. M. Determining worker preferences among employee benefit programs. *Journal of Applied Psychology,* 1964, 48, 2-12. (a)

Nealey, S. M. Pay and benefit preferences. *Industrial Relations,* 1964, 3, 17-28. (b)

Nealey, S. M., & Goodale, J. G. Worker preferences among time-off benefits and pay. *Journal of Applied Psychology,* 1967, 51, 357-361.

Neapolitan, J. Occupational change in mid-career: An exploratory investigation. *Journal of Vocational Behavior,* 1980, 16, 212-225.

Near, J. P., Rice, R. W., & Hunt, R. G. Work and extra-work correlates of life and job satisfaction. *Academy of Management Journal,* 1978, 21, 248-264.

Neugarten, B. L. Personality and the aging process. In R. H. Williams et al. (Eds.), *Process of aging,* Vol. 1. New York: Atherton, 1963.

Newbold, E. M. A contribution to the study of the human factor in the causation of accidents. In W. Haddon et al. (Eds.), *Accident research: Its methods and approaches.* New York: Harper & Row, 1964. (Reprinted from Report No. 34, 1926, Medical Research Committee, Industrial Fatigue Research Board.)

Newman, J. E. Understanding the organizational structure-job attitude relationship through perceptions of the work environment. *Organizational Behavior and Human Performance,* 1975, 14, 371-397.

Newsham, D. B. The challenge of change for the adult trainee. *Industrial Gerontology,* 1969, 3, 32-33.

Nicholson, N., Brown, C. A., & Chadwick-Jones, J. K. Absence from work and personal characteristics. *Journal of Applied Psychology,* 1977, 62, 319-327.

Nicholson, N., & Goodge, P. M. The influence of social, organizational and biographical factors on female absence. *Journal of Management Studies,* 1976, 13, 234-254.

O'Brien, G. E., & Dowling, P. Age and job satisfaction. *Australian Psychologist,* 1981, 16, 49-61.

O'Connor, E. J., Wexley, K. N., & Alexander, R. A. Single group validity: Fact or fallacy? *Journal of Applied Psychology,* 1975, 60, 352-355.

Oliver, R. L. Antecedents of salesman's compensation perceptions: A path analysis interpretation. *Journal of Applied Psychology,* 1977, 62(1), 20-28.

Olsen, L. H. New retirement options in Sweden. *Social Security Bulletin,* 1976, 39(3), 31-33.

Orbach, H. L. Social and institutional aspects of industrial workers' retirement patterns. In W. Donahue et al. (Eds.), *Trends in early retirement.* Ann Arbor: University of Michigan, 1969.

O'Rourke, J. F., & Friedman, H. L. An inter-union pre-retirement training program: Results and commentary. *Industrial Gerontology,* Spring 1972, 49-62.

Padley, R. Studies on age and wastage in industrial populations: I. Age and incidence. *British Journal of Occupational Medicine,* 1947, 1, 213-237.

Palmore, E. B. Retirement patterns among aged men: Findings of the 1963 Survey on the Aged. *Social Security Bulletin,* 1964, 27, 3-10.

Palmore, E. B. Differences in the retirement patterns of men and women. *The Gerontologist,* 1965, 5, 4-8.

Palmore, E. B. What can the USA learn from Japan about aging? *The Gerontologist,* 1975, 15(1), 64-67.

Palmore, E. B. When can age, period, and cohort be separated? *Social Forces,* 1978, 57, 282-295.

Palmore, E. B. (Ed.). *International handbook on aging: Contemporary developments and research.* Westport, CT: Greenwood Press, 1980.

Parnes, H. S. Middle-aged and older men in the labor force. *Aging,* 1980, 30, 25-29.

Parnes, H. S., Fleischer, B. M., Miljus, R. D., & Spitz, R. S. *The pre-retirement years: A longitudinal study of the labor market experience of men,* Vol. 1. Washington, DC: U.S. Department of Labor, 1970.

Parnes, H. S., & Nestel, G. Early retirement. In H. S. Parnes et al. (Eds.), *The pre-retirement years: Five years into the worklives of middle-aged men,* Vol. 4. Washington, DC: U.S. Department of Labor Manpower Research and Development, Monograph No. 15, 1975.

Parnes, H. S., & Nestel, G. The retirement experience. In H. S. Parnes et al. (Eds.), *Work and retirement: A longitudinal study of men.* Cambridge, MA: MIT Press, 1981.

Parker, D. F., & Dyer, L. Expectancy theory as a within-person behavioral choice model: An empirical test of some conceptual and methodological refinements. *Organizational Behavior and Human Performance,* 1976, 17, 97-117.

Pavard, F. Social Security financing through the contribution method. *International Social Security Review,* 1979, 32(4), 407-419.

Pechman, J. A., Aaron, H. J., & Taussig, M. K. *Social Security: Perspective for reform.* Washington, DC: The Brookings Institute, 1968.

Pelz, D. C., & Andrews, F. M. *Scientists in organizations: Productive climates for research and development.* New York: John Wiley, 1966.

Personnel Administrator. Many want to work past 65. Vol. 24, 1979.

Personnel Administrator. New survey reveals attitude toward retirement. Vol. 24(4), 1979.

Perspectives on Aging. Public policy agenda, 1979-80, Vol. 8(2), 1979.

Phillips, J. S., Barrett, G. V., & Rush, M. C. Job structure and age satisfaction. *Aging and Work,* 1978, 1, 109-119.

Pollman, A. W. Early retirement: A comparison of poor health to other retirement factors. *Journal of Gerontology,* 1971, 26(1), 41-45.

Pollman, A. W., & Johnson, A. C. Resistance to change, early retirement, and managerial decisions. *Industrial Gerontology,* 1974, 1(1), 33-41.

Poon, L. W. (Ed.). *Aging in the 1980's: Psychological issues.* Washington, DC: American Psychological Association, 1980.

Porter, L. W. A study of perceived need satisfaction in bottom and middle management jobs. *Journal of Applied Psychology,* 1961, 45, 1-10.

Porter, L. W. Job attitudes in management: I. Perceived deficiencies in need fulfillment as a function of job level. *Journal of Applied Psychology,* 1962, 46, 375-384.

Porter, L. W. Job attitudes in management: II. Perceived importance of needs as a function of job level. *Journal of Applied Psychology,* 1963, 47, 141-148.

Porter, L. W., Lawler, E. E. III, & Hackman, J. R. *Behavior in organizations.* New York: McGraw-Hill, 1975.

Porter, L. W., & Steers, R. M. Organizational, work, and personal factors in employee turnover and absenteeism. *Psychological Bulletin,* 1973, 80, 151-176.

Porter, L. W., Steers, R. M., Mowday, R. T., & Boulian, P. V. Organizational commitment, job satisfaction, and turnover among psychiatric technicians. *Journal of Applied Psychology,* 1974, 59, 603-609.

Powell, P. Age and occupational change among coal miners. *Occupational Psychology,* 1973, 47, 37-49.

Price, J. L. *The study of turnover.* Ames: Iowa State University Press, 1977.

Public papers of the Presidents: Lyndon B. Johnson. *Special message to the Congress proposing programs for older Americans* (Vol. 1, Paper No. 12). Washington, DC: Government Printing Office, 1968.

Pursell, D. E., & Torrence, W. D. The older woman and her search for employment. *Aging and Work,* 1980, 3(2), 121-128.

Pyron, H. C., & Manion, U. V. The company, the individual and the decision to retire. *Industrial Gerontology,* 1970, 4, 1-11.

Quinn, J. F. Microeconomic determinants of early retirement: A cross-sectional view of white married men. *Journal of Human Resources,* 1977, 12(3), 329-346.

Quinn, J. F. The extent and correlates of partial retirement. *The Gerontologist,* 1981, 21, 634-642.

Quinn, R. P., & Shepard, L. J. *The 1972-73 quality of employment survey.* Ann Arbor: University of Michigan, Survey Research Center, 1974.

Quinn, R. P., Staines, G. L., & McCullough, M. R. *Job satisfaction: Is there a trend?* Manpower Research Monograph No. 30, U.S. Department of Labor. Washington, DC: Government Printing Office, 1974.

Quirk, D. A., & Skinner, J. H. IHCS: Physical capacity, age and employment. *Industrial Gerontology,* 1973, 13, 49-62.

Rabinowitz, S., & Hall, D. T. Organizational research on job involvement. *Psychological Bulletin,* 1977, 84, 265-288.

Rabinowitz, S., & Hall, D. T. Changing correlates of job involvement in three career stages. *Journal of Vocational Behavior,* 1981, 18, 138-144.

Rabinowitz, S., Hall, D. T., & Goodale, J. G. Job scope and individual differences as predictors of job involvement: Independent or interactive? *Academy of Management Journal,* 1977, 20, 273-281.

Rahn, R. W., Reardon, P. A., Clarke, R. H., & Ortiz, G. T. *Special report: Economic impact of increases in Social Security tax rates.* Washington, DC: Chamber of Commerce of the United States, October 1981.

Reich, M. H. Group pre-retirement education programs. *Industrial Gerontology,* 1977, 4(1), 29-43.

Reitz, H. J., & Jewell, J. N. Sex, locus of control, and job involvement: A six-country investigation. *Academy of Management Journal,* 1979, 22, 72-80.

Rey, P. Various cases of job redesign for older workers. In *Job re-design and occupational training for older workers.* Paris: Organisation for Economic Cooperation and Development, 1965.

Rhodes, S. R., & Steers, R. M. *Summary tables of studies of employee absenteeism* (ONR Technical Report No. 13). Eugene: University of Oregon, 1978.

Rich v. Martin-Marietta, 522 F.2d at 350 (1977).

Richardson, I. M. Age and work: A study of 489 men in heavy industry. *British Journal of Industrial Medicine,* 1953, 10, 269-284.

Riley, M. W. Aging and cohort succession: Interpretations and misinterpretations. *Public Opinion Quarterly,* 1973, 37, 35-49.

Riley, M. W., & Foner, A. *Aging and society,* Vol. 1. New York: Russell Sage Foundation, 1968.

Riley, M., Johnson, M., & Foner, A. *Aging and society: A sociology of age stratification,* Vol. 3. New York: Russell Sage Foundation, 1972.

Robbins, S. P. *Organizational behavior: Concepts and controversies.* Englewood Cliffs, NJ: Prentice-Hall, 1979.

Robertson, I., & Downs, S. Learning and the prediction of performance: Development of trainability testing in the United Kingdom. *Journal of Applied Psychology,* 1979, 64(1), 42-50.

Robinson, D. D. Prediction of clerical turnover in banks by means of a weighted application blank. *Journal of Applied Psychology,* 1972, 56, 282.

Roe, A. Changes in scientific activities with age. *Science,* 1965, 150, 313-318.

Rokeach, M. *The nature of human values.* New York: Free Press, 1973.

Rones, P. L. Older men—The choice between work and retirement. *Monthly Labor Review,* 1978, 101, 3-10.

Root, N. Injuries at work are fewer among older employees. *Monthly Labor Review,* 1981, 104, 30-34.

Rose, C. L., & Mogey, J. M. Aging and preference for later retirement. *Aging and Human Development,* 1972, 3, 45-62.

Rosen, B. Management perception of the older worker. *Proceedings of the 30th Annual Winter Meeting of the Industrial Relations Research Association,* 1977.

Rosen, B., & Jerdee, T. H. The influence of age stereotypes on managerial decisions. *Journal of Applied Psychology,* 1976, 61, 428-432. (a)

Rosen, B., & Jerdee, T. H. The nature of job-related age stereotypes. *Journal of Applied Psychology,* 1976, 61, 180-183. (b)

Rosen, B., & Jerdee, T. H. Too old or not too old? *Harvard Business Review,* 1977, 55, 97-106.

Rosen, B., & Jerdee, T. H. Influence of employee age, sex, and job status on managerial recommendations for retirement. *Academy of Management Journal,* 1979, 22, 169-173.

Rosen, B., Jerdee, T. H., & Lunn, R. O. Effects of performance appraisal format, age, and performance level on retirement decisions. *Journal of Applied Psychology,* 1981, 66, 515-519.

Rosenthal, A. *The social programs of Sweden.* Minneapolis: University of Minnesota Press, 1967.

Rosow, I. What is a cohort and why? *Human Development,* 1978, 21, 65-75.

Rousseau, D. M. Characteristics of departments, positions, and individuals: Contexts for attitudes and behavior. *Administrative Science Quarterly,* 1978, 23, 521-539.

Ruch, F. L. The differentiative effects of age upon human learning. *Journal of General Psychology,* 1934, 11, 261-286.

Rush, J. C., Peacock, A. C., & Milkovich, G. T. Career stages: A partial test of Levinson's model of life/career stages. *Journal of Vocational Behavior,* 1980, 16, 347-359.

Rynes, S. L., Heneman, H. G. III, & Schwab, D. P. Individual reactions to organizational recruiting: A review. *Personnel Psychology,* 1980, 33, 529-547.

Saal, F. E. Job involvement: A multivariate approach. *Journal of Applied Psychology,* 1978, 63, 53-61.

Saleh, S. D., & Otis, J. L. Age and level of job satisfaction. *Personnel Psychology,* 1964, 17, 425-430.

Salvendy, G. Discrimination in performance assessments against the aged. *Perceptual and Motor Skills,* 1974, 39, 1087-1099.

Salvendy, G., & Pilitsis, J. Psychophysiological aspects of paced and unpaced performance as influenced by age. *Ergonomics,* 1971, 14, 703-711.

Sandman, B., & Urban, F. Employment testing and the law. *Labor Law Journal,* 1976, 27, 38-54.

Sarcini v. Missouri Pacific Railway Co., 431 F. Supp. 389, 393, 1977.

Schmidt, F. L., Berner, J. G., & Hunter, J. E. Racial differences in validity of employment tests: Reality or illusion? *Journal of Applied Psychology,* 1973, 58, 5-9.

Schmitt, N., Coyle, B. W., Rauschenberger, J., & White, J. K. Comparison of early retirees and non-retirees. *Personnel Psychology,* 1979, 32, 327-340.

Schmitt, N., & McCune, J. T. The relationship between job attitudes and the decision to retire. *Academy of Management Journal,* 1981, 24, 795-802.

Schneider, B. V. A. How capable are older workers? In *The Older Worker.* Berkeley: University of California, Institute of Industrial Relations, 1962.

Schottland, C. I. *The social security program in the United States.* New York: Meredith, 1980.

Schuler, R. S. *Determinants of job involvement: Individual vs. organization: An extension of the literature.* Paper presented at the meeting of the Academy of Management, New Orleans, August 1975.

Schulz, J. H. *The economics of aging.* Belmont, CA: Wadsworth, 1976.

Schulz, J. H., & Carrin, G. The role of savings and pension systems in maintaining living standards in retirement. *Journal of Human Resources,* 1972, 7, 343-365.

Schulz, J. H., Leavitt, T. D., & Kelly, L. Private pensions fall far short of preretirement income levels. *Monthly Labor Review,* 1979, 102, 28-31.

Schulzinger, M. S. *The accident syndrome.* Springfield, IL: C. Thomas, 1956.

Schuster, J. R. Another look at compensation preferences. *Industrial Management Review,* 1968, 10, 1-15.

Schuster, M. H., & Miller, C. S. Performance evaluations as evidence in ADEA cases. *Employee Relations Law Journal,* 1981, 4(4), 229-243.

Schuster, M. H., & Miller, C. S. Evaluating the older worker's use of employer appraisal systems in age discrimination litigation. *Aging and Work,* 1982, 4, 229-243.

Schwab, D. P. Impact of alternative compensation systems on pay valence and instrumentality perceptions. *Journal of Applied Psychology,* 1973, 58, 308-312.

Schwab, D. P., & Heneman, H. G. III. Age and satisfaction with dimensions of work. *Journal of Vocational Behavior,* 1977, 10, 212-220. (a)

Schwab, D. P., & Heneman, H. G. III. Effects of age and experience on productivity. *Industrial Gerontology,* 1977, 4, 113-117. (b)

Schwab, D. P., & Heneman, H. G. III. Age stereotyping in performance appraisal. *Journal of Applied Psychology,* 1978, 63, 573-578.

Schwab, D. P., & Wallace, M. J., Jr. Correlates of employee satisfaction with pay. *Industrial Relations,* 1974, 13, 78-89.

Schwyhart, W. R., & Smith, P. C. Factors in the job involvement of middle managers. *Journal of Applied Psychology,* 1972, 56, 227-233.

Sellet, L. R. Age and absenteeism. *Personnel Journal,* 1964, 43, 309-313.

Seybolt, J. W. Career development: State of the art among the grass roots. *Training and Development Journal,* 1979, 33(4), 16-21.

Shearer, R. L., & Steger, J. A. Manpower obsolescence: A new definition and empirical investigation of personal variables. *Academy of Management Journal,* 1975, 18, 263-275.

Sheldon, M. E. Investments and involvements as mechanisms producing commitment to the organization. *Administrative Science Quarterly,* 1971, 16, 142-150.

Shepherd, R. D., & Walker, J. Absence and the physical conditions of work. *British Journal of Industrial Medicine,* 1957, 14, 266-274.

Shepherd, R. D., & Walker, J. Absence from work in relation to wage level and family responsibility. *British Journal of Industrial Medicine,* 1958, 15, 52-61.

Sheppard, H. L. Work and retirement. In R. H. Binstock & E. Shanas (Eds.), *Handbook of aging and the social sciences.* New York: Van Nostrand Reinhold, 1976.

Sheridan, J. E., & Vredenburgh, D. J. Usefulness of leadership behavior and social power variables in predicting job tension, performance, and turnover of nursing employees. *Journal of Applied Psychology,* 1978, 63, 89-95.

Shkop, Y. M. The impact of job modification options on retirement plans. *Industrial Relations,* 1982, 21, 261-267.

Shott, G. L., Albright, L. E., & Glennon, J. R. Predicting turnover in an automated office situation. *Personnel Psychology,* 1963, 16, 213-219.

Siassi, I., Crocetti, G., & Spiro, H. R. Emotional health, life, and job satisfaction in aging workers. *Industrial Gerontology,* 1975, 2, 289-296.

Siegel, S. R., & Rives, J. M. Characteristics of existing and planned retirement programs. *Aging and Work,* 1978, 1, 93-99.

Sieman, J. R. Programmed material as a training tool for older persons. *Industrial Gerontology,* 1976, 3, 183-190.

Simonds, R. H., & Shafai-Sahrai, Y. Factors apparently affecting injury frequency in eleven matched pairs of companies. *Journal of Safety Research,* 1977, 9, 120-127.

Smiley, J. A. A clinical study of a group of accident prone workers. *British Journal of Industrial Medicine,* 1955, 12, 263-278.

Smith, N. W. Older worker efficiency in jobs of various types. *Personnel Journal,* 1953, 32, 19-23.

Snyder, R. A., Howard, A., & Hammer, T. H. Mid-career change in academia: The decision to become an administrator. *Journal of Vocational Behavior,* 1978, 13, 229-241.

Social security news. Belgium: Working after retirement. *International Social Security Review,* 1978, 31(1), 71.

Social security news. France: Generalization of social security coverage. *International Social Security Review,* 1978, 31(2), 227. (a)

Social security news. France: New agreement on early retirement at 60. *International Social Security Review,* 1978, 31(1), 75. (b)

Social security news. Sweden: Social security developments in 1977. *International Social Security Review,* 1978, 31(3), 341. (c)

Social security news. Sweden: Evolution of the partial retirement scheme. *International Social Security Review,* 1979, 32(2), 202-205. (a)

Social security news. Sweden: Extension of pension rights. *International Social Security Review,* 1979, 32(3), 330. (b)

Social security news. USSR: Measures taken in 1980 to improve social security. *International Social Security Review,* 1980, 33(3-4), 400-403.

Solovieu, A. G. The employment of pensioners in the national economy of the USSR. *International Social Security Review,* 1980, 33(2), 155-164.

Sonnenfeld, J., & Kotter, J. P. The maturation of career theory. *Human Relations,* 1982, 35, 19-46.

Spencer, D. G., & Steers, R. M. The influence of personal factors and perceived work experiences on employee turnover and absenteeism. *Academy of Management Journal,* 1980, 23, 567-572.

Stagner, R. Boredom on the assembly line: Age and personality variables. *Industrial Gerontology,* 1975, 2, 23-44.

Staines, G. L., & Quinn, R. P. American workers evaluate the quality of their jobs.

Monthly Labor Review, 1979, 102, 3-12.

Stanford, E. P. Retirement anticipation in the military. *The Gerontologist,* 1971, 11, 37-42.

Steers, R. M. Antecedents and outcomes of organizational commitment. *Administrative Science Quarterly,* 1977, 22, 46-56.

Steers, R. M., & Rhodes, S. R. Major influences on employee attendance: A process model. *Journal of Applied Psychology,* 1978, 63, 391-407.

Stern, J. A., Oster, P. J., & Newpart, K. Reaction time measures, hemispheric specialization, and age. In L. W. Poon (Ed.), *Aging in the 1980's: Psychological issues.* Washington, DC: American Psychological Association, 1980.

Stevens, A. F. Accidents of older workers: Relation of age to extent of disability. *Personnel Journal,* 1929, 8, 138-145.

Stevens, J. M., Beyer, J. M., & Trice, H. M. Assessing personal, role, and organizational predictors of managerial commitment. *Academy of Management Journal,* 1978, 21, 380-396.

Stewart, C. D. The older worker in Japan: Realities and possibilities. *Industrial Gerontology,* 1974, 1(1), 60-75.

Stewart, J. S. Retraining older workers for upgraded jobs. *Industrial Gerontology,* 1969, 2, 26-31.

Stone, T. H., & Athelstan, G. T. The SVIB for women and demographic variables in the prediction of occupational tenure. *Journal of Applied Psychology,* 1969, 53, 408-412.

Streib, G. F., & Schneider, C. J. *Retirement in American society: Impact and process.* Ithaca, NY: Cornell University Press, 1971.

Streib, G. F., & Thompson, W. E. Personal and social adjustment in retirement. In W. Donahue and C. Tibbetts (Eds.), *The new frontiers of aging.* Ann Arbor: University of Michigan Press, 1957.

Stumpf, S. A., & Dawley, P. K. Predicting voluntary and involuntary turnover using absenteeism and performance indices. *Academy of Management Journal,* 1981, 24, 148-163.

Stumpf, S. A., & Rabinowitz, S. Career stage as a moderator of performance relationship with facets of job satisfaction and role perceptions. *Journal of Vocational Behavior,* 1981, 18, 202-218.

Super, D. E. *The psychology of careers.* New York: Harper & Row, 1957.

Super, D. E. A life-span, life-space approach to career development. *Journal of Vocational Behavior,* 1980, 16, 282-298.

Super, D. E., & Hall, D. T. Career development: Exploration and planning. In M. R. Rosenzweig and L. W. Porter (Eds.), *Annual Review of Psychology,* 1978, 29, 333-372.

Super, D. E., Crites, J., Hummel, R., Moser, H., Overstreet, P., & Warnath, C. *Vocational development: A framework for research.* New York: Teachers College Press, 1957.

Surry, J. *Industrial accident research: A human engineering appraisal.* Canada: University of Toronto Press, 1969.

Surry, J. *Industrial accident research.* Toronto: Labour Safety Council, 1977.

Sutherland, I., Harris, C. G., & Smithers, A. Studies in occupational morbidity: Part III. *British Journal of Industrial Medicine,* 1950, 7, 140-144.

Suzuki, H. Age, seniority and wages. *International Labour Review,* 1976, 113(1), 67-84.

Tax Foundation, Inc. *The future role of social security* (Government Finance Brief No. 19, March 1970). Washington, DC: Author, 1970.

Taylor, K. E., & Weiss, D. J. Prediction of individual job termination from measured job satisfaction and biographical data. *Journal of Vocational Behavior,* 1972, 2, 123-132.

Taylor, R. N., & Thompson, M. Work value systems of young workers. *Academy of Management Journal,* 1976, 19, 522-536.

Thomas, L. E. A typology of mid-life career changers. *Journal of Vocational Behavior,* 1980, 16, 173-182.

Thomas, L. E., & Robbins, P. I. Personality and work environment congruence of mid-life career changers. *Journal of Occupational Psychology,* 1979, 52, 177-183.

Thompson, P. H., & Dalton, G. W. Are R & D organizations obsolete? *Harvard Business Review,* 1976, 54, 105-116.

Thorndike, E. L. *Adult learning.* New York: MacMillan, 1928.

Thornton, G. C. III. Differential effects of career planning on internals and externals. *Personnel Psychology,* 1978, 31, 471-476.

Tiffin, J., & McCormick, E. J. *Industrial psychology.* Englewood Cliffs, NJ: Prentice-Hall, 1952.

Tracy, M. *Retirement age practices in ten industrial societies, 1960-1976.* New York: International Social Security Assoc. (ISSA), 1979. (a)

Tracy, M. Trends in retirement. *International Social Security Review,* 1979, 32, 131-159. (b)

Treas, J. Socialist organization and economic development in China: Latent consequences for the aged. *Gerontologist,* 1979, 19, 34-43.

Tucker, H. I., & Lotz, J. F. Absenteeism: Experience with a liberal paid-absence plan. *Personnel,* 1957, 33, 327-336.

U.S. Department of Health, Education and Welfare. *Mandating private pensions: A study of the European experience.* Research Report No. 51, 1978.

U.S. Department of Health and Human Services. *Social security programs throughout the world, 1979.* Research Report No. 54, 1980.

U.S. Department of Labor, Bureau of Labor Statistics. *Comparative job performance by age: Office workers* (Bulletin No. 1273). Washington, DC: Government Printing Office, 1960.

U.S. Department of Labor, Bureau of Labor Statistics. *New labor force projections to 1990.* Special Labor Force Report 197, 1976.

U.S. Department of Labor, Bureau of Labor Statistics. *Occupational injuries and illness in the United States by industry, 1975.* Washington, DC: Government Printing Office, 1978.

U.S. Department of Labor, Employment and Training Administration. *Employment-related problems of older workers: A research strategy.* Washington, DC: Government Printing Office, 1979.

U.S. House of Representatives. *Demographic trends and the social security system.* Briefing before the Subcommittee on Social Security of the Committee on Ways and Means, Dec. 2, 1980. (a)

U.S. House of Representatives. *Social security: A critique of recommendations to tax benefits and to raise the eligibility age for retirement benefits.* A Report by the Subcommittee on Retirement Income and Employment of the Select Committee on Aging, Sept. 1980. (b)

U.S. Senate. *Social security financing hearings before the Subcommittee on Social Security of the Committee on Finance,* Feb. 22 and 25, 1980.

U.S. Senate. *Social security financing and options for the future.* Hearing before the Subcommittee on Social Security and Income Maintenance Programs of the Committee on Finance, July 7, 9, 10, 1981.

Usher, C. E. Alternative work options for older workers: Part I—Employees' interest. *Aging and Work,* 1981, 4(2), 74-81.

Van Gorkom, J. W. *Social security—The long-term deficit.* Washington, DC: American Enterprise Institute for Public Policy Research, 1976.

Val Zelst, R. H. The effect of age and experience upon accident rate. *Journal of Applied Psychology,* 1954, 38, 313-317.

Vecchio, R. P. The function and meaning of work and the job: Morse and Weiss (1955) revisited. *Academy of Management Journal,* 1980, 23, 361-367.

Vernon, H. M. *Accidents and their prevention.* New York: MacMillan, 1936.

Vernon, H. M. Prevention of accidents. *British Journal of Industrial Medicine,* 1945, 2, 1-9.

Vig, G. Scandinavian experiences in health and social services for older people. *Meeting the Problems of Older People.* The New York Academy of Medicine, April 30-May 1, 1973.

Villars, C. Ninth Amendment to the Swiss old age survivors insurance. *International Social Security Review,* 1979, 32(1), 72-79. (a)

Villars, C. Old-age, survivor's and invalid insurance in Switzerland. *International Social Security Review,* 1979, 32(4), 465-493. (b)

Vroom, V. H. *Work and motivation.* New York: John Wiley, 1964.

Wagner, L. A., & Bakerman, T. Wage earners' opinions of insurance fringe benefits. *Journal of Insurance,* 1960, 27(2), 17-28.

Walker, J. The job performance of federal mail sorters by age. *Monthly Labor Review,* 1964, 87, 296-301.

Walker, J. W., & Price, K. F. The impact of vesting, early retirement, rising cost of living and other factors on projected retirement patterns: A manpower planning model. *Industrial Gerontology,* 1974, 1(13), 35-48.

Walsh, W. B. Vocational behavior and career development, 1978: A review. *Journal of Vocational Behavior,* 1979, 15, 119-154.

Wanous, J. P. The role of individual differences in human reactions to job characteristics. *Journal of Applied Psychology,* 1974, 59(5), 616-622.

Wanous, J. P. Organizational entry: Newcomers moving from outside to inside. *Psychology Bulletin,* 1977, 84, 601-618.

Wanous, J. P., Stumpf, S. A., & Bedrosian, H. Job survival of new employees. *Personnel Psychology,* 1979, 32, 651-662.

Warr, P., Cook, J., & Wall, T. Scales for the measurement of some work attitudes and aspect of psychological well-being. *Journal of Occupational Psychology,* 1979, 52, 129-148.

Waters, L. K., Roach, D., & Waters, C. W. Estimates of future tenure, satisfaction, and biographical variables as predictors of termination. *Personnel Psychology,* 1976, 29, 57-60.

Watson, C. J. An evaluation of some aspects of the Steers and Rhodes model of employee attendance. *Journal of Applied Psychology,* 1981, 66, 385-389.

Weaver, C. N. Sex differences in the determinants of job satisfaction. *Academy of Management Journal,* 1978, 21, 265-274.

Weaver, C. N. Job satisfaction in the United States in the 1970s. *Journal of Applied Psychology,* 1980, 65, 364-367.

Weaver, C. N., & Holmes, S. L. On the use of sick leave by female employees. *Personnel Administration and Public Personnel Review,* 1972, 1(2), 46-50.

Welford, A. T. *Aging and human skill.* London: Oxford University Press, 1958.

Welford, A. T., Motor performance. In J. E. Birren & K. W. Schaie (Eds.), *Handbook of the psychology of aging.* New York: Van Nostrand Reinhold, 1977.

Welsch, H. P., & LaVan, H. Inter-relationships between organizational commitment and job characteristics, job satisfaction, professional behavior, and organizational climate. *Human Relations,* 1981, 34, 1079-1089.

White, J. K. Individual differences and the job quality-worker response relationship: Review, integration, and comments. *Academy of Management Review,* 1978, 3, 267-280.

Whitfield, J. W. Individual differences in accident susceptibility among coal miners. *British Journal of Industrial Medicine,* 1954, 11, 126-137.

Wiener, Y., & Vaitenas, R. Personality correlates of voluntary midcareer change in enterprising occupations. *Journal of Applied Psychology,* 1977, 62, 706-712.

Williams, A., Livy, B., Silverstone, R., & Adams, P. Factors associated with labour turnover among ancillary staff in two London hospitals. *Journal of Occupational Psychology,* 1979, 52, 1-16.

Willis, S. L., & Baltes, P. B. Intelligence in adulthood and aging: Contemporary issues. In L. W. Poon (Ed.), *Aging in the 1980s: Psychological issues.* Washington, DC: American Psychological Association, 1980.

Wolff, E. Accident proneness: A serious problem. *Industrial Medicine and Surgery,* 1950, 19, 419-426.

World almanac and book of facts, 1982. New York: Newspaper Enterprise Association, 1981.

Wounded executives fight back on age bias. *Business Week,* July 21, 1980, 109-114.

Wright, J. D., & Hamilton, R. F. Work satisfaction and age: Some evidence for the "job change" hypothesis. *Social Forces,* 1978, 56, 1140-1158.

Yahalem, M. R. Employee-benefit plans, 1975. *Social Security Bulletin,* 1977, 40, 19-38.

Youry, M. GULHEMP: What workers can do. *Manpower,* 1975, 7(6), 4-10.

Zakharov, M., & Tsivilyou, R. *Social security in the USSR.* Moscow: Progress, 1978.

Zey-Ferrell, M. Predictors of faculty intent to exit the organization: Potential turnover in a large university. *Human Relations,* 1982, 35, 349-372.

INDEX

Aaron, H. J., 353, 367
Abilities and skills, 85-89, 112
    ability to learn,112
    memory, 87-88
    speed of behavior, 87
Ability to learn and age, 112
Abrams, A. J., 80, 97, 99, 353
Absenteeism, 44-45, 54, 65-69, 81,
    187-188
    and accidents, 69
    and age, 65-69
    avoidable, 65-66, 68
    cost of, 65
    importance of, 65
    and job satisfaction, 44-45
    unavoidable, 65-66, 69
Accidents, 69, 74-80, 81, 187-188
    and age, 75-79
    causes of injuries, 78
    costs of, 74-75
    duration of disability, 77
    and fatalities, 77
    frequency, 75-77
    importance of, 74-76
    nature of injuries, 78
    and permanent disability, 77-78
    proneness, 79
Adams, P., 375
Age Discrimination in Employment Act
    (ADEA), 15-20, 87-88, 90, 93, 142
    coverage, 16
    exceptions to, 17
    and pension plans, 142
    performance appraisal, 92-94
    proving age discrimination, 18-19
Age-Related Differences, 21
    affects of aging, 21, 49-50, 52, 60
    biological aging, 21
    cohort effects, 22, 49-50, 52, 60
    period effects, 22
    separation of, 22-23
Aging effect, 21, 49, 50, 52, 60

Albright, L. E., 371
Aldag, R. J., 32, 36, 46, 55-58, 99-100,
    196, 202, 208, 211, 233, 236, 238,
    299, 353
Alderfer, C. P., 36, 107, 209, 304, 353
Alexander, R. A., 354, 366
Allen, R. T., 168, 353
Altimus, C. A., 136, 220, 223, 227,
    230, 353
Alvarez, M. G., 356
Andrews, F. M., 62-63, 247-248, 367
Andrews, I. R., 128, 136, 321, 353
Andrisani, P. J., 52-53, 353
Angle, H. L., 57-58, 239, 353
Appelbaum, E., 353
Arenberg, D., 64, 86-87, 353, 359
Armstrong, J. C., 109-110, 309, 353
Arnold, H. J., 57-59, 71, 240, 243, 278,
    353
Arvey, R. D., 51, 62, 90-92, 103, 249,
    294, 353, 357
Asher, J. J., 91, 353
Athelstan, G. T., 83, 372
Atkinson, J. W., 364
Attitudes, 31, 43-58, 85, 187
    defined, 43
    internal work motivation, 56-57
    job involvement, 54-56
    organizational commitment, 57-58
    overall job satisfaction, 43-50
    satisfaction with co-workers, 45, 50-
        51
    satisfaction with pay, 45, 50
    satisfaction with promotions, 45, 50-
        51
    satisfaction with supervision, 45, 50-
        51
    satisfaction with work itself, 45, 50-
        51
    toward older workers, 85

Babzhin, V., 171, 172, 354

Baker, R. L., 365
Bakerman, T., 129-131, 135, 316, 374
Baltes, P. B., 21, 65, 86, 88, 359, 375
Banas, P. A., 357
Barber, J. W., 114, 354
Barfield, R., 149, 155-157, 159, 161-
   164, 325-326, 329, 335, 341, 344,
   348, 350, 352, 354, 362
Barkin, S., 75, 77-78, 279, 285-288,
   354
Barrett, G. V., 75-76, 283, 354, 367
Bass, A. R., 94-95, 296, 354, 365
Bass, B. M., 365
Bassett, G. A., 70, 273, 354
Batten, M. D., 96, 354
Baugher, D., 88, 354
Baumgartel, H., 254, 262, 354
Bayley, G. A., 358
Bayley, S. M., 358
Beattie, W., Jr., 354
Beatty, J. R., 256, 354
Beatty, R. W., 256, 354
Bedrosian, H., 374
Beehr, T. A., 59, 71, 241, 275, 359
Behavioral intentions (see also turnover
   intentions), 59-60, 187
Belbin, R. M., 113, 157, 169, 329, 354
Bell, B., 358
Bell, D., 141-142, 354
Benecki, T. J., 357
Berkowitz, M., 75, 354
Berlew, D. E., 101, 354
Berman, H. J., 155, 157, 160, 325-326,
   329, 335, 354
Bernardin, H. J., 265, 354
Berner, J. G., 370
Berniger, J., 70, 272, 358
Beveridge, W. E., 115-116, 314, 354
Beyer, J. M., 372
Biological aging, 21
Birren, J. E., 64-65, 86-87, 113, 354-
   355
Bixby, L. E., 183, 355
Blood, M. R., 32, 355
Bluedorn, A. C., 57-59, 71, 240, 243,
   278, 355
Blumberg, M., 55, 235, 260, 355
Boskin, M. J., 149, 156, 159, 160, 162-
   164, 326, 336, 341, 350, 355

Bosse, R., 358
Botwinick, J., 86-88, 355
Boulian, P. V., 368
Bowers, W. H., 62, 244, 355
Bratthall, K., 355
Bray, D. W., 54, 355
Brayfield, A. H., 44, 355
Breaugh, J. A., 89-90, 355
Breen, L. Z., 62, 246, 355
Brewer, M. B., 25, 357
Brief, A. P., 32, 36, 46, 55-58, 99-100,
   196, 202, 208, 211, 233, 236, 238,
   299, 353
Brito V. Zia Co. (1973), 93, 355
Britton, J. O., 61, 85-86, 88, 292, 355
Broberg, M., 355
Brown, C. A., 366
Brown, J., 168, 356
Bruni, J. R., 362
Buchholz v. Symons Manufacturing Co.
   (1978), 93, 355
Buchholz, R. A., 32, 33, 202, 207, 355
Bureau of Labor Statistics (BLS), 12,
   142
Burkhauser, R. V., 149, 157, 159-161,
   163-164, 329, 333, 336, 341, 350,
   355
Buzzard, R. R., 252, 355

Cafeteria systems, 127-128, 134
   benefit to older workers, 128
   research results, 134
   selection by aerospace employees,
      127-128
Campbell, H., 356
Campbell, J., 90, 356
Campbell, R. J., 355
Capwell, D. R., 360
Career change (see middle career period)
Career planning and development, 105-
   119, 188
   implications for, 194
   intervention effectiveness, 111-112
   future research needs, 199
   summary, 188
Career stage(s), 100-101, 106
Career stage model, 107-108
Carrin, G., 143, 146, 370
Chadwick-Jones, J. K., 366

Chandler, H. R., 124, 356
Chapman, J. B., 132-133, 319, 356
Characteristics of the older workers, 29-83, 187-188, 198
  psychological, 31-60
  research needs, 198
  summary, 187-188
  work behaviors, 61-83
Charles, D. C., 116, 314, 356
Chelius, J. R., 75, 283, 356
Cherrington, D. J., 32-34, 38, 42, 202-205, 356
Choudhuri, P. K., 318, 363
Chown, S. M., 62, 68, 149, 248, 356
Clark, F. L., 157, 169, 329, 354
Clark, R. A., 364
Clarke, R. H., 368
Clay, H. M., 62, 99, 245, 356
Clemente, F., 249, 356
Cleveland, J. N., 63, 94-95, 251, 298, 356
Clopton, W., 109-110, 306, 356
Cobb, B. B., 62, 64, 249, 364
Cognition and age, 87-88
Cohort effect, 22, 49-50, 52, 60
  interaction with age and period effects, 23
Cohorts, 22
  and age plus learnings profile, 125-126
Cole, S., 62-63, 250, 356
Collins, K., 168, 356
Compensation, 121-139, 188-189
  definition of, 121
  employee preferences, 127, 134
  employee services, 121
  fringe benefits, 121
  function in the organization, 121, 127
  implications for, 194-195
  noneconomic rewards, 121
  performance by age, 130
  research needs, 199-200
  summary, 188-189
  wages and salaries, 121
Condie, S. J., 356
Connor, C. L., 92, 356
Constas, K., 66-67, 260, 356
Cook, J., 36, 58, 209, 239, 356, 374
Cooper, R., 255, 263, 356

Corso, J. F., 86, 357
Costa, P. T., 358
Coworker satisfaction, 45, 51, 60
  and age, 51
  and turnover, 45
Cox, S. R., 180, 357
Coyle, B. W., 370
Craft, J. A., 61, 85, 88, 293, 357
Craik, F. I. M., 87, 357
Crandall, N. F., 131, 319-320, 357
Crano, W. D., 24, 357
Crites, J., 372
Crocetti, G., 371
Crockett, W. H., 44, 355
Crooks, L., 356
Cunningham, W. R., 64, 87, 357

Dalton, G. W., 62-63, 70, 106, 109, 117, 248, 304, 357, 373
Darrow, C., 363
Davis, D. L., 313, 357
Dawley, P. K., 71, 271, 277, 372
Decision to retire, 148-166
  and age, 149, 155
  amount of work, 162
  autonomy, 163
  climate preference, 160-161
  co-workers, 163
  dependents, 155-156
  desire for leisure, 161
  education, 156
  financial factors, 159-160
  gender, 156-157
  growth needs, 161
  health, 161-162
  job change, 163
  job satisfaction, 162
  job strain and job tension/stress, 163
  locus of control, 162
  marital status, 157
  occupation, 157-158
  organizational factors, 162-164
  pay/extrinsic rewards, 163-164
  performance, 164
  place of residence, 158-159
  pressure to retire, 164
  promotions, 164
  race, 159

tenure, 159
work commitment, 162
de le Mare, G., 254, 262, 357
Demographics, 12
    labor force changes, 12
    older population, 12
Dennis, W., 62-63, 244, 248, 357
Dewhirst, H. D., 51, 353
Discovery method, 113, 118
Doctors, S. I., 357
Dodd, B., 113, 312, 357
Dowling, P., 49, 52-53, 60, 217, 218, 366
Downs, S., 70, 91, 114, 273, 295, 357, 369
Dubin, R., 54, 357
Dunham, R. B., 360
Dunnette, M. D., 95, 101, 357, 362
Dyer, L., 138, 142, 148, 155, 157, 325, 329, 357, 367

Eden, D., 73, 149, 155, 161-164, 324, 341, 344, 348-349, 351-352, 357
Eidsenberg, J., 62-63, 250, 357
Ekerdt, D. J., 155, 324, 358
Employee Compensation, 121
    age effects, 9
    among married workers, 132
    among men and women, 128
    education effects on, 132
    effect of dependents, 133
    for executives, 133
    for union workers, 129-130
    medical insurance benefits, 128
    modifying factors on, 131-132
    preferences, 127-128
    ranking of fringe benefits, 130-131
    research issues on, 9-10
Employee earnings, 123
    and age-education interaction, 124
    computer programmers, 124-125
    implications for management, 126-127
    international comparisons, 123
    men and women, 123
    older men versus younger men, 125-128
    post-World War II baby boom, 125
Eng, J. E., 112, 311, 358

England, J. L., 356
Equal Employment Opportunity Commission (EEOC), 18, 20
Eran, M., 148, 150, 155, 157, 159-164, 324, 328-329, 334, 337, 342, 344, 350-351, 361
Evans, M. G., 36, 59, 209, 241, 358

Fair Labor Standards Act (FLSA), 18
Farr, J. L., 95, 363
Farris, G. F., 70, 273, 358
Federico, J. M., 83, 358
Federico, P., 358
Feild, H. S., 90, 358, 360
Feld, S., 359
Feldman, D. C., 57-59, 71, 240, 243, 278, 353
Fishbein, M., 31, 59, 358
Flanagan, R. J., 67, 256, 358
Fleishman, E. A., 70, 272, 358
Foner, A., 149, 369
Ford Administration, 182
Foster, K., 356
Foster, L. W., 356
Fowler, W. M., Jr., 86, 363
Fox, H., 90, 358
Fozard, J. L., 64-65, 86-87, 358
France, 123
    earnings level by age and sex, 124
    employee earnings, 123
Freeman, R. B., 125-126, 358
Friedman, H. L., 116-117, 314, 367
Fringe benefits, 127-130, 134
    implications for, 194-195
Froggatt, P., 66, 264, 358
Frumkin, R., 142, 358

Gael, S., 90, 358
Garrison, K. R., 66-67, 256, 358
Giambra, L. M., 64, 359
Gibson, J. L., 45-46, 48, 50-51, 136-137, 211, 219, 226, 229, 359
Glamser, F. D., 116-117, 315, 359
Glenn, N. D., 23, 46, 49-50, 53, 60, 212-213, 359
Glennon, J. R., 371
Glueck, W. F., 90, 105, 121, 359
Goldstein, I. L., 86, 113, 359
Goodale, J. G., 133, 135, 318, 366, 368

Goodge, P. M., 66-68, 256, 265, 366
Gordus, J. P., 149, 359
Gottfredson, G. D., 109-110, 306, 359
Gottsdanker, J. S., 112, 311, 358
Gould, S., 99-102, 106, 108, 302, 305, 359
Goulet, L. R., 21, 359
Government regulation, 15-20, 142, 168, 179-180
   Age Discrimination in Employment Act (ADEA), 15-19, 142, 179
   disability insurance, 180
   Fair Labor Standards Act, 18
   Medicare, 180
   Old Age Security Pension, 168
Grant, D. L., 355, 358
Great Britain, 123
   earnings level by age and sex, 124
   employee earnings, 123
Green, R. F., 88, 359
Greenberg, L., 62, 246, 359
Greenhalgh, L., 73, 359
Griew, S., 75-76, 188, 282-283, 359
Griffeth, R. W., 44, 365
Grimaldi, J., 74, 359
Gruenfeld, L. W., 128, 317, 359
Grusky, O., 70, 359
GULHEMP, person-job matching system, 96
Gupta, N., 59, 71, 241, 275, 359
Gurin, G., 54, 232, 359
Gutteridge, T., 105, 359
Guzzo, R. A., 36, 107, 209, 304, 353

Haberlandt, K. F., 86-87, 359
Hackman, J. R., 36, 208, 359, 368
Haefner, J. E., 61, 85, 88, 92, 293, 360
Hagerty, K. V., 114, 360
Hale, A. R., 75, 360
Hale, M., 75, 360
Hall, A., 148, 156, 158-161, 360
Hall, D. T., 31, 35, 37, 38, 42, 54-56, 99, 101-102, 105-107, 191-192, 232, 236, 303, 327-328, 330, 332, 337, 342, 354, 360, 368, 372
Hall, J. L., 360
Hamilton, R. F., 36-38, 42, 52, 375
Hammer, T. H., 55, 57-58, 66, 235, 239, 260, 263, 360, 371

Hand, H. H., 365
Handyside, J. D., 210, 360
Hanman, B., 96, 360
Hanson, P. M., 96, 363
Harris, C. G., 372
Hearing and age, 85
Heijbel, C. J. A., 99, 360
Heinrich, H. W., 75, 360
Heinz, C. H., 75-77, 281, 286, 360
Hellriegel, D., 83, 360
Helmers, D., 170, 360
Heneman, H. G., III, 50-52, 62, 64, 94-95, 136-138, 221, 224, 227-228, 231, 249, 297, 323, 360, 369-370
Henry, M. M., 128, 136, 321, 353
Herman, J. B., 50, 52, 55, 220, 232, 360
Herzberg, F. I., 44-45, 134, 360
Hewes, A., 75-76, 279, 360
Hill, M., 255, 264, 360
Holland, J. L., 110, 360
Hollenback, J. H., 259, 361
Holley, B. B., 360
Holley, W. H., 35-36, 62, 208, 249, 360
Hollingsworth, A. T., 72, 365
Holmes, S. L., 256, 374
Holtzman, J. M., 155, 157, 160, 325-326, 329, 335, 354
Hom, P. W., 50, 222, 360
Horlick, M., 361
Horner, S. O., 72, 365
House, R. J., 358
Howard, A., 371
Hrebinick, L. G., 57-58, 237, 361
Hulin, C. L., 45, 50, 136, 219, 223, 226, 229, 321, 360-361, 365
Human resource planning and forecasting, implications for, 193
Hummel, R., 372
Hunt, J. G., 59, 242-243, 364
Hunt, J. S., 45-46, 48, 50-51, 136-137, 211, 220-221, 223, 227, 230, 322, 361
Hunt, R. G., 366
Hunter, J. E., 370
Hyden, S. O., 170, 360

Ilgen, D. R., 259, 361
Internal work motivation, 56-57, 60, 187
   and age, 56-57

defined, 56
importance of, 56
International Federation of Aging, 174-176, 361
International Social Security Administration (ISSA), 172-173, 178
Interview, selection, 92
Isambert-Jamati, V., 69, 263, 361
Ivancevich, J. M., 265, 361

Jabes, J., 43, 361
Jacobson, D., 73, 148-150, 155-164, 324, 328-329, 331, 334, 337, 341-342, 344, 348-352, 357, 361
Jaffe, A. J., 166, 327, 361
Jamal, M., 57-59, 239, 243, 361
James, L. R., 50, 55, 222, 235, 361-362
Jamieson, G. H., 113, 312, 361
Japan
    earnings level by age and sex, 124
    employee earnings, 123
Jerdee, T. H., 61, 85-86, 88, 92, 292-293, 369
Jewell, J. N., 55, 235, 368
Job characteristics and age, 36-42
Job design, 96-103, 191-193
    implications for, 191-193
    physical demands of the job, 97-99
    reactions to task characteristics, 99-103
Job involvement, 31, 60, 187
    and absenteeism, 54
    and age, 54-56
    defined, 54
    importance of, 54
    and job performance, 54
    and job satisfaction, 54
    and turnover, 54
Job performance, 61-65, 80-81, 187
    and decision to retire, 164
    and experience, 64-65
    and job involvement, 54
    and job satisfaction, 44
    post-training, 113-114
Job redesign, 97
Job satisfaction, 33, 43-54, 102-103, 110, 162
    and absenteeism, 44

and age, 45-54
and career change, 110
consequences of, 44-45
and decision to retire, 162
defined, 43
dimensions of, 45, 50-51
and expectations, 44
importance of, 44-45
and needs, 44
and performance, 44
and task characteristics, 102-103
and tenure, 46-49
and turnover, 44
and values, 44
Johns, G., 66-67, 259, 270, 361
Johnson, A. C., 148, 163, 166, 339, 349, 367
Johnson, Lyndon, 15
Johnson, M., 369
Johnson, T. R., 148, 156, 158-161, 327-328, 330, 332, 337, 342, 360
Johnston, D. F., 12, 361
Jones, A. P., 50, 54-55, 222, 233, 235, 361-362
Jurgenson, C. E., 128-129, 131-133, 316, 319, 362

Kamerman, S. B., 362
Kaplan, R. S., 182-183, 362
Kasschau, P. L., 114-116, 362
Katerberg, R., 365
Katona, G., 159, 164, 337, 352, 362
Katz, R., 71, 99, 102, 275, 300-301, 362
Kaufman, H. G., 109, 362
Kejner, J., 54, 232, 364
Kelleher, C. H., 114, 362
Kelly, L., 370
Kerr, E. A., 96, 364
Kidron, A., 31, 57-58, 238, 362
Kiggundu, M. N., 358
Kii, T., 173-174, 362
King, H. F., 62, 75, 78-79, 245, 282, 289-290, 362
Kirchner, W. K., 90, 95, 362
Klebba, J., 75, 77-78, 280, 286-287, 362
Klein, E., 363

Klein, S. M., 45-46, 48, 50-51, 136-137, 211, 219, 226, 229, 359
Klores, M. S., 62, 94, 247, 296, 362
Koch, J. L., 57, 71, 277, 363
Koppel, R., 353
Kossoris, M. D., 75-77, 252-253, 280-281, 285-287, 363
Kotter, J. P., 111, 371
Koyl, L. F., 96, 363
Kuh, C., 96, 363
Kutscher, R. E., 62, 64, 246, 363

Labor force
    by age in U.S., 15-16
    changes in U.S. population, 12
Lahiri, D. K., 318, 363
Landau, J. C., 360
Landy, F. J., 63, 94-95, 251, 298, 356, 363
Lanser, H. P., 133, 319, 363
Lantzev, M., 363
LaRoque, P., 173, 363
Laufer, A. C., 86, 363
LaVan, H., 57-58, 240, 375
Lawler, E. E. III, 36, 56, 65, 70, 134, 138, 359, 363, 365, 368
Lawrence, B. S., 109, 308, 363
Layton, B., 64, 86, 88, 363
Leavitt, T. D., 370
Lee, S. M., 57-58, 237, 363
Lefkovitz, J., 90, 358
Lehman, H. C., 62-63, 244, 363
Levinson, D. J., 106, 108, 363
Levinson, M., 363
Lewellen, W. G., 133, 319, 363
Ley, R., 70, 272, 363
Life expectancy, 181
Linn, R. L., 90, 363
Litzelman, D. K., 356
Liu, Y., 363
Livy, B., 375
Locke, E. A., 43-45, 364
Lodahl, T. M., 54, 232, 364
Lorence, J., 34, 42, 365
Lotz, J. F., 253, 262, 373
Louis Harris and Associates, 143
Lowell, E. L., 364
Lundgren, E. F., 116, 314, 364
Lundquist, G. W., 358

Lundstrom, A. B., 131, 320, 357
Lunn, R. O., 369
Lykova, L., 172, 364

Maddox, G. L., 23, 364
Maeda, P., 355
Maher, H., 62, 94, 245, 296, 364
Mahoney, M., 356
Mandatory retirement, 20
    effect on career planning, 20
    Japan, 173-174
    raising of age of, 20
Mangione, T. W., 71, 274, 364
Manion, U. V., 368
Mann, J., 75-76, 280, 364
Mannari, H., 71, 274, 364
Mannheim, B., 54, 233, 364
Mansfield, R., 35, 37-38, 42, 54, 56, 232, 236, 360
Mark, J. A., 62, 245, 364
Marsh, R. M., 71, 274, 364
Marshall v. Goodyear Tire and Rubber Co., 19
Martin, J., 66-67, 255, 265, 364
Martin, T. N., 58-59, 71, 239, 242-243, 364
Martin, T. N., Jr., 59, 242, 364
Maslow, A., 35, 364
Mathews, J. J., 62, 64, 249, 364
Mausner, B., 360
McClelland, D. C., 44, 364
McCormack, R., 356
McCormick, E. J., 75, 373
McCullough, M. R., 368
McCune, J. T., 149, 156-162, 166, 325, 327-328, 330, 332-334, 339, 343, 346, 370
McDonnell-Douglas Corp. v. Green, 19
McFarland, R. A., 75, 96, 358, 364
McKain, W. C., Jr., 158, 332, 364
McKee, B., 363
McMahon, J. T., 265, 361
Meglino, B. M., 365
Meier, E. L., 96, 364
Melching, D. E., 355
Meltzer, H., 136, 321, 365
Memory and age, 87-88
Messer, E. F., 161, 340, 342, 345, 365

Michaels, C. E., 57-59, 71-72, 240, 243, 278, 365
Middle career period, 106-111
    exploration and planning, 107-109
    job satisfaction, 109
    mid-career changers, 109-111
    motivation for, 109-110
    and personality/environment congruence, 110-111
    voluntary and involuntary, 111
Mihal, W. L., 354, 365
Milkovich, G. T., 369
Miljus, R. C., 353
Miller, C. S., 93-94, 370
Miller, H. E., 59, 71, 242, 276, 365
Miller, J. A., 111-112, 310, 365
Miner, M. G., 105, 365
Minor, F. J., 70, 272, 365
Mirvis, P. H., 65, 70, 365
Mistretta v. Sandia Corporation (1977), 93, 365
Mobley, W. H., 44-45, 59, 70-72, 241, 274-276, 365
Mogey, J. M., 148-149, 157, 159-160, 163-164, 166, 325, 327, 332, 334, 340, 345, 351, 369
Monczyka, R. M., 135-136, 322, 365
Morgan, J. N., 149, 155-157, 159, 161-164, 325-326, 329, 335, 341, 344, 348, 350, 352, 354, 362
Morris, J. H., 57-58, 239, 365
Morrison, P. A., 181-182, 365
Morrison, R. F., 108, 365
Morrow, P. C., 116, 315, 365
Morse, N. C., 33, 365
Mortimer, J. T., 34, 42, 365
Moser, H., 372
Mowday, R. T., 57, 275, 365-366, 368
Muchinsky, P. M., 50-51, 66-67, 136-137, 221, 225, 228, 231, 256, 323, 358, 366
Murrell, K. F. H., 80, 366
Mussio, S., 62, 90-91, 249, 294, 353

Namorsky, J. D., 142, 366
National Council for the Case of the Elderly, 17-18, 169, 171
Naylor, J. E., 253, 366

Nealey, S. M., 129, 130-133, 135, 317-318, 366
Neapolitan, J., 73, 109-111, 308, 366
Near, J. P., 46, 48, 213, 366
Needs, 34-36, 44, 107-108
    and age, 35-36
    defined, 34
    growth, 35-36, 107-108
    and job satisfaction, 44
    upward mobility, 107-108
Nestel, G., 148-149, 155-164, 324, 326-327, 330-331, 333, 338, 343, 345, 347, 351, 367
Neugarten, B. L., 68, 366
New Uniform Guidelines, 92-93
Newbold, E.M., 75-76, 279, 366
Newman, J. E., 50-52, 55, 221, 224, 227, 230, 233, 366
Newpart, K., 372
Newsham, D. B., 114, 366
Newstrom, J. W., 365
Nicholson, N., 66-68, 256-259, 265-269, 366
Nougaim, K. E., 54, 360

O'Brien, G. E., 49, 52-53, 60, 217-218, 366
Obsolescence, 109
O'Connor, E. J., 90, 366
Oldham, G. R., 36, 208, 359
Oliver, 1R. L., 136, 139, 323, 366
Olsen, L. H., 366
Orbach, H. L., 148, 158-159, 331, 367
Organizational commitment, 56-58, 60, 187
    and absenteeism, 57
    and age, 57-58
    defined, 57
    importance of, 57
    performance and, 57
    and turnover, 57
Organization design implications for, 191-193
O'Rourke, J. F., 116-117, 314, 367
Ortiz, G. T., 368
Oster, P. J., 372
Otis, J. L., 45, 210, 369
Ottemann, R., 132-133, 319, 356

Overstreet, P., 372

Padley, R., 75, 78, 281, 289, 367
Palmore, E. B., 23, 56, 161, 175-176,
    196, 340, 342, 367
Panek, P. E., 354
Parker, D. F., 148, 155, 157, 325, 329,
    367
Parnes, H. S., 148-149, 155-164, 324,
    326-327, 330-331, 333, 338, 342-
    343, 345, 347, 351, 367
Pavard, F., 367
Pay, 121, 135-138
    and decision to retire, 163-164
    expectancy model, 138
    lack of relationship, 137
    preferences for, 134
    relationship with age, 136, 137
    relationship with performance, 138
    satisfaction with, 37, 60, 135-136
Payne, R., 255, 263, 356
Payroll taxes, 168, 173, 175-178
Peacock, A. C., 369
Pechman, J. A., 159, 338, 367
Pelz, D. C., 62-63, 247-248, 367
Pension plans
    ADEA effects on, 142
    adequacy of benefits, 143-145
    Belgium, 177-178
    Canada, 167
    characteristics and trends, 141
    and early retirement, 170, 172-173,
        175-177
    effects of inflation, 145-146
    employer contributions to, 141-142
    Great Britain, 168
    incidence of, 141
    Japanese, 173
    Norway, 169-170
    Old Age Security Pension, 168
    People's Republic of China, 178
    preference for, 129
    research needs, 199-220
    Soviet Union, 171-173
    summary, 188-189
    Sweden, 169
    Switzerland, 176-177
    West Germany, 175

Perception and age, 85, 87-88
Performance (see job performance)
Performance appraisal, 92-95
Period effect, 22
Perry, J. I., 57-58, 239, 353
Person-job matching strategies, 95-103
    Personnel research implications for,
        190-191
Peterson, R. O., 360
Phillips, J. S., 53, 99-100, 301, 367
Pilitsis, J., 53, 370
Placement, 96
Podolsky, S., 358
Pollman, A. W., 148, 159-161, 163,
    166, 338-340, 343, 349, 367
Poon, L. W., 64-65, 86, 367
Porter, L. W., 35, 37-38, 42, 44-45,
    57, 70-71, 83, 138, 191-274, 363,
    365-368
Powell, P., 69, 76, 368
Preretirement programs, 114-117
    effectiveness, 116
    goals for, 114-115
    topics included, 115
President Reagan, 182
Price, J. L., 44-45, 368
Price, K. F., 374
Price, P. L., 357
Promotion, 37, 60
    and age, 37
    and decision to retire, 164
    satisfaction with, 60
    and turnover, 60
Protestant work ethic, 32-33
Public Papers of the President, 15
Public Policy Agenda, 143
Pursell, D. E., 89, 368
Pyron, H. C., 368

Quinn, J. F., 155, 158-159, 161, 163,
    326, 331, 339, 343, 348, 368
Quinn, R. P., 44-47, 60, 215, 368, 372
Quirk, D. A., 96, 114, 368

Rabinowitz, S., 31, 54-56, 62, 99, 101-
    102, 234, 251, 303, 368, 372
Rahn, R. W., 368
Rauschenburger, J., 370

Reardon, P. A., 368
Recruitment, 89-90
Reich, M. H., 115, 368
Reif, W. E., 365
Reimanis, G., 88, 359
Reitz, H. J., 55, 235, 368
Renner, V. J., 64-65, 87, 355
Research method issues, 195-198
    definition and operationalization of
        age, 195-196
    population and sample sizes, 197
    reporting of research results,
        197-198
    research design issues, 196
    statistical techniques, 197
    theoretical grounding, 196
Research needs, 198-200
Retirement, 142
    (see Decision to retire)
    factors affecting, 143
    income levels, 143
    and inflation, 145, 146
    and human resource management,
        146
    and personal savings, 146
    and quality of life, 143
    research needs, 199-200
    summary, 188-189
Retirement policies
    Belgium, 177-178
    Canada, 167-168
    China, 178-179
    France, 172-173
    Great Britain, 168-169
    Japan, 173-175
    Norway, 170-171
    Soviet Union, 171-172
    Sweden, 169-170
    Switzerland, 176-177
    U.S., 18-183
    West Germany, 175-176
Rey, P., 80, 368
Rhodes, S. R., 44-45, 65, 71, 277, 363,
    368, 372
Rice, R. W., 366
Rich Martin-Marietta (1977), 93, 368
Richardson, I. M., 79, 368
Riley, M. W., 22, 149, 369

Ritchie, R. J., 358
Rives, J. M., 115, 371
Roach, D., 374
Robbins, P. I., 73, 109-111, 307, 373
Robbins, S. P., 34, 369
Robertson, I., 91, 295, 369
Robertson-Tchabo, E. A., 86-87, 353
Robinson, D. D., 70, 273, 369
Rock, D., 356
Roe, A., 62-63, 247, 369
Rokeach, M., 31, 43, 369
Rones, P. L., 369
Root, N., 75, 77, 284, 287-288, 290-
    291, 369
Rose, C. L., 148-149, 157, 159-160,
    163-164, 166, 325, 327, 332, 334,
    340, 345, 351, 358, 369
Rosen, B., 61, 85-86, 88, 92, 292-293,
    369
Rosenthal, A., 170, 369
Rosow, I., 22, 369
Rousseau, D. M., 59, 66, 242, 270,
    369
Ruch, F. L., 112, 369
Rush, J. C., 106-108, 305, 369
Rush, M. C., 367
Rynes, S. L., 89, 369

Saal, F. E., 234, 369
Saleh, S. D., 45, 210, 369
Salvendy, G., 53, 91, 294-295, 370
Sandman, B., 90, 370
Sarcini Missouri Railway Co. (1977),
    93, 370
Saul, P. N., 45-46, 48, 50-51, 136-137,
    211, 220-221, 223, 227, 230, 234,
    322, 361
Schaie, K. W., 64-65, 86, 355
Schmidt, F. L., 90, 370
Schmitt, D., 142, 358
Schmitt, N., 149, 155-163, 166, 325-
    328, 330, 332-334, 339, 341, 343,
    345-348, 370
Schneider, B.V.A., 370
Schneider, C. J., 149, 156-157, 161,
    327, 330, 332, 344, 372
Schottland, C. I., 370
Schuler, R. S., 54, 233, 370

Schulz, J. H., 143-146, 370
Schulzinger, M. S., 75, 282, 370
Schuster, J. R., 127-128, 318, 370
Schuster, M. H., 93-94, 370
Schwab, D. P., 50-52, 62, 64, 94-95,
    136-137, 139, 142, 221, 224, 227-
    228, 231, 249, 297, 322-323, 357,
    369-370
Schweiker, R., 182
Schwyhart, W. R., 54, 232, 370
Sciarrino, J. A., 91, 353
Selection interview (see Interview
    selection)
Selection testing, 90-91
    validity of, 90
Sellett, L. R., 252, 263, 370
Sergean, R., 254, 262, 357
Seybolt, J. W., 106, 370
Shafai-Sharai, Y., 75, 283, 371
Shaw, W. J., 252, 355
Shearer, R. L., 109, 304, 370
Sheldon, M. E., 57-58, 237, 371
Shepard, L. J., 60, 368
Shepherd, R. D., 253, 371
Sheppard, H. L., 149, 371
Sheridan, J. E., 71, 275, 371
Sherman, J. D., 57-58, 239, 365
Shkop, Y. M., 357, 371
Shott, G. L., 70, 272, 371
Siassi, I., 46, 48, 212, 371
Siegel, S. R., 115, 371
Sieman, J. R., 113, 313, 371
Silverstone, R., 375
Simonds, R. H., 74-75, 283, 359, 371
Skinner, J. H., 96, 368
Smiley, J. A., 79, 291, 371
Smith, N. W., 62, 244, 371
Smith, P. C., 45, 50, 54, 136, 219,
    223, 226, 229, 232, 321, 361, 370
Smithers, A., 372
Snyder, R. A., 109-110, 307, 371
Sobol, R., 254, 262, 354
Social Security, 144-145, 180-181
    amendments to, 180-181
    inflation effects on, 145
    policy options for, 181-182
    problems with, 180
Solovieu, A. G., 172, 371

Sonnenfeld, J., 111, 371
Spaeth, J. L., 62, 246, 355
Speakman, D., 75, 362
Spector, P. E., 57-59, 71-72, 240, 243,
    278, 365
Speed of behavior and age, 87
Spencer, D. G., 66-67, 71, 260, 277,
    371
Spiro, H. R., 371
Staffing, 85-103, 188
    future research nneds, 199
    implications for, 193-194
Stagner, R., 46, 53, 212, 372
Staines, G. L., 45-47, 215, 368, 372
Stanford, E. P., 161, 325, 344, 372
Statistical techniques, 24-25
    correlations, 25
    multiple regression, 25
    research method issues, 197
    statistical significance, 25
Steers, R. M., 44-45, 57-58, 65-67, 70-
    71, 83, 237, 239, 260, 273, 277,
    363, 365-366, 368, 371-372
Steger, J. A., 109, 304, 370
Stern, J. A., 87, 372
Stern, R. N., 360
Sterns, H. L., 354
Stevens, A. F., 77, 285, 372
Stevens, J. M., 55, 57-58, 234, 238,
    372
Stewart, C. D., 175, 372
Stewart, J. S., 312, 372
Stone, E. F., 365
Stone, T. H., 83, 372
Strauss, G., 358
Strieb, G. F., 149, 156-157, 161-162,
    327, 330, 332, 344, 347, 372
Stumpf, A. A., 62, 71, 251, 271, 277,
    372, 374
Super, D. E., 21, 100-101, 105-106,
    108, 372
Supervision, 45, 51, 60
    and age, 51
    satisfaction with, 45, 51, 60
    and turnover, 45
Surry, J., 75-76, 78, 283, 287, 372
Survivor phenomenon effect, 65, 104
Sutherland, I., 75-76, 281, 372

Suzuki, H., 123-125, 373

Taussig, M. K., 367
Taylor, K. E., 71, 274, 373
Taylor, P. D., 359
Taylor, R. N., 33, 42, 203-204, 206,
    373
Taylor, W., 313, 357
Tersine, R. J., 136, 220, 223, 227,
    230, 353
Theriault, R., 138, 357
Thomas, K. R., 61, 85-86, 88, 242,
    355
Thomas, L. E., 73, 109-111, 307, 309,
    373
Thompson, M., 33, 42, 203-204, 206,
    373
Thompson, P. H., 62-63, 109, 117,
    248, 304, 357, 373
Thompson, W. E., 149, 162, 347, 372
Thorndike, E. L., 112, 373
Thornton, G. C. III, 311, 373
Tiffin, J., 75, 373
Todor, W. D., 70, 357
Torrence, W. D., 89, 368
Tracy, M., 170-171, 173, 176, 373
Training
    implications for, 194
    and learning, 112-113
    and post-training performance, 113
Trainability tests, 91
Treas, J., 178, 373
Trice, H. M., 372
Tsivilyou, R., 171-172, 375
Tucker, H. I., 253, 262, 373
Turner, J. N., 94-95, 296, 354
Turnover, 54, 69-74, 81, 187
    and age, 70-74
    costs of, 70
    importance of, 70
    and job performance, 70, 72
    and job satisfaction, 44, 72-73
Turnover intentions, 60, 187
    and age, 59
    importance of, 59
    and turnover, 59

Ulman, L., 358
Urban, F., 90, 370

United States, 12, 14-16, 123
    compensation in, 123
    earnings level by age and sex, 124
    labor force by age in, 12, 15-16
    population, 12, 14
U.S. Deparment of Health and Human
    Service, 168, 170-172, 175-179
U.S. Department of Labor, 65, 74
U.S. House of Representatives,
    180-182
House of Representatives Select
    Committee on Aging, 182
U.S. Senate, 182-183
Usher, E. E., 148, 156, 329, 374

Vaitenas, R., 109-111, 307, 375
Values, 31-34, 59-60
    and age, 32-34
    defined, 31
    importance of, 31-32
    Protestant work ethic, 32-33
Van Gorkom, J. W., 181, 374
Van Zelst, R. H., 75-76, 282, 374
Vecchio, R. P., 33, 203, 374
Vernon, H. M., 75-76, 280, 374
Veroff, J., 359
Vichas, R. P., 66-67, 260, 356
Vig, G., 171, 374
Villars, C., 177, 374
Vincent, N. L., 253, 366
Vision and age, 86
Vredenburgh, D. J., 71, 275, 371
Vroom, V. H., 44, 374

Wagner, L. A., 129-131, 135, 316, 374
Walker, J. F., 62, 64, 246-247, 253,
    363, 371, 374
Walker, J. W., 374
Wall, T., 36, 58, 209, 239, 356, 374
Wallace, M. J., Jr., 136-137, 322, 370
Walsh, R. P., 356
Walsh, W. B., 112, 374
Wanous, J. P., 35, 71, 89, 276, 374
Warnath, C., 372
Warr, P., 36, 55-56, 209, 235-236,
    374
Waters, C. W., 374
Waters, L. K., 59, 71, 241, 274, 374
Watson, C. J., 66-67, 261, 374

Weaver, C. N., 45-46, 50, 214-216, 256, 359, 374
Weiss, D. J., 71, 274, 373
Weiss, R. S., 33, 365
Welford, A. T., 86, 375
Welsch, H. P., 57-58, 240, 375
Wexley, K. N., 366
White, G. A., 83 360
White, J. K., 32, 35-36, 370, 375
Whitfield, J. W., 75, 76, 79, 281, 291, 375
Wiener, Y., 109-111, 307, 375
Wiley, J., 23, 364
Williams, A., 71, 277, 375
Williams, M. V., 86-87, 355
Willis, S. L., 65, 86, 88, 375

Wolf, E., 358
Wolff, E., 79, 291, 375
Woods, A. M., 355
Wooten, P. R., 180, 357
Work
    and age, 50
    satisfaction with, 45, 50, 60, 187
    and turnover, 45
Work behaviors, 81, 187-188
Wright, J. D., 36-38, 42, 52, 375

Yaholem, M. R., 144, 375
Youry, M., 96, 375

Zakhavor, M., 171-172, 375
Zey-Ferrell, M., 59, 243, 375

ABOUT THE AUTHORS

Mildred Doering is an Associate Professor of Personnel and Industrial Relations in the School of Management and a research associate at the All-University Gerontology Center, Syracuse University. She received her Ph.D. in Industrial Relations from the University of Minnesota. In addition to teaching staffing, training, career planning and development, and compensation administration, her current major research centers on the determinants of career change and retirement.

Susan R. Rhodes (Ph.D., University of Oregon, 1978) is an Associate Professor of Personnel and Industrial Relations in the School of Management and a research associate at the All-University Gerontology Center, Syracuse University. In addition to issues of aging and work, her research interests include employee ownership and control of organizations, employee absenteeism, and career change. Her articles have appeared in the *Journal of Applied Psychology, Journal of Vocational Behavior, Human Relations,* and *Personnel Administrator.*

Michael Schuster (J.D.-Ph.D., Syracuse University, 1979) is an Associate Professor of Personnel and Industrial Relations in the School of Management at Syracuse University. He spent the 1982-83 academic year as a Senior Fulbright Scholar at the London School of Economics and Political Science. Professor Schuster teaches courses in personnel, labor and employment law, and collective bargaining. His articles have appeared in *Aging and Work, Employee Relations Law Journal,* and *Law and Policy Quarterly.*